Mysteries
of
Life, Death, and Futurity

Mysteries
of
Life, Death, and Futurity

Horace Welby

Athens ✢ Manchester

Mysteries of Life, Death, and Futurity

Old Book Publishing Ltd

Book Cover Design: Old Book Publishing Ltd

Copyright © 2011 Old Book Publishing Ltd
All rights reserved.

Title of original: Mysteries of Life, Death, and Futurity
Originally published in 1863

ISBN–10: 1-78107-057-1
ISBN–13: 978-1-78107-057-4

EDITOR'S NOTE

Old Book Publishing Ltd takes care in preserving the wording and images of the original books. For this reason we have invested in technology that enables us to enhance the quality of such reproduction. This investment helps overcome problems encountered when reproducing old books, such as stains, coloured paper, discolouration of ink, yellowed pages, see-through and onion skin type paper.

This reproduction book, produced from digital images of the original, may contain occasional defects such as missing pages or blemishes due to the original source content or were introduced by the scanning process.

These are scanned pages and the quality of print represents accurately the print quality of the original book, though we may have been able to enhance it.

As this book has been scanned and/or reformatted from the original we cannot guarantee that it is error-free or contains the full content of the original.

However, we believe that this work is culturally important, and despite its imperfections, have elected to bring it back into print as part of our commitment to the preservation of printed works.

Old Book Publishing

THE SEVEN AGES OF MAN.

From a Block Print in the British Museum.
15th Century.

MYSTERIES

OF

LIFE, DEATH, AND FUTURITY:

ILLUSTRATED FROM

THE BEST AND LATEST AUTHORITIES.

BY

HORACE WELBY,
AUTHOR OF "PREDICTIONS REALIZED," "SIGNS BEFORE DEATH," ETC.

NEW YORK:
JOHN BRADBURN, 49 WALKER STREET.
SUCCESSOR TO M. DOOLADY.
MDCCCLXIII.

PREFACE.

Few of those persons who are accustomed to watch the religious tendencies of the age, need be reminded that its characteristics are freedom of inquiry, thought, and discussion, and these with greater latitude than can be traced in the history of any former period. The adage that "thinking nurseth thinking" is every day strongly exemplified; and if it be hard to estimate the actual results at their true value to society, it must be allowed that in the conflict of opinions, Truths may be abundantly garnered—the wheat gathered from the enemy's tares; and their importance and interest of the good part inculcated with greater effect than by ordinary means.

To bring the consideration of the three paramount subjects named in the annexed title-page within the limits of a single volume, may appear a pretentious object for a *Layman* to attempt; more especially when we remember how many splendid intellects have, through countless ages, been devoted to the rearing of the safe-guards of our belief, and the eternal interests of mankind. In comparison with such labors, which are the highest aspirations of the human mind, the present work has very humble claim to notice. It has been undertaken with the view of concentrating within its focus the views and opinions of some of the leading writers of the present day, and placing them before the reader in so popular a form and setting as to adapt them for a larger class than would be likely to consult the authorities themselves, whence the substance of this volume has been derived. Facts, anecdotes, personal traits of character, and well-grounded arguments and opinions, are the staple of the work; and special care being taken to give each statement its mint-mark of its authority. In virtue of the Scriptural character of the subjects, the rewards will be a special blessing on those who read and understand them; the interpretations and inferences, in many instances, being the deductions of men venerated for their piety and learning in ministering the most precious of all knowledge—the inestimable comfort of the Hope that is in us.

The writer has employed the word MYSTERY in its ordinary acceptation—a thing unintelligible or concealed—as well as in the Scriptural meaning—something that had been unknown, but in due time was revealed by the inspiration of God. Thus it is applied to the principles of the Gospel, and to the circumstances of the General Resurrection; as well as to denote an emblem of revealed truth.*

Surrounded as we are by Mysteries (says a contemporary), and helpless as we find ourselves amid them, we are irresistibly prompted to seek an explanation of them. The applications of natural science for this purpose are too striking a characteristic of this age of inquiry to have been neglected throughout the following pages; the writer having endeavored to profit by the sound opinions of Dr. Whewell, who has set the service of science, in this case, in the proper light: "Science," he tells

---

* See *A Scripture and Prayer-book Glossary.* By the Rev. John Booker, M. A.

Preface. 5

us, "teaches us our ignorance, as well as the elevation of our nature. Those misrepresent it much who describe it in other terms; for the lessons of science implant reverence and gratitude for the past, hope for the future, and humility in our own estimation."

As the aim of the writer is to render his book acceptable to a wide number of readers, he has endeavored to make it attractive by the notes and comments of expositors of our own time, as well as from those sacred treasures of learning, and those studies of Scripture, which strongly reveal to us the relation of God to man. The most reverential regard for things sacred has been fostered throughout the work; and although the stores of classic thought and fancy have been occasionally resorted to for embellishment and illustration, these have been employed as subsidiary to the Spirit and the Truth.

In conclusion, it may be remarked, that although the reader may receive from these pages many impressions of the transitory nature of man's life, it is hoped that they will lead him to thoughts of "the Great Mystery of Godliness," and fill his heart with "a gracious composition of love, and joy, and wonder;" thus to induce him to the meditation of the infinitely glorious work of our Redemption—and so make him both the happier and the better man.* H. W.

---

* Addison says: "Will any man be so impertinently officious as to tell me all prospect of a future state is only fancy and delusion? Is there any merit in being the messenger of ill-news? If it is a dream, let me enjoy it, since it makes me both the happier and the better man."

The Seven Ages of Man.

(See the Frontispiece.)

BEFORE we describe this quaint Illustration of the Progress of the Life of Man, it may be as well to say a few words of the Division of Man's Life into Stages, which appears to have been treated by various authors through a period of two thousand years.

The subject has long occupied the thoughts of the physician, the moralist, the speculative philosopher, and the poet. Instances may be found in the literature and art of all countries, and from the earliest periods. In Rosellini's *Monumenti dell' Egitto e della Nubia*, a very curious instance occurs of a date far anterior to any previously mentioned.

The earliest instance which Mr. John Winter Jones could find of the division of human life into stages occurs in the Greek verses attributed to Solon, who flourished about six hundred years before Christ, and which are introduced by Philo-Judæus into his *Liber de mundi opificio;* wherein also occurs, "Hippocrates says that there are *seven* ages;" and we find this division in the Midrach or Ecclesiastes, written about the ninth century, where, in six stages, man is compared to some animal.

In a beautiful Hebrew poem of the twelfth century, we find man's life divided into *ten* stages. Mr. Winter Jones describes two curious illustrations in ten stages, from Germany and Holland.

Sir Thomas More, when a boy, designed for his father's house in London, a hanging of painted cloths, with Man's Life in nine pageants, and verses over.

The division into *seven* years is suspected to have been derived from the speculations of cabalistic philosophers upon the secret powers of numbers, and upon the climacterical year.

Lady Calcott described in the cathedral of Sienna, in one of the side chapels seven figures, each in a compartment, inlaid in the pavement, representing the Seven Ages of Man, supposed to have been executed by Antonio Frederighi, in 1476.

Shakspeare's charming illustration of Man's Seven Ages in the mouth of the melancholy Jaques, in *As you like it*, have become familiar as "household words."

We now come to the original of our Frontispiece—a coarse but spirited woodcut, of about the middle of the fifteenth century, and roughly colored: it was found pasted inside what had been the covers of an old edition or manuscript of the *Moralia super Bibliam*, of N. de Lyra; and was purchased for the library of the British Museum by M. Panizzi.

The centre is occupied by a large wheel, on the inner circle of which are the words (in Latin), "The wheel of Life, which is called fortune." Between this and the outer circle is the form of a naked man; the arms extended, and grasping two of the upper spokes, and the legs apart against two corresponding spokes below. (The several inscriptions are in Latin: we give only the English translation.) On the outer circle of the wheel are the words: "Thus adorned, they are born in this mortal Life. Life decaying, they glide away like water."

Around the wheel are the figures of a man in his *seven stages*. Commencing on the left side, and proceeding upward, there is a label with the word "Generation" upon it.

Immediately above this is a cradle, in or rather upon which lies an infant in swaddling clothes; and at the foot of the cradle stands a little naked boy clapping his hands.

Next in order is a naked child, holding a toy-windmill, such as amuses children to the present day: a rudely drawn dog (more like a pig) stands on its hind feet, and rests against the child's leg. Underneath is a scroll, inscribed, "An infant to seven years."

Immediately above is a label inscribed, "Children to Fifteen years," illustrated by a youth holding a falcon on his right fist, and what appears to be a bag of money in his left hand—emblems of the love of pleasure and enjoyment natural to this stage of man's life. Above the head of this youth, and perhaps with reference to the same figure, there is another label, with the words, "Adolescence to twenty-five years."

The Frontispiece. 9

This brings us to the top of the print, at the left-hand side. In the upper centre, and sitting astride upon the wheel, there is a figure with a feather in his cap, and armed with spear and shield: on a label above him are the words, "Youth to thirty-five years."

At the top of the right side of the print is a label inscribed, "Manhood to fifty years:" beneath is a figure seated at a table, counting money,—evidently the worldly man, who, having passed through the stages of pleasure and war, is now occupied with the acquisition of wealth. Under his feet is a label with the words, "Old age to seventy years."

The next figure, descending, is that of an old man leaning on a staff, under which is a label inscribed, "Decrepit until death."

The dead body is next represented, lying in a coffin, under which is a label with the word "Corruption."

In the centre, at the foot of the print, is a winged figure with flowing drapery, the wings expanded, and the hands resting upon the two labels, bearing the inscriptions, "Generation" and "Corruption." Under the left hand of this figure is the name of the artist, "Clau;" with this punning device, three claws on a shield. At the bottom are eight lines in monkish verse (omitted in the Frontispiece), which may be thus rendered into plain prose:

"The state of man is exemplified in a flower:
The flower falls and perishes, so shall man also become ashes.
If thou couldst know who thou art, and whence thou comest,
Thou wouldst never smile, but ever weep.
There are three things which often make me lament
First, it is a hard thing to know that I must die;
Secondly, I fear because I do not know when I shall die;
Thirdly, I weep because I do not know what will become of me hereafter."*

Such are the details of this curious print: the design is superior to the execution, and is a very interesting Illustration of Man's Progress from the Cradle to the Grave.

* See the paper by Mr. Thos. Winter Jones, of the British Museum, in *Archaeologia*, vol. xxxv., pp. 167–189, 1858. The whole is extremely interesting.

A Hymn.

OH, thou great Power! in whom I move,
For whom I live, to whom I die,
Behold me through thy beams of love,
Whilst on this couch of tears I lie;
    And cleanse my sordid soul within,
      By thy Christ's blood, the bath of sin.

No hallow'd oyls, no grains I need,
No rays of saints, no purging fire;
One rosie drop from David's seed
Was worlds of seas to quench thine ire:
    O precious ransome! which once paid,
      That *Consummatum est* was said.

And said by Him that said no more,
But seal'd it with his sacred breath:
Thou, then, that has dispong'd my score,
And dying wast the death of Death,
    Be to me now, on thee I call,
      My life, my strength, my joy, my all!

SIR HENRY WOTTON.

CONTENTS.

                                                                              PAGES

LIFE AND TIME..15—58

What is Life? 15.—The Author of our Being, 16.—The Divine Eternity, 18.—The Divine Perfections, 19.—Change-bearing Laws of Nature, 20.—The Creation of Matter, 21.—The Mosaic and Geologic Creation, 22.—Origin of Life—Darwin's Theory, 27.—Unity of the Human Race, 30.—The Embryo under the Microscope, 32.—The Development Theory—Chemistry cannot create an Organism, 33.—Man and his Dwelling-place, 35.—Plurality of Worlds, 37.—Identity of the Vital Principle of Animals and Vegetables, 38.—Chain of Being, 39.—The Kingdoms of Nature, 41.—Numbers in Nature, 42.—Adaptation of Color to the Wants of the Animal, 43.—The Tree of Life, 44.—Eve's Apple-tree, 46.—How Cain killed Abel, 47.—Family Likenesses, 48.—Average of Human Life, 49.—Space and Time, 50.—Climacterics, 51.—Fragments of Time, 53.—Curious Statistical Results, 54.—Life Assurance; Sir William Hamilton on Phrenology, 55.—Consumption and Longevity; Man's proper Place in Creation, 57.

NATURE OF THE SOUL..59—75

On the Soul, by the Ancients, 59.—The Imprisoned Soul, 62.—The Soul and the Magnetic Needle, 62.—Symbols of the Soul, 65.—Personality of God—the Soul God's great Organ, 67.—Pre-existence of Souls, 68.—Transmigration of Souls and Sacredness of Animals, 75.

SPIRITUAL LIFE..76—92

Spiritual Reclamation, 76.—"Excelsior," 77.—Notions of Angels, 77.—Spiritual Natures, 83.—Permanent Impressions by Spiritual Powers, 85.—Materialism and Spiritualism—Personal Identity, 87.—Mesmerism and Somnambulism, 90.—Clairvoyance, 92.

MENTAL PHENOMENA..93—129

Mind and Body, 93.—Mental Processes of which we are unconscious, 94.—The Voltaic Battery, Electric Eel, and Brain of Man, 95.—A Galvanized Human Body, 96.—Changes in the Nervous System, 96.—Working of the Brain, 98.—What is Memory? 99.—How the Function of Memory takes place, 101.—Persistence of Impressions, 102.—Value of Memory—Registration, 104.—Decay of Memory, 105.—Intuitions, 107.—What is Genius? 108.—Mental Abstraction, 109.—Effects of Emotion on the Intellect, 110.—Melancholy or Poetic Feeling, 111.—Gay Melancholy, 113.—Insane Impulses, 116.—Keep the Brain fallow in Childhood, 118.—Perverted Reason: What is Madness? 119.—Intellectuality and Insanity, 120.—How the Egyptians treated their Insane, 124.—Operation of Mind—"the Great Book," 125.—Discipline of the Intellect, 126.—The Child Father to the Man, 127.—Life not greater than its Reflex, 128.

Contents.

PAGES

BELIEF AND SCEPTICISM .... 130—145

What is Faith? 130.—What is Revelation? 131.—Childish Desires, 132.—Weak Belief, 133.—Real Growth, 135.—Experience Fallible, 136.—Intolerance and Unbelief, 137.—How Men become Sceptics, 137.—Infidelity Irrational, 138.—Confessions of Sceptics, 138.—Renunciation of Infidelity, 142.—Materialism of the Development Theory, 143.—Combustion—the Metempsychosis, 144.

WHAT IS SUPERSTITION? .... 146—154

"To die childless," 146.—High Spirits a Presage of Evil, 150.—"Thirteen to Dinner," 152.—What is Chance? 153.

PREMATURE INTERMENT .... 155—161

Trance, 155.

PHENOMENA OF DEATH .... 162—228

Hours fatal to Life, 162.—Premonitions of Death, 163.—Death of Lord Lyttelton, 174.—Death of Archbishop Leighton, 177.—Old Age and Death, 178.—Death at Will; Sleep and Death, 179.—Does the Soul Sleep?—Contrition of the Ancients at the point of Death, 181.—Man's Reluctance to think of God, 183.—State of Mind preceding Death, 186.—How Man Dies, 187.—Death from Heart Disease, 196.—Broken Hearts, 197.—The Death-bed, by Owen Feltham, 198.—Death-bed Repentance, 199.—The last Moments and Words of Distinguished Persons, 202. —The Soul going forth from the Body, 208.—The Passing Bell, 210.—Beauty of Death, 212.—Grief for the Dead, 214.—Interferences of the Dead with the Living, 216.—Death Customs, 216.—Antiquity of Burial Clubs, 217.—"God's Acre," 218. —Emblems on Tombs, 219.—Antiseptic Burial Soils, 219.—Decay of the Human Body, 221.—Emblem of the Resurrection, 222.—Flowers on Graves, 223.

SIN AND PUNISHMENT .... 229—238

The Earliest Sin; the Great Sin, 229.—Special Providences, 230.—Nemesis, or Retribution, 231.—Representations of "the Devil," 233.—Picture of Hell—Utter Darkness, 234.—The Wheel of Eternal Punishment, 236.—The Fallen Angel, 238.

THE CRUCIFIXION OF OUR LORD .... 239—247

Crucifixion, 239.—Knowledge of God before the time of Christ, 244.—"Christ the Moral Saviour," 246.

THE END OF THE WORLD FORETOLD .... 248—253

Epidemic Terrors, 248.—Geological Future of the Universe, 252.

MAN AFTER DEATH .... 254—263

The Dead know not any thing, 254.—Prayers for the Dead, 254.—Condition of Man after Death, 256.—"To the Holy Spirit," 260.—Life after Death—Re-union of the Soul and Body, 262.

THE INTERMEDIATE STATE .... 264—275

What is the Intermediate State? 264.—Opinions concerning the State of the Dead, 267.—Paradise and Heaven, 269.—Heathen Philosophy of the Immortality of the Soul, 271.—That Man must be Immortal, 273.

Contents. 13

                                                                      PAGES

THE CHRISTIAN RESURRECTION...................................276—280

    The Resurrection, 276.—Resurrection of the same Body, 279.

THE FUTURE STATES...281—284

    The Day of Judgment, 281.—The Happiness of Heaven, 283.

THE RECOGNITION OF EACH OTHER BY THE BLESSED........285—298

    Evidences of the Recognition, 285.—Bishops King and Mant, 285.—David, St. Paul, the Transfiguration, 286.—Lazarus in Abraham's Bosom, 287.—Ulysses, Achilles, Agamemnon, Antigone, Darius, Socrates, Æneas, 288.—Anchises, Cicero, American Chiefs, Hindoos, 289.—Kings of Dahomey and Guinea ; Love of the Dead; Cyprian at Carthage, 290.—Translation of Enoch, 291.—" Marriages are made in Heaven," 292.—" Business of the Saints in Heaven," 293.—The New Heavens and Earth; Bishop Mant, 294.—Bishop Courtenay, 296.—Abodes of the Blest, 297.

ADVERSARIA..299—332

    Study of the Bible, 299.—Serpent Worship, 301.—Symbolical Figures from Nineveh, 302.—Evidences of Christianity, 303.—Changes in Opinion, 304.—Christian Revelation, why first given to the West, 305.—Holy Thorn at Glastonbury, 306.—The Christian Mission, 306.—The True Course of Christian Life, 310.—True and False Buddhism, 311.—Platonic Love, 314.—Platonism and Christianity, 315.—Religion happily adapted to the Mind of Man, 317.—Power of Religion over Difficulties, 319. —Attributes of the Deity, 320.—On Atheism, by South; Preparing for another World, 321.—Remoteness of Universal Christianity, 324.—Eternal Punishment, 325.—Boyish or Manly Happiness; God's Ancient People, 326.—Latin or Mediæval Christianity, 328.—Origin of the Litany ; Vital Force; What is Materialism? 330.—Mysteries and Miracles, 332.

PILGRIM'S PROGRESS, THE...333—337

    Authorship of, 333.—Bunyan's Vindication, 335.—Dr. Adam Clarke, 335.—Voyage of the Wandering Knight, 336.—Bunyan's Escapes, 337.

APPENDIX..338—351

    Lambton Family Tradition, 338.—Lord Bacon's Dream, 338.—Last Sonnet of Mrs. Hemans, 341.—Chartley Tradition, 339.—Lord Chesterfield, 340.—Dr. Johnson on Death, 340.—Latin Hymn, 341.—Capt. Kidd and Lord Byron, 341.—Grimaldi's dread of Friday, 342.—Cawnpore, Death at, 342.—Watching for the Dead, 342.—Dirge by Faber, 343.—Literary History of Madmen, 344.

"THERE are those to whom a sense of religion has come in storm and tempest; and there are those whom it has summoned amid scenes of revelry and idle vanity; there are those who have heard its 'still small voice' amid rural leisure and placid contentment. But perhaps the knowledge which cometh not to err is most frequently impressed upon the mind during seasons of affliction; and tears are the softening showers which cause the seed of heaven to spring and take root in the human heart."—*Sir Walter Scott.*

MYSTERIES,

ETC.

Life and Time.

WHAT IS LIFE?

> We're ill by these Grammarians us'd;
> We are abus'd by Words, grossly abus'd;
> From the Maternal Tomb,
> To the Grave's fruitful Womb,
> We call her Life, but Life's a name
> That nothing here can truly claim.

COWLEY, in a note to his Pindaric Ode, whence the above lines are quoted, says:

Plato, in *Timæus*, makes this distinction: "That which is, but is not generated; and that which is generated, but is not." This he took from Trismegistus, whose sentence of God was written in the Egyptian temples, "I am all that was, is, or shall be." This doctrine of Plato, that *nothing truly is but God*, is approved by all the Fathers. Simplicius explains it thus: That which has more degrees of privation, or not-being, than of being (which is the case of all creatures), is not properly said to be; and again, that which is a perpetual *fieri*, or making, never is quite made, and, therefore, never properly is.

Leaving the old "Grammarian," we pass to the science of our own times. M. Geoffroy St. Hilaire, in his *Histoire Naturelle générale des Règnes Organiques*, in the chapter on the definitions of Life, refutes the common mistake of supposing that vital force suspends or destroys physical action. If these vitalists had but taken the trouble of decomposing each complex question into its elements, instead of cutting the knot which they could not loosen, they would have seen their error. Thus, an animal, while living, "resists" cold, does not "obey" the physical laws of temperature, but keeps constantly above the temperature of the surrounding medium. When dead, this resistance ceases. Does this prove that vital force destroys physical action? Does it prove that the living animal is enfranchised from those physical laws which regulate the transmission of heat? Not in the least. The more complex conditions have produced a phenomenon different from that witnessed under simpler conditions; but an inorganic substance may manifest an analogous independence (or what seems such) of these laws of transmission, if it be heated by a galvanic current, or by an internal chemical reaction. Again, when we see an animal leap into the air, has he enfranchised himself from the laws of gravitation? Not more than the needle when it leaps to the magnet.*

Physiologists appear to have made this mistake in speaking of Life: they have enumerated certain functions, and have called such enumeration *life;* now function is not life, but the result of life; it is vital organ in action. Bichat defined life as "the sum total of the functions which resist death:" which amounts merely to this—that life is life. Bichat's definition of life is manifestly faulty in this—that it ignores the essential co-operation of the medium or surrounding circumstances in which organization is placed, and is, therefore, as one-sided and useless as any definition would be which might ignore the organism, and enumerate the circumstances as life; circumstances and individual are correlative, both in psychical and organic life; and man's life, mental and organic, is the result of such correlation. This is what Coleridge indicated, when, in his *Hints toward the Formation of a more comprehensive Theory of Life*, he defined life as "the Principle of Individuation." This is a plagiarism from the Germans (in this case from Schelling), as was most of Coleridge's philosophy.

THE AUTHOR OF OUR BEING.

Dr. Thomas Woods, of Parsonstown, observes: "If we look at the constitution of matter, the impossibility of a mass being

* *Saturday Review*, April 25, 1857.

formed, even though atoms might have been in existence, without the interference of some agency different from any at present operating; viewing its arrangements, measured out and bounded with mathematical precision, we must admit that some Being greater than any on this earth, and more powerful than the supposed laws of nature, has formed it. Seeing, also, that in all departments of creation, the object pre-eminently provided for is the welfare and preservation of man, and that the same method is everywhere manifested in carrying it out, we must likewise conclude that the same power which made the arrangements in matter is also the Author of our being.

"As in the animate creation, the organization of every living thing is made from one type, so in creation generally, one plan is taken for the working out of all its details; and whether we examine the combustion of coal, the growth of the living body, or the final destination of the soul throughout eternity, we see the same principle followed out in the accomplishment of each, and we are forced to ascribe a common authorship to all. It is abundantly evident that one mind, and at one time, conceived and set in motion the entire fabric of creation ; and that every thing, from the smallest particle of matter to the highest organization and disposition of life and power, in every stage of its existence, depends for its continuance on Him, and that in every thing we do, or think we do, we only use the power He has given; and therefore, in all our ways we are indebted to Him, and in all our works, however unconsciously, we worship him. Whether we pride ourselves on the power of our steam-engines, the rapidity of the telegraph, or the beauty and excellence of photography—the results of Heat, Light, and Electricity—we only declare the wonder of the mechanism He has provided, and the perfection of the arrangements He has made. And as, by virtue of these arrangements, the coal and air, when favorably placed together, evolve heat, the zinc and acid electricity, and the sunbeam and sensible salt the photograph, so does food taken into the body, by virtue of the vital power, continue life, and enable the animal to move; and so the blood of Christ, applied to the soul, makes also that alive and capable of acting.

"In every word we speak, we praise Him—in every thing we do, we must acknowledge Him; we trace in all creation the same hand, in all its arrangements the same mind, and therefore in every thing we think or act, to Him be all the Glory."—*The Existence of the Deity evidenced by Power and Unity in Creation; from the Results of Modern Science.*

THE DIVINE ETERNITY.

There are many passages in the Bible, the tendency of which is to give us a view of the Divine Existence, far elevated above any successive duration similar to our own. The self-existent Jehovah* revealed his name to Moses as the "I AM," the abiding, not the on-moving existence. Our Divine Redeemer, during his mission on earth, spoke sometimes as man, at other times as God. When He spoke from his manhood, He spoke as a being of time, having a past, a present, a future. But when He spoke from his Godhead, He repeated the language of Jehovah to Moses: "Before Abraham was, I AM," not I was.

St. Peter's words, "One day is with the Lord as a thousand years, and a thousand years as one day," seem to be more than *relative*, in regard to the inadequacy of all periods of time, the longest as well as the shortest, to measure the Divine duration. May we not consider them *absolute*, as implying the entire absence of succession in that sublime existence which has neither beginning nor end? The same observation is applicable to the words of Moses in the 90th Psalm: "For a thousand years in thy sight are but as yesterday when it is past, and as a watch in the night."

As in God there can neither be past nor future, nor any succession of duration, it follows that in HIM there can be no series, or sequency of actions. For if in HIM there could be one act *after* another, then to Himself would some of his acts be past, and others future: and we should thus relapse into the misconception of attributing to Him a successive duration like our own.

What, as regards ourselves, is truly a series of acts or dispen-

---

* In Baron Bunsen's *Bible for the People*, the word JEHOVAH has its deep significance brought out by being rendered THE ETERNAL.

sations—the Creation of Man, the Deluge, the call of Abraham, the birth of the Messiah, the resurrection of the dead, the final judgment—all these must be to God, not a series of acts or dispensations, but one eternal, simultaneous energy. His perception of the successive development of his dispensations, as apprehended by his creatures, does not make them successive as regards Himself.

But these contemplations of the Divine Eternity reach no further than the negation of the limits and imperfections of all created minds. We can form no conception of the HOW of that glorious existence which *transcends* the relations of Time and Space. If the Cherubim themselves veil their eyes before the HOLY ONE, how much more must his glory be *incomprehensible* to man!—CRONHELM *on Predestination.*

THE DIVINE PERFECTIONS.

The "metaphysical qualms" entertained in the present day at our partial conceptions of the Divine Perfections are strangely contrasted with the language of the inspired Writers. They expatiate in wonder and praise on the little we can conceive—in awe and adoration on the much beyond our conception.

"The heavens declare the glory of God; and the firmament showeth his handywork. Day unto day uttereth speech, and night unto night showeth knowledge. There is no speech nor language where their voice is not heard. In them hath he set a tabernacle for the sun, which is as a bridegroom coming out of his chamber, and rejoiceth as a strong man to run a race. His going forth is from the end of the heaven, and his circuit unto the ends of it; and there is nothing hid from the heat thereof."

And then the Psalmist turns from the wonders of Creation to those of Revelation. "The law of the Lord is perfect, converting the soul: the testimony of the Lord is sure, making wise the simple. The statutes of the Lord are right, rejoicing the heart: the commandment of the Lord is pure, enlightening the eyes."

So, after a sublime effusion on the power and wisdom of the great Creator, Job concludes: "Lo, these are *parts* of his ways;

but how little a portion is heard of him! but the thunder of his power who can understand?"

So also St. Paul: "For we know in *part*, and we prophesy in part. But when that which is perfect is come, then that which is in part shall be done away. . . . For now we see through a glass, darkly; but then face to face: now I know in part; but then shall I know even as also I am known."

Far from denying the truth of our partial conceptions in this life, the Apostle points to their progressive development hereafter. The metaphor borrowed from the semi-opaque glass of the ancients, and the indistinct vision which it afforded, is singularly appropriate and instructive.—CRONHELM *on Predestination.*

CHANGE-BEARING LAWS OF NATURE.

Mr. Owen* thus ingeniously advocates the probability of the existence of what he terms "*change-bearing laws of nature.*" In a world whose characteristic is change, "and which, for aught we know, may continue to endure for countless ages, laws of such a character, self-adapted to a changeful state of things, may be regarded as of likely occurrence.

"Modern science is revealing to us glimpses that may brighten into positive proof of this hypothesis." Sir John Herschel, writing to Sir Charles Lyell, the geologist, and alluding to what he calls "that mystery of mysteries, the replacement of extinct species by others," says:

For my own part, I cannot but think it an inadequate conception of the Creator, to assume it as granted that His combinations are expanded upon any one of the theatres of their former exercise: though, in this, as all His other works, we are led by all analogy to suppose that He operates through a series of intermediate causes, and that, in consequence, the origination of fresh species, could it ever come under our cognizance, would be found to be a natural, in contradistinction to a miraculous, process; although we may perceive no indication of any process, actually in progress, which is likely to issue in such a result. —*Sir John Herschel's Letter*, Feb. 20, 1836: *Ninth Bridgewater Treatise*, by *Babbage*.

* In his *Footfalls on the Boundary of another World.* 1860.

THE CREATION OF MATTER.

The Atomic Theory of Democritus, as defined by Boscovich, and since more fully developed by that eminent philosopher, the late Dr. Samuel Brown, offers an hypothesis for the Creation of Matter, which, in a subject so far beyond the region of certainty, possesses many features of probability; particularly in getting rid of the vexed question of the substratum.

That the primary atoms are merely centres of force, *i. e.*, mathematical points encircled with powers of repulsion and attraction, and that from the endless variety of combinations of repulsive and attractive forces, the whole material universe is constructed—is a theory alike simple, comprehensive, and sublime. To accomplish the dissolution of Nature, her Almighty Creator would only have to cancel the repulsive and attractive forces that encircle the Atomic centres; and instantaneously, without an audible crash, without a visible wreck, the glorious fabric of the earth and the heavens would disapppear from existence!*

When, in past ages, it was supposed that matter was perishable, it became a difficulty of belief that such material origin could escape material extinction. The discoveries of chemistry† have, however, gradually dissipated these fears. We are now satisfied of *the indestructibility of matter*, and that although substances may be decomposed and disappear, they do not cease to be, but pass into other forms of existence.

Whatever incredulity remained resolved itself into a questioning of His ability to raise the Human Dead: but

> Sure the same power
> That reared the piece at first, and took it down,
> Can reassemble the loose scattered parts,
> And put them as they were.

There is ONE, "in whom we live, and move, and have our

---

* Cronhelm *on Predestination*.
† As a first principle of all chemistry, it is to be kept in mind that *no matter is either created or lost*, whatever the changes or combinations taking place. In clearly fixing this principle, which was imperfectly apprehended before, Lavoisier rendered an invaluable service to science. Plutarch ascribes to Empedocles a passage which is well descriptive of this great principle of chemistry.—*Quarterly Review*, vol. lxxxiii.

being," and who works, on our behalf, this standing miracle; and can we suppose Him incapable of resuscitating after death whatever he had once made actively and consciously existent? "Is any thing too hard for God?"

But matter, it may be said, if indestructible, by its changes, loses its *identity*, and how can the substance remain the same in the lapse of ages which may intervene between death and the described resurrection? But the Humanity which rises again will be the same Humanity with that which ran on earth its mortal career; but only as the man of fourscore years and upwards, committed to the tomb, is the same with him who commenced life as an infant. Though a corporeity still, it will then be a *celestial* corporeity. "St. Paul, it is plain," says Cromwell, "regarded this change as the one passport of the Humanity that had lived in this world, to unending life in the world to prove as endless, when the Author of Life shall be pleased to consummate His eternal plan."*

THE MOSAIC AND GEOLOGIC CREATION.

The freedom with which the Biblical account of the Creation is discussed in these scientific times, presents a striking contrast with the fate of those who, in a former age, ventured to discuss such vital questions. One instance must suffice. About two centuries since, one Isaac la Peyrere, a French Protestant, published, in Latin, anonymously, a book entitled: " Man before Adam, or a Discourse upon Romans v. 12–14, by which are proved that the first Men were created before Adam, with a Theological System upon that Presupposition." 8vo. London. 1656. The author was discovered, and thrown into prison on account of his book; it caused considerable sensation, and several answers to it were published.

The school-books of the present day, while they teach the child that the earth moves, yet assure him that it is a little less than six thousand years old, and that it was made in six days. On the other hand, geologists of all creeds are agreed that the earth has existed for an immense series of years—to be counted by millions rather

---

* *The Soul and the Future Life—the Philosophic Argument.* 1859.

than by thousands; and that indubitably more than six days elapsed from its first creation to the appearance of man upon its surface. By this broad discrepancy between old and new doctrine is the modern mind startled, as were the men of the sixteenth century when told that the earth moved.*

The great object of the writers of our time is to show that the Biblical account of the Creation is strictly in accordance with the teachings of modern science. The notion put forth by Dr. Kurtz, Coleridge, Hugh Miller, and some others, is, that *the process of Creation was revealed to Moses in a series of visions.* About seven years since, Dr. J. C. Fisher proved that Hugh Miller, in his lecture, "The Two Records—the Mosaic and the Geologic," so far from using the classification by geologists of the rocks on the earth's surface into " palæozoic, secondary, and tertiary," to illustrate the striking coincidence between the two records, in an unauthorized manner, was perfectly justified in showing that this classification, *made without any reference to the Scriptures* whatever, in a most wonderful manner, agrees with them. By taking the most prominent fact in each of these periods, Mr. Miller only followed the course which Moses has taken with each of the other so-called days; while he does not state that these are *the only facts,* but the most prominent and characteristic.

Theologians and geologists have sought to reconcile Miller's *Testimony of the Rocks* and our version of the first chapter of Genesis, by two or perhaps three general schemes. The first one supposes that between the first verse and the second there was an undefined and enormous interval of time, in which the various geological changes, such as we now find upon the earth, took place; that the earth was then brought into the chaotic state described in the second verse; and then it was, in six days of twenty-four hours each, prepared for the habitation of man, who was at that time placed upon it. This was the plan of reconciliation of Dr. Chalmers, and, with a single exception, that of Dr. John Pye Smith, who thought that the chaos described in the second verse, and the work of creation in the rest of the chapter, extended over but a small part of the earth's surface; and that outside of

---

* Professor Baden Powell.

that area, the rest of the earth continued to enjoy the light of the sun, and plants and animals lived, and grew, and have continued by an unbroken series of generations to our own times. The progress of geological discovery has caused the scheme of Dr. Chalmers to be laid aside, for it does not meet the wants of the case; and that of Dr. Smith is opposed to the record of Moses, in making no provision for the creation of the heavens.

The second method supposes, that the days were periods of great and indefinite extent, each embracing vast ages, in which the various geological changes occurred. With some few modifications, this is now adopted by the great majority of modern geologists. There is little, if any doubt, that so far at least as the length of the days is concerned, this scheme is strictly in consonance with the meaning of the Scriptures. Almost all geologists and theologians, however, commit the mistake of confining this description of the creation to the earth alone, although the sacred narrative as plainly asserts that "in the beginning God created the *heavens* and the earth," and at its close declares, "thus the *heavens* and the earth were finished, and all the host of them."

Dr. Fisher's proofs extend through some half-dozen pages of argument, in which the translation of certain words is a distinctive feature. At the close, he proceeds to recapitulate the work of the several days, and shows how they agree with the teachings of the works of God.

In the beginning,[*] God created the substance of the heavens and the earth, and this substance was without form and void, or diffused throughout space; it was dark, and the Spirit of God caused a motion to commence in it. God endued a part of it with luminous properties, and a part He left dark; He then caused the light to separate from the dark matter, and named the light mat-

---

[*] "The word *beginning*," says Dr. Buckland, adopting the mode originally brought into vogue by Dr. Chalmers, "as applied by Moses in the first verse of the book of Genesis, expresses an undefined period of time, which was antecedent to the last great change that affected the surface of the earth, and to the creation of its present animal and vegetable inhabitants; during which period a long series of operations may have been going on, and which, as they are wholly unconnected with the history of the human race. are passed over in silence by the sacred historian." . . . "This *beginning* may have been an epoch at an unmeasured distance, followed by periods of undefined duration, during which all the physical operations disclosed by geology were going on." . . . "Millions of millions of years may have occupied the indefinite interval, between *the beginning* in which God created the heaven and the earth, and the evening or commencement of the first day of the Mosaic narrative."

The Mosaic and Geologic Creation. 25

ter day, or the warmth-producing matter; and the dark He called night, or the moving-around matter. This constituted *the first day*. On *the second day*, He caused the matter of the heavens and the earth, or of the universe, to separate and divide into distinct masses; and to the space which contained these masses, together with the masses themselves, He gave the name of heaven. This was the work of the second day. On *the third day*, He caused the masses of matter to become consolidated, and gave to the one which we inhabit the specific name of earth, and to its collections of waters, seas. He then clothed the earth abundantly with verdure of all kinds, and commenced its preparation for the residence of man upon it; this was the work of the third day. On *the fourth day*, He arranged the motions of the heavenly bodies, both with reference to the earth and to each other. On the *fifth and sixth days*, the preparation of the earth for the residence of man was completed, and man was placed upon it. We have thus a clear, definite, and intelligible narrative, which agrees throughout with the teachings of the most perfect science.

We have not space now to review the various phenomena of nature which bear us out in the assertion; but those who have studied the subject will understand the full force of the declaration, that if one should seek to give a sketch in the fewest words of the *Celestial Mechanism* of Laplace, the *Cosmos* of Humboldt, and the geology of the latest and best authorities, he would do it in the very language of Moses. Here, then, we have presented to us the wonderful spectacle of all the grandest conclusions of science epitomized, arranged, and accounted for ages ago, at a time when we are accustomed to look upon the world as in its infancy; and when all nations, except the one to which this wonderful writer belonged, were plunged in the darkest and most degrading idolatry. Where did Moses get this knowledge so absolutely perfect? Was it not from God? and is not this chapter, over which such a premature shout of triumph has been sent up, the most convincing proof of the inspiration of the Scriptures?

In the *Genesis of the Earth and of Man*, second edition, 1860, the Editor, Mr. Reginald Stuart Poole, in his ably written Preface, thus treats this much disputed question:

The common opinion, that man was first created six or seven thousand years ago, is considered by all who have in any degree mastered the subject to be no longer tenable. Two new theories have been offered in its place. One clings to the one origin of our race, but assigns to it an enormous antiquity. The other suggests the existence of a Pre-Adamite race, and supposes the Biblical narrative to refer especially to a higher and later stock. No third theory seems possible.

The two theories have one thing in common: they both assert the great antiquity of man, the fact upon which the rejection of the current opinion depends. I advisedly call it a fact, since it is proved in a conclusive manner, by evidence of a very various character, the most important point of which is the discovery of flint-implements in tracts of drift, and in bone-caves; in both cases with the bones of animals now extinct. What we may consider certain is the immense antiquity of man, and his having been in the remoter age of his existence in a state of great barbarism.*

Baron Bunsen, who may be considered the representative of a school, takes, apparently on grounds of sentiment, the unity of origin of the human race as the basis of his theory. He then examines the relation of languages on the supposition of their original unity, and roughly determines the length of man's dwelling on the earth by the time required for the origination and growth of the many varieties of human speech. He defines this period as about twenty thousand years B. C., divided midway by the Flood; and it is probable that those who belong to his school would not greatly shorten this vast space of time. Yet even this scheme is not sufficient without nullifying the Flood, as destructive of the descendants of Adam; for ten thousand years is not enough, in his opinion, for the development of language. But it is a serious question whether any space of time would meet the difficulties of the case.

The author of the above work, taking up the subject with entire freedom from bias, first examines the Biblical data. In them he finds strong evidence of the existence of a non-Adamite race both before and

---

* It appears that weapons of flint have since been found near Abbeville in beds of gravel lying in chalk, and mingled with the remains of elephants. This, if the age of the gravel and chalk be accepted as incontrovertible facts, gives a remote antiquity to the race whose implements they have entombed. The following decision has been given by Sir Charles Lyell, and is considered to be an authoritative conclusion:

"Although the accompanying shells are of living species, I believe the antiquity of the Abbeville and Amiens flint instruments to be great indeed, if compared to the times of history or tradition. I consider the gravel to be of fluviatile origin, but I could detect nothing in the structure of its several parts indicating cataclysmal action, nothing that might not be due to such river-floods as we have witnessed in Scotland during the last half-century. It must have required a long period for the wearing down of the chalk which supplied the broken flints for the formation of so much gravel at various heights, sometimes 100 feet above the present level of the Somme, for the deposition of fine sediment including entire shells, both terrestrial and aquatic, and also for the denudation which the entire mass of stratified drift has undergone, portions having been swept away, so that what remains of it often terminates abruptly in old river cliffs, besides being covered by a newer unstratified drift. To explain these changes I should infer considerable oscillations in the level of the land in that part of France—slow movements of upheaval and subsidence, deranging but not wholly displacing the course of the ancient rivers. Lastly, the disappearance of the elephant, rhinoceros, and other genera of quadrupeds now foreign to Europe, implies, in like manner, a vast lapse of ages, separating the era in which the fossil implements were framed, and that of the invasion of Gaul by the Romans."

after the Flood. The reader must see in the book itself how he reconciles this inference with the statements in the Bible supposed to declare the unity of our race *in origin*, upon which one point the whole difficulty rests. Passing from the Bible to human knowledge, the author examines ethnology, chronology, history, and philology, each independently, in illustration of the controversy. From ethnology, he finds that the varieties of our species may be reduced to two stocks, but scarcely, except on the supposition of an unrecorded miracle, to one. In history, he sees that every civilized race tells us of a barbarous race expelled or subdued by its ancestors. In Pagan religions, when all traces of primeval revelation have been set aside, he perceives, in the case of nearly every one, two distinct elements; one intellectually very low, the other always much higher; the worship of stones and trees, combined with the adoration of the great luminaries, or of intelligences. Philology, in like manner, leads him to the conclusion that many languages exhibit traces more or less clear of two sources of human speech widely distinct in character. In the case of the ancient Egyptians, which is of great importance from our having specimens of it four thousand years old, he discovers an example of the first contact of these two elements, which, mixed but not fused, like oil and water, compose this very ancient form of speech. This duality has never yet been explained in connection with the theory of the unity of our race.

There is yet another view. The late M. D'Orbigny has demonstrated, in his *Prodrome de Palæontologie*, after an elaborate examination of a vast number of fossils, that there have been at least twenty-nine distinct periods of animal and vegetable existence—that is, twenty-nine creations separated one from another by catastrophes which have swept away the species existing at the time, with very few solitary exceptions, never exceeding one and a-half per cent. of the whole number discovered, which have either survived the catastrophe, or have been erroneously designated. But not a single species of the preceding period survived the last of these catastrophes, and this closed the Tertiary period and ushered in the Human period. The evidence adduced by M. D'Orbigny shows that both plants and animals appeared in every one of those twenty-nine periods. The notion, therefore, that the "days" of Genesis represent periods of creation from the beginning of things is at once refuted. The parallel is destroyed, both in the number of the periods (thirty, including the Azoic, instead of six), and also in the character of the things created. No argument could be more complete; and yet the writer of the *Præ-Adamite Earth*, in Dr. Lardner's *Museum of Science*, sums up the above lucid sketch of M. D'Orbigny's researches, by referring the account in the first chapter of Genesis to the whole Creation from the beginning of all things, a *selection* of epochs being made, as he imagines, for the six days or periods.—ARCHDEACON PRATT'S *Science and Scripture not at Variance.*

ORIGIN OF LIFE—DARWIN'S THEORY.

For nearly a quarter of a century, Mr. Charles Darwin, favorably known to the public by more than one published work of natural history and science, has been engaged upon a most important inquiry, "On the Origin of Species by means of Natural Selection, or the Preservation of Favored Races in the Struggle for Life." A portion or summary of this work has appeared; and the author's conclusions, if established by the completing section, will cause an entire revolution in the fundamental doctrines of natural history, and trench upon the territory of established religious belief. With regard to the origin of the human race, he attempts to prove that the moral and spiritual faculties of man have been gradually developed by the working of matter upon matter; but, says an acute critic, "no conceivable amount of evidence, derived from the growth of the structure of animals and plants, would have the slightest bearing upon our convictions in regard to the origin of conscience, or man's belief in a Supreme Being and the immortality of his own soul."

Mr. Darwin's theory may be stated in a few words.* All organic beings are liable to vary in some degree, and tend to transmit such variations to their offspring. All at the same time tend to increase at a very rapid rate, and their increase is kept in check by the excessive competition of other individuals of the same species; or by physical conditions injurious to each organism; or to its power of bearing healthy offspring. Whatever variation, occurring among the individuals of the same species of animals or plants, is in any way advantageous in the struggle for existence, will give to these individuals an advantage over their fellows, which will be inherited by their offspring until the modified variety supplants the parent species. This process, which is termed *natural selection*, is incessantly at work, and all organized beings are undergoing its operation. By the steady accumulation, during long ages of time, of slight differences, each in some way beneficial to the individual, arise the various modifications of structure by which the countless forms of animal and vegetable life are distinguished from each other. All existing animals have descended from at most four or five progenitors, and plants from an equal or lesser number. Analogy (which Mr. Darwin admits to be a deceitful judge) would even lead him to infer that "all the or-

---

* Abridged from the *Saturday Review*.

ganic beings which have ever lived on this earth have descended from some one primordial form, into which life was at first breathed."

Archbishop Whately has reduced this "transmutation theory," as he terms it, to a skeleton, as follows:

1st. *Species* are *not permanent; varieties* are the beginning of new species.

2d. Nature began from the simplest forms—probably from one form —the primæval *monad,* the parent of all organic life.

3d. There has been a continual ascent on the organic scale, till organic nature became what it is, by one continued and unbroken stream of onward movement.

4th. The organic ascent is secured by a Malthusian principle through nature,—by a battle of life, in which the best in organization (the best varieties of plants and animals) encroach upon and drive off the less perfect. This is called the theory of *Natural Selection.* . . .

5th. We do not mark any great organic changes *now*, because they are so slow that even a few thousand years may produce no changes that have fixed the notice of naturalists.

6th. But *time is the agent,* and we can mark the effects of time by the organic changes on the great geological scale. And on every part of that scale, where the organic changes are great in two contiguous deposits of the scale, there must have been a corresponding lapse of time between the periods of their deposition—perhaps millions of years.

The foregoing heads give the substance of Darwin's theory; and the great broad facts of geology are directly opposed to it.

Dr. Whately objects that this new theory is not *inductive,*—not based on a series of acknowledged facts pointing to a *general conclusion,*—not a proposition evolved out of the facts, logically, and of course including them. The theory is as a vast pyramid resting on its apex, and that apex a mathematical point. The only facts Darwin pretends to adduce, as true elements of proof, are the *varieties* produced by domestication, or the *human artifice* of cross-breeding, which in the old world could have had no existence; whilst the varieties of domestication and human design are insufficient to undermine the continuity of true species. Species have been constant for thousands of years, and time would never change them, as long as the conditions remained constant.

In endeavoring to fit his principles to the facts of geology, Mr. Darwin urges, first, the extremely imperfect character of the geological record, in the organic remains found in each successive formation; secondly, the enormous lapse of time that must be

allowed for each formation, and for the intervals between them.
In this part of his case he fails; he enormously overrates the
amount of time which can be legitimately demanded to account
for the geological phenomena; and to obtain the space which he
requires to account for the existence of an enormous mass of
formations, he points to a period as far removed from the commencement of organic life in the earliest known palæozoic rocks
as these are from our era. His witnesses, he admits, are drowned;
they are the successive forms of primitive fauna and flora, which
have been silently entombed throughout millions of ages; through
which, however, no volcano, or other elevatory force, has ever
brought a single fragment of these buried continents to the light
of day!

Dr. Whately acutely observes, in conclusion:

> The pretended physical philosophy of modern days strips Man of all
> his moral attributes, or holds them of no account in the estimate of his
> origin and place in the created world. A cold atheistical materialism
> is the tendency of the so-called material philosophy of the present day.
> Not that I believe that Darwin is an atheist; though I cannot but regard his materialism as atheistical; because it ignores all rational conception of a final cause. I think it untrue, because opposed to the obvious course of Nature, and the very opposite of inductive truth. I therefore think it intensely mischievous.
>
> Any startling and (supposed) novel paradox—maintained very boldly
> and with an imposing plausibility, derived from a great array of facts
> all interpreted hypothetically—produces, in some minds, a kind of pleasing excitement, which predisposes them in its favor; and if they are
> unused to careful reflection, and averse to the labor of accurate investigation, they will be likely to conclude that what is (apparently) *original*
> must be a production of original *genius*, and that any thing very much opposed to prevailing notions must be a grand *discovery*,—in short, that
> whatever comes from "the bottom of a well" must be the "truth" which
> has been long hidden there.

UNITY OF THE HUMAN RACE.

Blumenbach is the father of Ethnology. Before his labors
this science had no existence. In various verse men murmured—

> The noblest study of mankind is man—

but they had not yet hit upon the proper method of studying him.
The history of the human race was far less accurately known than

Unity of the Human Race. 31

the history of dogs and horses. It was perplexed with errors of three kinds—physical, social, and moral. Blumenbach appeared, banished the physical errors, or at any rate destroyed our confidence in them; and by that one service he destroyed our confidence in all the others. The question of races was opened. Ethnology grew to be a science.

Blumenbach died on the 18th of January, 1840, having lived nearly a century, and having left his name forever marked in the history of science, as that of the man who first proved the unity of the human race. Pliny seriously speaks of men with but one leg, with eyes on their shoulders, and

> Anthropophagi, and men whose heads
> Do grow beneath their shoulders.

In the sixteenth century, Rondelet, the excellent naturalist, gravely described *marine men*, living in the sea, with beards of seaweed and coverings of scales. In the eighteenth century, Maupertius is eloquent on Patagonian giants, whose conceptions are as vast as their bodies. Even Linnæus classed the orang-outang in the same family as man. It was reserved for Blumenbach to prove the *physical unity* of the whole human race, and to demarcate the human from all other races.

The human race, as is well known, consists of a considerable number of varieties, differing from one another in personal appearance, character, language; in their average degree of moral and intellectual powers, and in their geographical distribution. Those whose observations have been mainly confined to the extremes of form and color, and who have not reflected on the wonderful changes to which all organized beings are subject by various external physical causes, have viewed the differences observed among the members of the human family, not as characteristics of so many varieties of a single species, but as marks distinguishing different species of the same genus. We have, however, the authority of the greatest observer of nature, as developed in the animal kingdom, in opposition to this doctrine.

" The permanence of certain types, in the midst of most opposite influences," says Humboldt, " especially of climate, appeared to favor this view, notwithstanding the shortness of the time to which the historical evidence applied; but in my opinion more powerful reasons lend their weight to the other side of the question, and corroborate the unity of the human race." Humboldt refers to the many intermediate gradations of the tint of the skin and the form of the skull; and adds, "The greater part of the supposed contrasts, to which so much weight was formerly assigned, have disappeared before the laborious investigation of Tiedmann on the brain of negroes and Europeans, and of the anatomical researches of Vrolik and Weber, on the form of the pelvis." "If we compare the dark-colored African nations with the natives of the Australasian Islands, and with the Papuas and Alfarous, we see that a black tint of skin, woolly hair, and negro features, are by no means invariably associated. So long as the western nations were acquainted with only a small part of the earth's surface, partial views almost necessarily prevailed. Tropical heat, and a black color of the skin, appeared inseparable. The campaigns of Alexander, in which so many subjects connected with physical geography were originally brought into notice, occasioned the first discussion on the problematical influence of climate on nations and races." (*Cosmos*.)

Thus, it appears that according to the principles admitted by the most eminent physiologists and naturalists, whether assenting or not to the doctrines of Christianity, there is nothing in the natural differences observable between different parts of the human race distributed over the globe, which is incompatible with the part of the origin of mankind, consigned to the Hebrew Scriptures, which *traces the whole human race to a single pair*, and constitutes them therefore as members of a common family.

THE EMBRYO UNDER THE MICROSCOPE.

How thrilling is the revelation of an embryo moving inside the egg, when placed under a microscope! There lie hundreds of eggs, which, to the naked eye, present the aspect of a single body, about the size of a pin's head. Every one of these eggs contains an embryo in process of development. In one we see nothing but a mass of granules. In another, something is moving. At first it moves with pendulum motion,—afterwards it moves round and round in the egg by means of long hairs which are vibrating with great activity—we are watching the beginnings of Life! Or take up this globule of jelly—under the Microscope you see a long worm-like body coiled round the globule, the head being very large in proportion. It is a young vertebrate animal, still in the egg; and as you watch, you observe a *rustling* current in one direction, and a *pulsating* current in another. This is the circulation of the blood; and if you are fortunate, you will see the heart, or pulsating sac, in incessant action. Can a planet be a finer sight than this? (*Saturday Review*, No. 40.)

Nevertheless, we must remember that, in the words of Sir Benjamin Brodie, "neither our unassisted vision, nor the microscope, nor chemical analysis, nor any analogy, nor any other means at our disposal, enable us to form any kind of notion as to the actual changes in the brain or spinal chord on which any other nervous phenomena depend."

THE DEVELOPMENT THEORY—CHEMISTRY CANNOT CREATE AN ORGANIC GERM. *

The amateurs of this theory maintain that in the course of an infinite series of years, the vast variety presented in the organic creation, was gradually *developed* from the lowest form of organization, a simple cell. Plants and animals formed an unbroken chain, and transitions from the one to the other could not be disputed.

But, whence is the origin of the first organic cell? This one cell, they tell us, was called into existence by the fiat of the Creator, and all others were developed from it. This school of physiologists thus presume that it was more conformable to the purposes of the Creator to bestow vitality on this one cell than

---

* "The Development Theory" of Lamarck, it will be remembered, formed the basis of the theory of the author of the *Vestiges of Creation*, the publication of which produced great effect, a few years since. Two arbitrary hypotheses were added: that "the creation of life, wherever it takes place, is a chemico-electric operation, by which simple germinal vesicles are produced;" and that all animated beings, "from the simplest and oldest up to the highest and most recent, are the results, *first*, of an inherent impulse in the forms of life to advance, in definite times, through grades of organization terminating in the highest dicotyledons and mammalia: secondly, of external physical circumstances, operating reactively upon the central impulse to produce the requisite peculiarities of exterior organization."

on many; and, having created it, to leave to time and chance the full unfolding and development of organic nature from this one cell. Exact scientific investigation, however, ignores the existence of a connected chain of organic life. What then becomes of the first created cell?

Superficial inquirers reply, that organic nature is formed of carbon, water, nitrogen, oxygen, and sulphur; that in the constant interchange taking place among these elements, it may possibly so have happened that, by their own inherent power, they united and formed the cell, and so the organic structure. The chemist can in his laboratory prepare a number of substances, formerly obtained only from living plants and animals. He can make sugar from wood, he can prepare urea and the taurine of bile: why then may carbon, water, and other elements not unite of their own accord, and produce a germ?

But what these superficial observers designate organic substances are only chemical compounds containing organic elements. The taurine extracted from bile cannot be distinguished from that made in the laboratory: they are both formed by a chemical, not by an organic force. It is self-evident, that chemical forces are in operation in the living body. Chemistry now proves what she asserted thirty years ago without the ability to offer proof. Under the influence of a cause which is not chemical, we see chemical forces acting in the living organism. As the intelligent will of the chemist forces the elements external to the body to combine into the products urea, taurine, &c., so within the body those same elements unite to form those same products, not by any inherent power of their own, but by the controlling action of this vital cause. It will be within the chemist's power to form quinine, caffeine, the coloring matter of plants, and all other compounds which possess chemical but not vital properties, the smallest particles of which, in arranging themselves into a crystalline form, are not under the influence of an organic force;—but he will never succeed in constructing in the laboratory a cell, a muscular fibre, a nerve, or in short any one single portion of the organic frame possessed of vital properties. Whoever has seen carbonate of ammonia, carbonate and phosphate of lime, an iron-ore, an alkaline mineral, will at once pronounce, that it is impossible by means of heat, electricity, or any other natural force, to form from these substances an organic germ capable of further development and propagation.

Inorganic bodies produce only inorganic substances; but organic bodies, with their peculiar forms so different from crystals, and endowed with vital properties, owe their origin to a higher force acting in the living body, and which presses into its service the inorganic forces.

A hundred years ago, it was believed that fishes and frogs were spontaneously produced in bogs, and that plants and all kinds of insects were formed in fermenting and putrefying mixtures, and in moist sawdust. Had this been true, then doubtless might a man under similar circumstances have been also spontaneously produced; inquiry, however, proved that all these opinions regarded as facts were based upon false and frivolous observations. In every well-investigated case, germs and seeds of plants, and eggs of animals, were discovered, which were developed in mould; but an egg, a seed, has its origin in a living organism.

Many philosophers have asserted, that life, like matter, has existed from all eternity. Exact inquiry has, however, proved, that at a certain period, the earth possessed a temperature which was incompatible with organic life; for congelation of the blood takes place at 172° Fahr. Organic life must, therefore, have had a beginning.—*Liebig's Familiar Letters.*

MAN AND HIS DWELLING-PLACE.

In 1859, there appeared a remarkable book with this title, with certain new views, or views which, if old, have a new face. The author understands by "Man" the human race, and by his "Dwelling-place" what we usually call the material universe. He claims to have hit upon an hypothesis relating to the world in which we live which will supply the key to its various perplexities. His fundamental proposition is, that man is in a defective condition, so that he does not feel things as they are, but otherwise than they are. Hence he argues that that enormous number of phenomena, the aggregate of which makes up what we call the external world—including, we suppose, our own bodies—are merely such a manifestation of certain unspeakable spiritual or living entities as our defective condition enables us to perceive. What those entities may be he does not pretend to say; but he thinks it possible that, if we once realize the fact that the inertness, or, as he prefers to describe it, the *deadness* which we are accustomed to ascribe to all natural objects, is in ourselves, and not in them—that we are looking at living beings through dead spectacles—we may ultimately be able, by the ordinary processes of reasoning, to arrive at some sort of conception of them not altogether inadequate. The unreality of the world of phenomena is of course a very old doctrine; nor can it surprise any one who is familiar with Plato, with Berkeley, with Mr. Mill, or even with Comte. Probably no one who has any claims to accuracy of thought believes in matter at the present day in the sense in which its existence was denied by Berkeley.*

The peculiarity of the view maintained in the work before us lies in its theory about man. The author repeats over and over again that man is dead—that it is our deadness which colors all our view of nature, and makes us think that nature is dead and physical, instead of being, as he says it is, living and spiritual. We are like people on a railway, who see the landscape flying past them—like our ancestors when they refused to believe that the earth moved, and that the sun stood still—like any one who transfers conditions affecting himself to what is outside of him. Man being dead, and that which we call the world being the shadow of some ineffably glorious spiritual being, which our incapacity only allows us to see and feel in that dead shape in which it appears to us, Christianity is a wakening of man to his proper life. The isolated event usually called death is falsely so called. It is comparatively unimportant, and has little or no moral significance. If we could only see it, we are in heaven now, and need no other change than the change from death to life to realize the fact.

Such, in a very compressed shape indeed, is the doctrine of this

---

* It has been stated that "a person possessed with a hallucination realizes up to a certain point the supposition of the Berkeleians, who pretend to decide that it is not positively necessary that the existence of the universe should be real, in order that we should perceive it as it appears to our senses."—*Octave Delepierre.*

curious book. We may say shortly, that the author considers that it embraces the various truths partially perceived by the idealist who denied that phenomena were realities—by the disciple of Reid, who maintained that the world was not an assemblage of ideas—by the Positivist, who denied that we have any knowledge of Being, properly so called—and by the Mystic, who maintained that if consciousness could prove the existence of a dead material substratum to natural objects, it could prove any thing and every thing, in the assertions that phenomena, being unreal in themselves, imply the existence of an external and substantial, but immaterial and spiritual world, of which we have no knowledge, though we may hereafter attain to it—and that our consciousness which falsely asserted the existence of a natural substratum, is the very first element which we must correct in all our speculations on these subjects.—*Abridged from the Saturday Review*, Feb. 5, 1859.

PLURALITY OF WORLDS.

The doctrine that there are more worlds than one has been maintained by nearly all the distinguished astronomers and writers who have flourished since the true figure of the earth was determined. Giordano Bruna of Nola, Kepler, and Tycho Brahe, believed in it; and Cardinal Cusa and Bruno, before the discovery of binary systems among the stars, believed also that the stars were inhabited. Sir Isaac Newton likewise adopted the belief; and Dr. Bentley, Master of Trinity College, Cambridge, ably maintained the same doctrine. In our day, we number among its supporters the distinguished names of La Place, Sir William and Sir John Herschel, Dr. Chalmers, Isaac Taylor, and M. Arago. It has been opposed by Dr. Whewell on theological as well as scientific grounds; he does not pretend to disprove the plurality of worlds; but he denies that any argument makes the doctrine probable, adding, that "it is too remote from knowledge to be either proved or disproved."

The great advocate of the doctrine, which has been revived of late years, is Sir David Brewster, who has replied to Dr. Whewell, emphatically maintaining that analogy strongly countenances the idea of all the solar planets, if not all worlds in the universe, being peopled with creatures not dissimilar in being and nature to the inhabitants of the earth. This view is supported in *Scientific Certainties of Planetary Life*, by T. C. Simon, who well treats one point of the argument—that mere distance of the planets from the central sun does not determine the condition as to light and heat, but that the density of the ethereal medium enters largely into the calculation. Mr. Simon's general conclusion is, that "neither on account of deficient or excessive heat, nor with regard to the density of the materials, nor with regard to the force of gravity on the surface, is there the slightest pretext for supposing that all the planets of our system are not inhabited by intellectual creatures with animal bodies like ourselves,—moral beings, who know and love their great Maker, and who wait, like the rest of His creation, upon His providence and upon His care."

Sir Isaac Newton, in a conversation with Conduitt, said he took " all the planets to be composed of the same matter with the earth, viz., earth, water, and stone, but variously concocted."

IDENTITY OF THE VITAL PRINCIPLE OF ANIMALS AND VEGETABLES.

Sir J. E. Smith, the distinguished botanist, advocates this hypothesis upon heat, both in animals and plants, seeming to have the closest possible connection with the vital principle, " as evident in every organized body, from our own elaborate frame to the humblest moss or fungus. Those different fluids, so fine and transparent, separated from each other by membranes as fine, which compose the eye, all retain their proper situations (though each fluid individually is perpetually removed and renewed) for sixty, eighty, or a hundred years, or more, while *life* remains. So do the infinitely small vessels of an almost invisible insect, the fine and pellucid tubes of a plant, all hold their destined fluids, conveying or changing them according to fixed laws, but never permitting them to run into confusion, so long as the vital principle animates their various forms. But no sooner does *death* happen, than, without any alteration of structure, any apparent change in their *material* configuration, all is reversed. The eye loses its form and brightness, its membranes let go their contents, which mix in confusion, and thenceforth yield to the laws of chemistry alone. Just so it happens, sooner or later, to the other parts of the animal as well as vegetable frame. Chemical changes, putrefaction and destruction, immediately follow the total privation of life, the importance of which becomes instantly evident when it is no more. I humbly conceive, therefore, that if the human understanding can, in any case, flatter itself with obtaining, in the natural world, a glimpse of the *immediate agency* of the Deity, it is in the contemplation of this *vital principle*, which seems independent of material organization, and an impulse of its own divine energy. Nor am I ashamed to confess, that I can no more explain the physiology of vegetables, than of animals, without this hypothesis, as I allow it to be, of a living principle in both."

CHAIN OF BEING.

The doctrine of *one gradual scale, one unbroken chain* in Nature, extending from Infinite being to Nonentity, was held by all Antiquity. The Ancients regarded the World as a *Cosmos* or Orderly System in which there was no vacuum, but all the parts of which were linked closely together, and each link subordinate, fixed, and necessary. To this doctrine in great measure we owe the belief in Elemental Spirits, Genii, Nymphs, Sylphs, and Fairies.

The admirable pietist John Arndt says:

God so disposes and orders things that the inferior creatures receive of the superior, and all Nature hangs together as it were in *One Chain*. And this connection of Nature and Providence is finely described by the prophet Hosea, ii. 21, 22. "It shall come to pass in that day, saith the Lord, I will hear the Heavens, and they shall hear the Earth; and the Earth shall hear the corn, and the wine, and the oil; and they shall hear Jezreel." In this place the Prophet presents us with the entire Order of Nature, beginning at the First Cause, which is God, &c.—*True Christianity*.

It was the opinion of Wesley (says Southey), that there is a *Chain of Being* advancing by degrees from the lowest to the highest point—from an atom of organized matter to the highest of the Archangels: an opinion consonant to the philosophy of the Bards, and confirmed by Science as far as our physiological knowledge extends.

As to this Chain of Nature, Professor Sedgwick observes:

"Independently of any evidence we derive from palæontology, a conception of this kind is so grateful to the imagination, and is so obviously suggested by the clear gradations of living Nature, that our Ideal Organic Scale has been for ages past a subject of speculation. I profess not to trace its history; but Dr. Johnson tells us that it took its rise among the Oriental metaphysicians and physiologists. In the former half of last century it was a favorite theme with our moralists and poets. It was adorned by the beautiful prose of Addison, and the glittering poetry of Pope; and it was tortured into the service of infidelity by Bolingbroke. Lastly, it was taken up by Soame Jenyns, in his acute and elegant, but very unsatisfactory, *Inquiry into the Nature and Origin of Evil*.*

"In the hypothetical scheme of the Authors just alluded to, 'The Universe is a system whose very essence consists in subordination—a Scale of Beings descending by insensible degrees from infinite perfection to absolute nothing; in which, though we may justly expect to find perfection in *the Whole*, could we possibly comprehend it; yet would it be the highest absurdity to hope for it in all its *parts*, because the beauty and happiness of the whole depend altogether on the just inferiority of its parts, &c.....' It is, moreover, highly probable (we are told) that there is such a connection between all ranks and orders by subordinate degrees, that they mutually support each other's existence; and every one in its place is absolutely necessary toward sustaining the whole magnificent fabric."

---

* See an interesting paper on "the Golden Chain of Homer—the Hermetic or Mercurial Chain," in *Curiosities of Science*, Second Series (*Things not generally Known*), pp. 32–88. The idea of the "Chain of Being" extends beyond the views held as to the Typical Forms in the Animal Kingdom, which show that while no single plan of combination is applicable to all animals, there is, nevertheless, a certain uniformity of organization observable in each primary division.

THE KINGDOMS OF NATURE.

Did it ever occur to the reader to inquire into the origin of that distribution of Nature into three Kingdoms, Mineral, Vegetable, and Animal? Naturalists have been scrupulous in recording the date of the establishment of each class in the animal and vegetable world; and beside the names of the species they have frequently recorded the names of the discoverers of these species. But scruples stopped there. The men who tell you the history of every genus, nay, of every species, of insects, polypes, and mosses, do not, because they cannot, tell you to whom the great primary groupings—those familiar "Kingdoms"—are due. Who first divided nature into three Kingdoms? Who first gave the name of Kingdom? Linnæus is silent—Cuvier has no word of explanation for his *Règne Animal*. Daubenton, indeed, did once intimate that our knowledge on this point was a blank; and a blank he left it. We are so familiarized with the division into Mineral, Plant, and Animal, that it is with difficulty we can conceive the division not to have always been accepted. But open Aristotle, who represents the whole science of antiquity, and you find him making the division to be that of *animate* and *inanimate* —a division accepted by all his followers—and, let us add, a division which, in spite of M. St. Hilaire, seems to us by far the most philosophical, seeing that the phenomena of organic substances are so intimately allied, and so broadly demarcated from those of inorganic substances, as to demand being grouped together in one division.

Where, then, is this division into three kingdoms to be found? To the surprise of M. St. Hilaire, and doubtless to that of all his readers, it is found in the writings of the alchemists. In the hermetical philosophy there is a strange combination of Pythagorean and Christian doctrines, and hence the employment of *septenary* and *ternary* divisions—the septenary, because of the seven days spoken of in Genesis, whence the seven planets, seven meteors, seven metals, seven precious stones, seven vital parts of man, seven notes of music, and so on—the ternary, because everywhere in creation the image of the Creator, the Three in One, the *tri-unitas* is impressed. Hence the three kingdoms.

But whence the name *kingdom?* The alchemists seem to have been royalists *quand même*. They always spoke of the sun as the king of the stars; of gold as the king of metals; of man as the king of animals. How these names became repeated until familiarity forced them into scientific use, and how they gradually became adopted in systematic treatises, must be read in M. St. Hilaire's curious chapter, where also will be found an account of the various divisions since proposed by eminent authors—Daubenton, Oken, Carus, and De Candolle, advocating *four*, Bory de Saint Vincent *five*, and Bischoff *seven.*—*Abridged from the Saturday Review*, April 25, 1857.

NUMBERS IN NATURE.

Physical science shows that numbers have a significancy in every department of nature. *Two* appears as the typical number in the lowest class of plants, and regulates that pairing or marriage of plants and animals which is one of the fundamental laws of the organic kingdoms. *Three* is the characteristic number of that class of plants which has parallel veined leaves, and is the number of joints in the typical digit. *Four* is the significant number of those beautiful crystals which show that minerals (as well as stars) have their geometry. *Five* is the model number of the highest class of plants,—those with reticulated veins and branches,—is the typical number of the fingers and toes of vertebrated animals, and is of frequent occurrence among star-fishes. *Six* is the proportional number of carbon in chemistry, and 3×2 is a common number in the floral organs of monocotyledonous plants, such as lilies. *Seven* appears as significant only in a single order of plants (Heptandria), but has an importance in the animal kingdom, where it is the number of vertebræ in the neck of mammalia; and, according to Mr. Edwards, the typical number of rings in the head, in the thorax, and in the abdomen of crustacea. *Eight* is the definite number in chemical composition for oxygen, the most universal element in nature, and is very common in the

Adaptation of Color.

organs of sea-jellies. *Nine* seems to be rare in the organic kingdom. *Ten*, or 5 × 2, is found in star-fishes, and is the number of digits on the fore and hind limbs of animals.

Without going over any more individual numbers, we find multiple numbers acting an important part in chemical compositions, and in the organs of flowers; for the elements unite in multiple relations, and the stamens are often the multiples of the petals. In the arrangement of the appendages of the plant we have a strange series, 1, 2, 3, 5, 8, 13, 21, 34, which was supposed to possess virtues of an old date, and before it was discovered in the plant.

ADAPTATION OF COLOR TO THE WANTS OF THE ANIMAL.

Upon this interesting inquiry, Mr. Broderip adduces the following evidences:

Throughout the animal creation, the adaptation of the color of the creature to its haunts is worthy of admiration, as tending to its preservation. The colors of insects, of a multitude of the smaller animals, contribute to their concealment. Caterpillars which feed on leaves, are generally either green, or have a large proportion of that hue in the color of their coats. As long as it remains still, how difficult it is to distinguish a grasshopper or young locust from the herbage or leaf on which it rests. The butterflies that flit about among flowers are colored like them. The small birds which frequent hedges have backs of a brownish or brownish-green hue, and their bellies are generally whitish, or light-colored, so as to harmonize with the sky. Thus, they become less visible to the hawk or cat that passes above or below them. The wayfarer across the fields almost treads upon the skylark before he sees it warbling to heaven's gate. The goldfinch or thistle-finch passes much of its time among flowers, and is vividly colored accordingly. The partridge can hardly be distinguished from the fallow or stubble upon or among which it crouches; and it is considered an accomplishment among sportsmen to have a good eye for finding a hare sitting. In northern countries, the winter dress of the hares and ptarmigans is white, to prevent detection among the snows of those inclement regions.

If we turn to the waters, the same design is evident. Frogs even vary their color according to that of the mud or sand that forms the bottoms of the ponds or streams which they frequent; nay, the tree-frog (*Hyla viridis*) takes its specific name from the color, which renders it so difficult to see among the leaves, where it adheres by the cupping-glass-like processes at the end of its toes. It is the same with fish, especially those which inhabit the fresh waters. Their backs, with the exception of gold and silver fish, and a few others, are comparatively dark; and some practice is required before they are satisfactorily made out. It is difficult to detect "the ravenous hue," as old Izaak calls the pike, with its dark-green and mottled back and sides, from the similarly tinted weeds among which that fresh-water shark lies at the watch, as motionless as they. Even when a tearing old trout, a six or seven pounder, sails in his wantonness, leisurely up the stream, with his back-fin partly above the surface, on the look-out for a fly, few, except a well-entered fisherman, can tell what shadowy form it is that ripples the whimpling water.

Nor is this design less manifest in the color and appearance of some of the largest terrestrial animals; for the same principle seems to be kept in view, whether regard be had to the smallest insects, or the quadrupedal giants of the land.

THE TREE OF LIFE.

The correspondence of religious symbols used by some of the ancient nations with those found on Christian monuments, and still more or less employed, would induce one to believe as much in the original unity of religious doctrine as in the unity of the human species. In illustration of this Dr. Barlow, in a communication to *The Builder*, Oct. 30, 1858, takes the palm-tree (*Phœnix dactylifera*), the sacred tree, *the tree of life*, among the Egyptians, the Assyrians, and the Jews. That the Egyptians, at a comparatively early period of their monumental history, represented the date-palm in this sense, we have a most interesting illustration on a stele in the Berlin Museum, which Dr. Lepsius found in the village of Abousir, near the great Pyramid. From the stem of the tree proceed two arms,—one administering, to a figure kneeling below, the fruit or bread of life; the other pouring from a vase the water of life, which the recipient guides to his mouth. This stele is at least anterior to the fifteenth century before Christ. On a more recent stele the tree of life, among the Egyptians, is figured by the *Ficus sycamorus*, the sycamore-tree of the Bible; or, occasionally, by the persica, among the boughs of which the goddess Nutpe appears with her hieroglyphical name, "Abyss of Heaven," administering to immortal souls the food and drink of the celestial regions.

The date-palm was largely introduced by the Jews in the decoration of Solomon's Temple, being represented on the walls, fur-

The Tree of Life. 45

niture, and vessels. In the last chapter of the *Apocalypse* there is a distinct reference to the palm-tree as the tree of life in the heavenly Jerusalem. For the tree here described (Rev. xxii. 1, 2), "which bare twelve manner of fruits, and yielded her fruit every month, and the leaves of the tree were for the healing of the nations," is evidently intended for the palm-tree, popularly believed to put forth a shoot every month, and the leaves of which were used for writing on. Accordingly, we find the palm-tree figuring in Christian mosaics as the tree of life in Paradise. A very good illustration of this is found in the Apsis of S. Giovanni Laterano. We have here an enclosure, the entrance to which is guarded by an angel; and within appears the palm-tree, on which is perched the phœnix, with a glory of rays, God the Father standing on one side of the tree, God the Son on the other. The palm-tree was also represented as synonymous with the cross, and with Christ. This may be seen in the illuminated frontispiece to an Evangelium, probably of the ninth century, in the library of the British Museum. Here the symbols of the four Evangelists, placed over corresponding columns of lessons from their gospels, are shown looking up to a palm-tree that rises from the centre, and on the top of which is placed a cross, having suspended from its arms the symbolical letters, Alpha and Omega.

In Christian ichnography the cross is considered as identical with Christ. So we have here the source of the Divine life symbolized by the palm-tree, as among the ancient Egyptians before their system had degenerated into idolatry.

These remarks were necessary in order to illustrate the meaning of the pine-cone in the hands of the Assyrian winged figures, or personified symbolical principles of Deity, placed on each side of the Assyrian sacred tree on our Nineveh monuments.

It will be observed that the tree here represented is a conventional form of the palm-tree, and it is surrounded by an enclosure of palmettes, or abbreviated forms of this tree, as in a garden of Paradise. The pine-cones are held toward the tree as having a significant connection with it, symbolizing the Divine principle of eternal life; and they are held toward the tree of life to indicate the source whence that life is derived.

The Evangelist St. John has sometimes been represented with

wings and an eagle's head, not unlike the Assyrian figures on the Nineveh marbles,—*apropos* of which might be quoted the curious fragment of the Zoroastrian oracles preserved by Eusebius (Præp. Evang. l. 1, c. x.): "God is he that has the head of a hawk. He is the first indestructible, eternal, unbegotten," &c. According to Dr. Layard, *Nisroch*, in whose temple Sennacherib was slain by his sons, was neither more nor less than such a symbolical personified Deity, as *Nisr*, we are told, signifies an eagle in all the Semitic languages, and the graver's tool might easily confound the head of an eagle with that of a hawk.

Pine-cones, it may be remarked, are also held in the hands of the Assyrian winged figures, in situations corresponding to those in which the symbolical divinities of the Egyptian theology hold the *crux-ansata*, the well-known symbol of eternal life, with which the pine-cone is shown to be synonymous.

Thus we find the same fundamental truth lying at the root of all religious teaching, as indicated by the remains of art and its records, among Egyptians, Assyrians, Jews, and Christians.

EVE'S APPLE-TREE.

It has been asked, What is the origin of the common mistake of calling the fruit of the forbidden tree an apple? No such phrase occurs in the Scripture. The mistake is, probably, due in part to a not very correct translation of the Latin word *pomum*. From *pomum Adami* we get *Adam's apple*. Other circumstances have helped the error. The idea that the fruit of Eden was an apple seems also to have found countenance in former days among the learned Jews. Thus, in the Song of Solomon (ii. 5), "comfort me with *apples*." The Targum has "apples of *the garden of Eden*." (See also Song viii. 5.)

It has long been known that there grows in parts of Palestine a tree supposed to bear the identical kind of fruit by eating which our first parents fell. Dr. Robinson, in his *Biblical Researches*, describes this tree as the *Asclepias gigantea*, the fruit of which, though beautiful to the eye, is a mere puff-ball, and collapses on being touched; and this fruit, says the learned Doctor, externally resembles a large smooth *apple* or orange. May not the *deceptive* appearance of this fruit have caused it to be associated with the forbidden fruit of Paradise, by which deceit, sin, and suffering were brought into the world?

We find, however, the tree more exactly described as one of the plants of Ceylon. Its native name is *Diuri Kaduru;* Kaduru signifying "forbidden," and Diuri "tigers." It is found near Colombo: the flower emits a fine scent; the color of the fruit is very beautiful, being orange on the outside and a deep crimson within; the fruit itself presenting the singular appearance of having *a piece bitten out of it.* This circumstance, together with the fact of its being a deadly poison, led the Mohammedans, on their first discovery of Ceylon (which they assigned as the site of Paradise), to represent it as "the forbidden fruit" of the garden of Eden; for although the finest and most tempting in appearance of any, it had been impressed, such was their idea, with the mark of Eve's having bitten it, to warn men from meddling with a substance possessing such noxious properties. These particulars are stated by Sir Alexander Johnston, who has so ably illustrated the history of Ceylon.

The traditions which connect the history of our first parents with various localities in Ceylon, are of very ancient date. Adam is represented by the Moormen or Mohammedans of Ceylon, on his expulsion from Paradise, to have lamented his offence, standing with one foot on the summit of the mountain which now bears his name. The figure of *a foot* is still to be traced there; but this, the Buddhists claim as a relic of their deity. Again, the reef of rocks connecting Ceylon with the island of Rámiseram, is usually called Adam's Bridge; and the two large monuments, like Mohammedan tombs, on the island of Rámiseram, are represented by the Mohammedans to be the tombs of Cain and Abel.

HOW CAIN KILLED ABEL.

I saw him fling the stone, as if he meant
At once his murder and his monument.

Cowley, in whose sacred poem of *Davideis* the above lines occur, notes that Cain was the first and greatest example of envy in this world; who slew his brother because his sacrifice was more acceptable to God than his own; at which, the Scripture says, he was sorely angered, and his countenance cast down. It is hard to guess what it was in Cain's sacrifice that displeased God. The Septuagint makes it to be a defect in the quality or quantity of the offering; if thou *hast offered right, but not rightly divided, hast thou not sinned?* But this translation neither the Vulgar edition, nor ours, nor almost any follows. We must, therefore, be content to be ignorant of the cause, since it hath pleased God not to declare it. Neither is it declared in what manner he slew his brother; and, therefore, I had the liberty to choose that which I thought most probable; which is, that he knocked him on the head with some great stone, which was one of the most ordinary and most natural weapons of anger; that this stone was big enough to be the monument or tombstone of Abel is not so hyperbolical as what Virgil says of Turnus:—

> Then, as he roll'd his troubled eyes around,
> An antique stone he saw; the common bound
> Of neighb'ring fields; and barrier of the ground:
> So vast, that twelve strong men of modern days,
> Th' enormous weight from earth cou'd hardly raise.
> He heav'd it at a lift: and pois'd on high,
> Ran stagg'ring on, against his enemy.
> *Æneid* xii.—*Dryden trans.*

FAMILY LIKENESSES.

Southey, in a letter to Sir Edgerton Brydges, says: "Did you ever observe how remarkably old age brings out family likenesses, —which, having been kept, as it were, in abeyance while the passions and business of the world engrossed the parties, come forth again in age (as in infancy), the features settling into their primary characters before dissolution? I have seen some affecting instances of this; a brother and sister, than whom no two persons in middle life could have been more unlike in countenance or in character, becoming like as twins at last. I now see my father's lineaments in the looking-glass, where they never used to appear."

Jeremy Taylor has this beautiful comparison of an aged man

to architectural remains: "It is true he was in the declension of his age and health; but his very ruins were goodly; they who saw the broken heaps of Pompey's theatre, and the crushed obelisks, and the old face of beauteous Philœnium, could not but admire the disordered glories of such magnificent structures, which were venerable in their very dust."

AVERAGE OF HUMAN LIFE.

The average of Human Life is about 33 years. One quarter die previous to the age of seven years; one half before reaching 17; and those who pass this age enjoy a felicity refused to one half the human species. To every 1,000 persons, only one reaches 100 years of life; to every 100, only six reach the age of sixty-five; and not more than one in 500 lives to eighty years of age. There are on earth 1,000,000,000 inhabitants, and of these, 333,333,333 die every year, 91,824 every day, 3,730 every hour, and 60 every minute, or one every second. These losses are about balanced by an equal number of births. The married are longer lived than the single; and, above all, those who observe a sober and industrious conduct. Tall men live longer than short ones. Women have more chances of life in their favor previous to being fifty years of age than men have, but fewer afterwards. The number of marriages is in proportion of 75 to every 1,000 individuals. Marriages are more frequently after the equinoxes; that is, during the months of June and December. Those born in the spring are generally more robust than others. Births and deaths are more frequent by night than by day.—*Quarterly Review.*

Of children born, certainly not more than one in ten thousand lives to a hundred; and of those who attain to the advanced age of a century, as certainly not more than one in twenty thousand has his life prolonged to 150: consequently, not more than one child out of twenty millions lives to the latter age.

By Gompertz's law of mortality, the sum of all the people who have as yet lived upon the earth, does not warrant the expectation of an individual attaining the greatest age which history actually reveals as having been reached; hence mathematical reasoning upon increasing numbers might lead us to infer that man is really immortal, and death but accidental. To medical science, however, death appears as inevitable as growth; and as the child is developed from the boy and grows to be a man, so the man in his turn as certainly retrogrades to senility and death. When age, unaccompanied with disease, sets in, the appetite gradually and increasingly fails, nutrition and assimilation gradually lessen; and the capacity to generate force and heat diminishes. At last, nervous power fails, and the patient silently passes into the sleep of death. To this end is man born, and must submit; for as sure as the endogenous tree grows itself to death, so does man, by virtue of some changes in his organization, cease to evince the powers of health, and finally of life.—SMEE *on General Debility and Defective Nutrition.*

SPACE AND TIME.

Dr. Reid has candidly confessed, "We are at a loss to what category or class of things we ought to refer Space and Time. They are not beings, but rather the receptacles of all created beings, without which they could not have had the possibility of existence."

Upon this it is asked: "Will no one venture to suggest that, in the beginning *God created space and time, as the receptacles of all beings to be called into existence by His Almighty fiat?*" But objections, such as these, will be made.

Where was God before the creation of space? *Where* is He now? Does not His omnipresence mean that He is everywhere? Was He nowhere before Creation? And is He not somewhere now? Is there not a local Paradise? Is there not a local Heaven in space where His presence and glory are manifested?

To such questions as these the answers are: The very word *where* is inapplicable to Him who cannot resemble His creatures in their relations to space. His omnipresence pervades the universe in knowledge and power, not in the diffusion of His essence. There is a local Heaven, where the Holy Angels are, with three human beings, Enoch and Elijah, who never died, and the Divine Redeemer, the first who triumphed over Death—the three witnesses of immortality, under the Patriarchal, the Mosaic, and the

Gospel dispensation. There is a local Paradise, where the spirits of the redeemed await the resurrection of their bodies, and their final admission into Heaven. And God's glory, which is manifested everywhere, is especially manifested there, in the transfigured humanity of Christ, the visible temple for evermore of the invisible God.—CRONHELM *on Predestination.*

CLIMACTERICS.

The superstition respecting Climacterics, or critical periods of life, was very strong during the Middle Ages; and even down to rather recent times, the mystic numbers 7 and 9, so frequently occurring in the Bible, and the combination of these numbers, have had their influence with many persons. It was believed that the constitution of man changed every seven years; and that during every septime the whole of the solids and fluids of the body were periodically renewed—the old cast off, and new matter formed. Periods of seven years were looked upon as steps or stages in life. At seven years of age, a child had left infancy; at twice seven, or fourteen, he had attained puberty; at three times seven, or twenty-one, he had reached majority, and so on. But as people advanced in years, the more critical points were approached, and the *Grand Climacteric* was looked forward to with some anxiety. Combinations of the numbers 3, 7, and 9 were mostly employed, and $3 \times 7 = 21$, $7 \times 7 = 49$, $7 \times 9 = 63$, and $9 \times 9 = 81$, were important periods. In the *Thesaurus Linguæ Romanæ et Britannicæ*, 1578, we have:

Climactericus annus. The perilous or dangerous yeare of one's lyfe.
Climactera.—The perilous time of one's life, at euery seven yeres' ende; or after other, at the ende of 63 yeres; at which tyme he is in some perill of body or minde.

In Florio's *Worlde of Worldes*, 1598, we read:

Climacterico, the dangerous and perilous year of one's life, comonly the year 63.

Blount, in his *Glossography*, gives: "the most dangerous and climacterical year at the age of 63, because both accounts meet in this number, namely, 7 × 9 = 63, and 9 × 7 = 63."

Kersey, in his *Dictionarium Anglo-Britannicum*, Third edition, 1722, gives:

Climacterical, belonging to the steps or rounds of a Ladder; as Climacterical Years, *i. e.*, certain remarkable Years, whereby Man's Life gets up, as it were, to its appointed period. Thus, every Seventh and Ninth Year is said to be Climacterical, wherein, if any sickness happen, it is counted very dangerous, especially the 63d and 81st, which are termed *Grand Climacterics*.

Johnson, in his Dictionary, refers to Cotgrave, who says:

Climactore; every seventh, ninth, or the sixty-third year of a man's life; all very dangerous, but the last most.
Death might have taken such, and her deferr'd,
Until the time she had been climacter'd,
When she would have been three score years and three,
Such as our best at three and twenty be.
DRAYTON, *on the Death of Lady Clifton*.

In the 59th number of the *Tattler*, a jocose old gentleman remarks, that having attained to sixty-four, he has passed his grand climacteric.

Sir Thomas Browne has a chapter in *Vulgar Errors*—"Of the Great Climacterical Year, that is Sixty-three;" in which he decides upon two climacterics, 63 and 81. He dwells upon the power and secret virtues of numbers, as taught by Pythagoras and Plato; and Philo the learned Jew, "who hath acted this part, even to superstition." These observations and researches extend to 20 pages.

Browne's foreign authorities are not more explicit than our own as to the numbers. Several French, Spanish, Italian, and Dutch writers harp upon the numbers 7 and 9; but we have no clear ideas of the meaning of the word climacteric.

The vital statistics of our time favor the 63d year as the period liable to severe sickness. Dr. Southwood Smith has shown from physiological views, and from Finlaison's tables, the age 63 to be very susceptible of sickness; for, taking a million of males, members of London benefit societies, it appears that there are not more persons on the sick-list at 53 than at 43 years of age; whilst *at 63 the number of sick is more than double*.

FRAGMENTS OF TIME.

Betwixt the more stated employments and important occurrences of humane life, there usually happens to be interposed certain intervals of time, which, though they are wont to be neglected, as being singly, or within the compass of one day, inconsiderable, yet in a man's whole life they may amount to no contemptible portion of it. Now these uncertain parentheses or interludes, that happen to come between the more solemn passages (whether business or recreations) of humane life, are wont to be lost by most men, for want of a value for them, and even by good men for want of skill to preserve them; for though they do not properly despise them, yet they neglect or lose them, for want of knowing how to rescue them, or what to do with them. But although grains of sand and ashes be apart, but of a despicable smallness, and very easy and liable to be scattered and blown away; yet the skilled artificer, by a vehement fire, brings numbers of these to afford him that noble substance, glass, by whose help we may both see ourselves and our blemishes lively represented (as in looking-glasses), and discern celestial objects (as with telescopes), and with the sunbeams, kindle disposed materials (as with burning-glasses), so when these little fragments or parcels of time, which, if not carefully look'd to, would be dissipated, and lost, come to be managed by a skilful contemplator, and to be improved by the celestial fire of devotion, they may be so ordered, as to afford us both looking-glasses to dress our souls by, and perspectives to discover heavenly wonders, and incentives to inflame our hearts with charity and zeal; and since goldsmiths and refiners are wont all the year long carefully to save the very sweepings of their shops, because they may contain in them some filings or dust of those richer metals, gold and silver, I see not why a Christian may not be as careful not to lose the fragments and lesser intervals of a thing incomparably more precious than any metal—time: especially when the improvement of them may not only redeem so many portions of our life, but turn them to pious uses, and particularly to the great advantage of devotion.—*Hon. Robert Boyle's Occasional Reflections, Oxford edit.,* 1848.

CURIOUS STATISTICAL RESULTS.

Researches in the modern science of Statistics have proved that the effects of the free-will of individuals composing large societies completely neutralize each other; and that such communities, taken collectively, act as if the whole body had by common consent agreed to follow a certain prescribed course of conduct, not only in matters which might be imagined to be more or less of common interest, but even in those in which no feeling could be imagined to be engaged, save the will, taste, personal inclination, or even caprice of the individual.

Not only, however, are voluntary acts subject to this numerical regularity. Collectively speaking, *persons remember and forget certain things with as much regularity as if memory and attention were the result of wheelwork.* A very common instance of forgetfulness is presented by persons posting letters without any address written upon them. The number of times this act of obliviousness annually happens is known with the greatest precision, inasmuch as such letters are specially recorded in each post-office. Now, it is found by the Post-office returns in England and France, that the number of these unaddressed letters in each country is almost exactly the same from year to year. In London, the number of such letters is about 2,000, being at the rate of above six per day. But, connected with this is another circumstance equally remarkable. A certain proportion of these letters is found to contain money, and other valuable enclosures; and, like the whole number, this proportion is also invariable.

The conclusion at which we arrive then is, that the great principle, in virtue of which the Author of nature carries out His purposes by the operation of general laws, is not, as it would at first appear, incompatible with the freedom of human agency, and, therefore, with man's moral responsibility. The same character of generality attaches to the laws which govern the moral and intellectual phenomena of human actions, considered collectively, as those which attach to mere physical phenomena. But these laws not being applicable to human actions, considered individually, leave free-will and moral responsibility inviolate.

LIFE ASSURANCE.

One of the most remarkable examples of the value of general laws is to be found in Life Assurances; for what, apparently, can be more precarious and uncertain than the duration of human life in any individual? Yet, in the aggregate, mortality is so regular that it has been said, by an eminent mathematician, that there is no investment so certain as that of a prudently conducted Assurance Society. If we take 5,000 persons in the prime of life, 600 die in the first ten years, 700 in the second ten years, 850 in the third. The experience under different circumstances varies but little, as Jenkin Jones, Neisson, and Farren have shown; and it is a curious fact, that lives which might be called first-class lives are as prone to disease as those which appear to belong to hardly so high a class.—*Alfred Smee*, F. R. S.

SIR WILLIAM HAMILTON ON PHRENOLOGY.

Sir W. Hamilton was a stalwart opponent of this new science. Gall had taken credit for the discovery that the cerebellum is the organ of the sexual passion, and supported the doctrine by asserting that it bears a much larger proportion to the brain proper in adults than in the young. By "an induction from an average of thirty-six brains and skulls of children, compared with an average of several hundred brains and skulls of adults," Sir W. Hamilton satisfied himself that the brain reaches its full size about seven years of age. "If it be not so, then am I a deliberate deceiver." After this we can ask but one question:—Why does the man need a larger hat than the child? The answer is, that "the greater development of bones, muscles, and hair renders the adult head considerably larger than that of the child at seven." Another inquirer tried to refute this by another induction and table of brains. But the Professor detected that the difference of sex had been overlooked, or, as he phrases it, in triumphant scorn of his adversary—and, for once, in round Saxon —"he lumps the male and female brains together!"

As another instance of the value of independent observation, he notices that, whereas he found a common fowl's brain to be to its body as 1 to 500, some twenty physiologists, including Cuvier, had followed each other in making it as 1 to 25, owing to an original mismeasurement by one-half, and a subsequent loss of a cipher. Such is the "sequacity" of anatomical authors. Yet, on the agreeable subject of maggots breeding in the frontal sinus, or cavity of the human forehead, Sir W. Hamilton thought it worth while, after an affected apology for his medical ignorance, to give a list of seventy-five writers who have discussed the matter, including "Olaus Wormius, who himself ejected a worm from the nose, Smetius, who relates his own case," &c. The import of this passage, which it would be unpleasant to quote, is to show the absurdity of phrenologists in ranging seventeen of the smallest organs, "like peas in a pod," along that part of the head where there is an empty space within, such that "no one can predict, from external observation, whether it shall be a lodging scanty for a fly, or roomy for a mouse."

Nor were his experiments confined to probing the foreheads of the dead, or "weighing the brain of a young and healthy convict, who was hanged, and afterwards weighing the sand which his prepared cranium contained." His own person was not spared. To test the association of ideas, he made his friends repeatedly wake him when dozing off in an arm-chair—a self-sacrifice which those who indulge that habit will appreciate. To try whether the mind is always active, he caused himself to be roused at different seasons of the night, and had the satisfaction of finding that he was always in the middle of a dream. To determine how many objects at once the mind can distinctly survey, he set himself to attend to marbles on the floor, and by an effort took in seven at most, beating Abraham Tucker by three, Degerando by two, and Bonnet and Destutt Tracy by one. Perhaps his most remarkable discovery of this kind is a law of mind which he has thus enunciated:—

"Knowledge and feeling, *perception* and *sensation*, though always co-existent, are always in the inverse ratio of each other. Thus, in sight there is more perception, less sensation; in smell there is more sensation, less perception. In the finger-points, tactile perception is at its height; but there is hardly another part of the body in which sensation is not more acute."

Sir W. Hamilton was not aware that this law had been announced and referred to its cause (the passive nature of sensation and active nature of perception) by De Biran, now nearly half a century ago. With what qualifications it is true of the sense of touch, is examined in the notes to Reid. Here again, with his usual zeal, Sir W. Hamilton seemed to have tried upon various parts of his own body the effect of "pressure with a subacute point" and of "puncture." The latter, in seeming contradiction to the law, produced most pain in the tongue and finger, where perception is also the highest. But an explanation was soon ready. Either nerves of feeling lie beneath the nerves of touch, or the same nerves "commence their energy as feeling only at the pitch where their energy as touch concludes." At any rate, he was reassured by finding that, in proportion to the soreness of the tongue or the finger under such treatment, it is incapacitated for the time as an organ of external touch.*

CONSUMPTION AND LONGEVITY.

Sir Edward Wilmot the physician was, when a youth, so far gone in a consumption, that Dr. Radcliffe, whom he consulted, gave his friends no hope of his recovery, yet he lived to the age of 93; and Dr. Heberden notes—"this has been the case with some others who had many symptoms of consumption in youth."

MAN'S PROPER PLACE IN CREATION.

Professor Daubeny has observed, with equal force and beauty:

When we reflect within what a narrow area our researches are necessarily circumscribed; when we perceive that we are bounded in space almost to the surface of the planet in which we reside, itself merely a speck in the universe, one of innumerable worlds invisible from the nearest of the fixed stars; when we recollect, too, that we are limited in point of time to a few short years of life and activity—that our records

* Selected and abridged from the *Saturday Review*.

of the past history of the globe and of its inhabitants, are comprised within a minute portion of the latest of the many epochs which the world has gone through; and that, with regard to the future, the most durable monuments we can raise to hand down our names to posterity are liable at any time to be overthrown by an earthquake, and would be obliterated as if they had never been by any of those processes of metamorphic action which geology tells us form a part of the cycle of changes which the globe is destined to undergo,—the more lost in wonder we may be at the vast fecundity of nature, which within so narrow a sphere can crowd together phenomena so various and so imposing,—the more sensible shall we become of the small proportion which our highest powers and their happiest results bear, not only to the cause of all causation, but even to other created beings, higher in the scale than ourselves, which we may conceive to exist.

Nature of the Soul.

It was a dictum of Aristotle's, that "in infancy the soul of man differs *in nothing* from that of the brutes." But then he also says that "one animal alone, man, can reflect and deliberate;" and the latter statement has found most favor with modern philosophers. Thus we are now informed that "the brute is sensitive but not self-conscious;" and powers and faculties are continually pointed to in man, which it is positively asserted can be found in none lower than himself. May we not ask the assertors how they know these things? Have they ever visited the chambers of thought within the penetralia of the brute? They are hardly likely to be right, if Sir Benjamin Brodie apprehends correctly, that "the mental principle in animals is of *the same essence* as that of human beings; so that even in the humbler classes we may trace the rudiments of those faculties to which, in their state of more complete development, we are indebted for the grandest results of human genius."—(*Psychological Inquiries*, p. 164.) Again: "I am inclined to believe that the minds of the inferior animals are *essentially of the same nature* with that of the human race." --(*Ibid.*, p. 166.)

The Rev. John Wesley's conclusion as to the nature of "the living soul" imparted to Adam was, that "God gave him such *life as other animals enjoy*."—(*Notes to the New Testament*, p. 497.)

Dr. Cromwell, in "the Philosophic Argument" of his work, *The Soul and the Future Life*, introduces, in a note, the following definitions of "spirit," or, as he terms it, "abstract self-subsistence."

Substances, said Dr. Watts, speaking after the schoolmen (*Philosophical Essays*, p. 51), are "such *things*, or *beings*, which we conceive as the subjects or supporters of distinct qualities, and which *subsist of themselves*, without dependence upon any creature." This notion of substance is commonly accepted by Immaterialists as applying to man's soul. Coleridge. in his *Theory of Life* (p. 94), admits that he regards the soul as "*a thing, a self-subsistent hypostasis.*" Belsham, much less consistently, either with Priestley, whom he professed to follow, or himself, defined Spirit as "thinking *substance.*" (*Elements of the Philosophy of the Mind, prefixed to a Compendium of Logic.*) Stewart saw an objection to the word "substance," but it was only "as implying a greater degree of knowledge of the *nature* of mind than our faculties are fitted to attain" (*Dissertation, Sir William Hamilton's,* ed. p 116); and his proposed substitute, "thinking *being.*" can be admitted to offer no material alteration. Reid also preferred, throughout his Inquiry into the Human Mind, such expressions as "thinking *being*" and "thinking *principle.*" But Sir William Hamilton continued to employ the old scholastic term. With him Mind was still "hyperphysical *substance*" (*Discussions on Philosophy,* &c., p. 307); notwithstanding his remark, made with equal reference to Mind and Matter, that "absolute substance and absolute quality are both inconceivable as more than negations of the conceivable." (Ibid., p. 605.)

Plato instituted a classification into the soul of the appetites, that of the passions, and that of the knowing faculties, each having its own seat in the body, and each its peculiar motions; and Aristotle had his souls, vegetable, sentient, and rational. Under all Grecian physiology and psychology lay the assumption that whatever was self-motional was life or soul, matter being essentially inactive. And thus it became necessary to suppose a *vital agent,* wherever *activity* was manifested, and that equally in the cases of mere physical function, sentience, and intellect; this being the supposition on which alike rested Plato's *three kinds of soul* and Aristotle's *three souls;* for to so much the theory of the last-mentioned philosopher seems very nearly, if not literally, to amount. Galen limited the term "soul" to the agent of the sentient and intelligent functions, and made "nature" the operator in the simply physical: but Aristotle reigned over the schools; and his doctrine of the vegetable, sentient, and rational souls, variously modified, may be traced in very many medico-physiological theories down to recent times. The Stagirite's "vegetable soul" especially, as Galen had merely given it another name in calling it "nature," or "the natural faculties," so was it substantially one with the "archæus," or "governing principle" of Paracelsus and Helmont; and "the animating and organizing principle" of Harvey. Yet, more lately, Müller has set up an "organic force," which "exists even in the germ, and *creates* in it the essential parts of the future animal;" and Prout, an

Nature of the Soul.

"organic agent," or "ultimate principle," "endowed with a faculty little short of *intelligence*," &c. And if Hunter, in his theory of Life, did not commit the last-cited extravagance, yet his "highly-attenuated substance" pervaded and gave vital properties to both solids and fluids; and, according to his zealous disciple and successor, the late Mr. Abernethy, "*actually constructed* the various means by which it carried on its various processes."

The discovery of Electricity made known a new class of beings or entities which seemed to exist between the opposite confines of matter and spirit, and to partake in a degree of the nature of both. Dr. Prichard says:

> The "vital principle" was imagined to be a substance of a similar kind in many respects, if not to be absolutely identified with the electric fluid. As the electric fluid appears to be endowed with the property of modifying, under particular circumstances, the ordinary influence of chemical affinity, and of controlling in a certain degree the usual operation of its laws, so "the vital principle," which was supposed to be diffused through the body in the living state, and to pervade every texture and every part, was imagined to protect the whole from the chemical agencies of the surrounding elements.—*Review of the Doctrine of a Vital Principle*, sect. ii.

This passage gives a fair exposition of the doctrine inculcated by Mr. Abernethy on the subject of Life, as taught by Hunter; and Abernethy imagined that if philosophers once saw reason to believe that Life was something of an invisible and active nature superadded to organization,—

> "They would see equal reason to believe that Mind might be superadded to Life, as life is to structure. They would then, indeed, still further perceive how Mind and Matter might reciprocally operate on each other, by means of an inhering substance" (viz., the "matter of life"). *Phys. Lect. and Disc.*, p. 95. (Again: "The consideration of the phenomena of Mind, as well as that of the phenomena of Life, equally enforces the opinion of *their* distinct and independent nature. . . . . Uneducated reason, and the most scientific research, equally induce us to believe that we are composed of an assemblage of organs formed of common inert matter, a principle of life and action, *and* a sentient and rational faculty; all intimately connected, yet each distinct from the other."—*Phys. Lect. and Disc.*, p. 401.)

Yet, adds Dr. Cromwell, "the notion of *any* distinct agent or principle, to account for Life at least, has already become obsolete, and is now commonly abandoned." (*The Soul and the Future Life*, p. 40.)

THE IMPRISONED SOUL.

Cowley, in his *Davideis*, book iv., says of Saul:

> His soul was ne'er unbent from weighty care;
> But active as some mind that turns a sphere.

Upon which he notes—"According to the old senseless opinion, that the heavens were divided into several orbs or spheres, and that a particular Intelligence or Angel was assigned to each of them, to turn it round (like a mill-horse, as Scaliger says), to all eternity."

In his Pindaric Ode—Life, Cowley thus describes the imprisoned soul. Upon the text from Euripides: "Who knows whether to *live* be not to *die;* and to *die* to *live?*" he says:

> We grow at last by custom to believe
>   That really we live:
> While all these shadows that for things we take,
> Are but the empty dreams which in death's sleep we make.
> But these fantastic errors of our dreams
>   Lead us to solid wrong;
> We pray God our friends' torments to prolong,
>   And wish uncharitably for them
> To be as long a dying as Methusalem.
> The ripened soul longs from his pris'n to come,
> But we would seal, and sow up, if we could, the womb.
> We seek to close and plaster up by art
> The cracks and breaches of th' extended shell,
>   And in that narrow cell
>   Would rudely force to dwell
> The noble bird, already wing'd to part.

Archbishop Leighton, in his *Commentary on St. Peter*, says: "It was a strange proof of Plato's Discourse of the Soul's Immortality, that moved a young man, on reading it, to throw himself into the sea, that he might leap through it to that Immortality."

THE SOUL AND THE MAGNETIC NEEDLE.

This strange metaphor occurs in the following passage from one of Archbishop Leighton's *Sermons:*

The Soul and the Magnetic Needle.

"The heart touched by the Spirit of God, as the needle touched with the loadstone, looks straight and speedily to God, yet still with trembling, being filled with holy fear."

There is a passage in Bishop Jeremy Taylor's sermon on "Growth in Sin," which amplifies the same thought:

"But as the needle of a compass, when it is directed to its beloved star, at the first addresses waves on either side, and seems indifferent in its courtship of the rising or declining sun, and when it seems first determined to the north stands awhile trembling, as if it suffered inconvenience in the first fruition of its desires, and stands not still in full enjoyment, till after first a great variety of motion, and then an undisturbed posture; so is the piety, and so is the conversion of a man wrought by degrees and several steps of imperfection; and at first our choices are wavering, convinced by the grace of God, and yet not persuaded; and then persuaded but not resolved; and then resolved, but deferring to begin; and then beginning, but as all beginnings are, in weakness and uncertainty," &c.

Of similar purport, though from a very different source, is the following:

> As still to the star of its worship, though clouded,
> The needle points faithfully o'er the dim sea!
> So dark as I roam, in this wintry world shrouded,
> The hope of my spirit turns trembling to thee.
> MOORE'S *Sacred Songs*.

Norris of Bemerton employs this simile in "The Aspiration:"

> How cold this clime! and yet my sense
> Perceives even here Thy influence.
> Even here Thy strong magnetic charms I feel,
> And pant and tremble like the amorous steel.
> To lower good, and beauties less divine,
> Sometimes my erroneous needle does decline;
>   But yet (so strong the sympathy)
>   It turns, and points again to Thee.

Again, in his "Contemplation and Love:"

"Man is not as a body, forever rolling or in an infinite vacuity; or, as a *needle continually trembling* for an embrace."

Then, a stanza on a loose slab in Bishop Joceline's crypt in Glasgow Cathedral commences:

> Our life's a flying shadow, God is the pole,
> The needle pointing to Him is our soul.

Quarles has these beautiful lines:

> Even as the needle that directs the hour,
> (Touch'd with the loadstone) by the secret power
> Of hidden Nature, points upon the pole;
> Even so the wavering powers of my soul,
> Touch'd by the virtue of Thy Spirit, flee
> From what is earth, and point alone to Thee.

In the song of "Sweet William's Farewell," the sailor, with great propriety, adopts a nautical term from his own art:

> Change as ye list, ye winds; my heart shall be
> The faithful compass that still points to Thee.

Quarles has likewise a poem in which is enshrined the same idea as Jeremy Taylor:

> Like to the Arctick needle that doth guide
>   The wand'ring shade by his magnetick power,
> And leaves his silken gnomon to decide
>   The question of the controverted hour,
> First franticks up and down, from side to side,
>   And restless beats his crystal'd iv'ry case
>   With vain impatience; jets from place to place,
> And seeks the bosom of his frozen bride:
>   At length he slacks his motion, and doth rest
> His trembling point at his bright Pole's beloved breast.
>
> E'en so my soul, being hurried here and there,
>   By ev'ry object that presents delight,
> Fain would be settled, but she knows not where;
>   She likes at morning what she loathes at night:
> She bows to honour; then she lends an ear
>   To that sweet swan-like voice of dying pleasure,
>   Then tumbles in the scatter'd heaps of treasure;
> Now flatter'd with false hope; now foyl'd with fear:
>   Thus finding all the world's delight to be
> But empty toys, good God, she points alone to thee.
>
> But hath the virtued steel a power to move?
>   Or can the untouch'd needle point aright?
> Or can my wand'ring thoughts forbear to rove,
>   Unguided by the virtue of thy sp'rit?
> O hath my leaden soul the art t' improve
>   Her wasted talent, and, unrais'd, aspire
>   In this sad moulting time of her desire?
> Not first belov'd, have I the power to love;
>   I cannot but stir, but as thou please to move me,
> Nor can my heart return thee love, until thou love me

The same metaphor also occurs in the 18th Emblem of Quarles's 1st Book:

> Like as the am'rous needle joys to bend
> To her magnetic friend, &c.

A much older author than either yet quoted, Raimond Lull, of Majorca, who died in 1315, says:

As the needle turneth by nature to the north, when it is touched by the magnet, so it behoves that thy servant should turn to praise his Lord God, and to serve Him, since out of love to him, He willed to endure sore griefs and heavy sufferings in this world.—NEANDER'S *Memorials of Christian Life.*

Southey, in his *Omniana* (vol. i., p. 210), cites a passage from the *Partidas*, in which the magnetic needle is used in illustration. This is especially worthy of attention, as having been written half a century before the supposed invention of the Mariner's Compass at Amalfi; and as Southey remarks, "it must have been well known and in general use before it would thus be referred to as a familiar illustration."—See *Notes and Queries*, vols. 6 & 8.

SYMBOLS OF THE SOUL.

The immortal Christian soul has been figured both by the Peacock and the Dove, but more frequently by the latter. We may see the disciples of our Lord represented as doves, on the apsidial cross in S. Clemente. As doves, Christian souls are found figured on mural tablets, on baptismal fonts, and on sarcophagi. Less frequently they appear as peacocks—rarely on sarcophagi; however, the Gentiles thus represented them on the walls of sepulchral chambers, and in scenes of the Paradise of Osiris. On a sarcophagus in the Museum of the Vatican, are two doves on a cross, surrounded by the monogram of Christ within a wreath. This device may frequently be seen.

On the unique ivory tabernacle preserved in the sacristy of the Cathedral of Sens, we see a pine-cone taking the place of the Cross, or the diagram of Christ, and on each side of it a peacock representing not the souls of Christians merely, but the souls of martyrs, for each peacock has a small palm-branch attached to its neck.

The Egyptian conventional symbol for the soul was, as every archæologist knows, a sparrow-hawk, with a human head. In later times, and among the Romans, the souls of the departed in the Paradise of Osiris, were figured as doves and peacocks. In a fresco painting that once existed at Pompeii (a copy of which was engraved at Naples in 1833), symbolical souls, as doves and peacocks, are represented as perched on the sacred trees, the palm and the peach-tree, in the Paradise of Osiris and Isis. In this fresco was also represented the heron, the symbol, according to the Vicomte de Rongé, of the first transformation of the soul in this mysterious Paradise.

Dr. Barlow has communicated to the *Builder*, Sept. 18, 1858, these interesting notes on the occasional identity of symbolical meaning between the Peacock and the Dove. Upon this the Editor of the journal observes: " Higgins also points, in his *Anacalypsis*, at the above identity. He speaks of the dove of Venus as 'a maenad or fanatic bird, crucified on a wheel with four spokes,' the dove called also *Inyx;* and in correlation with these symbols, also he alludes to Semiramis, described to have fled away, changed into this dove when conquered by Staurobates, who had threatened to 'nail her to a cross,' which is identified with the four-spoked wheel in 'the eternal crucifixion of Ixion, the accursed,' or the wheel of execution described by Pindar. The dove, crucified on a wheeled cross, is curious as a heathen symbol, in connection with what Dr. Barlow describes as a frequent Christian symbol, namely, two doves on a cross. If the peacock and dove be symbolically identical, may it not be questioned whether the symbolical meaning of either really be the *Soul*, and not the *Holy Spirit;* for the dove, in fact, does denote the Holy Spirit; and is it not more probable that doves, indicating our Lord's disciples, did so as signifying that each of them possessed that Spirit, than that these doves denoted their own souls? Even among the heathen, the dove denoted a spirit of prophecy, or divine *afflatus;* and the oracles were called doves—*columbæ*, by the Latins, for example."

In France, from the twelfth to the sixteenth century, there are many monuments where the soul is seen conveyed in a sheet by angels to heaven. In a church at Axminster is a monument where a lady holds between her hands a figure like a little doll, swathed in a close garment, with its hands uplifted, and this figure represents her soul. So, too, in the church of Hitchenden, near High Wycombe, there is an altar-tomb of the sixteenth century, without inscription, representing a man in his shroud, and on his open breast a little figure with hands raised, representing his soul.

PERSONALITY OF GOD—THE SOUL GOD'S GREAT ORGAN.

Mr. T. E. Poynting, in his able work, *Glimpses of the Heaven that lies about us*, states:

> How often has a poor doubting mind confessed to me, "You say that God is constantly with us, and gives his Holy Spirit to those who ask Him. Yet I look back through all my life, and I am not aware of any inspiration, any revelation, any suggestion, that has not come, like all my thoughts and feelings, by my ordinary faculties and instincts. It seems to me that I have been left alone with my own mind, and God has not at all interfered in its workings." I never saw that what we call the ordinary working of the mind itself, the law of its faculties, the movement of its impulses, was the very flowing of the Holy Spirit.

The same doubt is met with the same answer, as follows:

> We have watched our minds, we have prayed and striven, but we have been able to detect no trace of any stirring in our spirits beyond the natural action of our faculties and instincts.
>
> Let us then consider these ordinary impulses and faculties. When we feel the impulse of Benevolence, the love of the Beautiful, the love of Knowledge, when we feel the Sentiment of Conscience approving or disapproving, when we feel the Reason leading us on from step to step of truth, we know not how,—whence do these impulses and movements come? What is their fountain? Do *we* invent these movements? Do we originate or direct them ourselves? No, the movements seem to come in upon us like streams of life from a source outside our Will. Now, what is the *source* from which these streams or movements come? Is there an inexhaustible supply of such streams, powers, impulses, shut up in secret wells within us; and is there some mechanical contrivance for unlocking these wells at our need, and letting these streams flow in upon our consciousness? I reply, we know of no such wells; we cannot, indeed, imagine them. We have never had experience of any such contrivance. On the other hand, there is a Cause, a real known cause at hand all around us—God himself, the Eternal fountain of Life and Power —quite sufficient to account for the phenomena.

PRE-EXISTENCE OF SOULS.

That the Deity, at the beginning of the world, created the souls of all men, which, however, were not united to the body till the individuals for which they were destined, were born into the world—was (to omit any reference to Plato and his followers) a very general belief among the Jewish Kabbalists, a common opinion in our Saviour's time, and holden and taught by many fathers of the Christian Church,—as Justin Martyr, Origen, and others. It was, however, opposed by Tertullian.

Mede, in chap. iii. of his *Mystery of Godliness*, combats the vulgar opinion of a "daily creation of souls" at the time the bodies are produced which they are to inform. He calls "the reasonable doctrine" of pre-existence "a key for some of the main mysteries of Providence, which no other can so handsomely unlock." Sir Harry Vane is said by Burnet to have maintained this doctrine. Joseph Glanvil, Rector of Bath (the friend of Meric Casaubon and of Baxter, and a metaphysician of singular vigor and acuteness), published in 1662, but without his name, a treatise to prove the reasonableness of the doctrine.* It was afterwards republished, with annotations, by Dr. Henry More.

In 1762, the Rev. Capel Berrow published *A Pre-existent Lapse of Human Souls demonstrated ;* and in the *European Magazine* for September, 1801, is a letter from Bishop Warburton to the author, in which he says: "The idea of a *pre-existence* has been espoused by many learned and ingenious men in every age, as bidding fair to resolve many difficulties."

Southey, in his published Letters, says: "I have a strong and lively faith in a state of continued consciousness from this stage of existence, and that we shall *recover the consciousness of some lower stages through which we may previously have passed* seems to me not improbable." Again : "The system of *progressive existence* seems, of all others, the most benevolent ; and all that we do understand is so wise and so good, and all we do, or do not, so

---

* Among the Baxter MSS. in the Red-cross-street Library, Cripplegate, is a long letter, full of curious learning, from Glanvil to Baxter, in defence of the doctrine of the soul's pre-existence.

perfectly and overwhelmingly wonderful, that the most benevolent system is the most probable." Traces of belief in this doctrine also occur in Wordsworth's "Ode on the Intimation of Immortality in Childhood."

> Our birth is but a sleep and a forgetting:
> The soul that rises in us, our life's star,
> Has had elsewhere its setting,
> And cometh from afar.

Elsewhere, our metaphysical poet sings:

> My eyes are dim with childish tears,
> My heart is idly stirr'd;
> For the same sound is in my ears
> Which in those days I heard.
>
> Thus fares it still in our decay;
> And yet the wiser mind
> Mourns less for what time takes away,
> Than what he leaves behind.

The notion enters more or less into the majority of Oriental creeds and philosophies, and found a believer in Plato: indeed, it is a doctrine Platonic, that *all knowledge is recollection.*

Hence, it has been asked, whether it is not very possible, that previously to this life, *the human soul has passed through different phases of existence*, and that it is destined to pass through many more before it arrives at its final rest. Thus, Pythagoras recollected his former self in the majestic person of a herald named Æthalides; Euphorbus, the Trojan; and others; and he even pointed out, in the temple of Juno, at Argos, the shield he used when he attacked Patroclus.

Milton, who imbibed from his college friend, Henry More, an early bias to the study of Plato, hints at the same opinion in his *Comus*:

> The soul grows dotted by contagion,
> Imbodies and imbrutes, till she quite lose
> *The divine property of her first being.*
> Such are those thick and gloomy shadows damp,
> Oft seen in charnel vaults and sepulchres,
> Lingering and sitting by a new-made grave,
> As loth to leave the body that it loved.

In the first volume of Dodsley's *Miscellaneous Poems* is a poem in Miltonic blank verse, entitled *Pre-existence*. Gray called it "nonsense in all her attitudes;" but it contains some fine things in the midst of a great deal of wild turgidity. (*Atlas, May* 28, 1859.)

In *Chambers's Edinburgh Journal*, No. 93, New Series, this "Sentiment of Pre-existence" is stated to have been first described by Sir Walter Scott: this may be correct as to the *expression*, but not as to the phenomenon to which it is applied, as we have already shown. Scott, it will be remembered, was highly *susceptible* upon psychological matters. The description is thrown into the mouth of Henry Bertram on his return to Ellangowan Castle: "How often," he says, "do we find ourselves in society which we have never before met, and yet feel impressed with a mysterious and ill-defined consciousness that neither the scene, the speakers, nor the subject are entirely new; nay, feel as if we could anticipate that part of the conversation which has not yet taken place!"

We find the following entry in Scott's diary, under the date February 17, 1828.

> I cannot, I am sure, tell if it is worth marking down, that yesterday, at dinner-time, I was strongly haunted by what I would call the sense of pre-existence, in a confirmed idea that nothing which passed was said for the first time; that the same topics had been discussed, and the same persons had stated the same opinions on them. . . . The sensation was so strong as to resemble what is called a *mirage* in the desert, or a calenture on board a ship. . . . It was very distressing yesterday, and brought to my mind the fancies of Bishop Berkeley about an ideal world. There was a vile sense of want of reality in all I did and said.—LOCKHART'S *Life of Scott*.

It appears from a passage in the *Wool-gatherer*, a tale by James Hogg, that that extraordinary son of genius was occasionally conscious of the same feeling.

Sir Bulwer Lytton, in his *Godolphin*, thus notices this day-dream:

> How strange it is that at times a feeling comes over us, as we gaze upon certain places, which associates the scene either with some dim-remembered and dream-like images of the Past, or with a prophetic and fearful omen of the future! . . . Every one has known a similar strange, indistinct feeling, at certain times and places, and with a similar inability to trace the cause.

Elsewhere the same writer describes the same feeling of reminiscence as "that strange kind of inner and spiritual memory which often recalls to us places and persons we have never seen before, and which Platonists would resolve to be the unquenched and struggling consciousness of a former life."

In fewer words, the feeling may be described as seeing and hearing, apparently for the first time, what we have seen or heard before, though our reason assures us of the contrary. Can anything be more expressive of the *sameness* of human existence ?

> Moreover something is, or seems,
> That teaches me with mystic gleams,
> *Like glimpses of forgotten dreams—*
> Of something felt, like something here;
> Of something done, I know not where;
> Such as no language may declare.—*Tennyson.*

Mr. Dickens, in his *Pictures from Italy*, mentions this instance on his first sight of Ferrara:

On the foreground was a group of silent peasant-girls, leaning over the parapet of a little bridge, looking now up at the sky, now down into the water ; in the distance a deep bell; the shadow of approaching night on everything. If I had been murdered there on some former life I could not have seemed to remember the place more thoroughly, or with more emphatic chilling of the blood; and the real remembrance of it acquired in that minute is so strengthened by the imaginary recollection, that I hardly think I could forget it.

We could multiply these instances manifold : but proceed to attempt the explanation of the mystery.

In a curious and original book, entitled *The Duality of the Mind*, written by Dr. Wigan, and published in 1844, this strange sentiment is adduced as an evidence in favor of the conclusion aimed at,—that the Mind is double in its whole structure, correspondently with the duplicity of the structure of the Brain. "It is a sudden feeling, as if the scene we have just witnessed (although from the very nature of things it could never have been seen before) had been present to our eyes on a former occasion, when the very same speakers, seated in the very same positions, uttered the same sentiments in the same words—the postures, the expression of countenance, the gestures, the tone of voice, all seem to be *remembered*, and to be now attracting attention for the second time: *never* is it supposed to be the third time. This delusion," pursues the writer, " occurs only when the mind has been exhausted by excitement, or is, from indisposition or any other cause, languid, and only slightly attentive to the conversation. The persuasion of the scene being a repetition, comes on when the attention has been roused by some accidental circumstance, and we become, as the phrase is, wide awake. I believe the explanation to be this: only one brain has been used in the immediately preceding part of the scene; the other brain has been asleep, or in an analogous state nearly approaching it. When the attention of both brains is roused to the topic, there is the same vague consciousness that the ideas have passed through the mind before, which takes place on perusing the page we had read while thinking on some other subject. The ideas *have* passed through the mind before; and as there was not sufficient consciousness to fix them in the memory without a renewal, we have no means of knowing the length of time that had elapsed between the *faint* impression received by the single brain, and the *distinct* impression received by the double brain. It may seem to have been many years. I have often noticed this in children, and believe they have sometimes been punished for the involuntary error, in the belief that they have been guilty of deliberate falsehood."

The strongest example of this delusion I ever recollect in my own person was on the occasion of the funeral of the Princess Charlotte. The circumstances connected with that event formed in every respect a most extraordinary psychological curiosity, and afforded an instructive view of the moral feelings pervading a whole nation, and showing themselves without restraint or disguise. There is, perhaps, no example in history of so intense and so universal a sympathy, for almost every conceivable misfortune to one party is a source of joy, satisfaction or advantage to another. The event was attended by the strange peculiarity, that it could be a subject of joy or satisfaction to no one. It is difficult to imagine another instance of a calamity by which none could derive any possible benefit; for in the then state of succession to the throne no one was apparently brought a step nearer to it. One mighty all-absorbing grief possessed the whole nation, and was aggravated in each individual by the sympathy of his neighbor, till the whole people became infected with an amiable insanity, and incapable of estimating the real extent of their loss. No one under five-and-thirty or forty years of age can form a conception of the universal paroxysm of grief which then superseded every other feeling.

I had obtained permission to be present on the occasion of the funeral, as one of the lord chamberlain's staff. Several disturbed nights previous to that ceremony, and the almost total privation of rest on the night immediately preceding it, had put my mind into a state of hysterical irritability, which was still further increased by grief, and by exhaustion from want of food; for between breakfast and the hour of interment at midnight, such was the confusion in the town of Windsor, that no expenditure of money could procure refreshment.

I had been standing four hours, and on taking my place by the side of the coffin, in St. George's chapel, was only prevented from fainting by the interest of the scene. All that our truncated ceremonies could bestow of pomp was there, and the exquisite music produced a sort of hallucination. Suddenly, after the pathetic Miserere of Mozart, the music ceased, and there was an absolute silence. The coffin, placed on a kind of altar covered with black cloth (united to the black cloth which covered the pavement), sank down so slowly through the floor, that it was only in measuring its progress by some brilliant object beyond it that any motion could be perceived. I had fallen into a sort of torpid reverie, when I was recalled to consciousness by a paroxysm of violent grief on the part of the bereaved husband, as his eye suddenly caught the coffin sinking into its black grave, formed by the inverted covering of the altar. In an instant I felt not merely an *impression*, but a *conviction* that I had seen the whole scene before on some former occasion, and had heard even the very words addressed to myself by Sir George Nayler.

The author thus concludes—Often did I discuss this matter with my talented friend, the late Dr. Gooch, who always took great interest in subjects occupying the debatable region between physics and metaphysics; but we could never devise an explanation satisfactory to either of us. I cannot but think that the theory of two brains affords a sufficient solution of the otherwise inexplicable phenomenon. It is probable that some of the examples of religious mysticism, which we generally set down as imposture, may have their origin in similar hallucinations, and that in the uneducated mind these apparent recollections of past scenes, similar to the present, may give to an enthusiast the idea of inspiration, especially where one brain has a decided tendency to insanity, as is often the case with such persons.

Dr. Wigan's theory has been much controverted: but we think there is some probability in the view by Mr. W. L. Nichols, in *Notes and Queries*, Second Series, No. 55, that the cause is "some incongruous action of the double structure of the brain, to which perfect unity of action belongs in a healthy state."

Sir Benjamin Brodie describes Dr. Wigan's mind to have had in it more of ingenuity than of philosophy, and the object of his work to be to prove that each hemisphere of the cerebrum has a separate mind, and that on these occasions the two hemispheres might be considered as conversing with each other. Sir Benjamin does not believe this hypothesis, or, rather, he adds, "I should say that it is not in my nature to believe it. It seems to me that the question as to the oneness and individuality of the mind is very clearly and unanswerably stated by Father Buffier. It is one of those fundamental truths which are inherent in us, and defy all argument; which I can no more help believing than I can help believing in the external world, or even in my own existence."—*Pyschological Inquiries*, p. 23.

This disclaimer, however, leaves where it was, the explanation of the phenomenon which has been so often attested by reliable authorities in past and present times.

Sir Henry Holland repudiates the leading idea of Dr. Wigan's theory; although he assents to the still stranger notion that there is a duality of *natures* in the individual human being.

Combe's phrenological doctrine that "there are two organs for each mental power, one in each hemisphere," may seem to help the species of duality contended for by Dr. Wigan.—*Dr. Cromwell.*

A curious instance of *Duality of Heart* is stated to occur in the Elephants, in captivity, when their temper cannot be relied on, and they are subject to occasional fits of stubbornness. Hence a popular belief recorded by Phile, a Greek writer, of the 14th century, who in a poem (from which Sir Emerson Tennent gives extracts in his *Natural History of Ceylon*), to the effect that the elephant has *two hearts*, by the use of one of which he is used to gentleness, by the other to ferocity and resistance. Upon this, a writer in the *National Review* observes: "This legend of the two hearts of the elephant is a striking expression of that duality of the physical nature which seems to distinguish tamable from untamable animals. In an animal of the latter class, whether in its wild state or in captivity, the whole bent of its nature is single and unwavering; it may be crushed by outer violence, but it admits of no internal division, and the influence of man finds no place in the permanent nature of the beast. In the tamable animal, on the contrary, there is an original duality which furnishes a foot-hold for the power of man. There is one part of the creature's nature that struggles with the other, and thus strangely mimics the moral nature of man, with its conflicts between the higher and the lower principles in him, and like that moral nature is amenable to the power of rewards and punishments." The writer then instances the dog as exhibiting this quality in the highest degree; but considers that the same thing, in lesser degrees, characterizes all animals that are capable of being tamed, and not merely subdued to be held in by present force.

Mrs. Elizabeth Rowe, the friend of Bishop Ken, and of Dr. Isaac Watts, has left, in allusion to the "Pre-existence of Souls,"

A HYMN ON HEAVEN.

Ye starry mansions, hail! my native skies!
Here in my happy, pre-existent state,

(A spotless mind,) I led the life of gods.
But passing, I salute you, and advance
To yonder brighter realms, allowed access.
  Hail, the splendid city of the Almighty King!
Celestial Salem, situate above, &c.

TRANSMIGRATION OF SOULS AND SACREDNESS OF ANIMALS.

The Egyptians maintained that after death the soul, being immortal, transmigrated into bodies of all kinds of animals, whether birds, beasts, or fishes; and that after the space of three thousand years it again returned to the body which it left, provided that body was preserved from destruction during the long period of its absence. The Egyptians also held that the gods took refuge in the bodies of animals from the wickedness and violence of men; they therefore regarded such animals as sacred, and accordingly worshipped them as containing the divinities whom they revered. This led to the bestowing on them the honor of embalming, while it explains the reason why the mummies of so many animals are found to this day preserved in their catacombs. They placed particular gods in particular animals: thus, Apollo was in the hawk, Mercury in the ibis, Mars in the fish, Diana in the cat, Bacchus in the goat, Hercules in the colt, Vulcan in the ox, &c. These animals, with many others, or parts of them, are accordingly found embalmed with the bodies of the human race in the Egyptian tombs; but they were not all worshipped during the early history of Egypt.

Spiritual Life.

SPIRITUAL RECLAMATION.

THE progress of souls from darkness to light, from ignorance to knowledge, is among the more beautiful spectacles of our spiritual life. And, soon or late, this is a consummation which awaits us all. Yet, spiritual reclamation, whether on the large scale or the small, demands concentration of purpose, energy, and intelligence.

Would we realize heaven, let us begin now. The paradise of our aspirations has its foundations here, and the capacities of the future are grounded on those of the present life.

> A twofold cosmos, natural things and spiritual,
> Must go to a perfect world.
>   For whoso separates those two,
> In arts, in morals, or the social drift,
> Tears up the bond of nature and brings death.

As we love here, we shall love in a degree hereafter, as we feel and think now, so must we in somewise feel and think forever.

The unseen world, with all its momentous transactions, let us be assured, is simple and natural as that in which we dwell. Ascetic horrors and ascetic gloom, travestying and deforming with frightful, yet vain imaginings, the beautiful city of God, are sorry preparatives for heaven. How, indeed, should sourness and formality, convictions on which no ray of imagination or feeling seems to shine, consort with the angelic amenities, the transporting assurances of the life to come. For this, let us be well assured, is not as some inquisition torture-chamber, reformatory hulk, or condemned cell. In the celestial life, as here, so surely as God is light, and truth, and love, goal shall succeed goal, and quest follow quest, forever. A new iris shall spring up, not to foil past efforts, but to allure us on to new, a constant becoming of which the perfect realization is never. There, indeed, the great-souled patriot shall freedom find at last, there each self-denying saint the sanctities which lie folded within the inner life, and of which the perfect home is heaven.—*Dr. McCormack's Aspirations of the Inner Life.*

"EXCELSIOR."

This is the motto of the United States of America: it signifies literally "Higher," and may be considered to denote the aspiring character of that nation. "Excelsior" is also the title of a sublime poem by Longfellow, whose meaning is thus interpreted by a classic friend:

"Longfellow, in my mind, has a feeling in that beautiful poem not unlike the feeling of his Psalm of Life under *every* aspect. It is, I take it, an *ideo-religion* of Longfellow's own fine imagination and truly poetic art, and I read the effusion as his view of the *interior career of man*. EXCELSIOR, starting from that sublime point of departure wherein the human soul was placed by the Almighty, 'paulo minus ab angelis,' the individual who wishes to improve himself never finds a halting place on earth. His career is upward, in one sense, whatever it may appear to be. His very degradations are means of increased ennoblement, because of incessant compurgation and purity. And in *one* respect the human almost surpasses the angelic lot; because the one, being perfect in its kind, does not, *perhaps*, admit of progress, and the other does indefinitely. The yearning to fufil this progressive lot engenders a noble discontent, and that discontent is expressed by the word *Excelsior*. Observe, it is not *Excelsius;* it is therefore entirely interior; whereas *Excelsius* would refer to the *circumstances*, rather than to him who was in them."—*Miles Gerald Keon; Things not Generally Known, First Series*, page 91.

NOTIONS OF ANGELS.

The word Angel (*angelos* in Greek, *malak* in Hebrew), literally signifies "a person sent," or a "messenger." Dr. Lee remarks, in his Hebrew Lexicon: "As man is incapable of receiving any communication from God in his abstract and incomprehensible character of deity, if a revelation was to be made to man by any visible personage, it must have been by the intervention of some *being* fitted to sustain such office;" and such was the person emphatically styled "the Angel of Jehovah," in Exodus xxiii. 20, to whom are ascribed the acts and reverence attributable to none but God himself; for, it is added, v. 21, "*my name* (person) is *within him.*" In a lower sense, angel denotes a spiritual being employed in occasional offices; and lastly, men of office, as priests or bishops. The "angel of the congregation," among the Jews, was the chief of the synagogue. Such is the Scriptural usage of a term, which, in common parlance, is now limited to its principal meaning, and denotes only the happy inhabitants of heaven.

The apostle of the Gentiles speaks of the angels as "ministering spirits, sent forth to minister for them who shall be heirs of salvation," in strict keeping with the import of the term itself. In Mark i. 2, it is applied to John the Baptist. "Behold, I send my messenger (angel) before my face," and the word is the same ("malak") in the corresponding prophecy of Malachi. In Hebrews xii. 22, 24, we read: "Ye have come to an innumerable company of angels, to the spirits of the just," &c., and this idea of their great number is sustained by the words of our Lord himself, where, for example, he declares that "twelve legions" of them were ready upon his demand: the full Roman Legion numbered about 6,000 men. They are also called the "armies" of heaven. Their song of praise is described as "the voice of a great multitude, and as the voice of many waters, and as the voice of mighty thunderings." (Rev. xix. 6.) In fine, the sense of number is overwhelmed in the effort to compute them: "I heard the voice of many angels round about the throne, and the beasts and the elders: and the number of them was ten thousand times ten thousand, and thousands of thousands." (Rev. v. 11.)

The nature of angels is essentially the same as that of man; for not only are understanding and will attributed to them, but they have been mistaken for man when they appeared, and Paul represents them as capable of disobedience. (Heb. ii. 7, 16.) The latter possibility is exhibited in its greatest extent by Jude, who speaks of "the angels which kept not their first estate, but left their own habitation" (v. 6); and upon this belief is founded the whole system of tradition concerning angels and demons: the former term was gradually limited to mean only the obedient ministers of the will of the Almighty, and the influence of evil angels was sublimed into the office of the great adversary of all good, the devil, or Satan. These ideas were common to the whole Eastern world, and were probably derived by the Jewish people from the Assyrians. The Pharisees charged the Saviour with casting out devils "by Beelzebub, the prince of the devils." (Matt. xii. 24.) But that evil spirits acted in multitudes under one person appears from Mark x. 9, where the evil spirit being asked his name, answered: "My name is 'Legion,' for we are *many*."

The book of Tobias speaks of *seven angels* superior to all the rest; and this has been constantly believed, according to the letter, by the ancient Jews and Christians. So, the seven that have the greatest power, the first-born angels (Tob. xii. 15): "I am Raphael, one of the *seven holy angels*, which present the prayers of the saints, and go in and out before the glory of the Holy One." And this Daniel may very well be thought to mean when he says, chap. x. 13, &c.: "Michael, one of the chief princes, came to help me." That some angels were under the command of others may be collected out of Zechariah ii. and iii., where one angel commands another, "Run, speak to this young man," &c.; and out of Rev. xii., 7, where Michael and his angels fought with the dragon and his angels. The number of just seven supreme angels Grotius conceived to be drawn from the seven chief princes of the Persian empire; but it may be doubted whether the seven there were so ancient as this tradition. Three names of these seven the Scripture affords—Michael, Gabriel, and Raphael; but for the other four—Oriphiel, Zachariel, Samael, and Anael, let the authors of them answer, as likewise for their presiding over the seven planets.—*Cowley's Notes to Davideis.*

In the Roman Catholic services, St. Michael is invoked as a most glorious and warlike prince; "chief officer of Paradise," "captain of God's hosts," "the receiver of souls," and the "vanquisher of evil spirits." His design, according to Randle Holme, is a banner hanging on a cross: and he is armed as representing victory, with a dart in one hand, and a cross on his forehead. Bishop Horsely and others consider Michael only another designation for the son of God. We may add, as a certain Biblical truth, that the Lord Himself is always meant, in an eminent sense, by any angel named as his minister; and He is called the Angel of the Covenant, because He embodied in his own person the whole power and representation of the angelic kingdom, as the messenger, not of separate and temporary commands, but of the whole Word in its fulness.

Paul speaks of a "third heaven," which must be understood not as a distinct order of created intelligence, but in the same sense as the Lord's declaration, "In my Father's house are many mansions." For Jesus Christ always speaks of his kingdom as essentially *one*, even in both worlds, the spiritual and natural. The rhetorical passage (Rom. vii. 28, 30), "neither death, nor life, nor angels, nor *principalities*, can separate us from the love of God," makes excellent sense, however it may be understood.

Dionysius, or St. Denis, the supposed Areopagite, describes three hierarchies of angels in nine choirs, thus: Seraphim, Cherubim, Thrones, Dominions, Principalities, Powers, Virtues, Angels, and Archangels.

Vartar, the Armenian poet and historian of the thirteenth century, describes Angels under the same terms, but expressly states, "these orders differ from one another in situation, and degree of glory, just as there are different ranks among men, *though they are all of one nature*." He also remarks that the first order are attracted to the Deity by love; and hardly attributes *place* to them, but *states* of desire and love, while the heaven which contains the whole host is above the *primum mobile*, which, again, is superior to the starry firmament. This description, and all others resembling it, the twelve heavenly worlds of Plato, and the heaven succeeding heaven of the Chinese, for example, are but as landmarks serving to denote the heights which the restless waves of human intelligence have reached at various times in the attempt to represent the eternal and infinite in precise terms. Böhme (Behmen), regards "the whole deep between the stars" as the heaven of one of the three hierarchies, and places the other two above it; "in the midst of which," he says, "is the son of God:

not part of either is farther or nearer to Him, yet are the three kingdoms circular about Him." The Revelations of Swedenborg date a century later and begin all these subjects *de novo*.

The division of angels into nine orders, or three hierarchies, was held in the Middle Ages, and gave the prevalent character to much of their symbolism. With it was held the doctrine of their separate creation, and the tradition of the rebellious hierarchy, headed by Lucifer, the whole of which is rendered familiar to the popular mind by the Epic of Milton.

The Persian, Jewish, and Mohammedan accounts of angels all evince a common origin, and they alike admit a difference of sex. In the latter the name of "Azaril" is given to the hierarchy nearest the throne of God, to which the Mohammedan Satan ("Eblis" or "Haris") is supposed to have belonged; also "Azrael," the angel of death, and "Azrafil," the angel of the resurrection. The examiners "Moukir" and "Nakir" are subordinate angels of terrible aspect, armed with whips of iron and fire, who interrogate recently deceased souls as to their lives. The parallel to this tradition in the Talmud is an account of seven angels who beset the paths of death. The Koran also assigns two angels to every man, one to record his good and the other his evil actions; they are so merciful that if an evil action has been done, it is not recorded till the man has slept, and if in that interval he repents, they place on the record that God has pardoned him.

The Christian fathers, for the most part, believed that angels possessed bodies of heavenly substance. (Tertullian calls it "angelified flesh"), and if not, that they could assume a coporeal presence at their pleasure. The most decisive description of an angel contained in the whole Word is: "And I, John, saw these things and heard them. And when I had heard and seen, I fell down to worship before the feet of the angel that showed me these things. Then saith he unto me, See thou do it not: *for I am thy fellow servant, and of thy brethren the prophets*, and of them that keep the sayings of this book: worship God." (Rev. xxii. 8, 9.) This passage may well supply the place of any lengthened argument against the invocation of angels and supposed saints, whatever the love and service they bestow upon us; for they are but the agents of the All-merciful, and, like ourselves.

the subjects of his supreme government. The same passage establishes that angels are the beatified spirits of good men, and in a word, justifies the highest speculations of philosophy, and the dearest hopes of the Christian.

The remarkable passage, "Take heed that ye despise not one of these little ones; for I say unto you, that in heaven *their angels* do always behold the face of my Father which is in heaven" (Matt. xviii. 10), has been the subject of much comment. It is generally held to establish the fact of ministering angels; and at any rate, will be admitted to bear the construction, that the innocent are the happiest of all, and most immediately under the divine view.*

We now come to the broadest and most popular notion of an Angel. The Rev. John Eagles, in one of his ingenious Essays, says:

> I have often tried to make out the exact ideas the poor people have of Angels, for they talk a great deal about them. The best that I can make of it is, that they are children, or children's heads and shoulders winged, as represented in church paintings, and in plaster of Paris on ceilings. It is notorious and Scriptural, poor people think, that the body dies, but nothing being said about the head and shoulders, they have a sort of belief that they are preserved to angels, which are no other but dead young children.

Adam Littleton, in his *Dictionary*, has this odd sentence: "There is no reason for fancying Angels more of one sex than of the other, since amongst them there is no such distinction; but they may as well be imagined female as male."

Bishop Hall, in *The Invisible World: Of God and his Angels*, thus speaks of the portage of souls:

> The main care, and most officious endeavors of these blessed spirits, are employed about the better part, the soul—in the instilling of good motions; enlightening the understanding, repelling of temptations. furthering our opportunities of good, preventing occasions of sin, comforting our sorrows, quickening our dulness, encouraging our weakness: and lastly, after all careful attendance here below, conveying the souls of their charge to their glory, and presenting them to the hands of their faithful Creator.

It is somewhat too hard to believe, that there have been ocular witnesses of these happy convoys; who lists may credit that which *Hieron* tells us, that *Antony* the Hermit saw the soul of his partner in

---

* Selected and abridged from *The Occult Sciences*, by Elihu Rich.

that solitude (Paul) carried up by them to heaven; that *Severinus*, Bishop of *Colein*, saw the soul of St. Martin thus transported, as Gregory reports in his Dialogues; that *Benedict* saw the soul of *Germanus* in the form of a fiery globe thus conveyed: what though I speak of the souls of the Holy Martyrs, *Tiburtius, Valerian, Maximus, Marcellinus, Justus, Quintinus, Severus*, and others: we may if we please (we need not unless we list), give way to these reports, to which our faith obligeth us not. In these cases, we go not by eye-sight; but we are well assured the soul of *Lazarus* was by these glorious spirits carried up into the bosom of *Abraham*, neither was this any privilege of his above all other the saints of God; all which as they land in one common harbor of blessedness, so they all participate of one happy means of portage.

SPIRITUAL NATURES.

In Sir Humphrey Davy's posthumous *Consolations in Travel*, we find this picture of spiritual power. "Listen," said the Genius of the Vision, "whilst I reveal to you the mysteries of spiritual natures; but I almost fear that with the mortal veil of your senses surrounding you, these mysteries can never be made perfectly intelligible to your mind. Spiritual natures are eternal and invisible, but their modes of being are as infinitely varied as their forms of matter. They have no relation to space, and in their transitions no dependence upon time, so that they can pass from one part of the universe to another, by laws entirely independent of their motion. The quantity or the number of spiritual essences, like the quantity or number of the atoms of the material world, are always the same; but their arrangements, like those of the materials which they are destined to guide or govern, are infinitely diversified; they are, in fact, parts more or less inferior of the infinite mind, and in the planetary systems, to one of which the globe you inhabit belongs, are in a state of probation, continually aiming at, and generally rising to a higher state of existence. Were it permitted me to extend your vision to the fates of intellectual existences, I could show you the same spirit, which in the form of Socrates developed the foundations of moral and social virtue, in the Czar Peter possessed of supreme power and enjoying exalted felicity in improving a rude people. I could show you the monad or spirit which, with the organ of Newton, displayed an intelligence almost above humanity now in a higher and better state of planetary existence, drinking intellectual light from a purer source, and approaching nearer to the infinite and divine mind."

To this succeeds a glimpse of those states, which the highest intellectual beings that have belonged to the earth enjoy after death, in their transition to new and more exalted natures. "These beings," said the Genius, "so grand, so glorious with functions to you incomprehensible, once belonged to the earth; their spiritual natures have risen through different stages of planetary life, leaving their dust behind them, carrying with them only their intellectual power. You ask me if they have any knowledge or recollection of their transitions? Tell me of your own recollections in the womb of your mother, and I will answer you. It is the law of divine wisdom, that no spirit carries with it into another state and being, any habit or mental qualities except those which may be connected with its new wants and enjoyments; and knowledge relating to the earth would be no more useful to these glorified beings than their earthly system of organized dust, which would be instantly resolved into its ultimate atoms at such a temperature: even on the earth the butterfly does not transport with it into the air the organs or the appetites of the crawling worm from which it sprung.

"There is, however, one sentiment or passion which the monad or spiritual essence carries with it into all its stages of being, and which, in these happy and elevated creatures, is continually exalted: the love of knowledge or of intellectual power, which is, in fact, in its most ultimate and perfect development, the love of infinite wisdom and unbounded power, or the love of God. Even in the imperfect life that belongs to the earth, this passion exists in a considerable degree; increases even with age: outlives the perfection of the corporeal faculties; and at the moment of death is felt by the conscious being; and its future destinies depend upon the manner in which it has been exercised and exalted.

* * * * *

Your vision (said the Genius), must end with this glorious view of the inhabitants of the cometary worlds: I cannot show you the beings of the system to which I myself belong, that of the sun: your organs would perish before our brightness; and I am only permitted to be present to you as a sound or intellectual voice. *We* are likewise in progression, but we see and know something of the place of infinite wisdom: we feel the personal presence of that supreme Deity which you only imagine; to you belongs faith, to us knowledge; and our greatest delight results from the conviction that we are lights kindled by his light, and that we belong to his substance. To obey, to love, to wonder and adore forms our relations to the infinite Intelligence. We feel his laws are those of eternal justice, and that they govern all things, from the most glorious intellectual natures belonging to the sun and fixed stars, to the meanest spark of life animating an atom crawling in the dust of your earth. We know all things begin from, and end in, his everlasting essence, the cause of causes, the power of powers."

PERMANENT IMPRESSIONS BY SPIRITUAL POWERS.

Dr. Ferriar, in his *Essay toward a Theory of Apparitions*, relates a remarkable Trial of Dr. Pordage, a clergyman in Berkshire, which was published under the frightful title of *Demonium Meridionem*, or *Satan at Noonday*, &c. Dr. Ferriar remarks: "The development of this story, which is not necessary for my purpose, exhibits the combined effects of Mysticism, Superstition, and Sensuality, which evidently produced a disordered state of the sensorium, and gave rise to the visions, which were admitted by all the parties."

The book quoted by Dr. Ferriar (published in 1655), is one written by a most determined opponent of Dr. Pordage, in reply to Dr. P.'s own book (published in 1864). Had Dr. Ferriar consulted *that*, he would have found the following passage, which would have required quite another theory than the one he has offered to explain it. It will be seen that it affirms the fact of *permanent impressions*, caused by the spiritual powers, *upon objects in nature*. Such impressions, of course, could be judged of by the senses of other persons than the parties immediately concerned:—

Now, besides these appearances within, the spirits made some wonderful *impressions upon visible bodies without*, as figures of men and beasts upon the glass windows and the ceilings of the house, *some of which yet remain*. But what was most remarkable, was the whole invisible world, represented by the spirits upon the bricks of a chimney, in the form of two half globes, as in the maps. After which, upon other bricks of the same chimney, were figured a coach and four horses, with persons in it, and a footman attending, all seeming to be in motion, with many other such images, which were wonderfully exactly done. Now fearing lest there might be any danger in these images, through unknown conjuration and false magic, we endeavored to wash them out with wet cloths, but could not, finding them engraven in the substance of the bricks; which, indeed, might have continued until this day had not our fear and suspicion of whichcraft, and some evil design of the devil against us in it, caused us to deface and obliterate them with hammers.

It is difficult to see how what is commonly called *delusion* could have any place here. The affirmations, from their nature, if not truths, must be *intentional falsehoods;* yet they are most deliberately put forth, and that too, not by any one wholly obscure, but by a man well known amongst those who are interested in the mystic writers, as being of some eminence in that class; and, moreover, he makes these statements in a book written to clear himself from charges which had been of the most serious consequences to him.—*Notes and Queries*, Second Series, No. 166.

Dr. South has this remarkable passage upon "The Mind of Man in Spiritual affected by External objects:"

The mind of man in spirituals, acts with a corporeal dependence, and so is helped or hindered in its operations according to the different quality of external objects that incur into the senses; and perhaps, sometimes, the sight of the altar, and those decent preparations for the work of devotion, may compose and recover the wandering mind much more effectually than a sermon or rational discourse: for these things, in a manner, preach to the eye, when the ear is dull and will not hear; and the eye dictates to the imagination, and that at last moves the affections. And if these little impulses set the great wheels of devotion at work, the largeness and height of that shall not be at all prejudiced by the smallness of its occasion. If the fire burns brightly and vigorously, it's no matter by what means it was at first kindled; there is the same force and the same refreshing virtue in it, kindled by a spark from a flint, as if it were kindled by a beam from the sun.

Perhaps, the most remarkable manifestation of material attributes by presumed spiritualities is that narrated by Damascius, a stoic philosopher of Syria, who flourished in the time of Justinian. Speaking of him, Dr. Lardner writes: "He says expressly that in a battle fought near Rome with the Scythians commanded by Attila, in the time of Valentinian (the third) who succeeded Honorius (in the year 425) the slaughter on both sides was so great, that none on either side escaped, except the generals and a few of their attendants. And which is very strange," he says, "when the *bodies* were fallen, the *souls* stood upright, and continued fighting three whole days and nights, nothing inferior to living men either for the activity of their hands or the fierceness of their minds;" . . . . . they were "both seen and heard, fighting together, and clashing with their armor."—*Works*, viii. 143. Southey thought this passage sufficiently curious for insertion in his *Commonplace Book*, page 143.

MATERIALISM AND SPIRITUALISM—PERSONAL IDENTITY.

Isaac Taylor has well observed, in his *Physical Theory of Another Life:* "The doctrine of the materialists, if it were followed out to its extreme consequences, and consistently held, is plainly atheistic, and is therefore incompatible with any and with every form of religious belief. It is so because, in affirming that *mind is nothing more than the product of animal organization*, it excludes the belief of a pure and uncreated mind—the cause of all things; for if there be a supreme mind, absolutely independent of matter, then, unquestionably, there may be created minds, also independent."

The question has been thus ably illustrated by Dr. Lardner, in his popular *Museum of Science and Art*, vol. 8:

"Man's nature, it is admitted, is a compound of the material and the intellectual. According to some, to whom, on that account, the name of *Materialists* has been given, the intellectual is a mere function or property of the material part of our nature. According to others, the intellectual is a function of a spiritual essence, which is independent of our material organization, though inseparably connected with it during human life.

"Our nature being thus compound, let us see how far we can

trace the connection between its mere physical part and the thinking and intelligent principle which abides in it.

"There is a principle called in metaphysics *Personal Identity*, which consists in the internal consciousness by which each individual knows his past existence, so as to be able, with the greatest certainty of which the judgment of our minds is susceptible, to identify himself existing at any given moment with himself existing at any former time and place. Nothing in human judgment can exceed the clear certitude which attends this consciousness. The Duke of Wellington, on the eve of his death, at Walmer, had an assured certainty that he was himself the same individual intelligent thinking being, who, on the 18th of June, 1815, commanded at Waterloo the allied armies. Now, to what did this intense conviction and consciousness of identity apply? What was there in common between the individuals who died at Walmer and who commanded at Waterloo? To reply to this question we must recur, for a moment, to our physical organization.

"The human body consists of bones, flesh, and blood, each of which is, however, itself a compound substance, and the whole is largely impregnated with water. The ultimate materials of the average human body are 14 lbs. of charcoal and 10 lbs. of lime, impregnated with 116 lbs. of water, and 14 lbs. weight of the gases which form air and water, that is, oxygen, nitrogen, and hydrogen.

"Now, those who think that the intellectual principle residing in the human body is nothing more than a quality or a property arrising from the matter composing it, must be able to imagine how 14 lbs. of charcoal, 10 lbs. of lime, and 116 lbs. of water can be so mixed up with 14 lbs. of air as to make a material thing—machine, let us call it—which can feel, think, judge and remember, and reason. This power of intelligence, we know, is ascribed to the organization of the materials; but we are still left as far as ever from any explanation as to how the mere arrangement and peculiar juxtaposition of the material atoms thus composing such a body, can produce the prodigious powers of intellect.

"But even admitting a supposition apparently so impossible, the question of *Personal Identity* will raise an insuperable objection to it. Physiologists and anatomists have proved that the

Materialism and Spiritualism.

matter which composes our bodies is subject to continual change with varying rapidity, according to the habitudes and occupations of individuals. According to some authorities the average length of the interval within which the change takes place does not exceed thirty days. It is, however, generally agreed that it is a very brief period.

"This, then, being the case, let us again ask, what is it that was identical in the Duke of Wellington dying at Walmer in Sept., 1852, with the Duke of Wellington commanding at Waterloo in June, 1815? Assuredly, it was not possible that there should have been a single particle of matter common to his body on the two occasions. The interval consisting of 37 years and 3 months, the entire mass of matter composing his body must have undergone a complete change several hundred times—yet no one doubts that there was *something* there which *did not* undergo a change except in its relation to the mutable body, and which possessed the same thought, memory, and consciousness, and constituted the personal identity of the individual; and since it is as demonstrable as any problem in geometry, that *that something* which thus abode in the body, retaining the consciousness of the past, could not have been an atom, or any number of atoms, of matter, it must necessarily have been something not matter, that is to say, something *spiritual*—thus proving the existence of a spiritual essence connected with the human organization. Here the proof of the physical inquirer terminates. If there is nothing in the disorganization of the human body and the phenomena of death to demonstrate the simultaneous destruction of the spiritual principle, the existence of which is thus established, there is, on the other hand, nothing to prove its continued existence, and for that we are thrown upon the resources of revelation, which might, indeed, have been foreseen; for, if the continued existence of the spirit, or in other words, a future state, were capable of demonstration by the ordinary faculties of the mind, it would have been incompatible with the divine economy to have rendered it the subject of revelation. God does not suspend the laws of nature to reveal by miraculous means those truths which are discoverable by the exercise of our natural faculties."

MESMERISM AND SOMNAMBULISM.

In 1784, a Report was made to the King of France, signed, among other members of the Commission, by Franklin and Lavoisier. It speaks in strong terms of the Magnetism of this period, with its *baquets*, its *crises*, and its convulsions—against Mesmer's theory, too, of a universal fluid with flux and reflux, the medium of influence by the celestial bodies on the human system, and a universal curative agent—they express no opinion whatever, favorable or unfavorable, in regard to Somnambulism properly so called.

It is equally admitted that somnambulism, with its attendant phenomena, in the form now known to us, was observed, for the first time, by the Marquis de Puysegur, on his estate of Buzancy, near Soissons, on the fourth of March, 1784; but his observations were not published until four months after the Commissioners' report was made. Bailly, and his associates, learned and candid as they were, did not condemn that which they had never seen nor heard of. To this fact Arago testifies as follows: "the Report of Bailly upsets from their foundations the ideas, the system, the practice, of Mesmer and his disciples:" but we have no right to evoke its authority against modern somnambulism, most of the phenomena of which were neither known nor announced in 1783. A magnetizer undoubtedly says one of the least probable things in the world when he tells us that such an individual, in a state of somnambulism, can see everything in perfect darkness, can read through a wall, or even without the aid of the eyes.

Bailly does not notice such marvels. The naturalist, the physician, or the more curious investigator of somnambulistic experiments, who inquires, whether, in certain states of nervous excitement, individuals are really endowed with extraordinary faculties —that, for instance, of reading through the epigastrium or the heel—who desires to ascertain positively up to what point the phenomena announced with so much assurance by modern magnetizers, belong only to the domain of the rogue or the conjuror; all such inquirers, we say, are not really opposing themselves to a Lavoisier, a Franklin, or a Bailly. They are entering upon a world entirely new, the very existence of which these illustrious sages did not suspect. A little further on, Arago adds: "My object has been to show that Somnambulism ought not to be rejected *à priori*, especially by those who have kept up with the progress of modern physical science."

In 1826, a Commission was appointed from among the Members of the Royal Academy of Medicine of Paris, to examine the subject of Animal Magnetism; and after five years' investigation (in 1831) this Commission reported unanimously in favor of the reality of certain somnambulic phenomena; among them, insensibility, vision with the eyes closed, prescience during sickness, and, in one case, perception of the diseases of others. Some years later (in 1837) a second Commission of the Academy reported, expressing their conviction that not one of these phenomena had any foundation except in the imagination of the observers. They reached this conclusion by examining two somnambules only. Still, the President of the Academy, on their first Report, observed on the conclusions of the second Report, that "the negative experiences thus obtained can never destroy the positive facts observed by the previous Commission; since, though diametrically opposed to each other, both may be equally true."

Arago, also, speaking of "the actual power which one man may exert over another without the intervention of any known physical agent," declares that even Bailly's Report against Mesmer's crude theory shows "how our faculties ought to be studied experimentally, and by what means psychology may one day obtain a place among the exact sciences." Cuvier, more familiar than Arago with the phenomena of animated nature, says: "it scarcely admits of further doubt that the proximity of two living bodies in certain circumstances and with certain movements, has a real effect, independently of all participation of the imagination of one of the two;" and he further adds: it appears now clearly enough that the effects are due to some communication established between their nervous systems." This is conceding the principle lying at the base of Mesmerism,—a concession which is sustained by countless observations, little reliable in some cases, but in others made by upright and capable experimentalists, on the contested ground of artificial somnambulism and kindred phenomona.*

* Abridged from Owen's *Footfalls*.

CLAIRVOYANCE.

Dr. Carpenter, in his *Principles of Human Physiology*, under the head "Mesmerism," discredits the higher phenomena of Clairvoyance, but admits, 1st, A state of complete insensibility, during which severe surgical operations may be performed without the consciousness of the patient. 2dly, Artificial somnambulism, with manifestation of the ordinary power of mind, but no recollection, in the waking state, of what has passed. 3dly, Exaltation of the senses, during such somnambulism, so that the somnambule perceives what in his natural condition he could not. 4thly, Action, during such somnambulism, on the muscular apparatus, so as to produce, for example, artificial catalepsy : and, 5thly, perhaps curative effects.

Dr. Carpenter adds : his mind is made up as to the reality of these phenomena, and that "he does not see why any discredit should attach to them."

Rogers, the poet, relates that, when he was in Paris, he went to Alexis, the clairvoyant, and desired him to describe the house in St. James's Place. "On my word," says Rogers, "he astonished me! He described most exactly the peculiarities of the staircase ; and that, not far from the window in the drawing-room, there was a picture of a man in armor (the painting by Giorgione), and so on. Colonel Gurwood, shortly before his death, assured me that he was reminded by Alexis of some circumstances that had happened to him in Spain, and which he could not conceive how any human being, except himself, should know. Still, I cannot believe in clairvoyance, because the thing is impossible." Not because the opportunities for observation were too few, and the experiments needed repetition ; but because *no* evidence would suffice. La Place, however, says : "It is exceedingly unphilosophical to deny magnet phenomena merely because they are inexplicable in the present state of our knowledge ;" and upon the above instance, Owen, in his *Footfalls*, observes : "It is remarkable enough that in a matter like this, usually deemed to savor of imagination, the mathematician should reprove the incredulity of the poet."

Mental Phenomena.

MIND AND BODY.

It has been observed that the mental powers, unlike the bodily, do not suffer from the effects of time, but continue, as life advances, to enlarge and exalt themselves. Lord Brougham says:

> It is an undoubted fact, and almost universally true, that the Mind, before extreme old age, becomes more sound, and is capable of greater things, during nearly thirty years of diminished bodily powers; that in most cases, it suffers no abatement of strength during ten years more of bodily decline; that in many cases, a few years more of bodily decrepitude produce no effect upon the mind; and that in some instances its faculties remain bright to the last, surviving almost totally the total extinction of the corporeal endowments. It is certain that the strength of the Body, its agility, its patience of fatigue, indeed, all its qualities, decline from thirty at the latest; and yet the mind is improving rapidly from thirty to fifty; suffers little or no decline before sixty; and therefore is better, when the body is enfeebled, at the age of fifty-eight or fifty-nine, than it was in the acme of the corporeal faculties thirty years before. It is equally certain that, while the body is rapidly decaying, between sixty or sixty-three and seventy, the mind suffers hardly any loss of strength in the generality of men; that men continue to seventy-five or seventy-six in the possession of all their mental powers, while few can then boast of more than the remains of physical strength; and instances are not wanting of persons, who, between eighty and ninety, or even older, when the body can hardly be said to live, possess every faculty of the mind unimpaired.
>
> We are authorized to conclude from these facts, that unless some unusual and violent accident interferes, such as a serious illness or a violent contusion, the ordinary course of life presents the mind and the body running courses widely different, and in great part of the time in opposite directions: and this affords strong proof, both that the mind is independent of the body, and that its destruction in the period of its entire vigor is contrary to the analogy of nature.—*Discourse of Natural Theology*, pp. 119–121.

Dr. Cromwell gives as the leading doctrine of his work, that Mind is *no* independent immaterial essence, but the most excellent and exalted among the numerous and varied phenomena of life. "Though," says Mr. Spencer, "we commonly regard mental and bodily life as distinct, it needs only to ascend somewhat above the ordinary point of view, to see that they are but subdivisions of life in general ; and that no line of demarcation can be drawn between them otherwise than arbitrarily." (*Elements of Psychology*, p. 349.) And if the oft-put question again follow, "*What is life ?*" we repeat that it cannot be more closely defined than as the expression by operation of the laws of the states, functions, and actions, by which an organism manifests itself to be alive.

MENTAL PROCESSES OF WHICH WE ARE UNCONSCIOUS.

It has long been our practice, in order to master a subject of difficulty, to assemble the facts and reasonings, to weigh and consider them thoroughly, and, having done so, to take leave of the matter until the next day, or for a short interval ; when, on returning to it, we have, invariably, been the better able to master the inquiry. This result may, perhaps, be attributed to returning to the subject with a fresh eye and recruited brain; but this is not precisely the explanation. In Sir Benjamin Brodie's *Psychological Inquiries*, we find it stated that a remarkable process takes place in the mind, which is independent of any direct act of volition ; "as if there were in the mind a principle of order which operates without our being at the time conscious of it." The explanation is thus given in the First Dialogue :

Crites. It has often happened to me to have been occupied by a particular subject of inquiry; to have accumulated a store of facts connected with it; but to have been able to proceed no further. Then, after an interval of time, without any addition to my stock of knowledge, I have found the obscurity and confusion in which the subject was originally enveloped, to have cleared away; the facts have seemed all to have settled themselves in their right places, and their mutual relations to have become apparent, although I have not been sensible of having made any distinct effort for that purpose.

Eubulus. What you have now described has occurred repeatedly to myself. It is certainly not very easy to comprehend the nature of this mental operation. Is it that the subject every now and then comes before us, and is considered without our recollecting it afterwards ?—or is it, as a philosophical friend has suggested, that in the first instance we are perplexed by the multiplicity of facts presented to us, and that after an interval of time, those of less importance fade away, while the memory retains those which are essential, in the subsequent arrangement or classification of which, being thus rendered more conspicuous, there is no difficulty?

Crites. The latter seems to be the more probable explanation of the two. At the same time, it must be admitted that they are not incompatible with each other.

Accordingly, as men possess this faculty of keeping the attention fixed on a particular object until we have, as it were, *looked all around it*, will be the success of taking cognizance of relations of which another mind has no perception. It is this, much more than any difference in the abstract power of reasoning, which constitutes the vast difference which exists between the minds of different individuals. "I keep the subject," said Sir Isaac Newton, "constantly before me, and wait until the first dawnings open by little and little into a full light." It was thus that, after long meditation, he was led to the invention of fluxions, and to the anticipation of the modern discovery of the combustibility of the diamond.

THE VOLTAIC BATTERY, THE ELECTRIC EEL, AND THE BRAIN OF MAN.

We boast of our Voltaic Battery; but when we compare it with the battery which Nature has given to the electrical eel and torpedo, how insignificant are human operations compared with those of the Architect of living beings! The stupendous electrical eel exhibited some years since at the Polytechnic Institution, when he sought to kill his prey, enclosed him in a circle; then by volition caused the voltaic force to be produced, and the hapless creature was instantly killed. It would probably require ten thousand artificial batteries to effect the same object, as the creature was killed *instanter* on receiving the shock. As much, however, as Smee's battery is inferior to that of the electric fish, so is man superior to the same animal. Man is endowed with a power of mind competent to appreciate the force of matter, and is thus enabled to make the battery. The eel can but use the specific apparatus which nature has bestowed upon it.

If the brain (says Sir John Herschel) be an electric pile constantly in action, it may be conceived to discharge itself at regular intervals, when the tension of the electricity reaches a certain point, along the nerves which communicate with the heart, and thus excite the pulsation of that organ.

A GALVANIZED HUMAN BODY.

The appearances produced by the agency of galvanism on the human body are of the most frightful nature, and awaken horrible fancies in the mind of the spectator: the eyes roll wildly, and the countenance is distorted with ghastly grins, whilst the limbs move in forcible and convulsive actions. The most successful effort to resuscitate by galvanism was that made on the body of John White, who was executed for a murder at Louisville. The body, after hanging twenty-five minutes, was cut down, and whilst yet warm, and even trembling, was subjected to the stimulus of galvanism. The man suddenly rose from the bench to a sitting posture, afterward stood on his feet, opened his eyes, and gave a terrific screech. His chest worked as if in respiration. One of the surgeons present exclaimed that he was alive. On another shock being given, he jumped up with a sudden bound, disengaged himself from the wires, and ran into a corner of the room. He frequently opened his eyes, and the breathing became so regular, that many addressed him, but he made no sign of understanding. Nevertheless, by the assistance of a medical student, he took a few steps on the floor, and seated himself in an arm-chair. He seemed like a man intoxicated, and overcome with the exertion he had made. Every effort was put in practice to equalize the circulation; but congestion of the brain eventually came on, and terminated his existence. A man named Clydesdale, who was executed for murder at Glasgow, was also made the subject of a similar experiment.—*Harrison on the Medical Aspects of Death.*

CHANGES IN THE NERVOUS SYSTEM.

Sir Benjamin Brodie considers it (1) very probable that the Nervous Force is some modification of the force which produces

Changes in the Nervous System. 97

the phenomena of electricity and magnetism; and he compares the generation of it by the oxygenated blood on the gray substance of the brain and spinal chord, to the production of the electric force by the action of the acid solution on the metallic plates in the cells of a voltaic battery.

2. We know that the solid parts of the body are in a state of perpetual change. There is a constant influx of new materials supplied by the digestive organs, and in other ways; and a corresponding efflux of the old materials by means of the various excretions, especially by that of the kidneys. The brain itself forms no exception to the general rule. We cannot otherwise account for its growth in the early part of life, nor for the alterations in its structure which arise as the consequence of disease, nor for those other changes which occur in extreme old age. The mind preserves its identity, but there is no corresponding identity of the corporeal organ with which it is associated; and we may even venture to assert that the brain of to-day is not precisely and in all respects the same with the brain of yesterday, and that it will not be the brain of to-morrow.

3. We cannot suppose that such deposition of new materials and abstraction of old ones can be effected by mere mechanical means, as you would take one brick from a building and substitute another in its place. The elements of which the nervous system is composed exist in the blood, but they must undergo a new chemical combination before they can be incorporated with it; and in like manner they must undergo a chemical change of an opposite kind before they can re-enter the current of the circulation. The precise character of these chemical changes we have no means of ascertaining; but whatever it may be, there is reason to believe that it must be in proportion as the nervous system is more or less exercised.

The nervous substance is distinguished from all the other tissues (with the exception of the bones) by the very large proportion of phosphorus which enters into its composition, amounting to 1·5 parts in 100, and to as much as one-thirteenth of the solid matter which remains after the evaporation of the water; and that one result of over-exercise of the nervous system is the elimination of an unusual quantity of salts containing phosphorus, by means of the secretions of the kidneys. This fact was first observed by Dr. Prout, who has given it as his opinion, "that the phosphorus in organized beings is in some measure connected with the nervous tissues and nervous action."

Lastly, Sir Benjamin Brodie considers that even if we had more perfect organs of sense, or, by more perfect microscopes, we could trace exactly the changes which took place in the brain, we should be just as far from identifying physical and mental phenomena with each other as we are at present. The link between them would still be wanting, and it would be as idle to speculate on the nature of the relation between mind and matter, as on the proximate cause of gravitation, or of magnetic attraction and repulsion.—*Selected and Abridged from Psychological Inquiries.*

Dr. Forbes Winslow has thus sketched what may be termed the ubiquitous existences of the Nervous System:

From the maggot that leaps from a nut as we crack it in our plate after dinner, and the caterpillar that eats up the leaves of our favorite convolvulus in the garden—from the fish that cleaves the green, translucent wave, and the bird that wings the breeze of incense-breathing morn—from the lion that roams the desert wild, and the horse that tramps the battle-field, or prances before the lady's equipage—up to Man, the master of them all, there is one all-pervading Nervous System, progressively diminishing in a downward scale of analytic exhaustion, till it ends in a mere microscopic globule of a brain, by which they all communicate and hold their relative and interdependent existences, according to their various forms and needs, and types of organization, function, growth, location, and pursuits.

WORKING OF THE BRAIN.

From several causes within medical experience, it would seem that Motion of the Brain is, at least, *coincident* with every mental operation. Thus, "in a case reported by Dr. Pierquin, observed by him in one of the hospitals of Montpellier, in 1821, he saw, in a female patient, part of whose skull had been removed, the brain motionless, and lying within the cranium, when she was in a dreamless sleep; in motion, and protruding without the skull, when she was agitated by dreams; more protruded in dreams reported by herself to be vivid; and still more so, when perfectly awake, and especially if engaged in active thought or sprightly conversation."—*Combe's Constitution of Man.*

A British captain, whilst giving orders on the quarter-deck of his ship at the Battle of the Nile, was struck on the head by a shot, and immediately became senseless. He was taken home, and removed to Greenwich Hospital, where for fifteen months he evinced no sign of intelligence. He was then trephined, and immediately upon the operation being performed, consciousness returned, and he immediately began busying himself to see the orders carried out that he had given during the battle fifteen months previously. The clockwork of the brain, unaware that it had stopped, upon being set going again, pointed to the exact minute at which it had left off. These sudden revivals of a lost intelligence almost rival in their dramatic effect the effect of the Prince's advent in the palace of the Sleeping Beauty, where, at the magic of a kiss, the inmates of the royal household, who had gone to sleep for a hundred years transfixed in their old attitudes, leapt suddenly into life and motion, as though they had only for a moment slept.—*Once a Week.*

WHAT IS MEMORY?

The eye, the ear, and the other organs of sense, are physical instruments by means of which impressions are communicated through the nerves to the brain. It does not, however, follow that the brain itself feels, or that it performs any other than a subordinate office, conveying the impressions received from the organs of sense to a superior principle in connection with it. *Memory is a recurrence of sensations, which existed formerly, produced by the operation of some internal changes, after the causes by which the first sensations were excited, have ceased to exist.* When renewed, sensations are (with some rare exceptions) fainter and less distinct than those in which they originated. There is also this difference between them, that the renewed sensations are subject to the influence of volition, vanishing at once on the slightest effort being made to direct the attention to any thing else; whereas, we have no such power over the impressions which are made on our senses by the immediate presence of external objects.

Notwithstanding these points of difference, it is plain that memory is closely allied to sensation, and the resemblance between the two orders of phenomena is so great as to justify the suspicion that the nervous system is instrumental in producing the one as well as the other; while a multitude of facts show that the suspicion is well founded. A blow on the head may destroy the memory altogether, or (which is more usual) it may destroy it partially, or it may interrupt its exercise for a certain time, after which it may be gradually, or even suddenly restored. After fever, also, and some other bodily ailments, the memory is not unfrequently impaired or lost. A blow on the head which causes insensibility, generally affects the memory so far that when the patient has recovered from the state of insensibility, he has no knowledge of the accident. (*See Page* 99.) But in some instances, the effect of a blow on the head is merely to disturb the memory, the other functions being unimpaired.

It seems to be a legitimate conclusion, that impressions made on the organs of sense, and transmitted to the brain, produce some actual change in the minute organization of the latter; and that this is subservient, and, in our present state of existence, essential to, the memory.

What the actual changes in the condition of the brain may be, it is impossible for us to comprehend.

It is clearly not sufficient that an impression should be transmitted to the brain to be remembered. An act of the mind itself is necessary for that purpose; and that, as Dr. Hooke has observed, is attention. It is only a small proportion of what we see, or hear, or feel, or imagine, that is not immediately forgotten, simply because there are very few of these things to which we pay more than a momentary attention, while to many of them we pay no attention at all. Now, attention implies volition: that is, it is that effort of volition by which an object, which would otherwise have immediately passed away, is kept present to the mind during a certain period of time. Sensation and volition are the two functions by means of which the mental principle is enabled to maintain its communication with the external world. It is under the influence of volition that the contraction of muscles takes place for locomotion, speech, the procuring of food, and other purposes, and that the torpedo discharges his electric battery. Here there is an impulse communicated from the mind to the brain, and from hence to the nerves, and from these to other organs, and producing a marked change in the condition of the latter; and, *à priori*, there is no reason to doubt that the operation of a similar cause may produce an equal change, though of another kind, and more prominent, in the minute structure of the brain itself.

It appears probable that there is a special organ in the brain for the purpose of memory, as well as for locomotion and speech. But there our knowledge ends. At present, we must be content to acknowledge that we know nothing as to the locality of the function, nor of the minute changes of organization which are connected with it.—*From Sir B. Brodie's Psychological Inquiries.*

HOW THE FUNCTION OF MEMORY TAKES PLACE.

Berzelius asks—Where, in the narrow emulsive mass of the Brain, lie those registers of the objects and occurrences of a man's life; those tablets which are the result of recitals or reading; the numberless words of many languages understood by the same individual; and the systems of facts belonging to the many sciences which he understands? Where is all this knowledge stored away ready for use? What part has the matter (the water, the albumen, and the cerebral fat) in that sublime activity, which, nevertheless, does not exist without it, and which, through its least derangement, is altered, or entirely lost?

The method of transforming the valuation of time into space by the rapid rotation of a cylinder rotating 1,000 times in a second, proposed by M. Fizeau, has been applied by M. Helmholtz to the measurement of the rapidity of nervous impulse. In this way it has been found by experiments made with the utmost care,—1. That sensations are transmitted to the brain with a rapidity of about 180 *feet per second*, or at one-fifth the rate of sound ; and this is nearly the same in all individuals. 2. The brain requires *one-tenth of a second* to transmit its orders to the nerves which preside over voluntary motion; but this amount varies much in different individuals, and in the same individual at different times, according to the disposition or the condition at the time, and is more regular the more sustained the attention. 3. The time required to transmit an order to the muscles by the motor nerves is nearly the same as that required by the nerves of sensation to pass a sensation; moreover, it passes nearly one-hundredth of a second before the muscles are put in motion. 4. The whole operation requires one and a quarter to two-tenths of a second. Consequently, when we speak of an active, ardent mind, or of one that is slow, cold, or apathetic, it is not a mere figure of rhetoric.—M. ULE, *Revue Suisse*.

PERSISTENCE OF IMPRESSIONS.

There is reason to believe that *no idea which ever existed in the mind can be lost*. It may seem to ourselves to be gone, since we have no power to recall it ; as is the case with the vast majority of our thoughts. But numerous facts show that it needs only some change in our physical or intellectual condition to restore the long-lost impression. A woman-servant, for instance, twenty-four years old, who could neither read nor write, in the paroxysm of a fever, commenced repeating, fluently and pompously, passages of Latin, Greek, and Hebrew; and it afterward appeared that, in her early days, a learned clergyman with whom she lived had been in the daily habit of walking through a portion of his house, that opened into the kitchen, and repeating aloud the very passages which the servant uttered in her fever. This extraordinary statement is made by Dr. E. Hitchcock, Boston, U. S.

Dr. Beattie tells of a gentleman who received a severe blow on the head, and completely lost for a time his knowledge of Greek, but did not appear to have lost any thing else. Dr. Gregory, again, tells of a clergyman, who, while laboring under an affection of the brain, could speak nothing but Hebrew, the language he had in part acquired. So, too, Dr. Prichard mentions a lady, who, after a fit of apoplexy, could only speak French for a time, but after that recovered her knowledge of English. The most curious instance, perhaps, is, however, that mentioned by Cuvier, in his Lectures, of a person who for some weeks lost the power of pronouncing substantives, but could pronounce all his adjectives as usual.*

That the brain constitutes the material organ which is immediately subjected to the operation of the mind, is unquestionable.

The human brain consists of a congeries of matter so extensive that its actual service has been computed to be equal to that of the whole body. Phrenologists have long assigned to each part of the brain a separate office, and have estimated the capacity of the mind by the relative quantities of the different portions of that organ on which they suppose it to act; but in what way it acts they have not explained. If the distribution they have made be well founded, it is obvious that a particular and distinctive part of this organ must be the immediate subject of each mental operation; and it may not be an unreasonable conjecture, that this widely-extended surface is the part acted on.

Take, for example, one of the simplest processes of the mind; the record it makes of the scenes which are presented to us. If an impression be made in early life, before the brain has been overtasked, it is always easily revived:—latent it may be for years, for many years; but so far is it from becoming extinct, that some accidental occurrence, the mention of a person or incident connected with it, immediately brings up the picture of the past in all its marked outlines, and with all its glowing colors.

And it does more: it brings up a hundred other pictures which have also lain in total obscurity, and which seem to have no further connection with each other than the views that are in the same portfolio. May we not suppose that the surface of certain organs or parts of the brain constitutes a living portfolio? The objects we look upon pass through that small but highly finished telescope, the eye, and paint their image on the retina; the retina

* *The Critic*, 1859.

does not retain the picture, but transmits it to the brain. Why should not the next operation be that of engraving it on the surface of that part of the brain which is appropriated for its preservation? and why should not the picture be actually indented on the brain, there to remain until the final destruction of that organ? How well does such a supposition correspond with the mental operation! A scene is viewed,—is recollected for years;—so vividly recollected, that we fancy the impression incapable of being strengthened:—the scene is again visited; how well does it correspond with the old impression, but for a time how much more vivid is the picture! How indelible, as we have already remarked, are the impressions which are made in early life when the brain is unoccupied! How evanescent are those which are made when every part is crowded with impressions—when the same ground has been occupied and reoccupied, until a confused blending takes place, and the outlines are too faint to be accurately retained, even for a short period, if they pass not away beyond the dawn of our earthly consciousness.

VALUE OF MEMORY.—REGISTRATION.

To estimate the value of Memory in regulating our proceedings, we should compare examples of powerful memories with other instances in which the faculty is lost. Mr. Smee relates a case of a poor fellow who could not tell what he had done the day before, or even on the morning he was examined; and he would, in a few minutes, totally forget any thing that was told to him. Where memory is lost, all the properties of the mind dependent upon it are also lost. The man without memory cannot compare a present event with a past event, or judge in any way of the difference. He cannot exercise the powers of reflection or imagination, and is said to be fatuous or foolish,—a state which destroys all that ennobles the man, and lowers him almost to the condition of a plant.

From various facts we know that memory entirely depends upon organization, which is the word used for mechanism contrived by the Infinite Cause. It is, therefore, a physical property arising from that mechanism. It ultimately resolves itself into an action, determined by some previous impression on the body, and, as such, can be obtained by human contrivances. Now, here a difficulty ensues; for if you pass a voltaic current through a solution, and so alter it that it ever afterward shows that phenomenon, you obtain the same effect which is produced in the brain by memory.

Mere registration may be imitated by mechanical means. At the Bank of England there are many presses for printing Banknotes; and every time the press acts, a communication is made to a series of numbers, and the event is registered; and the clerk who sits in an adjoining apartment has only to look to the numbers, when he can tell how many times the press has acted at any given moment of the day. This, however, is an instance of registration, not of memory. Memory involves a new tendency to act, while registration is a passive result; and we thus find that registration may exist without memory, although memory cannot act without registration.

Memory is a property of the mind of extreme importance. It is the basis of its other more noble qualities; and, as man possesses it, we must admit that it requires a mechanism so extensive as only to be exemplified in the glorious works of God.*

Nothing so strengthens memory as the exercise of it. We have heard of persons losing their powers of memory by the use of a Ready Reckoner, instead of exercising their own calculation. Mason, in his *Treatise on Self-knowledge*, says: "Recur to the help of a common-place book, according to Mr. Locke's method, and review it once a year. But take care that by confiding to your minutes or memorial aids, you do not excuse the labor of the memory; which is one disadvantage attending this method."

DECAY OF MEMORY.

In old age, the brain loses its power to receive new images, to restore bygone impressions, to connect different images, or to apply general laws to specific instances. That which ennobles the man has passed away: the outward form remains, but the inward structure has lost its power to act. Childhood again

---

* Smee on *Instinct and Reason*.

ensues—not to acquire new ideas, but to forget those before implanted. All that is beautiful and desirable in this world has passed away;—the brain has lost its power—the mind ceases—the very existence of the man is unknown to himself, till death gives rise to a new life, and discloses that new and glorious state in which our organization teaches us that man will be immaterial and immortal.*

Mr. Stewart conceives (says the Rev. Sydney Smith), and, as it appears to me, with great justice—that the decay of memory observable in old men, proceeds as frequently from the very little interest they take in what is passing around them, as in any bodily decay by which their powers of mind are weakened:—"In so far as this decay of memory, which old age brings along with it, is a necessary consequence of a physical change in the constitution, or a necessary consequence of a diminution of sensibility, it is the part of a wise man to submit cheerfully to the lot of his nature. But it is not unreasonable to think that something may be done by our own efforts to obviate the inconveniences which commonly result from it."

Sir Benjamin Brodie observes upon this point: "It is worthy of notice that, while in old age the recent impressions on the memory are evanescent, it is quite otherwise as to those which were made formerly; and hence it is that the old man, whose mind wanders when he speaks of what has happened to-day or yesterday, may be quite clear and coherent when he goes back to the scenes of his early life; and that it is on these especially that he loves to dwell during the day, while they form almost the entire subject of his dreams at night. At the same time, my own observations lead me to believe that the failure of the mind in old age is often more apparent than real. The old man is not stimulated by ambition, as when he felt that he might have many years of life before him. He has, probably, withdrawn from his former pursuits, and has substituted no others for them; and we know that the mind as well as the body requires constant exercise to maintain it in a healthy state. Where it is still occupied we frequently find it to survive the decay of the body, retaining its energy and vigor even to the last."

* Smee on *Instinct and Reason.*

INTUITIONS.

Animals carry out certain designs, which we infer to originate in their organization, because we observe, that, under all circumstances, the same species conduct their operations in a similar manner. Now, Man does not conduct any ordinary operation by instinct, but is guided by a knowledge of the properties of matter to obtain any given result.

Nevertheless, certain ideas are possessed in common by all mankind; and under all circumstances, in every clime and region of the world, are held both by educated men and savages. Various combinations of ideas give us other higher ideas. Thus, the ideas of personality and infinity give us the idea of the soul; pleasure and infinity, of good; pain and infinity, of evil; cause and infinity, of God; time and infinity, of eternity; infinity, pleasure, and time, of heaven; infinity, pain, and time, of hell. Personality, and all the units of sensation, give us the idea of the body; personality, infinity, and time, of immortality; personality, and other totalities of the senses, give us the idea of the mind; thought and infinity, of spirit; lastly, action, infinity, and pleasure, give us the idea of virtue; action, infinity, and pain, of vice.

Thus, we perceive that we know, from the very organization of our bodies, that we are immortal;—that God exists;—that there are vice and virtue,—a heaven and a hell. It is not in our power to define these ideas; and if we attempt to descend to particulars upon these mental conceptions, very different specific ideas are attached to the same point. That which is infinite must not be limited;—time must not be confounded with eternity, matter with space, the body with the soul, or material creations with God.

Many of these intuitive ideas cannot be deduced from the external world by any effort of reason. For instance, man knows that all mankind are mortal, but cannot deduce from experience that man has an immortal soul. It is, in like manner, impossible to prove by reason the existence of heaven and hell, of virtue and vice. But when man observes the insect deposit its egg blindly, to produce an offspring which it can never see, but which, nevertheless, comes to life and eats food which has been instinctively supplied by its parent; when man observes the bird to build its nest upon principles which never fail,—can he suppose that when he himself aims at attaining a future reward in heaven, which he intuitively believes, that he will be deceived? Can he believe that these ideas have been implanted in him as a mockery of Providence? and can he doubt the reality of his soul, and that his soul will live forever?

WHAT IS GENIUS?

From several pages of facts bearing on the faculty of attention, in Sir William Hamilton's *Lectures on Metaphysics*, we select the following illustrations:

To one who complimented Sir Isaac Newton on his genius, he replied, that if he had made any discoveries it was owing more to patient attention than to any other talent. There is but little analogy between mathematics and play-acting; but I heard the great Mrs. Siddons, in nearly the same language, attribute the whole superiority of her unrivalled talent to the more intense study which she bestowed on her parts. . . . "Genius," says Helvetius, "is nothing but a continued attention." "Genius," says Buffon, "is only a protracted patience." "In the exact sciences at least," says Cuvier, "it is the patience of a sound intellect, when invincible, which truly constitutes genius." And Chesterfield has also observed, that "the power of applying an attention, steady and undissipated, to a single object, is the sure mark of a superior genius."

Mr. Disraeli has, in his *Coningsby*, this striking passage:

Genius, when young, is divine. Why, the greatest captains of ancient and modern times both conquered Italy at twenty-five! Youth, extreme youth, overthrew the Persian empire. Don John of Austria won Lepanto at twenty-five—the greatest battle of modern time; had it not been for the jealousy of Philip, the next year he would have been Emperor of Mauritania. Gaston de Foix was only twenty-two when he stood a victor on the plain of Ravenna. Every one remembers Condé and Rocroy at the same age. Gustavus Adolphus died at thirty-eight. Look at his captains—that wonderful Duke of Weimar, only thirty-six when he died. Banèr himself, after all his miracles, died at forty-five.

Cortes was little more than thirty when he gazed upon the golden cupolas of Mexico. When Maurice of Saxony died at thirty-two, all Europe acknowledged the loss of the greatest captain and the profoundest statesman of the age. Then there is Nelson, Clive; but these are warriors, and perhaps you may think there are greater things than war. I do not. I worship the Lord of Hosts. But take the most illustrious achievements of civil prudence. Innocent III., the greatest of the popes, was the despot of Christendom at thirty-seven. John de Medici was a cardinal at fifteen, and, Guicciardini tells us, baffled with his craft Ferdinand of Aragon himself. He was Pope as Leo X. at thirty-seven. Luther robbed even him of his richest province at thirty-five. Take Ignatius Loyola and John Wesley—they worked with young brains. Ignatius was only thirty when he made his pilgrimage and wrote the *Spiritual Exercises*. Pascal wrote a great work at sixteen (the greatest of Frenchmen), and died at thirty-seven. Ah, that fatal thirty-seven! which reminds me of Byron—greater even as a man than a writer. Was it experience that guided the pencil of Raphael when he painted the palaces of Rome? He died at thirty-seven. Richelieu was secretary of state at thirty-one. Well, then, there are Bolingbroke and Pitt, both ministers before other men leave off cricket. Grotius was in practice at seventeen, and attorney-general at twenty-four; and Acquaviva—Acquaviva was General of the Jesuits—ruled every cabinet in Europe, and colonized America, before he was thirty-seven. What a career! the secret sway of Europe! That was indeed a position! but it is needless to multiply instances. The history of heroes is the history of youth.

MENTAL ABSTRACTION.

In some persons the power of abstraction almost degenerates into a habit akin to disease. . . . Archimedes was so absorbed in a geometrical meditation that he was first aware of the storming of Syracuse by his own death-wound. Joseph Scaliger, the most learned of men, when a Protestant student at Paris, was so engrossed in the study of Homer, that he became aware of the Massacre of St. Bartholomew and of his own escape only on the day subsequent to the catastrophe. The philosopher Carneades was liable to fits of meditation so profound, that to prevent him sinking from inanition, his maid found it necessary to feed him like a child. Newton sometimes forgot to dine. Cardan, one of the most illustrious of philosophers and mathematicians, was once upon a journey so lost in thought, that he forgot both his way and the object of his journey. To the questions of his driver whither he should proceed he made no answer; and, when he came to himself at nightfall, he was surprised to find the carriage at a standstill, and directly under a gallows. The mathematician Vieta was sometimes so buried in meditation, that for hours he bore more resemblance to a dead person than to a living. On the day of his marriage, the great Budæus forgot everything in his philological speculations; and he was only awakened to the affairs of the external world by a tardy embassy from the marriage-party, who found him absorbed in the composition of his *Commentarii.—Sir William Hamilton's Lectures.*

EFFECT OF EMOTION ON THE INTELLECT.

In a clever paper on the *Physiology of Laughter*, in *Macmillan's Magazine* for March, 1860, it is remarked:

All know how generally it happens that a large amount of emotion disturbs the action of the intellect, and greatly interferes with the power of expression. A speech delivered with great facility to tables and chairs, is by no means so easily delivered to an audience. And every schoolboy can testify that his trepidation, when standing before a master, has often disabled him from repeating a lesson which he had duly learnt. In explanation of this we commonly say that the attention is distracted—that the proper train of ideas is broken by the intrusion of ideas that are irrelevant. But the question is, in what manner unusual emotion produces this effect; and we are here supplied with a tolerably obvious answer. The repetition of a lesson or set speech previously thought out, implies the flow of a very moderate amount of nervous excitement through a comparatively narrow channel. The thing to be done is simply to call up in a given succession certain previously arranged ideas—a process in which no great amount of mental energy is expended. Hence when there is a large quantity of emotion, which must be discharged in some direction or other, and when, as usually happens, the restricted series of intellectual actions to be gone through does not suffice to carry it off, there result discharges along other channels besides the one prescribed; that is to say, there are aroused various ideas foreign to the train of thought to be pursued, and these tend to exclude from consciousness those which should occupy it.

And now, observe the meaning of those bodily actions spontaneously set up under these circumstances. The schoolboy saying his lesson commonly has his fingers actively engaged—perhaps in twisting about a broken pen, or perhaps in squeezing the angle of his jacket; and if he is forbidden thus to occupy his hands, he soon again falls into the same or a similar trick. Many anecdotes are current of public speakers having incurable automatic actions of this class; barristers who perpetually wound and unwound a piece of tape; members of Parliament ever putting on and taking off their spectacles. So long as such movements are unconscious they facilitate the mental actions. At least this seems a fair inference from the fact that confusion frequently results from putting a stop to them; witness the case narrated by Sir Walter Scott of his schoolfellow, who became unable to say his lesson after the removal of the waistcoat-button that he habitually fingered while in class. But why do they facilitate the mental actions? Clearly because they draw off a portion of the surplus nervous excitement. If, as above explained, the quantity of mental energy is greater than can find vent along the narrow channel of thought that is open to it; and if, in consequence, it is apt to produce confusion by rushing into other channels of thought; then by allowing it an exit through the motor nerves into the muscular system, the pressure is diminished, and irrelevant ideas are less likely to intrude upon consciousness.

Instantaneous impressions are very deceptive. A visitor to the Polytechnic Institution—a person of quick temperament—inadvertently placed his hand upon the head of one of the stuffed tigers in the gallery of the Institution. The affrighted gentleman turned quickly round, and started with horror; *at the instant*, he thought the tiger alive, an impression which another instant enabled him to correct.

The same susceptible person, whilst walking through one of the least frequented portions of Covent Garden Market, was followed by a famished dog; *at the instant*, he took from his pouch a penny, which he offered to the miserable animal. Here was the same emotion at work, which would have led him to relieve a starving man; if this was madness, there was some method in it.

MELANCHOLY OR POETIC FEELING.

Hypochondriacal feelings are, no doubt, in a great measure, connected with constitution or temperament. Melancholy is much more common than is generally conceived, and may be, perhaps, in some degree inseparable from a mind which highly appreciates the beautiful, has quick sympathies with all around, and a thoughtful regard to the possibilities and even probabilities of a changing world. On this account it has always been considered by the poets as a poetic feeling. Ben Jonson alludes to this notion, with respect to melancholy, as an accompaniment of sensibility, in his *Every Man in his Humour:*

Stephen. Ay, truly, sir, I am mightily given to melancholy.

Matthew. Oh! it's only fine humour, sir; your true melancholy breeds your perfect wine wit, sir. I am melancholy myself divers times, sir; and then do I no more but take pen and paper presently, and overflow you half a score or a dozen of sonnets at a sitting.—Act iii. sc. 1.

Again, Stephen says, in Act 1, "I will be more proud and melancholy, and gentlemanlike than I have been."

Sir Walter Scott, in his "Diary" (May, 1827), says:

Imagination renders us the victim of occasional low spirits. All belonging to this gifted, as it is called, but often unhappy class, must have felt, but for the dictates of religion, or the natural recoil of the mind from the idea of dissolution, there have been times when they would have been willing to throw away life, as a child does a broken toy. I am sure I know one who has often felt so.

In a letter to his daughter-in-law, Sir Walter says of Mathews, the comedian: "It is very odd—he is often subject to fits of melancholy."

A disposition to melancholy (says Mr. Harrison), is by no means, as might first be imagined, necessarily indicated by a staid and grave deportment. In a large proportion of instances, it is even coupled with an exuberance of spirits, which would seem to promise a perpetual sunshine of cheerfulness. The mind, however, which is alive to joy, is also, and perhaps equally, alive to sorrow; and often passes by quick transition from the one to the other. Lord Byron, in his *Corsair*, touches upon this peculiarity of mind:

> Strange though it seem, yet with extremest grief
> Is linked a mirth—it doth not bring relief.
> The playfulness of sorrow ne'er beguiles,
> And smiles in bitterness—but still it smiles.

Dr. Currie describes Burns, notwithstanding the gayety of his writings, as constitutionally a melancholy man, and subject "to those depressions of mind, which are perhaps not wholly separable from the sensibility of genius, but which, in him, rose to an uncommon degree." . . . . "Such a disposition is far from being at variance with social enjoyments. Those who have studied the affinities of mind, know that a melancholy of this description after a while seeks relief in the endearments of society, and that it has no distant connection with the flow of cheerfulness, or even the extravagance of mirth."

Mr. Liston, the celebrated comedian, the first sight of whom was wont to set the audience in a roar, is said to have been a melancholy man. This is not strictly correct. He, however, did really imagine he could be a tragic actor; and there were, undoubtedly, touches of pathos occasionally in his acting that seldom failed to draw tears from feeling hearts: his success was in great part the result of thought and study. He went into society but little; his attention to religion was marked by devout sincerity, and his knowledge of the Scriptures was very extensive.

Another phase of melancholy—that peculiar to youth—may be noticed here. The Rev. Dr. Temple, Head Master of Rugby School, in his admirable Essay on the *Education of the World*, observes:—" Young men are prone to extreme melancholy, even to disgust with life. A young preacher will preach upon afflictions much more often than an old one. A young poet will write more sadly. A young philosopher will moralize more gloomily. And this seems unreal sentiment, and is smiled at in after years. But it is real at the time; and perhaps is nearer the truth at all times than the contentedness of those who ridicule it. Youth, in fact, feels every thing more keenly; and as far as the keenness of feeling contributes to its truth, the feeling, whether it is pain or pleasure, is so much the truer."

GAY MELANCHOLY.

The history of Madge Wildfire, previous to her derangement, is well known to the legion of readers of Sir Walter Scott's *Heart of Midlothian*. Illicit love and its consequences, in a character of low extraction, whose beauty raised her above her station, were the predisposing causes of her malady. Her personal charms appear to have attracted much attention, and a considerable degree of vanity and self-love formed a prominent feature in her character. The ruling passion of her mind runs through the whole of her history when insane, and stamps all its workings with a peculiar feature. Facts teach us that persons in whom vanity or *amour-propre* forms a predominating part of the disposition, if afflicted with insanity, from whatever cause it may arise, have the ideas of health renewed in a modified and exalted form in the state of disease; and as the tenor of the mind, when awake, determines in a great measure the nature of our dreams, so does the stamp of the sane intellect throw the hue of its coloring over the imagination of the insane. The vain are apt, in this condition, to imagine themselves queens and princesses, and are more greedy of admiration than ambitious of power. This turn of the insane mind is peculiar to females. It is well exemplified in some of Madge's ditties:

> I'm Madge of the country, I'm Madge of the town,
> I'm Madge of the lad I'm blithest to own;
> The lady of Beaver in diamonds may shine,
> But has not a heart half so happy as mine.
> I'm queen of the wake, and I'm lady of May,
> And I head the blithe ring round the May-pole to-day;
> The wild-fire that dances so fair and so free,
> Was never so bright or so bonnie as me.

Bred at a distance from the Court, and in an obscure village, the imagination of Madge wonderfully adapts itself to the circumstances of her previous life. Had she been accustomed to society of a higher order, she would probably have fancied herself a royal queen; but the fancy having no materials of this kind to work upon, she exalts herself to that dignity which, in rural sport, is generally awarded to the most beautiful.

The death-bed of this sufferer is one of the most feeling scenes ever sketched. In the most violent and perfect maniacs, alarming disease very commonly partially or completely restores the mental faculties: the body acts by way of revulsion upon the mind, and the disorder appears to be removed from one by the action of disease in another. Most commonly this return of consciousness is rather an unsteady twinkling than a fixed and brilliant light. The mind seizes ideas which it fancies are not new, and looks upon objects in a truer light. The causes of its observation become apparent; and however gay the paroxysms of the disorder may have been, there is frequently a tinge of profound melancholy attends these periods of mental health, especially when the occasion of its overthrow has been crime or great misfortune. When these periods immediately precede dissolution, as they frequently do, there is always an instructive "persuasion" of its approach. The maniac is aware that his troubles are past, that his toils are at an end, that his grief and his gayety, the troubles of his spirit, and the wanderings of his imagination, will all sleep the sleep that knows no waking.* All the wanderings of Madge's partially restored mind upon her sick-bed centre in her approaching death, and the whole of the portions of old ballads, collected in her roving life, bear upon this point:

> Our work is over, over now:—
> The good man wipes his weary brow,
> The last long wain winds slowly away,
> And we are free to sport and play;
> The night comes on when sets the sun,
> And labor ends when day is done;
> When autumn's gone and winter's come
> We hold our jolly harvest home.

Again, in a strain of a different character:

> When the fight of grace is fought,
> When the marriage crest is wrought,
> When faith hath chased cold doubt away,
> And hope but sickens at delay.
> When charity, imprison'd here,
> Longs for a more extended sphere;
> Doff thy robes of sin and clay,
> Christian, rise! and come away.

The next snatches are extremely pathetic, and indicate a greater degree of consciousness than was exhibited by the former. Memory assumes more power, and the poor maniac, looking back with sorrow and shame at the crimes and misfortunes of her past life, and her once happy home, contrasts it with her present situation

---

* "It is rare" (says Foville) "that the insane die in a state of mental alienation: they generally fall victims to some bodily disorder, and the mind recovers, in some measure, its sanity before dissolution. Even where the most complete fatuity has been produced by long continued mental derangement, an unsteady glimmering of reason occasionally returns. The intellect appears to approach once more the throne of reason, to linger about the scenes in which she once delighted, and to recall for once more, and but for a moment, ideas which she once possessed, and which she is about to part with forever." How true is our author's character to nature!

as an outcast on the bed of charity; and prophesies that an evil and sudden termination of existence must attend the author of all her miseries:

> Cold is my bed, Lord Archibald,
>   And sad my sleep of sorrow;
> But thine shall be as sad and cold,
>   My false true love, to-morrow.
>
> And weep ye not, my maidens free,
>   Tho' death your mistress borrow:
> For he for whom I die to-day
>   Shall die for me to-morrow.

Her last words relate to her burial, which a strange mixture of ideas confused with her wedding:

> Tell me, thou bonnie bird,
>   When shall I marry thee?
> When six braw gentlemen
>   Kirkward shall carry ye.
>
> Who makes the bridal bed?
>   Birdie, say truly?
> The gray-headed sexton,
>   That delves the grave truly.
>
> The glow-worm o'er grave-stone,
>   Shall light there steady,
> The owl, from the steeple, sing
>   Welcome, proud lady!

Such is an example illustrating the imaginations of that form of mental derangement termed *mania mitis, amenomania*, or gay melancholy.—*The Analyst*, 1837.

INSANE IMPULSES.

Mr. Harrison speaks of these peculiar states of mind, which attend certain peculiarities of temperament, and though not incompatible with mental sanity, are yet to be considered as bordering upon derangement. These strange sensations are not common to everybody, and are far more frequent or powerful in the imaginative and eccentric, than in others.

Amongst this class of feelings may be placed the disposition which is sometimes manifested by those who stand on precipitous cliffs to throw themselves over; or when standing on the brink of deep water, to plunge into it; although such impulses are dreaded by the very persons who indulge them.

Shakspeare alludes to such a feeling, in *Hamlet*, when he is cautioned by Horatio not to follow the Ghost:

> What if it tempt you toward the flood, my lord,
> Or to the dreadful summit of the cliff,
> That beetles o'er his base into the sea;
> And there assume some other horrible form,
> Which might deprive your sovereignty of reason,
> And *draw you into madness?* Think of it—
> The very place puts toys of desperation,
> Without more motive, into every brain,
> That looks so many fathoms to the sea,
> And hears it roar beneath.

Mr. Harrison considers under this head the cases of suicide which seem to have been suggested by the contemplation of frightful precipices, lofty buildings, deadly poisons, or dangerous weapons. The same kind of feeling sometimes urges persons to contemplate scenes of suffering and distress, which are painful to be witnessed, or impels them on to acts which they at the time dread.

There are feelings sometimes, which are contradictory in their nature and objects. The mind is strangely perplexed in a war of emotions, which are cherished while they are painful. Actions are not always dictated by the simple feelings which seem to have given them birth. How many persecuting spirits have wept for those they have persecuted! There are those whose feelings of mercy and forgiveness have struggled hard, and yet yielded to pride and an ignoble revenge. Such contradictory feelings do indeed partake of an insane character, and there is a fine significance in the words of the poet:

> That to be wroth with those we love,
> Doth work like madness in the brain.

Such states of mind should be at once deprecated as unhealthy and insane feelings; since the proper control of the mind, which constitutes virtue, is in reality the most conducive to a sound understanding.

Goëthe speaks of an evil disposition of mind which often misleads us so far as to make us find a pleasure in tormenting those whom we love. He tells us how he abused the fondness of a young female by tyrannical and arbitrary caprices; and, secure of her affection, vented on her all the ill-humor caused by the failure of his poetical essays, and every thing else that occurred to vex him. He poisoned all her best days by groundless and unworthy jealousies; she long endured all these follies with angelic patience; but he had the cruelty to tire it out. (See Goëthe's *Characteristics*.)

Hazlitt observes, in his acute *Characteristics*, that men often take a perverse delight in acting, not only contrary to reason, but in opposition to their own inclination.

KEEP THE BRAIN FALLOW IN CHILDHOOD.

Mr. Arthur Helps makes the following suggestive remarks upon what may be termed the forcing system of early education:

When we are considering the health of children, it is imperative not to omit the importance of keeping their brains fallow, as it were, for several of the first years of their existence. The mischief perpetrated by a contrary course, in the shape of bad health, peevish temper, and developed vanity, is incalculable. Some infant prodigy, which is a standard of mischief throughout its neighborhood, misleads them. But parents may be assured that this early work is not, by any means, all gain, even in the way of work. I suspect it is a loss; and that children who begin their education late, as it would be called, will rapidly overtake those who have been in harness long before them. And what advantage can it be that a child knows more at six years old than its compeers, especially if this is to be gained by a sacrifice of health, which may never be regained? There may be some excuse for this early book-work in the case of those children who are to live by manual labor. It is worth while, perhaps, to run the risk of some physical injury to them, having only their early years in which we can teach them book-knowledge. The chance of mischief, too, will be less, being more likely to be counteracted by their after life. But for a child who is to be at book-work for the first twenty-one years of its life, what folly it is to exhaust in the least its mental energy, which, after all, is its surest implement!

Sir Henry Holland, in his book on *Mental Physiology*, has the following passage bearing upon this intellectual exhaustion:

> It is a fact well attested by experience, that the memory may be seriously injured by pressing upon it too hardly and continuously in early life. Whatever theory we hold as to this great function of our nature, it is certain that its powers are only gradually developed; and that if forced into premature exercise, they are impaired by the effort. This is a maxim, indeed, of general import, applying to the condition and culture of every faculty of body and mind; but singularly to the one we are now considering, which forms, in one sense, the foundation of intellectual life. A regulated exercise, short of fatigue, is improving to it, but we are bound to refrain from goading it by constant and laborious efforts in early life, and before the instrument is strengthened to its work, or it decays under our hands.

PERVERTED REASON.

In all cases of perverted reason (says Mr. Smee*), there appears to be an irregular action of the brain, analogous to the irregular action of machinery. If a steam-engine be subjected to the undue stimulus of heat, it will, like the over stimulated man, exhibit increased action; and if too much power were applied to the striking part of a clock, it might continue to strike independently of a corresponding action in the other parts of the machinery. So with contrivances for ascertaining force; as a mere spider's cord might materially interfere with the correct action of the vertical force of the magnetic needle, which is said by Professor Airy to appreciate the one-ten-millionth part of a grain. With all pieces of human mechanism we thus find that proper care must be taken, that they act correctly. The elaborate mechanism of the brain, formed by nature, requires that its action should be conducted upon the laws of the Creator. Whoever ventures to set at naught these laws, will most assuredly fall into the errors and delusions of perverted reason.

WHAT IS MADNESS?

Madness, like sense, admits of no adequate definition; no one

* In his popular work, *On Instinct and Reason*.

set of words will include all its grades and varieties. Some of the existent definitions of insanity would let loose half the inmates of Bedlam, while others are wide enough to place nine-tenths of the world in strait-jackets. The vulgar error consists in believing the powers of the mind to be *destroyed* by the malady, but general disturbance of the intellect is only one form. The aberration may be confined to a few objects or trains of ideas; sometimes the feelings, the passions, and even instincts of our nature may assume an undue ascendency over a mind not disjointed, but warped, urging it with resistless force to the commission of forbidden deeds, and to form the most consistent plans for their accomplishment.—*Quarterly Review.*

In a lecture delivered at the Royal Institution, Dr. Conolly, of the Hanwell Lunatic Asylum, speaking of the moral treatment of the insane, stated as the result of the experience of his whole life, that distorted views on religious subjects are the cause of at least two-thirds of the cases of mania in women, especially those belonging to the upper classes. Touching with all reverence on the proper study of religious books, Dr. Conolly lamented that morbid brooding over subjects of theology and points of doctrine, is such a fruitful cause of mental diseases: and he remarked that of all forms of insanity, religious monomania is the one most prone to lead its unfortunate possessor to the commission of suicide.

Among the most frequent sources of mental derangement is the mind *breaking down* under some heavy affliction; or its more gradually yielding to the apprehension of poverty, especially when it may arise from the misconduct of the individual; while, on the other hand, the unexpected acquisition of wealth, and overweening vanity and pride, overturn even a strong mind.

INTELLECTUALITY AND INSANITY.

The division between the intellectual and insane portion of mankind is by no means so broad as it appears on a cursory examination. There are minor aberrations of the mind, which do not come within the limits of actual madness; nor is real insanity so far dissevered from the more healthy operations of the mind as to be altogether incompatible with intermissions of extraordinary brightness. Dryden has sung with nervous truth:

Intellectuality and Insanity. 121

> Great wits are sure to madness near allied,
> And thin partitions do their bounds divide.

And, in the masterly satire whence these lines are quoted, how truly are insane workings portrayed in the character of "the false Achitophel:"

> A fiery soul, which, working out its way,
> Fretted the pigmy body to decay,
> And o'er-informed the tenements of clay.*

Mr. Harrison observes:† "It is well known that many of our eminent writers, especially those of an imaginative kind, were hypochondriacs. The unfortunate Cowper and Collins were of this class; and Chatterton and Haydon, it will be remembered, destroyed themselves under its influence. The Rev. Robert Hall had periods of actual insanity, and the elegant Charles Lamb probably escaped from his sister's fate only by the necessities of his position. Whitbread, Romilly, Londonderry, and Calcraft, put an end to their own existences; but the list is too great to particularize, and it is enough to know, that learning and genius are not removed from the worst of human calamities."

How tenderly has Johnson spoken of the affliction of Collins, in his letters to Joseph Warton:

"But how little can we venture to exult in any intellectual powers or literary attainments, when we consider the condition of poor Collins. I knew him a few years ago, full of hopes and full of projects, versed in many languages, high in fancy, and strong in retention. This busy and forcible mind is now under the government of those who lately would not have been able to comprehend the least and most narrow of its designs.

"The moralists all talk of the uncertainty of fortune, and the transitoriness of beauty; but it is yet more dreadful to consider that the powers of the mind are equally liable to change, that understanding may make its appearance and depart, that it may blaze and expire."

To the list of sufferers must be added Robert Southey, who,

---

* Absalom and Achitophel. This character of Shaftesbury (Achitophel), is drawn with as much truth as power. He hated a calm, lived all his life in intrigues, and in his sixty-second year his "fiery soul" wore out his small and fragile body. A curious parallel to these famous lines occurs in Fuller's *Profane State:* "He was of a lean body and visage, as if his eager soul, biting for anger at the clog of his body, desired to fret a passage through it."—*Bell's Annotated Edition of Dryden's Poetical Works.*
† *Medical Aspects of the Human Mind.*

in early life, professed a democratic and half-deistical creed; his overtasked mental faculties gave way, and he sank into a condition which gradually became one of deeper unconsciousness, in which state he died, after four years' suffering. The poet Moore, for the last three years of his life, was afflicted with a softening of the brain, which reduced him to a state of mental incapacity, though without pain.

The fate of Swift is well known; but even before the period at which his mind gave way, it is too probable that he inwardly labored under a mental infirmity which, in itself, might be nearly allied to his genius. His own account of the source of his affliction is curious. In a letter to Lord Bolingbroke, Swift says: "I remember when I was a little boy, I felt a great fish at the end of my line, which I drew up almost on the ground, but it dropt in, and the disappointment vexes me to this very day, and I believe it was the type of all my future disappointments."

This little incident (says Percival), perhaps gave the first wrong bias to a mind predisposed to such impressions; and by operating with so much strength and permanency, it might possibly lay the foundation of the Dean's subsequent peevishness, passion, misanthropy, and final insanity. The quickness of his sensibility furnished a sting to the slightest disappointment; and pride festered those wounds which self-government would instantly have healed. As children couple hobgoblins with darkness, every contradiction of his humor, every obstacle to his preferment, was, by him, associated with ideas of malignity and evil. By degrees, he acquired a contempt of human nature, and a hatred of mankind, which at last terminated in the total abolition of his rational faculties.

Swift himself, in the last document which we possess of him, as a rational and reflecting being, thus awfully foretells the catastrophe which shortly afterward took place:

"I have been very miserable all night, and to-day extremely deaf and full of pain. I am so stupid and confounded that I cannot express the mortification I am under, both in body and mind. All I say is, that I am not in torture; but I daily and hourly expect it. Pray let me know how your health is, and your family. I hardly understand one word I write. I am sure my days will be very few,—few and miserable they must be.

I am, for those few days, yours entirely,
If I do not blunder, it is Saturday.   J. SWIFT."

Intellectuality and Insanity. 123

Dr. Ferriar observes that what we call genius has often a degree of eccentricity connected with it, which, he hints, may even have an alliance with insanity. "No doubt," says he, "the same causes, which, in a strong degree, produce madness, may, in a lower, increase the natural powers of the mind."

Lord Byron has left a "trivial fond record" of a mind, rendered more subtle and more oppressed with thought and ambition, looking back even to its primitive simplicity, with a feeling little short of regret:

> I feel almost at times as I have felt
> In happy childhood; trees, and flowers, and brooks,
> Which do remember me of where I dwelt
> Ere my young mind was sacrificed to books,
> Come as of yore upon me, and can melt
> My heart with recognition of their looks.

Wordsworth thus expresses a feeling akin to the above:

> My eyes are dim with childish tears,
>   My heart is idly stirr'd;
> For the same sound is in my ears
>   Which in those days I heard.
> Thus fares it still in our decay;
>   And yet the wiser mind
> Mourns less for what time takes away
> Than what he leaves behind.

Personal attachment sometimes exists to a morbid degree in sensitive minds. Sheridan, in his play of *The Rivals*, apostrophizes Love as the tormentor and fiend, "whose influence acting on men of dull souls makes idiots of them, but meeting subtler spirits, betrays their courses, and urges sensibility to madness."

There are few persons who have not, at particular seasons, experienced the effect of certain *accidental associations*, which obtrude one impertinent idea, or set of ideas, on the mind, to the exclusion of every other. Locke has noticed this weakness, and he humorously describes it as "a childishness of the understanding, wherein, during the fit, it plays with and dandles some insignificant puppet, without any end in view." Thus, at times, a proverb, a scrap of poetry, or some other trivial object, will steal into the thoughts, and continue to possess them long after it ceases to be amusing. Persuasives to dismiss a guest that proves so troublesome, can hardly be necessary; and bodily exertion is generally the best remedy for this mental infirmity.

HOW THE EGYPTIANS TREATED THEIR INSANE.

How strange is it to find that the mild system now adopted in our asylums should have been that actually pursued in that "cradle of civilization," Egypt!

The system of treatment seems to have been excellent. At both extremities of Egypt were temples dedicated to Saturn, to which melancholics resorted in great numbers in quest of relief. In these abodes, surrounded by shady groves and beautiful gardens, varieties of games and recreations were established for the amusement of the mind and the invigoration of the body, while the imagination was impressed with the finest productions of the sculptor and painter. This was nothing less than the treatment which Pinel labored to restore when he struck off the chains from the lunatic, and by reverting to the system of a comparatively benighted age, destroyed that barbarous and cruel system which was disgracing the character and satirizing the vaunts of an advanced civilization. They were, indeed, wonderful people, those ancient Egyptians, with their tenets of a resurrection, a day of judgment, a future retribution and an incarnation of God; perhaps justice has scarcely been done them by those who owed so much to them. Thus Pythagoras, who was the first Greek philosopher who practised medicine, seems to have inherited most of his philosophy from them; and may well have introduced into Greece, with the doctrine of metempsychosis, the plan after which the Egyptians treated insanity. At any rate the method of Asclepiades, who is looked upon as the real founder of a psychical mode of cure among the Greeks, was Egyptian. "Music, love, wine, employment, exercising the memory, and fixing the attention, were his principal remedies."* He recommended that bodily restraint should be avoided as much as possible, and that none but the most dangerous should be confined by bonds. It was reserved, however, for more recent times to discover the ingenious plan of once for all disposing of lunatics by *burning them alive*, and to mingle with a barbarity scarcely paralleled in the most barbarous time, the degraded folly which discovered in some of them saints worthy of canonization. The cells, the whip, and the chains were of even yet more recent date;† but now, happily, resting on the solid basis of the highest moral law, we apply every comfort which humanity can suggest, and every instrument which science can devise, to relieve the unhappy beings whom destiny has so fearfully afflicted.‡

* Feuchterleben's *Medical Psychology*.
† Scarcely has half a century elapsed since the Parliamentary Inquiry was instituted, which led to the reform of the treatment of lunatics in Bethlem Hospital.
‡ *Journal of Mental Science*, July, 1860.

OPERATION OF MIND.—"THE GREAT BOOK."

Mr. Samuel Warren says: "I do not know how to express it, but I have several times had a transient consciousness of mere ordinary incidents then occurring having somehow or other happened before, accompanied by a vanishing idea of being able to predict the sequence. I once mentioned this to a man of powerful intellect, and he said, 'So have I.' Again, it may be that there is more of truth than one suspects in the assertion which I met with in a work of M. de Quincey's, that *forgetting*—absolute forgetting—is a thing not possible to the human mind. Some evidence of this may be derived from the fact of long-missed incidents and states of feeling suddenly being reproduced, and without any perceptible train of association. Were this to be so, the idea is very awful; and it has been suggested by a great thinker that merely perfect memory of every thing may constitute the *great book* which shall be opened in the last day, on which man has been distinctly told that the secrets of all hearts shall be made known; for *all things are naked and opened unto the eyes of him with whom we have to do.*" (Heb. iv. 18.)

Sir Francis Beaufort (in a letter published in the *Autobiography of Sir John Barrow*) describes what happened to himself when he was preserved from being drowned; when "every incident of his former life seemed to glance across his recollection in a retrograde succession, not in mere outline, but the picture being filled with every minute and collateral feature," forming "a kind of panoramic picture of his entire existence, each act of it accompanied by a sense of right and wrong." All this must have happened in the brief space of a very few minutes.

Other instances are related of individuals whose minds had been affected very much in the same way when they were suddenly placed in a situation which threatened immediate death, although they were not at all deprived of their sensibility and self-possession.

The accounts, however, given after recovery from drowning differ very much. Some, whatever they may have felt at the time, remember nothing except their having been overcome by a sense of insuperable drowsiness. In one instance, a sailor who had been snatched from the waves, after lying for some time insensible on the deck of the vessel, proclaimed on his recovery that he had been in Heaven, and complained bitterly of his being restored to life as a great hardship.

We may conclude that drowning, terrible as it appears to be, is not, after all, either morally or physically, a painful death; and this is confirmed by the experience of one who had nearly lost his life in this manner. He says that the last thing which he remembers is, looking at the pebbles and weeds at the bottom of the river, with little or no fear of what was about to happen, and no bodily suffering. (*Sir B. Brodie.*)

We remember to have heard the Bishop of Oxford relate from the pulpit of St. James's Church, Piccadilly, an incident which illustrates this consciousness. An acquaintance of his Lordship, a man of remarkably clear head, was crossing a railway in the country, when an express train, at full speed, appeared closely approaching him. He had just time to throw himself down in the centre of the road between the two lines of rails; and as the vast train passed over him, the sentiment of impending danger to his very existence, brought vividly into his recollection every incident of his former life—in such an array as that which is suggested by the promised opening of "the great book, at the last great day."

DISCIPLINE OF THE INTELLECT,

Dr. Temple has thus ably illustrated the importance of the teaching of discipline in mature life which is needed for the intellect even more than for the conduct: There are many men who, though they pass from the teaching of the outer law to that of the inner in regard to their practical life, never emerge from the former in regard to their speculative. They do not think; they are contented to let others think for them, and to accept the results. How far the average of men are from having attained the power of free independent thought, is shown by the staggering and stumbling of their intellects when a completely new subject of investigation tempts them to form a judgment of their own on a matter which they have not studied. In such cases a really educated intellect sees at once that no judgment is yet within its reach, and acquiesces in suspense. But the uneducated intellect hastens to account for the phenomenon; to discover new laws of nature, and new relations of truth; to decide, and predict, and perhaps to demand a remodelling of all previous knowledge. The discussions on table-turning, a few years ago, illustrated this want of intellects able to govern themselves. The whole analogy of physical science was not enough to induce that suspension of judgment which was effected in a week by the dictum of a known philosopher.—*The Education of the World; Essays and Reviews.*

THE CHILD FATHER TO THE MAN.

The outer law of childhood is often the best vehicle in which the inner law of mature life can be contained for its various purposes. The man remembers with affection, and keeps up with delight, the customs of the home of his childhood; tempted, perhaps, to over-estimate their value, but even when perfectly aware that they are no more than one form out of many which a well-ordered household might adopt, preferring them because of his long familiarity, and because of the memories with which they are associated. So, too, truth often seems to him richer and fuller when expressed in some favorite phrase of his mother's, or some maxim of his father's. He can give no better reason very often for much that he does every day of his life than that his father did it before him; and provided the custom is not a bad one the reason is valid. And he likes to go to the same church. He likes to use the same prayers. He likes to keep up the same festivities. There are limits to all this. But no man is quite free from the influence; and it is in many cases, perhaps in most, an influence of the highest moral value. There is great value in the removal of many indifferent matters out of the region of discussion into that of precedent. There is greater value still in the link of sympathy which binds the present with the past, and fills old age with the fresh feelings of childhood. If truth sometimes suffers in form, it unquestionably gains much in power; and if its onward progress is retarded, it gains immeasurably in solidity and in its hold on men's hearts.

We quote this exquisite and life-like sketch from Dr. Temple's essay on the *Education of the World*.

LIFE NOT GREATER THAN ITS REFLEX.

The opinion that Life in spontaneous unconscious evolution, is, relatively to us, or to life's progress, greater than its reflex—is thus eloquently controverted by Mr. A. Wilson, in the *Edinburgh Essays*, 1856:

As the flower on the mountain-side, and the crystal in the vein of the rock, may be more lovely and more perfect to us than the mountain itself, so individual souls may be, as it were, the flowers and highest perfection of the great existence of which they are a part, while these souls again have their flower and highest perfection in the ideal life which they project beyond the confines of the real. The highest life known to us exists not in the ages of our past, not in the distant stars, which look so blue and beautiful, while probably they are full of wildly conflicting forces, but in our own imaginings and longing dreams, which can harmonize all antagonisms, and shadow forth a perfect world. It is even this draping glorifying power of imaginative thought which renders possible our conscious recognition of things existent. Omnipotent Phantasy, that divinest goddess, is the true *mater gloriosa* and Queen of Heaven, the mistress of souls and the benefactress of mankind, ever gathering our knowledge and ignorance into shapes of beauty, weaving the rainbow across our path, and veiling the dark deep with lucid azure. From the cradle to the grave, what were the children of men but for her? Before the child's gaze, where the speculation is but small, she forms this our world as before the clear earnest eyes of the bravest man; and when the strong thought is about to slumber forever in the wearied brain, the heart of feeling beats faintly, and the dim eye is closing, she is *there*, painting the blessed fields, on the awful darkness, with the very mists of death. In her gift is an ordered world. How often, in her highest exercise, has she formed it anew for the races of men!—now giving, as centre, some misty Olympus, among the peaks of which are gods; now some unfathomable source of creative power, itself unmoved; now some omnipotent ruler—"Jehovah, Jove, or Lord." Slight her not, poor Thinker!—and worship at her nod, for without her there is only the blackness of darkness forever—the melancholy waste of waters on which no Columbus has found the New Land. Painful and dangerous is her service, *spes et præmia in ambiguo—certa, funera et luctus;* but even to him who is destroyed by it there is compensation; for in the very perception of genius—in its love penetrating to all stars, its sight, which vindicates existence, and hails the golden age,—there is a pure joy, an exceeding sense of glory, which can raise and transfigure it above the sufferings of earth.

After all, though you may look to your understanding for amusement, it is to the affections that we must trust for happiness. These imply a spirit of self-sacrifice; and often our virtues, like our children, are endeared to us by what we suffer for them. Conscience, even when it fails to govern our conduct, can disturb our peace of mind. Yes! it is neither paradoxical, nor merely poetical, to say

> That seeking other's good, we find our own.

This solid yet romantic maxim is found in no less a writer than Plato; who, sometimes, in his moral lessons, as well as in his theological, is almost, though not altogether, a Christian. These are the opinions of Richard Sharpe, a man of refined conversation and practical virtue.

Belief and Scepticism.

WHAT IS FAITH?

Sir William Hamilton, in his *Lectures on Metaphysics*, gives, as a joint reason for the desire of unity as one of the essential causes of philosophy, the existence of a corresponding unity in the order of nature, and the ultimate dependence of all effects on one cause, the Creator. That he did not believe the human mind capable of any direct knowledge of this highest unity is plain from his *Alphabet of Thought*. It would be vain to criticise his few words which remain:—

"We must believe in the infinity of God; but the infinite God cannot by us, in the present limitation of our faculties, be comprehended or conceived. A Deity understood would be no Deity at all; and it is blasphemy to say that God only is as we are able to think Him to be. We know God according to the finitude of our faculties, but we believe much that we are incompetent properly to know. The Infinite, the infinite God, is what, to use the words of Pascal, is infinitely inconceivable. Faith—Belief—is the organ by which we apprehend what is beyond our knowledge."

On the nature of this organ, Sir W. Hamilton has left us nothing. This has made his philosophy popular among those who do not seek a reason for the faith that is in them. With pardonable confusion of thought, many of them have also welcomed the work of the disciple, who has included Faith itself in the demonstration that the spirit of man has no direct knowledge of the Infinite Spirit. How far the teaching of Sir W. Hamilton tended to such conclusions, is a question which has excited much controversy.

Lord Erskine has left us this practical picture of Faith. "I can conceive a distressed but virtuous man, surrounded by his children, looking up to him for bread, when he has none to give them, sinking under the last day's labor and unequal to the next, yet still supported by confidence in the hour, when all tears shall be wiped from the eyes of affliction—bearing the burden laid upon him by a mysterious Providence, which he adores, and anticipating with exultation the revealed promises of his Creator, when he shall be greater than the greatest, and happier than the happiest of mankind."

WHAT IS REVELATION?

The idea of *a positive external Divine revelation* of some kind has formed the very basis of all hitherto received systems of Christian belief. The Romanist indeed regards that revelation as of the nature of a standing oracle accessible in the living voice of his Church; which, being infallible, of course sufficiently accredits all the doctrines it announces, and constitutes them divine. A more modified view has prevailed among a considerable section of Anglican theologians, who ground their faith on the same principles of Church authority, divested of its divine and infallible character. Most Protestants, with more or less difference of meaning, profess to regard revelation as once for all announced, long since finally closed, permanently removed, and accessible only in the written Divine word contained in the Scriptures. And the discussion with those outside the pale of belief has been entirely one as to the validity of those external marks and attestations by which the truth of the alleged fact of such communication of the Divine will was held to be substantiated.—*Prof. Baden Powell; Essays and Reviews.*

Mr. Locke says: "He that takes away Reason to make way for Revelation puts out the light of both; and does much about the same as if he would persuade a man to put out his eyes, the better to receive the remote light of an invisible star by a telescope."

Much scepticism has been engendered of late years by tyros in science straining after identities of physical truths with Scripture. "There are, indeed," observes the Rev. W. L. Harcourt, "certain common points in which Reason and Revelation mutually assist each other; but, in order that they may ever be capable of doing so, let us keep their *paths* distinct, and observe their *accordances* alone; otherwise our reasonings run round in a circle, while we endeavor to accommodate physical truth to Scripture, and Scripture to physical truth."

CHILDISH DESIRES.

Archbishop Leighton, speaking of unreasonable and childish Desires, says:

"And what would we have? Think we that Contentment lies in so much and no less? When that is attained, it shall be as far off as before. When children are at the foot of a high Hill, they think it reaches the Heavens, and yet, if they were there, they would find themselves as far off as before, or, at least, not sensibly nearer. Men think, Oh, had I this, I were well; and when it is reached, it is but an advanced standing, from which to look higher, and spy out for some other thing."—*Comment on St. Peter*.

Compare this with Norris's fine poem, entitled *The Infidel:*

>Farewell, Fruition, thou grand cruel cheat
>Which first our hopes dost raise, and then defeat;
>Farewell, thou midwife to abortive Bliss,
>Thou mystery of Fallacies;
>Distance presents the object fair,
>With charming features and a graceful air,
>But when we come to seize th' inviting prey,
>Like a shy Ghost, it vanishes away.
>
>So to th' unthinking Boy, the distant Sky
>Seems on some Mountain's surface to rely;
>He with ambitious haste climbs the ascent,
>Curious to touch the Firmament;
>But when with an unweary'd pace
>Arrived he is at the long-wished-for place,
>With sighs the sad defeat he does deplore,
>His Heaven is still as distant as before.

We conclude with a beautiful passage from Bishop Hickes's *Devotions:*

'Tis to be happy that we run after Pleasures; and cover (*sic*) in every thing our own proud Will. But we, alas! mistake our Happiness, and foolishly seek it where it is not to be found. As silly children think to catch the sun, when they see it setting at so near a distance. They travel on, and tire themselves in vain; for the thing they seek is in another World.

WEAK BELIEF.

There is in the world a great deal of this lukewarm reception of divine truths; it does not amount to unbelief, but it is thickly beset with its perils. "It is easy and agreeable to believe," said Bonnet, the learned Genevese: "to doubt requires an unpleasant effort." But how important is the conviction. There can be no reasonable doubt that it is better to believe too much than too little; since, as Boswell observes (most probably in Johnson's words), "a man may breathe in foul air, but he must die in an exhausted receiver."

How many, too, content themselves with expressing their sense of the importance of a firm religious belief, and a desire to attain it, rather than an assertion that they themselves have found all they sought. This shortcoming is very observable among leaders of science, and hence it has a baleful effect. What can be more encouraging on the one hand, and disheartening on the other, than the following eloquent declaration of Sir Humphrey Davy:

> I envy no qualities of the mind and intellect in others—nor genius, nor power, nor wit, nor fancy: but if I could choose what would be the most delightful, and, I believe, most useful to me, I should prefer a firm religious belief to every other blessing. For it makes life a discipline of goodness, creates new hopes when all earthly hopes vanish, and throws over the decay, the destruction of existence, the most gorgeous of all lights; awakens life in death, and calls out from corruption and decay beauty and everlasting glory.

Twenty years ago, it was sagaciously remarked that "an absence of religious principle and belief, similar to that which has, of late years, characterized so much of the popular literature of the day, appears in the speculations of several men of high intellectual endowments. And what is remarkable is, the productions of some of these philosophers have been received by the most amiable and popular of our contemporaries, with scarcely a remark upon the fact, that their speculations conducted directly to the dreary gulf of utter scepticism. . . . It is not to the appearance of such speculations that we are to look as characteristic of the age, but to the fact that their publication excites so little attention,—that they blend so readily, so much a matter of course, with the prevailing tone of its literature." (*British and Foreign Review*, 1840.) This omission to arrest, and apathy to correct, the progress of infidelity has progressively increased since the above was written; for, as our great moralist observed: "There are few persons who do not practise that which they cease to censure."

In the *Spirit of Truth*, by Delta, we find the following spirited rebuke of these restless and sceptical tendencies of the day:

> I mean what I say, and express it as a deliberate conviction, founded on an extensive observation of young men, that no book in the world was ever so generally possessed, and so little comprehended, as an English Bible in the present day. I do not say *English* Bible, with any reference to faults of translation, for whatever errors may cling to the authorized version of the Scriptures, I do not believe that *these* affect, in any appreciable degree, the question of its intelligent perusal. The evil lies much deeper. *Every thing*, in English society, is unfavorable to the profitable study of the Bible: the ceaseless activities of the good, and the restless insinuations of the bad,—textual preaching, and tormenting criticism,—the multiplication of books, and the mingling of things sacred and profane, *all* tend to keep men from feeding in green pastures, or reposing by the side of still waters. The result is—for that which affects the people affects the Priest—that while public worship was never [?] so well attended as at present, the pulpit was never so powerless; conduct in the counting-house never so independent of attention in the pew; scepticism never so rampant; and *happy* Christians never so rare.

Most unfortunately, in the present day, a very large class of persons are unsettled by others in their belief: they doubt unwillingly, but they cannot resist the difficulties thrust upon them. Of such an one the author of the *Eclipse of Faith* (Henry Rogers) gives the following as a confession:

> I have been rudely driven out of my old beliefs; my early Christian faith has given way to doubt; the little hut on the mountain-side in which I had thought to dwell with pastoral simplicity, has been shattered to the tempest, and I turned out to the blast without a shelter. I have wandered long and far, but have not found that rest which you tell me is to be obtained. As I examine all other theories, they seem to me pressed by at least equal difficulties with that I have abandoned. I

cannot make myself *contented*, as others do, with believing nothing; and yet I have nothing to believe. I have wrestled long and hard with my Titan foes, but not successfully. I have turned to every quarter of the universe, but in vain. I have interrogated my own soul, but it answers not. I have gazed upon nature, but its many voices speak no articulate language to me; and more especially when I gaze upon the bright page of the midnight heavens, those orbs gleam upon me with so cold a light, and amidst so portentous a silence, that I am, with Pascal, terrified with the spectacle of the infinite solitude.

The Hon. Robert Boyle has this *Occasional Meditation* upon the resemblance between those disturbers of belief,—profane and atheistical wits,—and the black cloud in a thunderstorm: as the clouds, when raised, afford flashes of light, so these irreligious wits are sometimes conspicuous enough to bring forth surprising notions; but as the same clouds, while they give us their own momentary light, obscure by darkness the sky, and hinder us from receiving the light of the sun, which is preferable to vanishing coruscations; so these wits, while they seem to enlighten those they dazzle, with their own new opinions, do really deprive them of the true heavenly light, that would else shine forth to them in the revealed Word of God; and as the light we do receive from the clouds may deceive and astonish us, but is not sufficient to travel by; so the admired reasonings of these sophisters may surprise and amaze us, but will never prove sufficient to be, like the Scripture, *a constant Lamp unto our feet and Light unto our paths.*—PSALM cxix. 105.

REAL GROWTH.

The only real growth is spiritual growth. Behind the physical the savage sees a demon, the civilized man a soul. Philosophy, indeed, will bake no bread, but it will procure us God, freedom, immortality. It is the marriage of nature with the human soul. The principles of psychology, of all philosophy, like those of all religion, all truth, have subsisted from the beginning; not so, however, man's appreciation of them, which is progressive.

The soul (observes a recent writer) in its attempts to bring the divine into closer union with the consciousness, has gradually built up its appreciation of the character of Christ. And thus it is more or less in all our delineations of greatness and goodness, our conceptions of the ideal, and its realization in man.

It has been asserted that psychology, in place of converting, ratifies the delusions of ordinary thought. This, however, must mean an erroneous psychology. Otherwise we may gladly subscribe to Ferrier's eloquent remark, that all God's truths and man's blessings lie in trodden ways, and that intellect and genius are but the power of discerning wonders in common things.—DR. M'CORMACK'S *Aspirations from the Inner Life*.

EXPERIENCE FALLIBLE.

In our searches after truth, we should bear in mind that the possibility of "*change-bearing laws*" having been established, then, in regard to any occurrence, strange, but coming to us well attested—we must not assert that, because contrary to past experience, it would be miraculous, and is consequently impossible.

Professor de Morgan has ably illustrated this position in the following paragraph :

The natural philosopher, when he imagines *a physical impossibility* which is not an inconceivability, merely states that his phenomenon is against all that has been hitherto known of the course of nature. Before he can compass an impossibility, he has a huge postulate to ask of his reader or hearer, a postulate which nature never taught: it is, that the future is always to agree with the past. How do you know that this sequence of phenomena always will be? Answer, Because it must be. How do you know that it must be? Answer, Because it always has been. But then, even granting that it always has been, how do you know that what always has been always will be? Answer, I feel my mind compelled to that conclusion. And how do you know that the bearings of your mind are always toward truth? Because I am infallible, the answer *ought to be*—but this answer is never given.—*Athenæum*, No. 1687.

INTOLERANCE AND UNBELIEF.

To tax any one with want of reverence (says Dr. Arnold, in his *Lectures on Modern History*), because he pays no respect to what we venerate, is either irrelevant, or is mere confusion. The fact, so far as it is true, is no reproach, but an honor; because to reverence all persons and all things, is absolutely wrong: reverence shown to that which does not deserve it is no virtue; no, nor even an amiable weakness, but a plain folly and sin. But if it be meant that he is wanting in proper reverence, not respecting what is really to be respected, that is assuming the whole question at issue, because what we call divine, he calls an idol; and as, supposing that we are in the right, we are bound to fall down and worship, so, supposing him to be in the right, he is no less bound to pull it to the ground and destroy it. Considering the ability of Dr. Arnold, considering his great influence, and considering his profession, his antecedents, and the character of the university in which he was speaking, it must be allowed that this is a remarkable passage, and one well worthy the notice of those who wish to study the tendency of the English mind during the present generation.

HOW MEN BECOME SCEPTICS.

Locke, in his profound *Essay on the Human Understanding*, book i., says:

> Men extending their inquiries beyond their capacities, and letting their thoughts wander into those depths where they can find no sure footing, it is no wonder that they raise questions, and multiply disputes; which, never coming to any clear resolution, are proper only to continue and increase their doubts, and *to confirm them at last in perfect scepticism.* Whereas, were the capacities of our understandings well considered, the extent of our knowledge once discovered, and the horizon found which sets the bounds between the enlightened and dark parts of things; between what is, and what is not, comprehensible by us, men would perhaps, with less scruple, acquiesce in the avowed ignorance of the one, and employ their thoughts and discourse with more advantage and satisfaction in the other.

INFIDELITY IRRATIONAL.

When speaking of infidelity, we usually mean the conduct of those persons who disbelieve the evidences of the Christian religion. Doubtless, a Deist may be a very good man;[*] and such were some of the philosophers of ancient times, and such were many of the Jews, who could not discern the person or terms of the Christ in the book that guided their moral and humane life. But whether an utter infidel can exist, one who beholds all the orderly arrangements of the celestial and terrestrial systems, and yet can discern no power more than human, is a problem indeed. Hannah More makes mention of the only atheist (poor Ayrey) that she ever knew. "He was an honest, good-natured man, which certainly," she observes, "he should not have been on his principles." Yet he was not without a belief. "He was a fatalist, and if he snuffed the candle, or stirred the fire, or took snuff, *he solemnly protested* he was compelled to do it." What made him believe in this necessity of things? must be our question. She adds: "He always confessed he was a coward, and had a natural fear of pain and death, though he knew he should be as if he never had been." This was, indeed, in him cowardly and irrational, and quite opposed in principle to the fear of death which a Christian may entertain. "God's purpose shall stand," said the devout Charles Simeon; "but our liability to fall and perish is precisely the same as ever it was: our security, as far as it relates to him, consists in *faith*, and as far as relates to ourselves, it consists in *fear*."

CONFESSIONS OF SCEPTICS.

Dr. Arnold, in his sermon *Of Christian Life, its Course, its Hindrances, and its Helps*, says:

[*] Because a Deist may be a good man, let it not be thought that any encouragement is held out to a profession of deism. There is a wide difference between the case of a heathen who has never heard of Christ, and a man in a Christian country who wilfully rejects evidences internal and external, the disbelief of which is sometimes attributable to defective moral constitution, but in the vast majority of cases to vitiated moral feeling, and a dislike of the humbling doctrines of the Cross.

One of the greatest men of our time has declared, that, in the early part of his life, he did not believe in the divinity of our Lord; but he has stated expressly, that he never, for a moment, persuaded himself that St. Paul or St. John did not believe it; their language, he thought, was clear enough upon the point; but the notion appeared to him so unreasonable in itself, that he disbelieved it in spite of their authority.... The language of the Scripture was as clear to him at first as it was afterwards; but in his early life he disbelieved it, while, in his latter life, he embraced it with all his heart and soul.

Now the "greatest man" here alluded to was Samuel Taylor Coleridge, and here is his confession:

Take myself, S. T. C., as a humble example. I was never so befooled as to think that the author of the fourth Gospel, or that St. Paul, ever taught the Priestleyan Psilanthropism, or that Unitarianism (presumptuously, nay, absurdly so called) was the doctrine of the New Testament generally. But during the sixteen months of my aberration from the Catholic faith, I presumed that the tenets of the divinity of Christ, the Redemption, and the like, were irrational, and that what was contradictory to reason could not have been revealed by the Supreme Reason. As soon as I discovered that these doctrines were not only consistent with reason, but themselves very reason, I returned, at once, to the literal interpretation of the Scriptures, and to the Faith.—*Notes on English Divines*, p. 179.

I owe, under God, my return to the faith, to my having gone much further than the Unitarians, and so having come round to the other side. I can truly say, I never falsified the Scripture: I always told them that their interpretations of the Scripture were intolerable upon any principles of sound criticism, and that if they were to offer to construe the will of a neighbor as they did that of their Maker, they would be scouted out of society. I said then plainly and openly that it was clear enough that John and Paul were not Unitarians. But at that time I had a strong sense of the repugnance of the doctrine of Vicarious Atonement to the moral being, and I thought nothing could counterbalance that.

The old Unitarians of Birmingham have never forgiven Coleridge these strictures.

Paley truly says: "No one in his heart derides religion long. What are we, any of us? Religion will soon be our only care and friend."

Charles Lamb has been accused of scepticism; but Coleridge has thus manfully rescued him from the heinous charge:

"No, no; Lamb's scepticism has not come lightly, nor is he a sceptic. The harsh reproof to Godwin, for his contemptuous allusion to Christ before a well-trained child, proves that he is not a sceptic. His mind, never prone to analysis, seems to have been disgusted with the hollow pretences, the false reasonings and absurdities of the rogues and fools with which all establishments, and all creeds seeking to become established, abound. I look upon Lamb as one hovering between earth and heaven; neither hoping much nor fearing any thing.

"It is curious that he should retain many usages which he learnt or adopted in the fervor of his early religious feelings, now that his faith is in a state of suspended animation. Believe me, who knew him well, that Lamb, say what he will, had more of the *essentials* of Christianity than ninety-nine out of a hundred professing Christians. He has all that would still have been Christian had Christ never lived or been made manifest upon earth."

We may here refer to the scepticism of Lord Bolingbroke, upon which some new light has been thrown of late by the publication of the Diary of one of his contemporaries. The opposition of his philosophical sentiments to revealed religion, and the system which he would substitute in its place, are principally detailed in the third of his *Essays on the Study of History*; and in his *Essays* addressed to Pope.

It appears from an entry in the *Diaries and Correspondence of the Rt. Hon. George Rose*, edited by the Rev. L. V. Harcourt, and published in 1860—that, by a letter of Lord Bolingbroke's, dated 1740, he had actually written some Essays dedicated to the Earl of Marchmont of a very different tendency from his former works. These essays, on his death, fell into the hands of Mr. Mallet, his executor, who had, at the latter end of his life, acquired a decided influence over him, and they did not appear among his lordship's works published by Mallet; nor have they since been heard of. From whence it must be naturally conjectured that they were destroyed by the latter, from what reason cannot now be known: possibly, to conceal from the world the change, such as it was, in his lordship's sentiments in the latter end of his life, and to avoid the discredit of his former works. In which respect, he might have been influenced either by regard for the noble Viscount's consistency, or by a desire not to impair the pecuniary advantage he expected from the publication of his lordship's works.

Upon this Mr. Harcourt observes:

The letter to Lord Marchmont here referred to, has a note appended to it by Sir George Rose, the editor of the *Marchmont Papers*, who takes a very different view of the contents from his father. He gravely remarks, that as the posthumous disclosures of Lord Bolingbroke's inveterate hostility to Christianity lays open to view as well the bitterness as the extent of it, so the manner of that disclosure precludes any doubt of the earnestness of his desire to give the utmost efficiency and publicity to that hostility, as soon as it could safely be done: that is, as soon as death should shield him against responsibility to man. Sir George saw plainly enough that when he promised in these essays to vindicate religion against divinity and God against man, he was retracting all that he had occasionally said against Christianity; he was upholding the religion of Theism against the doctrines of the Bible, and the God of nature against the revelation of God to man.

Bolingbroke was the last of the professed Deists.* It is painful to reflect upon this prostration of a splendid intellect, and we are but slightly relieved by Lord Chesterfield's statement in one of his letters (published by Lord Mahon, in his edition of Chesterfield's *Works*), that "Bolingbroke only doubted, and by no means rejected, a future state." Lord Brougham says:

The dreadful malady under which Bolingbroke lingered, and at length sank—a cancer in the face—he bore with exemplary fortitude, a fortitude drawn from the natural resources of his mind, and unhappily not aided by the consolation of any religion; for, having early cast off the belief in revelation, he had substituted, in its stead, a dark and gloomy naturalism, which even rejected those glimmerings of hope as to futurity not untasted by the wiser of the heathens.

We know that Bolingbroke denied to Pope his disbelief of the moral attributes of God, of which Pope told his friends with great joy. How ungrateful a return for this "excessive friendliness" was the indignation which Bolingbroke expressed at the priest having attended Pope in his last moments!

It will be recollected that the publication of Bolingbroke's posthumous works by his executor, Mallet, drew from Dr. Johnson the severe remark,—that "having loaded a blunderbuss and pointed it against Christianity, he had not the courage to discharge it himself, but left half-a-crown to a hungry Scotchman to pull the trigger after his death." To talk Deism had ceased to be fashionable as soon as it ceased to attract attention.

* Yet Bolingbroke encouraged the hope of better things: he occasionally visited the Countess of Huntingdon, who tells us that he was seldom in her company without discussing some topic beneficial to his eternal interests; and he always paid the utmost respect and deference to her ladyship's opinion. Bolingbroke's collected Works were presented as a nuisance by the grand jury of Middlesex in 1752.

It is now, we believe, admitted that Christianity has not found a very formidable or lasting opponent in Bolingbroke; his objections betray his half-learning, but their speciousness, in the latter half of the last century, proved very mischievous. His rashness was condemned even by that "mad assassin and low wretch," Lord Ferrers, who said, on his way to execution, "I always thought Lord Bolingbroke in the wrong to publish his notions on religion; I will not fall into the same error."—*Walpole.*

RENUNCIATION OF INFIDELITY.

Well directed efforts are unceasingly made to check the progress of infidelity, and this rather by steady and small-voiced operations than by more pretentious means. It affords us much pleasure to quote an instance of this progress (to use a cant word of the day), recorded in the *Times* journal of August 5, 1858:

"Some years ago there was rather a numerous society of persons at Nottingham, chiefly operatives, who professed to disbelieve the tenets of the Christian religion, and set up a peculiar creed of their own. Great numbers of the working people were from time to time attracted to the lectures of these free-thinkers, and some conversions were made; but after the first excitement of the thing was over the members of the party began to drop off, and under the influence of repeated discussions between the leaders of the sceptics and various religious ministers of the town, particularly the Rev. J. W. Brooks, the vicar, the society gradually collapsed, and last week its president, a framework knitter, named Jonathan Barber, publicly announced his secession from the doctrines he had so long advocated. After a lecture by the vicar in the school-room, Barkergate, Barber stated that it was about fourteen years since he and other infidels first met in that room, on the invitation of their much esteemed vicar, for the purpose of holding discussions on infidelity; and he now thought it right publicly to acknowledge in the same place, that throughout those discussions he had had misgivings in regard to the existence of a God, and that for the last five years he had been uneasy in his mind with respect to Christianity. This uneasiness increased when he found himself upon a sick-bed, and on reviewing his creed he found it worthless in the prospect of death. He had therefore determined, after a considerable struggle with his pride, to avow his entire renunciation of his infidel sentiments, and his belief in Divine revelation. A working man named Start, in proposing a vote of thanks to the vicar for his very able and convincing lecture, to which he had listened with the deepest attention, and found singularly useful to himself, avowed that he had held the same infidel sentiments as Barker, but had been led to see his error, and now publicly thanked God, who had in great mercy brought him out of darkness into his marvellous light. Two other men in the room admitted a similar change of sentiments. The infidel party in Nottingham is now broken up."

MATERIALISM OF THE DEVELOPMENT THEORY.

This theory (see pp. 33-35), when taken in its full extent, is manifest Materialism. The animals of lowest organization have been derived, it asserts, from inanimate matter by some ordinary and general process of nature; and those of higher forms have been derived from the lower, till man was finally arrived at, the crowning point. Thus, not only are all the ordinary phenomena of organic life, but likewise all our intellectual and moral attributes, derived primarily from inert matter by the operation of natural causes, without any separate creation, either of animal life, or of the spiritual life of man. The advocates of the theory will, doubtless, admit the former fluid and incandescent state of the globe; and it then follows, necessarily, from their theory, that the noblest qualities of man's intellect, the tenderest feelings of his heart, the deepest consciousness of his moral responsibilities, and his highest aspirations for the future, must all have been contained in a molten mass of matter, to be finally evolved from it by natural causes a few thousand years ago. Yet there are men who, in the confidence of their own intuitive insight into the Creator's ways, shrink not from conclusions which, we doubt not, will appear so preposterous to most of our readers.

These views present one of the alternatives if we reject the theory of successive creations, and the permanence of species in the animal and vegetable kingdoms. Such views differ from those of the author of an Essay on the *Philosophy of Creation*, by a distinguished member of the University of Oxford. According to this latter theory, the offensive part of the materialism is avoided, by regarding the spiritual part of man's nature as the special object of a separate and independent creation; while to the merely animal part he is indebted for the same material elements and natural causes as those from which the brute creation is supposed to derive its origin.

Though this theory avoids the more monstrous extravagance of development, which, in the *Vestiges of Creation*, assumed the unequivocal form of materialism,—it loses the greater simplicity of the more unrestricted theory; and still involves, what appears to us, the enormous difficulty of conceiving how the sensation, volition, memory, foresight, and all the instinct of animals, can be derivable from inanimate matter. We believe that a careful consideration of such theories must generally lead to increased confidence in that which maintains that the Creator, for the introduction of new classes of animate beings from time to time, has called into action powers altogether different from those which we recognize in the ordinary course of nature.—W. HOPKINS, F. R. S.; *Cambridge Essays.* 1857.

COMBUSTION—THE METEMPSYCHOSIS.

Berthollet, in his *Chemical Statics*, observes: "When bodies are burnt, none of their principles are destroyed; they had previously formed together one kind of compound, and they now separate from each other, at the high temperature to which they are exposed, in order to form others with the vital air in contact with them; and such of the principles as cannot unite with the vital air, viz., the earth, some saline and some metallic particles, compose the cinder. The new compounds formed are carbonic acid and water. The proportion of these varies according to the proportion of the carbonic particles, and of the hydrogen that had been contained in the inflammable body."

It was said of old, that the Creator *weighed* the dust and *measured* the water when he made the world. The first quantity is here still, and though man can gather and scatter, move, mix, and unmix, yet he can destroy nothing; the putrefaction of one thing is a preparation for the being, and the bloom, and the beauty of another. Something gathers up all fragments, and nothing is lost. Thus, the laws by which matter is modified, effect so many desirable purposes, and at the same time prevent the destruction of those elementary principles which are actually essential to the preservation of the world.

Combustion—The Metempsychosis.

Perhaps it was in some such light as this that Pythagoras meant the Metempsychosis to be understood. It might be a curious inquiry, whether or not he received the doctrine from the Egyptian priests, as they from the philosophers of India. An ancient Shastre, called the Geeta, has a beautiful stanza upon this subject, in which the varied form that nature assumes is compared to a change of dress. (See Halhed's *Account of the Hindoo Land.*) Ovid, in the speech he forms for Pythagoras, compares it to wax, where the substance is always the same though the outward form is varying. Dr. Darwin thus pursues the same idea:

> " Hence when a monarch or a mushroom dies,
> A while extinct the organic matter lies;
> But, as a few short hours or years revolve,
> Alchemic powers the changing mass dissolve;
> Emerging matter from the grave returns,
> Feels new desires, with new sensations burns:
> With youth's first bloom a finer sense acquires,
> And loves and pleasures from the rising fires."

Metempsychologic appellations are used in a good as well as bad sense. Thus, the designation of wolf has been applied to St. Paul; Christ is the lion of the tribe of Judah, although Satan, " as a roaring lion, walketh about seeking whom he may devour."

The doctrine of Pythagoras and Plato is humorously illustrated in the *Dreamer* (a series of dreams forming an indirect satire on the abuses of religion, literature, &c., by Dr. William King), by quotations from sacred as well as profane writers, *e. g.*, Isaiah lvi. 10, 11; Nahum ii. 12:

A judicious critic (Dr. King writes), or observant reader, will scarce allow that more than four or five, in the long catalogue of Roman Emperors, had any humanity; and although they might perhaps have a just claim to be styled Lords of the Earth, they had no right to the title of Man. There is an excellent dissertation in Erasmus on the princely qualities of the Eagle and the Lion; wherein that great wit has demonstrated that Emperors and Kings are very justly represented by those animals, or that there must be a similarity in their souls, as all their actions are similar and correspondent.

What is Superstition?

"TO DIE CHILDLESS."

THE origin of the word *Superstition* has been described as some mysterious belief respecting the relations between the Dead and the Living—the deceased and those who survive them—the World that is seen, and the World that is not seen.

Cicero thus defines the word: " Not only Philosophers, but all our forefathers dydde ever separate Superstition from true Religion; for they which prayed all day that theyr children mought overlyve them, were called superstitious: whiche name afterwards was larger extended."—*Old Translation.*

Lactantius, however, says "the word got its meaning from the worship of deceased parents and relatives, by the Superstites or Survivors; or from men holding the memory of the dead in superstitious veneration."

Cicero and Lactantius thus agree in connecting the word with some visionary notion respecting the relation between the Dead and the Living who *survive* them.

The question may be said to turn mainly upon the *rites of sepulture*. The Ancients believed that the manes of unburied men were restless and unhappy, and haunted the earth; and in this point of view they deemed it unfortunate not to have a child to close their eyes after death, and to perform duly the last solemn rites: accordingly, they even adopted children with this view, rather than die without survivors.

This may not seem a very satisfactory solution of the matter, as it might be asked, Why should one's own children be absolutely required? Could not others perform the last rites? The question then still remains: Why was it considered so terrible a misfortune

To Die Childless. 147

to survive one's children? It is obvious that there was something more at bottom than mere natural feelings.

Passing over the use of Prayers *to* the Dead,* and Prayers *for* the Dead, among the Ancients, we come to the Doctrine of Vicarious Sacrifice.

The Ancients believed that the Death of one person might be prevented by that of another. From hence came the custom of those Devotements we read of, made for the life of a friend, a nation, or a prince.

We now proceed to illustrate the belief of the Ancients in the importance of securing to themselves the rites of Sepulture by their surviving children. Solomon declares, in *Ecclesiastes* vi. 3:

If a man beget an hundred children, and live many years . . . *and that he have no burial:* I say that an *untimely birth is better than he.*

Bishop Pearson, in treating of the fifth Article of the Creed, in which, arguing that *Hades* is a *place*, and not a *state*, refers "to the judgment of the Ancient Greeks," because there were many which they believed to be dead, and to continue in the state of death, which yet they believed not to be in *Hades*, as *those who died before their time, and those whose bodies were unburied.*

The souls of the latter bodies were thought to be kept out of Hades till their funerals were performed; and the souls of those who died an untimely or violent death, were kept from the same place until the time of their natural death should come.

Bishop Pearson then quotes from Virgil's account of the souls who wander and flit about the shores of Hades for a hundred years. Thus he (Virgil) is understood in the description of the funeral of Polydorus, Æn. iii. 62:

> Ergo instauramus Polydoro funus, et ingens
> Aggeritur tumulo tellus: . . . .
> . . . . . . animamque sepulchro
> Condimus.

Not that *anima* does here signify the body, as some have ob-

---

* "When a father mourned grievously for his child that was taken away suddenly, he made an Image of him that was then dead, and worshipped him as a god, ordaining to those under him Ceremonies and Sacrifices. Thus, in process of time, this wicked custom prevailed, and was kept as a law."

served, but that the soul of Polydorus was at rest when his body had received funeral rites,—*ad quietem inferni*, according to the petition of Palinurus. And that the soul of Polydorus was so wandering about the place where his body lay unburied, appeareth out of Euripides in *Hecuba;* and in the *Troades* of the same poet, this is acknowledged by the Chorus. And when their bodies were buried, then their souls passed into Hades, to the rest. So was it with Polydorus, and that man mentioned in the history of the philosopher of Athenagoras, whose *umbra* or *phasma* (according to Pliny) walked about after his death.

A curious illustration of the wide prevalence of those ideas which lie at the root of Superstition, occurs in the narrative of the sufferings of Byron and the crew of H. M. Ship, *Wager*, on the coast of South America. The crew had disgraced themselves by rioting, mutiny, and recklessness, in the island upon which they were thrown, after a most tempestuous navigation. Long before they left the bay, the body was found of a man, supposed to have been murdered by some of the first gang who left the island. *The corpse had never been buried*, and to this neglect did the crew now ascribe the storms which had lately afflicted them; nor would they rest until the remains of their comrade were placed beneath the earth, when each (says the narrative) evidently felt as if some dreadful spell had been removed from his spirit.* "Few would expect to find many points of resemblance between the Grecian mariners of the heroic ages, who navigated the galleys described by Homer, to Troy, and the sailors of George II.; yet here, in these English seamen, was the same feeling regarding the *unburied dead* which prevailed in ancient times."

The desire for Posterity, though it seems, perhaps, hardly sufficient to account for the acts of the *Superstitiosi*, is so deeply implanted in the human heart, and is so connected with Man's instinctive longing and striving after Immortality, that, after all, it may possibly have been their ultimate and only motive. Hooker has forcibly said:

It is the demand of nature itself—"What shall we do to have Eternal

* "Yet, in Christian England (but the other day), we remember more than one unseemly squabble about the liabilit to bury a corpse—turning upon some obscu e point or parochial law!"

Life?" The desire of Immortality and the Knowledge of that whereby it may be attained, is so natural unto all men, that even they which are not persuaded that they shall, do, notwithstanding, wish that they might know a way *how to see no end of life*. A longing, therefore, to be saved, without understanding the true way how, hath been the cause of all the superstitions in the world.—*Hooker, Serm.* ii.

The erudite correspondent (Eirionnach) who has contributed to *Notes and Queries* the very interesting papers whence these details have been selected, proceeds to illustrate the subject from "the intense *humanity* and domesticity of minds such as Dr. Arnold's," whose tastes and feelings were strongly domestic; "he thought, and he taught, and he worked, and he played, and he looked at Sun, and Earth, and Sky, with a *domestic* heart. The horizon of family life mixed with the skyey life above, and the Earthly Landscape melted, by a quiet process of nature, into the Heavenly one."
—(*Christian Remembrancer*, 1844.)

Dr. Arnold himself declared:

I do not wonder that *it was thought a great misfortune to die childless in old times*, when they had not fuller light—*it seems so completely wiping a man out of existence*. . . . The anniversaries of domestic events—the passing away of successive generations, and the entrance of his sons on the several stages of their education—struck on the deepest chords of his nature, and made him blend with every prospect of the Future, the keen sense of the *continuance* (so to speak) of his own *existence in the good and evil fortunes of his children*, and to unite the thought of these with the yet more solemn feeling, with which he was at all times wont to regard "the blessing of a whole house transplanted entire from Earth to Heaven without one failure."—*Dr. Arnold's Life.*

This reminds one of what the Son of Sirach says:

He that teacheth his son grieveth the enemy; and before his friends he shall rejoice him. *Though his father die, yet he is as though he were not dead, for he hath left one behind him that is like himself.* While he lived, he saw and rejoiced in him; and when he died, he was not sorrowful. He left behind him an avenger against his enemies, some that shall *requite kindness to his friends.*—*Ecclus.* xxx. 3–6.

Bacon (*Essays*, xxvii.) uses similar language with regard to Friends:

It was a sparing speech for the Ancients to say "*That a Friend is another himself;*" for that a *Friend* is far more than *himself*. Men have their time, and die many times of some things which they principally take to heart; the bestowing of a Child, the finishing of a Work, or the like. If a man have a true friend, he may rest almost secure that the care of those things will continue after him; so that a man hath, as it were, two lives in his desires.

In the same Essay, Bacon mentions that Septimius Severus had such a friendship for Plautianus, that he preferred him to his own son, and wrote to the Senate, in the words of the *Superstitiosi*: "*I love this man so well, that I wish he may outlive me.*"

The *domesticity* of character to which we have just alluded would appear to be concentrated, as it were, in the *oneness* of conjugal life. How often do we read in the newspaper obituary lists of the death of a husband in a few days following that of his wife, and a wife that of her husband. These remarkable instances are in our recollection. On October 29, 1817, died Lady Romilly; and on November 2, following, Sir Samuel Romilly, in an aberration of mind, induced by grief for the loss of his wife, committed suicide. It is a singular coincidence, that in the church of St. Bride, Fleet Street, is a tablet with an inscription to the memory of Mr. Isaac Romilly, F. R. S., who was the uncle of Sir Samuel, and who died in 1759, of *a broken heart*, seven days after the decease of his beloved wife. There is still another coincidence connected with Sir Samuel Romilly's death: he had just been returned to Parliament for Westminster, after a severe contest, principally with the supporters of Sir Francis Burdett, who, twenty-seven years later, expired of grief for the loss of his wife —Lady Burdett having died thirteen days previously.

HIGH SPIRITS A PRESAGE OF EVIL.

Among the minor perplexities which beset life's thorny path, is this curious psychological question—whether high spirits do not often forebode evil, and fancied good fortune prove the forerunner of adversity.

Shakspeare (*Romeo and Juliet*, Act v. Sc. 3) has:

> How oft when men are at the point of death
> Have they been merry; which their Keepers call
> A lightning before death.

High Spirits a Presage of Evil. 151

This phenomenon has, however, a physiological explanation; but it may have favored the popular notion of high spirits presaging calamity. This historical incident has been pressed into the illustration of the above feeling: upon the morning of the day of the assassination of the Duke of Buckingham by Felton, his Grace "did rise up in a well-disposed humor, out of his bed, and cut a caper or two."—*Howell's Fam. Lett.*

Tytler, in his *History of Scotland*, tells us of the death of King James I.: "On this fatal evening (Feb. 20, 1436), the revels of the Court were kept up to a late hour. . . . The Prince himself appears to have been in unusually gay and cheerful spirits. He even jested, if we may believe the contemporary manuscript, about a prophecy which had declared that a King should that year be slain."

In *Guy Mannering*, chap. 9, "I think," said the old gardener to one of the maids, "the gauger's *fle*," by which words the common people express those violent spirits which they think a presage of death.

In the evidence given at the inquest upon the bodies of four persons killed by an explosion at a firework manufactory in Bermondsey, Oct. 12, 1849, one of the witnesses stated: "On Friday night, they were all very merry, and Mrs. B. said she feared something would happen before they went to bed, *because they were so happy.*"

We return to Shakspeare, in the *Second Part of King Henry IV.* Act. iv. Sc. 2.

Westmoreland. Health to my lord and gentle cousin, Mowbray.
Mowbray. You wish me health in very happy season:
For I am, on the sudden, something ill.
Archbishop of York. Against ill chance, men are ever merry;
But heaviness foreruns the good event.
West. Therefore be merry, cos; since sudden sorrow
Serves to say thus—some good thing comes to-morrow.
Arch. Believe me, I am passing light in spirit.
Mow. So much the worse, if your own rule be true.

In the last act of *Romeo and Juliet*, Sc. 1, Romeo comes on, saying:

If I may trust the flattering eye of sleep,
My dreams presage some joyful news at hand:

> My bosom's lord sits lightly on his throne;
> And all this day, an unaccustomed spirit
> Lifts me above the ground with cheerful thoughts.

Immediately, a messenger comes in to announce Juliet's death. In Act iii. Sc. 2, of *King Richard III.*, Hastings is represented as rising in the morning in unusually high spirits. Stanley says:

> The Lords at Pomfret, when they rode from London,
> Were jocund, and suppos'd their states were sure,
> And they, indeed, had no cause to mistrust;
> And yet, you see, how soon the day o'ercast.

This idea runs through the whole scene. Before dinner-time Hastings is beheaded.

Shelley, the poet, whose life was a dream of romance, a tale of mystery and grief, strongly entertained this feeling: "during all the time he spent in Leghorn, he was in brilliant spirits, *to him a sure prognostic of coming evil.*"

The following incident is strange, but scarcely comes within our purpose. At an inquest held in Feb., 1853, concerning the death of a poor girl, supposed to have been murdered by her paramour throwing her into the Regent's Canal, one of the witnesses deposed that the girl was in high spirits, and insisted upon singing the song, "I've wander'd by the brook-side." The deceased then left in company with the accused; and met with her death within half an hour after.

"THIRTEEN TO DINNER."

There is a prejudice existing, generally, on the pretended danger of being the thirteenth at table. If the probability be required, that out of thirteen persons of different ages one of them at least shall die within a year, it will be found that the chances are about one to one that one death at least will occur. This calculation, by means of a false interpretation, has given rise to the prejudice, no less ridiculous, that the danger will be avoided by inviting a greater number of guests, which can only have the effect of augmenting the probability of the event so much apprehended.—*Quetelet, on the Calculation of Probabilities.*

This superstition obtains in Italy and Russia, as well as in England. Moore, in his *Diary*, vol. ii. p. 206, mentions there being thirteen at dinner one day at Madame Catalani's, when a French countess, who lived with her upstairs, was sent for to remedy the grievance. Again, Lord L. said he had dined once abroad at Count Orloff's, who did not sit down to dinner, but kept walking from chair to chair, because "the Naristiken were at table, who, he knew, would rise instantly if they perceived the number *thirteen*, which Orloff would have made by sitting down himself."

The following instance is related by Rachel, the celebrated *tragédienne.* When she returned from Egypt, in the spring of 1857, she installed herself in a villa in the neighborhood of Montpellier. There she received the visit of the poet Ponsard, and Arsène Houssaye, who was making a tour as inspector of departmental museums. "Do you recollect the dinner we had at the house of Victor Hugo, at the close of the repetition of L'Angelo?" she said to the former director. "You remember there were *thirteen* of us? There was Hugo and his wife, you and your wife, Rebecca and I, Girardin and his wife, Gerard de Nerval, Pradier, Alfred de Musset, Perrée, of the *Siècle*, and the Count d'Orsay. Well! where to-day are the thirteen? Victor Hugo and his wife are in Jersey; your wife is dead; Madame de Girardin is dead; my poor Rebecca is dead; Gerard de Nerval, Pradier, Alfred de Musset, are dead. I—*say no more.* There remain but Girardin and you. Adieu! my friends. Never laugh at thirteen at a table."

WHAT IS CHANCE?

Chance is frequently personified and erected into a chimerical being, whom we conceive as acting arbitrarily, and producing all the effects the real causes of which do not appear to us; in which sense the word coincides with the $\tau \acute{v} \chi \eta$, *fortuna*, of the Ancients.

The ancient *sortilege* or *chance*, M. Placette observes, was instituted by God himself; and in the Old Testament we find several standing laws and express commands which prescribed its use on certain occasions. Hence the Scripture says, "The *lot* or *chance* fell on Matthias," when it was in question who should fill Judas's place in the apostolate; and hence also arose the *sortes sanctorum*, or method of determining things, among the ancient Christians, by opening some of the sacred books, and pitching on the first verse the eye rested on as a sure prognostic of what was to happen. The *sortes Homericæ, Virgilianæ, Prænestinæ*, and the like, used by the heathens, were resorted to with the same view, and in the same manner. St. Augustin seems to approve of this method of determining things future, and owns that he had practised it himself, grounding his doing so on the principle that God presides over *chance.*

Premature Interment.

TRANCE.

How prevalent is the fear of being "buried alive" may be gathered from the number of instances in which men have requested, that before the last offices are done for them, such wounds or mutilations should be inflicted upon their bodies as would effectually prevent the possibility of an awakening in the tomb. Dr. Dibdin relates that Francis Douce, the antiquary, requested, in his will, that Sir Anthony Carlisle, the surgeon, should sever his head from his body, or take out his heart, to prevent the return of vitality; and his co-residuary legatee, Mr. Kerrick, had also requested the same operation to be performed in the presence of his son.

> Sometimes the burning of the body has been enjoined as an assurance against living interment. Dr. Paris tells us, that the daughter of Henry Laurens, the first President of the American Congress, when an infant was laid out as dead of the small-pox; upon which the window of the apartment, that had been carefully closed during the progress of the disease, was thrown open to ventilate the chamber, when the fresh air revived the corpse, and restored her to her family: this circumstance occasioned in her father so powerful a dread of living interment, that he directed by will that his body should be burnt, and enjoined on his children the performance of this wish as a sacred duty.—*Medical Jurisprudence*, p. 5.

In 1708, a sermon was preached in the Presbyterian chapel of Lancaster, "On the Duty of the Relations of those who are in dangerous Illness, and the Hazard of Hasty Interment;" wherein it is stated by Dr. Hawes that thirty years previously, M. Bruhier, the physician, of Paris, in a work entitled *The Uncertainty of the Signs of Death*, clearly proved, from the testimonies of various authors, and attestations of unexceptionable witnesses, that many persons who have been buried alive, and were providentially discovered in that state, had been rescued from the grave, and lived for several years afterward. Notwithstanding these numerous instances, the custom then remained in full force. As soon as the *semblance of death* appears, the bed-clothes are removed, and the body is exposed to the air; which, when cold, *must extinguish the little spark of life* that may remain, and which, by a different *treatment*, might be kindled into flame.

Mrs. Godfrey, mistress of the Jewel Office, and sister of the great Duke of Marlborough, is stated to have lain *in a trance*, apparently dead, for seven days, and was even declared by her medical attendants to have been dead. Colonel Godfrey, her husband, would not allow her to be interred, or the body to be treated in the manner of a corpse; and on the eighth day she awoke, without any consciousness of her long insensibility. The authority assigned for this story is Mr. Peckard, Master of Magdalen College, Cambridge, in a work entitled *Further Observations on the Doctrine of an Intermediate State.*

Stories are also told of a Mr. Holland, improperly treated as dead, who revived—only to die, however, from the effects of exposure to cold in the grave-dress; and of a Mrs. Chaloner, a lady of Yorkshire, who was buried alive, and who was found, on the reopening of the vault in which she was interred, to have burst open the lid of her coffin, and to be sitting nearly upright in it.

Dr. Doddridge, at his birth, showed so little signs of life that he was laid aside as dead; but one of the attendants, perceiving some motion in the body, took the infant under her charge, and by her treatment the flame of life was gradually kindled.

In 1814, Anne Taylor, the daughter of a yeoman of Tiverton, being ill, lay six days insensible, and to all appearance dead: during the interval she had a dream, which her family called *a trance*, an account of which was subsequently printed. On awaking from her stupor, by her request a person wrote down all she had to relate, which she desired her father would cause to be printed. This request he evaded until, as she told him, it would be too late. She died the same evening. Next morning her voice was heard, by the person who wrote the narrative, inquiring if it was printed. Between ten and twelve o'clock the undertaker's men placed her in the coffin; and while the family were at dinner her voice was again heard, saying, "Father, it is not printed." This was attested by six witnesses; but after her death, Mr. Vowles, a dissenting minister of Tiverton, in a sermon, was considered to have proved the fraud of the whole story.

More veracious is the case of the Rev. Owen Manning, the historian of Surrey, who, during his residence at Cambridge University, caught small-pox, and was reduced by the disorder to a state of insensibility and apparent death. The body was laid out, and preparations were made for the funeral, when Mr. Manning's father, going into the chamber to take a last look at his son, raised the imagined corpse from its recumbent position, saying, "I will give my poor boy another chance;" upon which signs of vitality were apparent. He was therefore removed by his friend and fellow-student, Dr. Heberden, and ultimately restored to health. He had another narrow escape from death; for becoming subject to epilepsy, and being seized with a fit as he was walking beside the river Cam, he fell into the water, and was taken out apparently lifeless; Heberden, however, being called in, again became the means of Manning's restoration.

A monument in St. Giles's church, Cripplegate, has strangely been associated with a trance story. In the chancel is a tablet in memory of Constance Whitney, representing her rising from a coffin: and the story relates that she had been buried while in a trance, but was restored to life through the cupidity of the sexton, which induced him to disinter the body to obtain possession of a valuable ring left upon her finger.[*]

In Smith's *History of Cork*, vol. ii. p. 428, we find recorded that "Mr. John Goodman, of Cork, died in January, 1747, aged about fourscore; but what is remarkable of him, his mother was interred *while she lay in a trance;* having been buried in a vault which she found means to open, she walked home, and this Mr. Goodman was born some time after."

Raikes, in his Journal, under August 3d, 1837, mentions the horrible death of the Cardinal Somaglia, who recovered from his trance for one moment to put away the surgeon's knife, which

[*] From *Things not generally Known*, Second Series.

had begun the preparatory incision before embalming—and then died in agony.

Peter Klaus, the goatherd, a tradition of the Hartz, furnished Washington Irving with the plot of *Rip Van Winkle*. There are several German traditions and ballads which turn on the *unsuspected lapse of time under enchantment;* and we may remember, in connection with it, the ancient story of *the Seven Sleepers* of the fifth century. (*Gibbon*, vi. 32.) That tradition was adopted by Mahomet, and has, as Gibbon observes, been also adopted and adorned by the nations from Bengal to Africa, who profess the Mahometan religion. The next step is to animate the period dropt from real life—the parenthesis of existence—with characteristic adventures, as in the story of *the Elfin Grove* in Tieck's *Phansatus;* and as in *the Dean of Santiago*, a Spanish tale from the Condé Lucanor.

There is a very pretty story in the Turkish Tales (of a Sultan of Egypt and a Mahometan doctor), the *morale* of which is: The doctor took this occasion of instructing the Sultan that nothing was impossible with God; that He, with whom a thousand years are but as one day, can, if He pleases, make a single day, nay, a single moment, appear to any of His creatures as a thousand years.

Emerson, in *The Over-Soul*, says:

The Soul circumscribeth all things. It contradicts all experience. In like manner, it abolishes time and space. The influence of the Senses has, in most men, overpowered the mind to that degree that the walls of time and space have come to look solid, real, and insurmountable; and to speak with levity of those limits is, in the world, the sign of insanity. Yet time and space are but the inverse measures of the forces of the soul. A man is capable of abolishing them both. The spirit sports with time—

> Can crowd eternity into an hour,
> Or stretch an hour out to eternity.

We are often made to feel that there is another youth and age, than that which is measured from the year of our natural birth. Some thoughts always find us young, and keep us so. Such a thought is the love of the universal and eternal beauty. Every man parts from that contemplation with the feeling that it belongs rather to ages than to mortal life. The least activity of the intellectual powers redeems us, in a degree, from the influences of time. In sickness, in languor, give us a strain of poetry, or a profound sentence, and we are refreshed; or produce a volume of Plato or Shakspeare, or remind us of their names, and instantly we come into a feeling of longevity .... Always the soul's scale is one; the scale of the senses and the understanding is another. Before the great revelations of the Soul, time, space, and nature shrink away.

Trance legends beautifully illustrate the great truth that the soul is "its own place and time," and the sublime passage in the Apocalyptic Vision:

And the angel, which I saw stand upon the sea and upon the earth, lifted up his hand to heaven, and sware by Him that liveth for ever and ever, who created heaven and the things that therein are, and the earth and the things that therein are, and the sea and the things which are therein, that there should be time no longer

Lord Lindsay, in his work on *Christian Art*, refers to

A very beautiful legend of a monk on whose heart the benumbing thought had settled, "Must not the bliss of eternity pall at last, and shall we not weary of heaven?"—and who, after having been beguiled into a wood by a song of a bird, and having passed as it seemed an hour there listening to it, returned to the monastery to find a whole generation had passed away during his absence, and to learn by this experience, that an eternity will not suffice to exhaust the bliss of paradise.

According to the legend, the book which the monk was reading before his trance was the famous treatise of St. Austin, *De Civitate Dei*—(Of the City of God). The penult chapter of this noble work treats "Of the Quality of the Vision with which the Saints shall see God in the World to come;" and the last chapter treats "Of the Eternal Felicity of the City of God, and the Perpetual Sabbath."—See *Notes and Queries*, 2d S. No. 61.

Another trance legend is that of *Dornröschen* or *Thorn Rose*, commonly called the *Sleeping Beauty:* this is a Hessian story, which Mon. Grimm traces to the ancient tradition of the Restoration of Brynhilda by Sigurd, as narrated in the Edda of Sæsmund, in *Volsunga Saga*. The heroine fells a king in fight, but Odin strikes her head with the Sleepy Thorn (the Thorn-rose or Dog-rose), and says, she shall never be again victorious, and shall be hereafter wedded. Though the allusion to the Sleep-Rose is preserved in our heroine's name, she suffers from the wound of a spindle, as in the Pentamerone of G. B. Basil.

Trance legends afford momentary glimpses of eternity; and the ecstasy, or "Pylgrimage of the Sowle" out of itself, its rupture into spirit-land and beatific vision of the joys of paradise, and its sorrowful return into the prison of the body and the dominion of time and change, are set forth in countless instances, not forgetting that of Tirndall, treating of a vision supposed to have taken place in 1149. Trance legends comprise also those tales of the giants who are wrapt in a magic slumber in enchanted caves until the great day of doom; besides descriptions of terrestrial paradises: but the most interesting are those legends, the leading ideas of which are nullity of time as regards the soul when apart from the body; and, on the other hand, the manifold changes of this early life and the power of time.

In a rare work, printed by Wynkyn de Worde and Caxton—*The Art and Craft to lyve well and to dye well*, translated from the French, is a beautiful legend of "The Joyes of Paradise," which Longfellow has versified in his *Golden Legend*. This idea is also embodied in *The Seven Sleepers of Ephesus*, of which the popular German tale of the Slumbers of the Emperor Frederick Barbarossa is a late version; and the old Welsh tradition of King Arthur's enchanted slumber, from which he will awake before the last day arrives, and join in the holy wars of the times—bears a strong likeness to the German legend. The Welsh legend of Owen Lawgoch, the Red-handed,* corresponds with that of King Arthur. Mr. Faber has traced "the Origination of Romance from old Mythologic Idolatry." Thus with

"The legend of the wandering Jew; who, for insulting the Messiah while upon his mock trial, is doomed to await in the flesh the Second Advent. Like the fabled Great Father, he rambles over the face of the whole globe, and visits every region. At the close of each revolving century, bowed down with age, he sickens and falls into a deathlike slumber; but from this he speedily awakes in renovated youth and vigor, and acts over again the part which he has so repeatedly sustained. As these romances have originated from the periodical sleep of the Great Father and his family, so that of St. Antony has been copied from the various

---

* This Legend has some resemblance to the ancient legend of Epimenides, as related by Diogenes Laertius. See *Notes and Queries*, Nos. 267, 268.

terrific transformations exhibited in the funeral orgies of Dionusus, or Osiris, or Mithras."

The Eastern prediction, "The child shall die an hundred years old," is thus illustrated by Addison:

In the Koran it is said that the angel Gabriel took Mahomet out of his bed one morning, to give him a sight of all things in the seven heavens, in paradise, and in hell, which the prophet took a distinct view of, and after having held ninety thousand conferences with God, was brought back to his bed. All this, says the Koran, was transacted in so small a space of time, that Mahomet, on his return, found his bed still warm, and took up an earthen pitcher, which was thrown down at the very instant that the angel carried him away, before the water was spilt!

Apparent death is not always accompanied by a suspension of consciousness. In the *Psychological Magazine*, No. 5, we read that a young lady, after lying ill for some time, to all appearance died. She was laid in her coffin, and the day of her funeral was fixed. When the lid of the coffin was about to be screwed down, a perspiration was observed on the body; life soon appeared, and at length she opened her eyes, and uttered a most pitiable shriek. She said it seemed to her, as if in a dream she was really dead; yet she was perfectly conscious of all that happened around her in this dreadful state. She distinctly heard her friends speaking, and lamenting her death, at the side of her coffin. She felt them pull on the dead clothes, and lay her in them. This feeling produced a mental anxiety which was indescribable: she tried to cry, but her soul was without power, and could not act on her body. She had the contradictory feeling as if she were in her body, and yet not in it, at one and the same time. It was equally impossible for her to stretch out her arm, or to open her eyes, or to cry, although she continually endeavored to do so. The internal anguish of her mind was, however, at its utmost height, when the funeral hymns were being sung, and when the lid of the coffin was about to be screwed on. The thought that she was to be *buried alive* was the one that gave activity to her soul, and caused it to operate on her corporeal frame.

Phenomena of Death.

HOURS FATAL TO LIFE.

A WRITER in the *Quarterly Review* states: "We have ourselves ascertained the hour of death in 2,880 instances of all ages, and have arrived at interesting conclusions. We may remark that the population from which the *data* are derived is a mixed population in every respect, and that the deaths occurred during a period of several years. If the deaths of the 2,880 persons had occurred indifferently, at any hour during the twenty-four, 120 would have occurred at each hour. But this was by no means the case. There are two hours in which the proportion was remarkably below this, two *minima*, in fact, namely, from midnight to one o'clock, when the deaths were 53 per cent. below the average, and from noon to one o'clock, when they were 20¾ per cent. below. From three to six o'clock A. M. inclusive, and from three to seven o'clock P. M., there is a gradual increase; in the former of 28½ per cent. above the average; in the latter of 5½ per cent. The *maximum* of deaths is from five to six o'clock A. M., when it is 40 per cent. above the average; the next, during the hour before midnight, when it is 25 per cent. in excess; a third hour of excess is from nine to ten o'clock in the morning, being 17½ per cent. above the average. From ten A. M. to three o'clock P. M. the deaths are less numerous, being 16¼ per cent. below the average, the hour before noon being the most fatal. From three o'clock P. M. to seven P. M. the deaths rise to 5½ per cent. above the average, and then fall from that hour to eleven P. M., averaging 6¼ per cent. below the mean. During the hours from nine to eleven in the evening there is a *minimum* of 6¼ per cent. below the average. Thus, the least mortality is during the mid-day hours, namely, from ten to three o'clock; the greatest during early morning hours, from three to six o'clock. About one-third of the total deaths noted were children under five years of age, and they show the influence of the latter still more strikingly. At all the hours from ten in the morning until midnight the deaths are at or below the mean: the hours from ten to eleven A. M., four to five P. M., and nine to ten P. M., being *minima*, but the hour after midnight being the lowest *maximum;* at all the hours from two to ten A. M. the deaths are above the mean, attaining their *maximum* at from five to six A. M., when it is $45\frac{1}{2}$ per cent. above."

PREMONITIONS OF DEATH.

The first symptom of approaching death with some is the strong presentiment that they are about to die.

Ozanam, the mathematician, while in apparent health, rejected pupils, from the feeling that he was on the eve of resting from his labors; and he expired soon after of an apoplectic stroke.

Fletcher, the divine, had a dream which shadowed out his impending dissolution, and believing it to be the merciful warning of Heaven, he sent for a sculptor and ordered his tomb. "Begin your work forthwith," he said, at parting; "there is no time to lose." And unless the artist had obeyed the admonition, death would have proved the quicker man of the two.

The case of Wolsey was singular. After his arrest by the Earl of Northumberland, the Cardinal proceeded from Cawood Castle towards London on his mule, but by the way he was attacked with dysentery. As he entered the gate of the monastery at Leicester, he said, "Father Abbot, I am come to lay my bones among you;" and so the event proved: the monks carried him to his bed, upon which, three days afterward, he expired. The morning before he died he asked Cavendish, his gentleman-usher, the hour, and was answered, "Past eight." "Eight of the clock?" replied Wolsey, "that cannot be; eight of the clock— nay, nay, it cannot be eight of the clock, for by eight of the clock shall you lose your master." The day he miscalculated, the hour came true. On the following morning, as the clock struck eight, his troubled spirit passed from life. Cavendish and the bystanders thought he must have had a revelation of the time of his death; and from the way in which the fact had taken possession of his mind, we suspect that he relied on astrological prediction, which had the credit of a revelation in his own esteem.

Shakspeare has little altered the words Wolsey used on his death-bed, though they were spoken to Kingston, the lieutenant of the Tower, and not, as in the play, to Cromwell:

> Had I but served my God with half the zeal
> I served the King, he would not in mine age
> Have left me naked to mine enemies.
> *Henry VIII.* Act iii. Sc. i.

It is unnecessary, as well as uncharitable, to suppose, what there is no proof of, that Wolsey died of poison, either by himself or others. The obvious and proximate cause of his death was affliction. A great heart opprest with indignities, and beset with dangers, at length gave way, and Wolsey received the two last charities of a death-bed and a grave, with many circumstances affectingly told by Cavendish, in the Abbey of Leicester.

Of "The Renowned Confessor," Philip Howard, Earl of Arundel, who died in 1595, in the Tower of London, where he was imprisoned for high treason, we find an impressive narrative, in the Life of him, edited from the original MSS. by the late Duke of Norfolk, and published in 1857. The Earl's piety was remarkable. He constantly rose in the morning at five o'clock, and "as soon as he was risen out of bed, he fell down upon his bare knees, and breath'd forth in secret his first Devotions to Almighty God, his eyes and hands lifted up to heaven. With his kneeling in that manner then and at other times, his knees were grown very hard and black." . . . . "In those times which were allotted to walking or other recreation, his discourse and conversation, either with his Keeper, or the Lieutenant, or his own servants, was either tending to Piety, or some profitable discourse, as of the lives and examples of holy men, of the sufferances and constancy of the martyrs of ancient times, from which he would usually deduce some good document or other: as of the facility of a virtuous life, after a man had once overcome his sensuality; of the happiness of those that suffered any thing for our Saviour's sake, with such like; to which purpose he had writ with his own hand upon the wall of his chamber this Latin sentence: *Quanto plus afflictionis pro Christo in hoc sæculo, tanto plus gloriæ cum Christo in futuro.* The more affliction we endure for Christ in this world, the more glory we shall obtain with Christ in the next." The Earl's last moments are thus pathetically described:

The last night of his life he spent for the most part in prayer, sometimes saying his Beads, sometimes such Psalms and Prayers as he knew by heart. And oftentimes used these holy Aspirations: O Lord, into thy hands I commend my spirit. Lord, thou ar't my hope; and life. Very frequently, moreover, indicating the holy names of Jesus and Mary.

Seeing his servants in the morning stand by his bedside weeping in a mournful manner, he ask'd them what o'clock it was; they answering that it was eight, or there about. Why then, said he, I have almost run out my course, and come to the end of this miserable and mortal life, desiring them not to weep for him, since he did not doubt by the grace of God but all would go well with him. Which being said, he return'd to his Prayers upon his Beads again, though then with a very slow, hollow, and fainting voice, and so continued as long as he was able to draw so much breath as was sufficient to sound out the names of Jesus and the glorious Virgin, which were the last words which he was ever heard to speak. The last minute of his last hour being now come, lying on his back, eyes firmly fixt towards Heaven, and his long lean consumed armes out of the bed, his hand upon his breast laid in cross one upon the other, about twelve o'clock at noon, in which hour he was also born into this world, arraign'd, condemn'd, and adjudg'd unto death, upon Sunday the 19th of October, 1595, (after almost 11 years imprisonment in the Tower) in a most sweet manner, without any sign of grief or groan, only turning his head a little aside, as one falling into a pleasing sleep, he surrender'd his happy soul into the hands of Almighty God, who to his so great glory had created it.

Some have thought, and perhaps not improbably, that he had some fore knowledge of the day of his death, because about seven or eight days before, making certain notes (understood only by himself) in his Calendar, what Prayers and Devotions he intended to say upon every day of the week following, on Monday, Tuesday, &c.: *when he came to the Sunday on which he dy'd, he there made a pause, saying, Hitherto and no further:* this is enough: and so writ no more, as his servants who then heard his words, and saw him write, have often testified.

In the following chapter occurs this curious record:

I forgot to note in the due place, that upon the night precedent to the Earl's arraignment and condemnation, a Nitingale was heard to sing with great melody in a jessamine tree all y⁐ night long in the garden of Arundel House, where his Countess and children then did remain, the which may seem the more strange in regard the like was neither before, nor since that time ever heard in that place. Another thing as strange did happen in the Tower soon after his death; for two tame stags which the Lieutenant kept there for his pleasure falling into a fury, never desisted knocking their horns against the walls till their brains being beaten out they dy'd.

Foote, the dramatist, shortly prior to his death, stood contemplating the picture of a brother author, and exclaimed, his eyes full of tears, "Poor Weston!" In the same dejected tone he added, after a short pause : " Soon shall others say, ' Poor Foote !' " and, to the surprise of his friends, a few days proved the justice of his prognostication. While performing at the Haymarket theatre, he was seized with paralysis on the stage ; he shortly after went to Brighton, returned to London, set out for Paris, but died on his way, at Dover. The expectation of the event had a share in producing it ; for a slight shock completes the destruction of prostrate energies.

Another great artist, in a different department, convinced that his hand was about to lose its cunning, chose a subject emblematical of the coming event. His friends inquired the nature of his next design, and Hogarth replied, " The End of All Things." " In that case," rejoined one, " there will be an end of the painter." What was uttered in jest was answered in earnest, with a solemn look and a heavy sigh : "There will," he said, "and the sooner my work is done the better." He commenced next day, labored upon it with unremitting diligence, and when he had given it the last touch, seized his palette, broke it in pieces, and said : " I have finished." The print was published in March, under the title of " Finis," and in October the curious eyes which saw the manners in the face were closed in the dust. Our ancestors, who were prone to look in the air for causes which were to be found upon the earth, attributed these intimations to various supernatural agencies.

John Hunter has solved the mystery, if mystery it can be called, in a single sentence. "We sometimes," he says, "feel within ourselves that we shall not live ; for the living powers become weak, and the nerves communicate the intelligence to the brain." His own case has often been quoted among the marvels of which he offered this rational explanation.

Premonitions of Death. 167

Dr. Ridge, in an eloquently written Oration, delivered by him before the Hunterian Society, has introduced some valuable information on the nature of *gout* and *angina pectoris*, incidentally in his examination of the various attacks under which the great anatomist suffered, with many judicious remarks on the mental and bodily health, which left unmistakable evidence of the affection under which Hunter labored, and which at length suddenly terminated his most extraordinary and useful career. Dr. Ridge thus describes the death scene. "On the 16th of October, 1793," says Mr. Ottley, "the board was to meet; and Hunter prepared to fulfil his promise, though he was so well aware of the risk he incurred in undertaking a task which he felt would agitate him, that in mentioning the circumstance to a friend who called on him in the morning, he expressed his apprehension lest some unpleasant dispute might occur, and his conviction that, if it did, it would certainly prove fatal to him. At his accustomed hour he left his house to commence his morning rounds, and by accident forgot to take with him his list of appointments. He had left his house but a few minutes when it was discovered; and Mr. Cleft, who was residing in his house, hastened with it to York street, St. James's, the first place on the list, where he found the carriage waiting. Hunter now made his appearance, took the list, and in an animated tone, bade his coachman drive to St. George's. Arrived at the Hospital, he found the Board already assembled; and entering the room, presented the memorial of the young men, and proceeded to urge the propriety of their being admitted. In the course of his remarks he made some observation which one of his colleagues thought it necessary instantly and flatly to contradict. Hunter immediately ceased speaking, retired from the table, and, struggling to suppress the tumult of his passion, turned into the adjoining room, where he had scarcely reached, when, with a deep groan, he fell lifeless into the arms of Dr. Robertson, one of the physicians of the hospital, who chanced to be present."* Dr. Ridge has also traced the hereditary affection which Hunter inherited, to its fatal termination. He has discriminated the different results of the ordinary wear and tear of the organic functions, and the aggravated form, which, as in the case of John Hunter, was induced by too much mental application and the neglect of the ordinary means of health; at the same time, distinguishing some forms of disease (gout and angina pectoris), which were shown to be in the life of the illustrious John Hunter.

It is remarked in the *Phrenological Journal :*—There was every thing to lament in the circumstance, but nothing at which to wonder, except that any individual could show such disrespect to the great genius, a single year of whose existence was worth the united lives of his opponents. Hunter, in uttering the prediction, had only to take counsel in his own experience, without the intervention of invisible spirits. He had long labored under a disease

* He was carried to his house in Leicester-square, in a close chair belonging to the Hospital, and was interred on the Wednesday following in the public vault of St. Martin's-in-the-Fields, whence the coffin was removed, in 1859, to Westminster Abbey.

of the heart, and he felt the disorder had reached the point at which any sharp agitation would bring on the crisis.

Mrs. Schimmelpenninck, in her amusing Memoirs, relates the following well-attested instance.

"While Dr. Priestley occupied the post of librarian to Lord Shelburne, one day, Mr. Petty, the precocious and gifted youth, sent for Dr. Priestley (Lord Shelburne being then absent, I think, in London). When the doctor entered, Mr. Petty told him he had passed a very restless night, and had been much disturbed by uncomfortable dreams, which he wished to relate to Dr. Priestley, hoping that, by so doing, the painful impression would pass away. He then said he dreamed he had been very unwell, when suddenly the whole house was in preparation for a journey; he was too ill to sit up, but was carried lying down into the carriage; his surprise was extreme in seeing carriage after carriage in an almost interminable procession. He was alone, and could not speak; he could only gaze in astonishment. The procession at last wound slowly off. After pursuing the road for many miles toward London, it at last appeared to stop at the door of a church. It was the church at High Wycombe, which is the burial-place of the Shelburne family. It seemed, in Mr. Petty's dream, that he entered, or rather was carried into, the church; he looked back; he saw the procession which followed him was in black, and that the carriage from which he had been taken bore the semblance of a hearse. Here the dream ended, and he awoke. Dr. Priestley told him that his dream was the result of a feverish cold, and that the impression would soon pass off. Nevertheless, he thought it best to send for the family medical attendant. The next day Mr. Petty was much better; on the third day he was completely convalescent, so that the doctor permitted him to leave his room; but, as it was in January, and illness was prevalent, he desired him on no account to leave the house, and, with that precaution, took his leave. Late the next afternoon the medical man was returning from his other patients; his road lay by the gates of Bowood, and, as Lord Shelburne was away, he thought he might as well call to see Mr. Petty, and enforce his directions. What was his surprise, when he had passed the lodge, to see the youth himself, without his hat, playfully running

Premonitions of Death.   169

to meet him! The doctor was much astonished, as it was bitterly cold, and the ground covered with snow. He rode toward Mr. Petty to rebuke him for his imprudence, when suddenly he disappeared; whither, he knew not — but he seemed instantaneously to vanish. The doctor thought it very extraordinary, but that probably the youth had not wished to be found transgressing orders, and he rode on to the house; there he learnt that Mr. Petty had just expired."

Soldiers and sailors are remarkable for their presentiments of death. Here are three instances:

At the battle of Ramillies, was engaged a young officer, who had been intimate with Sir John Friend, executed by William of Orange for adherence to the interests of the exiled family. The officer assured his friends that he should not survive the battle. At its close, while the allied forces were pursuing the remains of the enemy, a knot of his acquaintance rallied him on his despondency, and congratulated him on his safety. "You speak," he replied, "as you think. I shall die yet." Scarcely had he said these words when the last cannon-ball fired by the enemy laid him dead on the spot. In his pocket was found a slip of paper, with these words, after a certain date: "Dreamed, or ————" (the blank was supposed to be intended for "was told by a spirit"), "that on May 22, 1706, Sir John Friend meets me." On that May 22 the battle of Ramillies was fought.

The following is related in Cadell's *Campaigns in Egypt*:—
"When the inlying pickets turned out in the morning, a soldier of my company (the Grenadiers), named M'Kinlay, came up to me, handing a paper, and said: 'Captain, here is my will; I am to be killed to-day, and I will all my arrears, and every thing I have, to my comrade, Hugh Swift.' 'What nonsense, M'Kinlay,' I replied to him; 'go into action, and do what you have always done: behave like a brave soldier.' He answered: 'I will do that, sir; but I am certain I am to be killed to-day, and I request you to take my will.' To satisfy him, I took it; and the man fought with the pickets during the whole day with great coolness and gallantry. In the afternoon, a little before the action was over, we rejoined the regiment; we had suffered much, but M'Kinlay was standing unhurt close to me; upon which I ob-

served to him: 'So, M'Kinlay, I suspect you are wrong this time.' The right of the regiment being posted on the round of a hill cut into steps for the vines, a body of the enemy's sharpshooters came close under us, and opened a fire to cover their retiring columns. M'Kinlay, seeing one of them taking aim over the arm of a fig-tree in our direction, exclaimed, 'Look at that rascal going to shoot our captain!' And, advancing one step down the hill, he presented at the Frenchman, who, however, was unfortunately too quick for him, for in an instant afterward poor M'Kinlay was shot through the neck, and killed on the spot. The same ball gave me a severe contusion on the breast, and I fell with the unfortunate man, and was actually covered with his blood. He was one of the best soldiers in the Grenadier company, and was much regretted; indeed, but for him, it is probable I should not have lived to tell this tale. The will was duly forwarded to the War Office, whence an order was issued for his comrade Swift to receive all that was due to him."

A correspondent of *Notes and Queries*, 2d S. No. 34, relates: "Having been several months in the Crimea during the severest period of the bombardment, I can state that many cases of *presentiment* were fulfilled: as also, that some were falsified. There were also many deaths without any accompanying presentiment having been made known. A sergeant in the Light Division, who was in the second boat which reached the shore before the Alma, and went through all the severest work up to the final storming, frequently, in his letters home, remarked, 'Something tells me I shall escape;' but, poor fellow, he was hit severely in two places, at the Redan. In one of his letters he stated: 'Many of our men knew when they would fall, and prepared accordingly by packing up letters and papers, and leaving instructions as to sending and writing to friends: *sure enough they did fall.*'"

It will be remembered that Dr. Johnson, in his *Rasselas*, puts into the mouth of the sage Imlac, these words:

That the dead are seen no more, I will not undertake to maintain against the concurrent testimony of all ages and all nations. There is no people, rude or unlearned, among whom apparitions of the dead are not related and believed. This opinion, which prevails as far as human nature is diffused, could become universal only by its truth: those that never heard of one another would not have agreed in a tale which nothing but experience could make credible. That it is doubted by single cavillers can very little weaken the general evidence; and some who deny it with their tongues, confess it with their fears.

To this passage Lord Byron thus alludes:

> I merely mean to say what Johnson said,
> That in the course of some six thousand years,
> All nations have believed that from the dead
> A visitant at intervals appears.
>
> And what is strangest upon this strange head
> Is, that, whatever bar the reason rears
> 'Gainst such belief, there's something stronger still
> In its behalf, let those deny who will.

Lord Byron was "superstitious:" he believed in the ill-luck of Friday, and was seriously disconcerted if any thing was to be done on that frightful day of the week. Yet he sometimes laughed at the idea of ghosts. In 1811, Byron, writing to Mr. Murray, says: "My old school and form-fellow Peel, the Irish secretary, told me he saw me in St. James's-street; I was then in Turkey. A day or two afterward he pointed out to his brother a person across the way, and said, 'There is the man I took for Byron:' his brother answered, 'Why, it is Byron, and no one else.' I was at this time *seen* to write my name in the Palace book. I was then ill of a malaria fever. If I had died, here would have been a ghost-story."

Not long after the death of Lord Byron, Sir Walter Scott was engaged in his study, during the darkening twilight of an autumnal evening, in reading a sketch of Byron's form and habits, his manners and opinions. On a sudden, he saw, as he laid down his book, and passed into his hall, the *eidolon* of his departed friend before him. He remained some time impressed by the intensity of the illusion, which had thus created a phantom out of skins, and scarfs, and plaids, hanging on a screen, in the gothic hall at Abbotsford.

Harriet Duchess of St. Alban's frequently expressed a wish that her own demise should take place on *a Sunday ;* which was fulfilled; she died on Sunday, Aug. 6, 1837. In reply to a question why she so fervently desired to die on the Sabbath, she said: " As it was on the Sunday after the Crucifixion that the Resurrection took place, those who would believe in their salvation by the Lord Jesus naturally wish to leave earth on the same day, in the humble hope of gaining admission where there are many mansions."

Burton, in his *Anatomy of Melancholy*, Part i. sec. 2, tells us that near Rupes Nova, in Finland, in the Kingdom of Sweden, there is a lake, in which, before the governor of the cattle dyes, *a spectrum*, in the habit of Arion with his harp, appears, and makes excellent musick, like those blocks in Cheshire, which (they say) presage death to the master of the family; or that oak in Lanthadran park in Cornwall, which foreshows as much. Many families in Europe are so put in mind of their last, by such predictions, and many men are forewarned (if we may believe Paracelsus) by familiar spirits in divers shapes, as cocks, crows, owls, which often hover about sick men's chambers, *ve quia morientium fœditatem sentient*, as Barcellus conjectures, *et ideo supertectum infirmorum crocitant*, because they smell a corse; or for that (as Bernardinus de Bustis thinketh) God permits the devil to appear in the form of crows, and such like creatures, to scare such as live wickedly here on earth. A little before Tullie's death (saith Plutarch) the crows made a mighty noise about him; *tumultuose perstrepentes*, they pulled the pillow from under his head. Of course, allowance must be made for the classic garniture of these prodigies.

Persons in health have died from the expectation of dying. It was once common for those who perished by violence to summon their destroyers to appear, within a stated time, before the tribunal of their God; and we have many perfectly attested instances in which, through fear and remorse, the perpetrators withered under the curse, and died. Pestilence does not kill with the rapidity of terror.

The profligate abbess of a convent, the Princess Gonzaga of Cleves and Guise, and the profligate Archbishop of Rheims, took it into their heads—for a jest—to visit one of the nuns by night, and exhort her as a person who was visibly dying. While in the performance of their heartless scheme they whispered to each other, "She is just departing," she departed in earnest. Her vigor, instead of detecting the trick, sank beneath the alarm; and the profane pair discovered, in the midst of their sport, that they were making merry with a corpse.—*Phrenological Journal.*

Mrs. Crawford relates in the *Metropolitan Magazine*, 1836, that Lord Chedworth (father of the late lord) had living with him the orphan daughter of a sister of his, a Miss Wright, from whom Mrs. Crawford heard this circumstance. Lord Chedworth had some lamentable doubts as to the existence of the soul in another world. He had a great friendship for a gentleman, who was as sceptical as himself. One morning, Miss Wright observed, on her uncle's joining her at the breakfast table, that he was very thoughtful, ate little, and was unusually silent. At last, he said, "Molly (for thus he familiarly called her), I had a strange visitor last night. My old friend B—— came to me." "How?" said Miss Wright, "did he come after I went to bed?" "*His spirit did,*" said Lord Chedworth, solemnly. "Oh, my dear uncle! how could the spirit of a living man appear?" said she, smiling. "He is dead, beyond doubt," replied his lordship; "listen, and then laugh as much as you please. I had not entered my bedroom many minutes, when he stood before me. Like you, I could not believe but that I was looking on the living man, and so accosted him; but he (the spirit) answered, 'Chedworth, I died this night at eight o'clock. I came to tell you there is another world beyond the grave; there is a righteous God that judgeth all.'"

"Depend upon it, uncle, it was only a dream;" but while Miss Wright was yet speaking, a groom on horseback rode up the avenue, and immediately afterward delivered a letter to Lord Chedworth, announcing the sudden death of his friend. The effect that it had upon the mind of Lord Chedworth was as happy as it was permanent: all his doubts were at once removed, and forever.

Haydon, the painter, in his *Journal*, February 15, 1815, has this extraordinary entry: "About this time, I had a most singular dream. I dreamt Wilkie and I were both climbing up an immensely high wall, at the top of which were sweet creatures smiling and welcoming us. He could scarcely keep hold, it was so steep and slippery: when all of a sudden he let go, and I saw him wind and curve in the air, and felt the horrible conviction that his body would be dashed to pieces. After a moment's grief

I persevered and reached the top, and there found Mrs. Wilkie and his sister, lamenting his death." Upon this Haydon subsequently noted: "This is like a presentiment of his (Wilkie's) dying first."—B. R. H. 1843.

DEATH OF LORD LYTTELTON.

The premonition said to have been received by Thomas Lord Lyttelton, a short time before his death, at the precise period foreshadowed, at Pitt Place, Epsom, is well known; but there are many versions of the circumstances. That most to be relied on is by Mr. William Russell, an organist, of Guildford, whose company was much courted on account of his musical talent, and who was a visitor at Pitt Place, on the night of Lord Lyttelton's death. We have in our possession Mr. Russell's narrative in his own handwriting, but it is incomplete as regards the dream in which the time of death was foretold. The circumstances are related, though with a difference, by a Correspondent of *Notes and Queries*, 2d Series, No. 113, who, however, received his version from a gentleman who had it from Mr. Russell.

The story ordinarily told is, that Lord Lyttelton dreamed the ghost of a lady whom he had seduced, appeared to him, and predicted his death at twelve at night on the third day following. The informant's version differs only thus far: that the supposed apparition was that of Mrs. Amphlett, the mother of the lady in question, who had died of a broken heart, in consequence of her daughter's dishonor. Lord Lyttelton was, at this time, in a very bad state of health, in consequence of his excesses, and was subject to "suffocating fits," probably nervous hysteria. Be this as it may, it appears that on the day of his death, the foretold third day, he had a party of friends at Pitt Place, among whom was Mr. Russell, the organist. He said that Lyttelton was in a state of some agitation, and had told the story of the dream to his friends. As the night wore on, and midnight approached, his nervousness increased painfully; and some of his visitors said, during his absence, "Lyttelton will frighten himself into another fit with this foolish ghost-story:" they determined to put a clock, which stood

Death of Lord Lyttelton. 175

in the room, forward; and when he returned to them they said,—" Hurrah, Lyttelton, twelve o'clock is past, you've jockeyed the ghost—now, the best thing to do, is to go quietly to bed, and in the morning you will be all right." He accordingly went upstairs; and while some of his guests were preparing to depart, his valet came down to fetch some mint-water which he was in the habit of taking, leaving his Lordship alone. At this period, the clock of the parish-church, which was not far off, and which, of course, could not have been touched, began slowly to peal forth the true midnight hour. The valet returned upstairs, and called out loudly; the company ran up, and found his lordship had fallen dead.

Now, the impression of the narrator was, that the sudden revulsion of feeling, from a state of fancied security to the finding of himself in the very instant of the dreaded danger, had caused such a reaction as to bring on the fits which carried his Lordship off. He, no doubt, had heard the first stroke of the clock, as well as others downstairs; and as each successive blow struck slowly upon the bell, the sense of danger, and the remembrance of the dream, became greater and greater—and to so weakened a frame, and so distressed a mind, no doubt, these caused the catastrophe.

It is also stated that Mrs. Amphlett died of grief at the precise time when the figure appeared to Lord Lyttelton; and that at the period of his Lordship's own dissolution, a figure answering his description appeared at the bedside of Miles Peter Andrews, Esq. (his Lordship's friend and companion), and suddenly throwing open the curtains, desired Mr. Andrews to come to him. The latter, not knowing that his Lordship had returned from Ireland, got up, when the phantom disappeared. Mr. Andrews (then at his partner's, Mr. Pigou, at Dartfort), had, in consequence, a short fit of illness; and in his subsequent visits to Pitt Place no solicitations could ever prevail on him to take a bed there; but he would invariably return, however late, to the Spread Eagle inn for the night. Mr. Croker, in his edition of Boswell's *Life of Johnson*, notes that he had heard Mr. Andrews relate these details, more than once, but always reluctantly, and with an evidently solemn conviction of their truth.

In *Notes and Queries*, 2d Series, No. 158, we find another version of the above story, copied from a MS. at least fifty years old, of a gentleman of Derbyshire, whose mother was a collateral descendant of Lord Lyttelton. This version states that his Lordship died at his house in Hill-street, Berkeley-square; but of the accuracy of Mr. Russell's statement, that his Lordship died at Pitt Place, there can be no doubt. This version repeats the statement, that the next post, on the morning after Lord Lyttelton's death, brought the account of the death of Mrs. Amphlett, "who departed precisely at the time Lord Lyttelton saw the vision."

We find the following narrative in the supplement to Nash's *History of Worcestershire:*

Thomas, the second Lord Lyttelton,* had great parts and ambition. He had all his father's foibles, but without his sound principles of religion and morality; for want of which, he fell into great enormities and vices. His pleasures were restrained by no ties of relationship, friendship, or decency. He was a great lover of gaming; in his younger years he was unsuccessful, but he afterward became more artful, and at his death he was supposed to have acquired 30,000*l.* by play. His constitution was feeble, and by his vices so enervated, that he died an old man at the age of 35. He was, like his father, a believer in ghosts, and many stories are told, with considerable confidence, which have relation to his death. About three days before he died, a female figure, with a bird on her hand,† appeared to him, as he imagined, and told him he should die in three days. The day of this supposed appearance he went to the House of Lords, and spoke with great earnestness on some business then in agitation. The next day, he went to a villa he had at Epsom, apparently as well as he had been some time before. The succeeding day he continued there, and was in as good health and spirits as usual, though the apparition still hung upon his mind. He spent the evening in company with the Miss Amphletts, Admiral Wolseley, Earl Fortescue, and some other persons; he seemed perfectly well, and pulling out his watch, said jocularly, it was ten o'clock, and if he lived two hours, he should *jockey* the ghost. In about an hour he retired to his chamber, and ordered his valet to bring his powder of rhubarb, which he frequently took

---

* Lord Lyttelton married, in 1772, Apphia, relict of Joseph Peach, Esq., Governor of Calcutta. She survived her lord 60 years, dying at Peach Field Lodge, Great Malvern, at the age of 96. With means comparatively slender she was eminently charitable; and the schools founded by her, the public walks laid out and improved, and the Home of Industry at Malvern, are interesting memorials of her beneficence.

† In Devonshire the appearance of a *white-breasted bird* has long been considered an omen of death. This belief has been traced to a circumstance stated to have happened to one of the Oxenham family in that county, and related by Howel in his *Familiar Letters:* wherein is the following monumental inscription : "Here lies John Oxenham, a goodly young man, in whose chamber, as he was struggling with the pangs of death, a bird, with a white breast, was seen fluttering about his bed, and so vanished." A similar circumstance is related of the death of his sister Mary, and two or three others of the family.

at night. His servant brought it, and forgetting to bring a spoon, was going to stir it with a key; upon which his Lordship called him a dirty fellow, and bid him fetch a spoon. Accordingly he went out, and returning in a few minutes, found his Lordship in the agonies of death.

DEATH OF ARCHBISHOP LEIGHTON.

Bishop Burnet records of the saintly Robert Leighton:

He often used to say that if he were to choose a place to die in, it should be an *Inn*. It looked like a Pilgrim's going Home, to whom this world was all as an Inn, and who was weary of the noise and confusion in it. He added that the officious tenderness and care of friends, was an entanglement to a dying man; and that the unconcerned attendance of those that could be procured in such a place would give less disturbance. And he obtained what he desired; for *he died at the Bell Inn, in Warwick-lane.*

Dr. Fall, who was well acquainted with Leighton, after a glowing eulogy on his holy life and "heavenly converse," proceeds:

Such a life, we may easily persuade ourselves, must make the thought of Death not only tolerable but desirable. Accordingly, it had this noble effect upon him. In a paper left under his own hand (since lost) he bespeaks that day in a most glorious and triumphant manner: his Expressions seem rapturous and ecstatic, as though his Wishes and Desires had anticipated the real and solemn celebration of his Nuptials with the Lamb of God. . . . . . He sometimes expressed his desire of not being troublesome to his friends at his Death; and God gratified to the full his modest humble choice: he dying at an Inn *in his sleep*. . . . So kind and condescending a Master do we serve, who not only enriches the souls of his faithful servants with His best Treasures, but often indulges them in lesser matters, and giveth to his beloved, even in their sleep.

Diodorus tells us that the Egyptians used to style the dwellings of the living "Inns," regarding the Life as the Journey of a Traveller toward his home. Cowley has a similar thought in one of his *Pindaric Odes*, of which the following is the first stanza:

LIFE.

Nascentes morimur.—Manil.

We're ill by those Grammarians us'd,
We are abus'd by *Words*, grossly abused;
From the Maternal Tomb
To the Grave's fruitful Womb,

We call here *Life;* but *Life's* a Name
That nothing here can truly claim:
This wretched *Inn,* where we scarce stay to bait,
  We call our *Dwelling-place;*
  We call one *Step* a *Race;*
But *Angels* in their full enlightened state,
Angels who Live, and know what 'tis to *Be,*
Who all the nonsense of our Language see,
Who speak *Things,* and our *Words* (their ill-drawn Pictures) scorn:
  When we by a foolish Figure say,
  Behold an old Man dead! then they
Speak properly, and cry: "*Behold a Man-child born!*"

OLD AGE AND DEATH.

M. Richerand, in his *Elements of Physiology,* has this pathetic picture of the closing scene:

New impressions are now less easily made, and the motions necessary to the operation of the understanding are performed with difficulty. Hence in decrepitude man returns, as far as relates to his intellectual faculties, to a state of *second childhood,* limited to certain recollections which are at first confused, and at last completely lost, incapable of judgment or will, or of new impressions.

The close of life is marked by phenomena similar to those with which it began. The circulation first manifested itself, and ceases last. The right auricle is the first to pulsate, and in death the last to retain its motion.

The following is the order in which the intellectual faculties cease and are decomposed—I am not here speaking of the immortal soul, of that divine emanation which outlives matter, and, freed from our perishable part, returns to the Almighty; I am speaking merely of those intellectual faculties which are common to man, and to those animals which, like him, are provided with a brain. Reason, the exclusive faculty of man, first forsakes him. He begins by losing the faculty of associating judgments, and then of comparing, bringing together, and of connecting, a number of ideas, so as to judge of their relation. The patient is then said to have lost his consciousness, or to be delirious. This delirium has generally for its subject the ideas that are most familiar to the patient, and his prevailing passion is easily recognized. The miser talks, in the most indiscreet manner, of his hidden treasure; the unbeliever dies haunted by religious apprehensions. Sweet recollections of a distant native land! then it is that ye return with your all-powerful energy and delight.

At last, he ceases to feel; but his senses vanish in succession, and in a determinate order. The taste and smell cease to give any sign of existence; the eyes become obscured by a dark and gloomy cloud; but the ear is yet sensible to sound and noise; and no doubt it was on this account that the Ancients, to ascertain that death had really taken place, were in the habit of calling loudly to the deceased.

A dying man, though no longer capable of smelling, tasting, hearing, and seeing, still retains the sense of touch; he tosses about in his bed, moves his arms in various directions, and is perpetually changing his posture.

DEATH AT WILL.

An instance of this kind, which may also be termed *voluntary trance*, is quoted by Mrs. Crowe, in her *Nightside of Nature*.

Doctor Cheyne, the Scottish physician, who died in 1742, relates the case of Colonel Townshend, who could, to all appearance, die whenever he pleased: his heart ceased to beat, there was no perceptible respiration, and his whole frame became cold and rigid as death itself; the features being shrunk and colorless, and the eye glazed and ghastly. He would continue in this state for several hours, and then gradually revive; but the revival does not appear to have been an effort of will, or rather, we are not informed whether it was so or not. The Doctor, who attended the Colonel, states that his patient said, he could "die or expire when he pleased;" and yet, by an effort, or *somehow*, he could come to life again. He performed the experiment in the presence of three medical men; one of whom kept his hand on his heart, another held his wrist, and the third placed a looking-glass before his lips: and they found that all traces of respiration and pulsation gradually ceased, insomuch that after consulting about his condition for some time, they were leaving the room, persuaded that he was really dead, when signs of life appeared, and he slowly revived. He did not die while repeating the experiment, as has been sometimes asserted.

SLEEP AND DEATH.[*]

Aristotle, who hath written a singular tract of sleep, hath not, methinks, thoroughly defined it; nor yet Galen, though he seem to have corrected it; for those *noctambulos* and night-walkers,

[*] From Sir Thomas Browne's *Religio Medici*, Part II. Sect. xii.

though in their sleep, do yet enjoy the action of their senses. We must, therefore, say that there is something in us that is not in the jurisdiction of Morpheus; and that those abstracted and ecstatic souls do walk about in their own corpses, as spirits with the bodies they assume, wherein they seem to hear, see, and feel; though indeed the organs are destitute of sense, and their natures of those faculties which should inform them.

We term sleep a death; and yet it is waking that kills us, and destroys those spirits that are the house of life. 'Tis indeed a part of life that best expresses death; for every man truly lives, so long as he acts his nature, or some way makes good the faculties of himself. Themistocles, therefore, that slew his soldier, was a merciful executioner; 'tis a kind of punishment the mildness of no laws hath invented: I wonder (says Sir T. Browne) the fancy of Lucan and Seneca did not discover it. It is that death by which we may be literally said to die daily; a death which Adam died before his mortality; a death whereby we live a middle and moderating point between life and death. In fine, so like death, I dare not trust it without my prayers, and an half adieu unto the world, and take my farewell in a colloquy with God:

>The night is come, like to the day;
>Depart not thou, great God, away.
>Let not my sins, black as the night,
>Eclipse the lustre of thy light.
>Keep still in my horizon; for to me
>The sun makes not the day, but thee.
>Thou whose nature cannot sleep,
>On my temples sentry keep;
>Guard me 'gainst those watchful foes,
>Whose eyes are open while mine close.
>Let no dreams my head infest,
>But such as Jacob's temples blest.
>While I do rest, my soul advance;
>Make my sleep a holy trance:
>That I may, my rest being wrought,
>Awake into some holy thought,
>And with as active vigor run
>My course as doth the nimble sun.
>Sleep is a death;—O make me try,
>By sleeping, what it is to die!
>And as gently lay my head
>On my grave as now my bed.

> Howe'er I rest, great God, let me
> Awake again at last with thee.
> And thus assur'd, behold I lie
> Securely, or to wake or die.
> These are my drowsy days; in vain
> I do now wake to sleep again:
> O come that hour, when I shall never
> Sleep again, but wake forever!

This is the dormitive I take to bedward: I need no other *laudanum* than this to make me sleep; after which I close mine eyes in security, content to take my leave of the sun, and sleep unto the resurrection.

DOES THE SOUL SLEEP?

The Cartesian doctrine, that the Soul never sleeps, it is extremely difficult if not impossible to test. If we imagine that the soul has need of rest, then we must admit that sleep will be found in the next world, as in this. This, however, does not accord with our ideas of an immortal spirit, which has thoughts and sensations, which we on earth apply to mental conditions which presuppose the action of the human brain; and our present existence furnishes us with no idea of the action of the soul without the action of the brain.

CONTRITION OF THE ANCIENTS AT THE POINT OF DEATH.

Diogenes Laertius relates of the atheistic philosopher, Bion, that on his deathbed he changed his opinion, and repented of the sins he had committed against God. The notion of penitence for offences against the gods scarcely ever presents itself in polytheism. Their offerings and prayers had regard to the conciliation of the deities, with a view to some prospective temporal benefit; for spiritual and eternal benefits do not seem at all to have occupied the heathen mind. Even the concluding scene of Socrates, depicted by Xenophon and Plato, leaves the result arrived at by Cicero, that philosophy can reckon a future state of rewards and punishments, only among the *probabilia*. The cultivated Greek, according to Tholuck, believed in no future state: as, for example, Polybius, Pausanias, and Simonides. The second Alcibiades (of Plato) is designed to show that prayer itself should be seldom, if at all, addressed to the gods, lest a person should unconsciously pray for great evils upon himself, whilst thinking that he prays for good; and lest the gods should not happen to be in a disposition to grant what he happens to pray for.

Particular prayers, as for rain, are objected to by Marcus Antoninus;[*] and Socrates prayed simply for what was good, leaving the gods to decide, as knowing better than himself, what was or was not for his good. Some of the philosophers decided not to pray at all. (See Tholuck on *Heathenism.*)—*J. T. Buckton; Notes and Queries*, 2d S., No. 112.

In the Introduction to the *Republic* of Plato, Cephalus is made to say:

> Be assured, Socrates, that when a man is nearly persuaded that he is going to die, he feels concerned about things which never affected him before. Till then he has laughed at those stories about the departed, which tell us that he who has done wrong here must suffer for it in the other world; but now his mind is tormented by the fear that these stories may possibly be true. And, either owing to the infirmities of old age, or because he is nearer to the confines of a future state, he has a clearer insight into these mysteries. However that may be, he becomes fuller of misgiving and apprehension, and sets himself to the task of calculating and reflecting whether he has done any wrong to any one. Hereupon, if he finds his life full of unjust deeds, he is apt to start out of sleep in terror, as children do, and he lives haunted by gloomy anticipations. But if his conscience reproaches him with no injustice, he enjoys the abiding presence of sweet Hope, that "kind nurse of old age," as Pindar calls it.

This passage (from Davis and Vaughan's excellent translation) is alone sufficient to prove the belief of *some* of the ancients in remorse or contrition for crimes at the approach of death; especially when taken in connection with Plato's constant recognition of a future state, in which "the rewards and honors that await a good man surpass in number and magnitude all that one experiences in this life." (*Rep.* 6, x. p. 614 n.)—*Notes and Queries*, 2d S., No. 115.

---

[*] Some Christians of the present day have not, in this respect, disdained to follow the practices of the Heathens. In the wet autumn of 1860, prayers for fine weather were objected to by certain correspondents of the newspapers of the day, as had been in the previous year prayers for rain.

MAN'S RELUCTANCE TO THINK UPON GOD.

A striking incidental illustration of the aversion of the unrenewed heart to meditate upon God occurs in Shakspeare's description of the Death-bed of Falstaff, for the hint of which the dramatist may have been indebted to some gossiping Mrs. Quickly, or to his own ever-wakeful observation, beside the bed of a dying person. "In other respects," says a writer in the *Christian Observer*, "graphic and vivid as it is—and so minutely correct in delineation that one can scarcely believe it is not a description of an actual occurrence—it is so painful to witness the solemnities of death portrayed for scenic effect, and even mixed up with associations of gross ribaldry, that it seems astonishing that persons of refined mind, even though unimpressed by religious feelings, do not shrink from such pictures in theatrical representations. Mrs. Siddons's mimicry (for what is it but mimicry?) of death is related to have been awfully natural; but is death, after which comes judgment, a subject for amusement? It is too solemn even for tragedy; in comedy it is revolting." Yet, how truthful is the following passage:

'A made a finer end, and went away as it had been any christom* child.

---

* "Chrystom," scilicet *chrisom.* From Mrs. Quickly's version of the word (for, doubtless, Shakspeare intended to give the popular dialect, and, it may be supposed, his spelling has been retained), we may conclude that uneducated persons, and perhaps others, confused the anointing *chrism,* and the baptismal robe, called *chrisom,* with *christen:* that is, man's unwarranted addition to Christ's sacrament, with the sacrament itself, whereby we are admitted visibly into the Christian church; in vernacular phrase, *christened.* The rite of *chrism* was retained in the first service-book of Edward VI., but happily it was expunged in the second. Chrisom was, in popular language, the holy robe, or chrisom-cloth put about, or upon, the child, at, or in token of, his baptism; and with which the women used to shroud it, if it died "within the month;" otherwise, it was usually brought to church on the day of the mother's purification. Hence, Chrisoms, in the bills of mortality, were properly such children as died within the month, or before they had left off the chrisom-cloth; but the parish-clerks, "in their ignorance," justly says Wheatly, mean by the word in those Bills, infants dying unbaptized, who, therefore, were *not* chrisoms. It came to be popularly used as Shakspeare makes Mrs. Quickly use it, in the sense of innocents—infants who had not committed sin after baptism. That wonderful man, Shakspeare, knew well the rites, and even the technical language of the church of Rome, to which he often alludes; as in the well-known lines of the ghost in *Hamlet:*

Cut off e'en in the blossom of my sins,
Unhousel'd, unanointed, unaasoil'd.

In some copies, "disappointed, unanealed." The word "soil" is still used in our Hymn in the Ordination office for priests: "Anoint and cheer our soiled face." The penitent was "cheered" by being "assoiled." The word "ousel" is Saxonic for the

'A parted even just before twelve and one, e'en at turning o' th' tide; for after I saw him fumble with the sheets, and play with flowers, and smile upon his fingers'-ends, I knew there was but one way: for his nose was as sharp as a pen, and 'a babbled of green fields. "How now, Sir John," quoth I: "what, man! be of good cheer." So 'a cried out, "God, God, God!" three or four times. Now I, to comfort him, bid him 'a should not think of God: I hoped there was no need to trouble himself with such thoughts yet. So 'a bade me lay more clothes on his feet: I put my hand into the bed, and felt them, and they were as cold as any stone.—*King Henry the Fifth*, Act ii. Sc. 3.

With incomparable skill—though the images are too painful to be gazed at without distress in fiction, by any person who has witnessed them in reality—has Shakspeare here brought together the visible prognosticators of dissolution. We have the *facies Hippocratica:* "his face was as sharp as a pen;" (?) and we have the peculiar and characteristic restlessness alluded to by Richer—and—"I saw him fumble with the sheets, play with the flowers, and smile upon his fingers'-ends,"—which Shakspeare well knew betokened that "there was but one way."

But, perhaps, the most striking part of the description is the half-disclosed intimation of what was passing in the dying man's mind, even in its incoherence, when he "cried out, God, God, God! three or four times;" with the counsel which the woman, with the utmost simplicity, tells us she gave him: "Now I, to comfort him, bid him 'a should not think of God; I hoped there was no need to trouble himself with any such thoughts yet." How wonderfully in these few words has Shakspeare exhibited the feelings of the unrenewed mind, which is "enmity with God;" and also the popular delusion, that it is not necessary to think upon God till it is too late to think of any thing else. The narrator dreams not that there could be two opinions upon the subject: she relates with perfect complacency the advice she gave; she does not conjecture that any person could suppose that a man would think upon God except as a matter of necessity; it

---

sacrament of the Lord's Supper.—Abridged from the *Christian Observer*. See Nares's *Glossary*, 1841, new edit. 1859, voce *Chrisome*, in which the Editor considers it plain that we should read "*chrisom child*;" unless Mrs. Quickly be supposed to disfigure the word, *chrisome child* is used where no suspicion of misuse can apply. The original use of this cloth was to prevent the rubbing off the *chrism*, or holy unguent, a part of the old baptismal office. It afterward came to signify the white mantle thrown over the whole infant. We retain the word *robe*, applied to the long frock in which the child is christened: it is often finely embroidered, and is very costly.

might be requisite if he were in the very article of death; but why should he "trouble himself"—a most apt expression to convey her idea—with such reflections, so long as any ray of hope remained? It comes out also—for Shakspeare is evidently painting from nature—that such was, and, it is feared, still is, the advice given by ignorant, officious persons to the sick and dying.

The language put by Shakspeare into the lips of Mrs. Quickly is the more striking, because he is making her speak in character, as an ignorant and irreligious woman; her being dissolute does not touch the question, for he might have caused her to speak thus without her being grossly vicious. And, a few pages further on, when Henry V., whom Shakspeare means to represent as a reflecting, religious, and high-souled man, is describing how a sick person should feel and act, very different are the sentiments. Speaking of the wicked lives of too many soldiers, before they entered the army, he says:

Now, if these men have defeated the law, and outrun native punishment, though they can outstrip man, they have no wings to fly from God: war is his beadle, war is his vengeance: so that men are here punished for before breach of the King's laws, in now the King's quarrel: where they feared death, they have borne life away; and where they would be safe, they perish. Then if they die unprovided, no more is the King guilty of their damnation, than he was before guilty of those impieties for the which they are now visited. Every subject's duty is the King's; but every subject's soul is his own. Therefore, should every soldier in the war *do as every sick man in his bed, wash every mote out of his conscience; and dying so, death is to him advantage; as not dying, the time was blessedly lost, wherein such preparation was gained;* and in him that escapes, it were not sin to think, that, making God so free an offer, he let him outlive that day to see his greatness, and to teach others how they should prepare.

In this passage, which might have been written by Jeremy Taylor, there is nothing of its being time enough to repent when we are dying. The time, he says, which men accounted lost, was "blessedly lost," wherein such preparation was gained. He vents no such folly as the popular notion, that a sick man is to seek his comfort in banishing serious reflection. Shakspeare, though irreligious himself, knew, as a matter of information, that it is the wicked who say unto God, "Depart from us; for we desire not the knowledge of thy ways." The righteous man—the true believer—finds comfort in thinking upon God: though alienated by nature, he is brought nigh by grace; though he fell in the first Adam, he is restored by the second; though he had destroyed himself, yet in God is his help; his offended Creator has become his reconciled Father in Christ Jesus; God is his shield, and his exceeding great reward; he has followed the advice which Eliphaz gave to Job in his affliction, and has enjoyed the blessing which he predicted should follow—" Acquaint now thyself with Him, and be at peace; thereby good shall come unto thee."—Abridged from the *Christian Observer*, 1841.

STATE OF MIND PRECEDING DEATH.

Sir Benjamin Brodie, as the result of his long observation, concludes that the mere act of Dying is seldom, in any sense of the word, a very painful process. It is true (he adds) that some persons die in a state of bodily torture, as in the case of tetanus; that the drunkard dying of *delirium tremens* is haunted by terrific visions; and that the victim of that most horrible of all diseases, hydrophobia, in addition to those peculiar bodily sufferings from which the disease has derived its name, may be in a state of terror from the supposed presence of frightful objects, which are presented to him as realities, even to the last. But the general rule is, that both mental and bodily sufferings terminate long before the scene is finally closed.

Then, as to the actual fear of death: it seems that the Author of our existence, for the most part, gives it to us when it is intended that we should live, and takes it away from us when it is intended that we should die. Those who have been long tormented by bodily pain are generally as anxious to die as they ever were to live. So it often is with those whose life has been protracted to an extreme old age, beyond the usual period of mortality, even when they labor under no actual disease. Sir Benjamin describes the dying of old age—

>Like ripe fruit to drop
>Into his mother's lap,

as seeming to be a happy conclusion of worldly cares and joys.

"It is like falling to sleep never to wake in this state of existence. Some die retaining all their faculties, and quite aware that their dissolution is at hand. Others offer no signs of recognition of external objects, so that it is impossible for us to form any positive opinion whether they do or do not retain their sensibility; and others, again, who appear to be insensible and unconscious, when carefully watched, are found not to be so in reality; but they die contentedly."

Sir Benjamin Brodie has never known but two instances in which, in the act of dying, there were manifest indications of the fear of death. The individuals alluded to were unexpectedly destroyed by hemorrhage, which it was impossible to suppress. The depressing effects which the gradual loss of blood produced on their corporeal systems seemed to influence their minds, and they died earnestly imploring that relief which art was unable to afford. Seneca might have chosen an easier death than that from opening his arteries.

With respect to the influence of religious sentiments on the minds of dying persons, Sir B. Brodie observes: "there is no doubt that a pure and simple religious faith, and a firm reliance on the Being who has placed us here, contribute more than anything besides to disarm death of its terrors, deprive 'the grave of its victory,' and smooth the passage of the humble and sincere believer to the termination of his worldly career. Nevertheless, according to my own experience, and what I have heard from others, the influence of religious feelings is, for the most part, not so much perceptible at the moment when death is actually impending, as it is at an earlier period, when the individual, who was previously in health, or supposed himself to be so, first discovers that it is probable that he shall die."

HOW MAN DIES.*

Although the fear of death is natural to man in some cases, illness gradually removes this dread, and the change is welcomed, and even earnestly desired; the sufferer has ceased to take an in-

* These additional illustrations are, in the main, selected and abridged from Mr. Harrison's excellent work on *The Medical Aspects of Death*.

terest in the things around him; they have lost all the charms they borrowed from hope and anticipation, and he has no future earthly prospect but the grave.

The fear of dying in sleep is not uncommon. The wife of Mr. Edgeworth expressed this dread. She soon fell asleep, and awakened smiling. "I am smiling," said she, "at my asking you to sit beside me as a sort of protection, and at my being afraid to *die in my sleep,* when I never felt afraid of dying when awake."

Sometimes, consciousness remains to the last moment of existence, and even when the tongue refuses to speak, the wistful eye and waving of the hand serve to impress the dying injunction. How touchingly has Sterne pictured this in the story of Lefevre, where the poor soldier looks first at his son, and then at my Uncle Toby; and the ligature, fine as it is, was never broken!

The changes which immediately precede death are, of course, more or less painful, according to their nature and severity; yet there can be no doubt but dissolution itself is the cessation of suffering. In some instances, the approach of death is betokened by strange and awful sensations; and it is probable that where consciousness remains to the last, the feelings are always peculiar and unmistakable.

The premonitions of death often give rise to a degree of restlessness and a wish for change, which is odd and capricious in its manifestations. Persons who have long remained tranquil will suddenly express a desire to be dressed and go down stairs, or have their beds moved to another position. Strange yearnings for particular places and old scenes sometimes arise, which seem like the shadowing forth of dim instincts, which have been concealed in the recesses of the mind.

With the exception of those who are worn down by long illness, or reduced to despair by mental anguish and misfortune, there are few who can believe that they have accomplished all the purposes of life; and we naturally look toward the infirmities of old age to wean us from the interests of the world. But even then we are reluctant to leave; and it is only when deserted by friends, that we can say—

> I have lived long enough; my way of life
> Is fall'n into the sear, the yellow leaf.

In speaking of others it is common to regard life as properly terminating when usefulness, activity, and fortune are declining. When reverses succeed a happy and prosperous career, we say that existence has been too protracted: it is on this account that the poets have spoken of the happiest moment of life as the most proper time for death; a notion more poetical than rational:

> Why did they
> Then not die ?—They had lived too long
> Should an hour come to bid them breathe apart.
> *Lord Byron's Don Juan,* canto iv.

And Shakspeare makes Othello exclaim:

> If I were now to die,
> 'Twere now to be most happy; for I fear
> My soul hath her content so absolute,
> That not another comfort like to this
> Succeeds in unknown fate.

The absence of respiration is the most ordinary sign of death, but at the same time the most likely to deceive. To ascertain whether the breathing be entirely suspended, it is a common practice to hold a looking-glass to the face:—

> Lend me a looking-glass;
> If that her breath will mist or stain the stone,
> Why, then she lives.—*King Lear,* Act v. Sc. 3.

For the same reason, the stirring of any light substance, such as down, which may rest about the mouth, has been regarded as a fine indication of the act of respiration: but this, like the mist on the looking-glass, is a deceptive or inaccurate method. Shakspeare represents Prince Henry as having been deceived when he carried off the crown from his father's pillow:

> By his gates of breath
> There lies a downy feather which stirs not;
> Did he suspire, that light and weightless down
> Perchance must move.

If the observance of the respiration be taken as the indication of life, and its absence as a proof of death, the exposure of the naked chest and abdomen would enable the spectator to form a much more accurate appreciation of it, especially if it be made carefully, and for a sufficient length of time.

Death may be said to *begin* at different parts of the body; and it will be found that the nature, symptoms, and peculiarities of the act of dying, are determined by the organ first mortally attacked. The alterations which directly occasion dissolution seem principally effective, either in the arrest of the *circulation* or the *respiration*.

As the heart is the great mover of the circulation, we can easily conceive that whatever brings it to stop must be fatal to life. Extensive losses of blood operate in this manner, and they furnish us with a good illustration of the manner in which death takes place. The sufferer becomes pale and faint, his lips white and trembling; after a while the breathing becomes distressed, and a rushing noise seems to fill the ears. The pulse is soft, feeble, and wavering; and the exhaustion and prostration are more and more alarming. Soon a curious restlessness takes place, and he tosses himself from side to side. At length, the pulse becomes uncertain, and the blood is feebly thrown to the brain. The surface assumes an icy coldness. The mind is yet untouched, and the sufferer knows himself to be dying. In vain the pulse is sought at the wrist—in vain efforts are made to re-excite warmth —the body is like a living corpse. Now, a few convulsive gaspings arise, and the countenance sets in the stiff image of death. Such are the more striking phenomena which attend the fatal hemorrhages.

The failure of the vital powers, from the withdrawal of blood, may be regarded as a sort of type of this mode of death, since the various symptoms which have been named, arise from the cessation of the healthy circulation.

A dread of the loss of blood may almost be considered as an instinctive feeling; at any rate, its importance is early impressed on the mind, and is never forgotten. In childhood, it is looked at with alarm; and the stoutest mind cannot but view with horror those perilous gushes of blood which bring us into the very jaws of destruction.

Byron has given a fearful description in his *Manfred* of the state which Mr. Harrison has just portrayed:

> *Abbot.* Alas! how pale thou art—thy lips are white,
> And thy breast heaves, and in thy gasping throat
> The accents rattle—give thy prayers to Heaven—
> Pray—albeit but in thought—but die not thus.
> *Manfred.* 'Tis over—my dull eyes can fix thee not;
> But all things swim around me, and the earth
> Heaves as it were beneath me. Fare thee well—
> Give me thy hand.

Independently of the mere loss of blood, other causes may depress the action of the heart: it may be arrested by a *shock*, or sudden impression on the nervous system—so frequent in cases of violent death, and disease in which life is extinguished with fearful rapidity.

In many accidents, there is little loss of blood; yet the injury is great, and its consequences are terrible. The sufferer turns pale—his countenance changes, and he feels that he is fatally wounded. Sickness and complete prostration follow, and the heart never rallies. In this manner, extensive burns and scalds, and dreadful blows, or internal lacerations, produce death. In the same way, the strong mineral acids, when taken internally, appear to destroy by their depressing influence on the heart.

The internal lesion of the stomach causes a sympathetic failure of the circulation.

But the effects of the *shock* are much more numerous and interesting than might at first be imagined. At least, impressions on the nervous system, analogous in their nature, play an important part in the fatal termination of many diseases. Violent inflammations seem, when fatal, to act by their depressing influence, by lowering the vital powers, and bringing the circulation to a stand.

The introduction of some poisons, also, is peculiarly inimical to the *vitality* of the blood. Thus, the death is truthfully described by Shakspeare, as commencing in the blood itself:

> It is too late; *the life of all his blood*
> Is touch'd corruptibly; and his pure brain,
> Which some suppose the soul's frail dwelling-house,
> Doth, by the idle comments that it makes,
> Foretell the ending of mortality.

Sir Benjamin Brodie states that he has been curious to watch the state of dying persons, and is satisfied that, where an ordinary observer would not for an instant doubt that the individual is in a state of complete stupor, *the mind is often very active even at the very moment of death.*

Dr. Baillie once said, that "all his observation of death-beds inclined him to believe that nature intended that we should go out of the world as unconscious as we came into it." "In all my experience," he added, "I have not seen one instance in fifty to the contrary." Yet, even in such a large experience, the occurrence of "one instance in fifty to the contrary" would invalidate the assumption that such was the law of nature (or "nature's intention," which, if it means any thing, means the same). The moment in which the spirit meets death is perhaps like the moment in which it is embraced by sleep. It never, I suppose (says Mrs. Jameson, whose observations we quote), happened to any one to be conscious of the immediate transition from the waking to the sleeping state.

The mode of death, though not one of pain, may have been preceded by considerable suffering, as in the case of burns and scalds. But the act of dying is one of relief; or if the sensations are uneasy and fearful, they cannot be termed painful in the common sense of the term.

When fluids taken by the patient flow back from his mouth, or fall heavily down his throat, as if poured into an ordinary tube, death is soon to be expected.

In young children a curious playing with the bed-clothes often attends fatal affections of the brain. Mr. Harrison relates that a little child, who had in her hand her handkerchief, spread it out repeatedly with apparent care, and in a fantastic manner, that would have been amusing but for its fatal import. The picking of bed-clothes and catching of the hands, as if at imaginary objects, are well known as terrible indications.

Chomel remarks, as of serious presage, the automatic manner in which a patient will unceasingly draw his hand to his side, in spite of the efforts of the physician to ascertain his pulse.

When death occurs in advanced and feeble age, the vital powers are so easily depressed, and the heart's action is brought to a stand in so imperceptible a manner, that it is common to speak of it as a quiet sleep:

> —and our little life
> Is rounded with a sleep.
> Shakspeare's *Tempest*, Act iv. Sc. 1.

Madame D'Arblay thus describes the death of her revered father, Dr. Burney: "An awful stillness pervaded his apartment, and so soft became his breathing, that I dropped my head by the side of his pillow, to be sure that he breathed at all. . . . Yet could I not believe that all had ceased thus suddenly, without a movement, without even a sigh."

The *stiffness of death* is often not fairly established until the body is already cold, and, when overcome by pressure, does not return, as the contractions which arise from nervous causes. The rigidity comes on with various degrees of rapidity, and its duration is also various. It usually commences in about seven hours; seldom if ever later, according to Sommer; but it may be deferred even to twenty and thirty hours. When the body is greatly weakened by disease, the rigidity comes on much sooner, but is more evanescent: it has been known to arise in fifteen or twenty minutes. Its duration is ordinarily from twenty-four to thirty-six hours; but it may continue many days. This stiffening of the body seems like the final act of life, and has been supposed to be the last effort of muscular power. Every one must be struck with the analogy it presents to the coagulation of the blood: indeed, it was long imagined by some physiologists to be dependent on that cause; but this is not the case. The rigidity does not seem to be confined to the external muscles of the body, but is particularly manifested in the heart and great blood-vessels. The walls of the heart contract forcibly after the external signs of death; the arteries also contract, and propel their contents into the veins.

According to Dr. Taylor, the average time of the body cooling after death is about fifteen or sixteen hours, when not warmly clad, and when the temperature is about 60°. He has known a body keep warm thirty or forty hours; the heat remaining longest when the death was violent, and the person robust. It is a curious fact in relation to the temperature of the body, that in cases of Asiatic cholera, the body, previously quite cold, has become warm immediately before or even after death.

The brightening-up of the mind previous to dissolution, or, to use the common expression, "the Lightness before Death," has led to a notion that dying persons are favored beyond others with a spiritualized conception of things not only relating to time, but likewise to eternity: or, in other words, that they have visions of angelic consolation. This lighting-up of the mind is stated by Mr. Madden to amount to "nothing more than a pleasurably excited condition of the mental faculties, following perhaps a state of previous torpor, and continuing a few hours, or oftentimes moments, before dissolution. This rousing up of the mind is probably produced by the stimulus of dark venous blood circulating through the arterial vessels of the brain, in consequence of the imperfect oxygenation of the blood in the lungs, whose delicate air-cells become impeded by the deposition of mucus on the surface, which there is not sufficient energy in the absorbents to remove; and hence arises the rattling in the throat which commonly precedes death."

Of the general forerunners of death Mr. Harrison* says: "When the evidences of dissolution begin to manifest themselves, a general failure of the temperature, with a cold dew on the skin, may be considered an indicative that the scene is about to close. In many cases it is easy to recognize the fatal turn which diseases take by the alterations which the symptoms undergo. Where internal inflammations are about to issue in death, there is mostly a striking change in the expression of the face, and sometimes a curious shrinking of the body. The nose and lips are very characteristic in dying; the lips become pale, the nostrils dilated and dark-looking, and the hairs about the lips seem more than usually apparent; the teeth look like pieces of ordinary bone, and the eyes seem to shadow through the eye-lids, or are partially turned under the lids; the nails appear dark, and the ends of the fingers sodden.

"Finally, convulsive twitchings often show themselves in the face, with singular elevations of the eyebrows, and starting of the eyes. A gasping attempt to breathe terminates the struggle.

"When coma is present, a mucous rattle is generally of fatal import; and, è contrario, when the lungs are affected, the supervention of coma is equally to be dreaded."

* *On the Medical Aspects of Death.*

How Man Dies.

From observations by D. A. T. Thomson, it is evident there are no certain signs that a person is truly dead, except the total cessation of respiration, and the commencing putrefaction of the body.

Take away but the pomps of death (says Jeremy Taylor), the disguises and solemn bugbears,* and the actings by candlelight, and proper and fantastic ceremonies, the minstrels and the noise-makers, the women and the weepers, the swoonings and the shriekings, the nurses and physicians, the dark room and the ministers, the kindred and the watches, and then to die is easy, ready and quit of its troubled circumstances.

How fearfully does the impressive poetry of Pope picture the closing scene:

THE DYING CHRISTIAN TO HIS SOUL.

Vital spark of heavenly flame,
Quit, oh, quit this mortal frame:
Trembling, hoping, lingering, flying—
Oh, the pain, the bliss of dying!
Cease, fond nature, cease thy strife,
And let me languish into life!

Hark, they whisper, angels say,
Sister spirit, come away!
What is this absorbs me quite?
Steals my senses, shuts my sight,
Drowns my spirit, draws my breath?
Tell me, my soul, can this be death?

The world recedes, it disappears!
Heaven opens on my eyes! my ears
  With sounds seraphic ring:
Lend, lend your wings! I mount! I fly!
O Grave! where is thy victory?
  O Death! where is thy sting?†

---

* When we read of these easy modes of shuffling off "the mortal coil," we are the more displeased with the vulgar emblems of Death—as the "bugbear" of the skull and cross-bones, or "Death's Head," which we owe to Pagan sensuality. "I wonder," says Bishop Hall, "at the practice of the ancient both Greeks and Romans, whose use was, to bring up a death's head, in the midst of their feasts, on purpose to stir up their guests to drink harder, and to frolic more: the sight whereof, one would think, should have rather abated their courage, and have tempered their jollity."—*Occasional Meditations.*

† A popular living poet, whose lyrics sing of the more cheerful aspects of life, has afforded us much gratification by declaring the above to be one of the most perfect embodiments of poetic genius in our literature.

DEATH FROM HEART DISEASE.

Fatal fainting is not unfrequently the result of actual disease of the heart, although death from affections of the heart is not always of a sudden or uncomplicated kind. The walls of the heart are sometimes thin and dilated, and there is a soft struggling palpitation, which has been aptly compared to the fluttering of a bird against the bars of its cage.

At other times, the heart is overloaded with fatty deposits, so that its natural fleshy structure is proportionally defective; and it is unable to propel the blood with sufficient force to meet the exigencies of the system. Occasionally, bony deposits are found in the heart and great vessels, and the natural contractions of the heart are painful and irregular. From these and other causes, which probably produce a spasm of the heart, arises the disease called *angina pectoris*.

John Hunter died of this disease. (*See page* 167.)

The benevolent and accomplished Dr. Arnold was taken from us by *angina pectoris*. He awoke in the morning with a sharp pain across his chest, which he had felt lightly on the preceding day, before and after bathing. He composed himself to sleep for a short time; but the pain seemed to increase, and to pass down the left arm, which called to Mrs. Arnold's remembrance what she had heard of this fatal disease. Their usual medical attendant, Dr. Bucknill, was sent for, and found Dr. Arnold lying on his back—his countenance much as usual—his pulse, though regular, was very quick, and there was cold perspiration on the brow and cheeks. He apologized in a cheerful manner for troubling Dr. Bucknill at so early an hour, and inquired as to the nature and danger of his illness; he was told it was a spasm of the heart. The physician quitted the house to furnish himself with remedies. On his return, Dr. Arnold said: "If the pain is again as severe as it was before you left, I do not know how I can bear it." He again questioned Dr. Bucknill as to the danger of his complaint —he was told of his danger—inquired as to the remedies, and on being told, answered, "Ah! very well!" The physician, who was dropping the laudanum into a glass, turned round, and saw him quite calm, but his eyes were shut. In another minute he heard a rattle in his throat, and a convulsive struggle—flew to the bed, and called to one of the servants to fetch Mrs. Arnold. The family soon arrived; but the sobs and cries of his children were unable to affect him—" the eyes were fixed, the countenance was unmoved: there was a heaving of the chest, deep gasps escaped at prolonged intervals, and just as the usual medical attendant arrived, and as the old school-house servant, in an agony of grief, rushed with the others into the room, in the hope of seeing his master once more, he breathed his last." This occurred shortly before eight in the morning. . . . " What that Sunday was in Rugby, it is hard fully to represent—the incredulity—the bewilderment—the agitating inquiries for every detail—the blank, more awful than sorrow, that prevailed through the vacant services of the long and dreary day—the feeling as if the very place had passed away with him who had so emphatically been in every sense its head—the sympathy which hardly dared to contemplate, and which yet could not but fix the thoughts and looks of all on the desolate house, where the fatherless family were gathered round the chamber of death."—*Arnold's Life*, vol. ii.

Mr. Harrison, in whose work are quoted these details, adds: "In Dr. Arnold's case, the heart was found soft and thin, but without any valvular disease." Mr. Harrison then relates a case of a gentleman, about fifty-five years of age, in impaired health, and who, from having been thin and muscular, was slightly tending to fat and corpulency. One day, at dinner, he felt an unusual pain in the region of the heart; he retired, warm applications were made to the chest, and the pain soon ceased altogether. He then begged to be left alone: in less than an hour, his wife found him lying upon the sofa, just in the position she had left him: she believed him asleep, but found him dead. The examination of his body disclosed nothing that could account for his death, but a thin, fat heart; fat was deposited on it at the expense of its muscular substance.

BROKEN HEARTS.

The term " broken heart," as commonly applied to death from

grief, is not a vulgar error, as generally supposed. On the contrary, though not a very common circumstance, there are many cases on record in medical works. This affection, it is believed, was first described by Harvey; but since his day several cases have been observed. Morgagni has recorded a few examples: amongst them, that of George II., who died suddenly, of this disease, in 1760; and, what is very curious, Morgagni himself fell a victim to the same malady. Dr. Elliotson, in his Lumleyan Lecture on Diseases of the Heart, in 1839, stated that he had only seen one instance; but in the *Cyclopædia of Practical Medicine*, Dr. Townsend gives a table of twenty-five cases, collected from various authors. Generally, this accident is consequent upon some organic disease, such as fatty degeneration; but it may arise from violent muscular exertion, or strong mental emotions.

THE DEATH-BED.—BY OWEN FELTHAM.

Feltham lived in the time of James I., and wrote a curious book of pious and moral treatises, called *Resolves*, rich in wit and fancy, not flung about in idle and unmeaning sport, but employed as the exponents of thoughts in themselves acute and profound. Feltham delighted in reflection, but was at the same time a man of the world—of a cheerful and lively temper, and always preserving a clear understanding. He has left this naturally eloquent picture of a death-bed:

'There is no spectacle more profitable, more terrible, or more humble, than the sight of a dying man, when he lies expiring his soul on his death-bed; to see how the ancient society of the body and the soul is divided; and yet to see how they struggle at the parting; being in some doubt what shall become of them after.

The spirits shrink inward, and retire to the anguished heart; as if, like sons pressed from an indulgent father, they would come for a sad vail, from that which was their life's maintenance; while that, in the meantime, parts with affrighting pangs, and the hands and feet, being the most remote from it, are, by degrees, encolded to a fashionable clay; as if death crept in at the nails, and by an insensible surprise, suffocated the environed heart.

To see how the mind would fain utter itself, when the organs of the voice are so debilitated that it cannot.

To see how the eye settles to a fixed dimness, which, a little before, was swift as the shoots of lightning, nimbler than the thought, and bright as the polished diamond: and in which this miracle was more eminent than in any of the other parts, that it being a material, earthly body, should yet be conveyed with quicker motion than the revolutions of an indefinite soul; so suddenly bringing the object to conceits, that one would think the apprehension of the heart were seated in the eye itself.

To see the countenance (through which, perhaps, there shined a lovely majesty, even to the captivating of admiring souls), now altered to a frightful paleness.

To think how that which commanded a family, nay, perhaps a kingdom, and kept all in awe with the moving of a spongy tongue, is now become a thing to be transmitted from all these enchanting blandishments, to the dark and noisome grave; where, instead of shaking the golden sceptre, it now lies imprisoned but in five feet of lead. There is even the difference of two several worlds between a king enamelled with his robes and jewels, sitting in his chair of state, and his condition in his bed of earth; and yet all this change without the loss of any visible, substantial, since all the limbs remain as they were, without the least sight either of dislocation or diminution. From hence it is, I think, Scaliger defines death to be the cessation of the functions of the soul; as if it were rather a restraint than a missive ill.

When thou shalt see all these things happen to one whose conversation had endeared him to thee; when thou shalt see the body put on death's sad and ashy countenance, in the dead age of night, when silent darkness does encompass the dim light of thy glimmering taper—tell me if thou canst then find a thought of thine, devoting thee to pleasure and the fugitable joys of life?—O what a bubble, what but a wink of life, is man!

When Hadrian asked Secundus what death was, he answered in these several truths: "it is a sleep eternal; the body's dissolution; the rich man's fear: the poor man's wish; an event inevitable; an uncertain journey; a thief that steals away man; sleep's father; life's flight; the departure of the living, and the resolution of all."

Who may not, from such sights and thoughts as these, learn, if he will, both humility and loftiness? the one to vilify the body, the other to advance the soul. As I would not care for too much indulgiating of the flesh, so I would ever be studious for such actions as may appear the issues of a divine and noble soul.

DEATH-BED REPENTANCE.

In "a further continuation" of his Meditations, the Hon. Robert Boyle adduces this Reflection on the great mistake of those that think a death-bed the fittest and opportunest place to begin repentance in: "But sure these men are very little acquainted, either with the disadvantages of a dangerous sickness, or the nature of repentance. 'Tis true that sin and death do more easily frighten one, when they are looked on as both together: but I much doubt whether the being frightened by hell, be sufficient to give a man a well-grounded hope of Heaven: for when we see sin and torment at one view, and so near one to another, 'tis not so easy to be sure which of the two it is that, as we presume, scares the sinner toward Heaven. And surely repentance, which ought to be the change of the whole man, and in some sense the work of the whole life, is very improperly begun, when men have finished that course, which it should have guided them in: nor have men cause to presume, that when God is severely punishing them for their sins, he will vouchsafe them so great a grace as that of repentance, which they would none of till it could not make them serviceable to him. And as for the opportunity 'tis hoped an expiring state may give men for repentance, they must needs be great strangers to great sickness, that can promise themselves so unlikely a matter: who can secure them, that the acuteness of the disease will not invade the brain? and as deliriums and phrensies are not unfrequent in fevers, and other acute diseases, so in case they happened to persevere, the wretched patient is cast into a desperate condition, even on this side the grave, and as near as the *body* is to its dissolution, the *man* may be dead a pretty while before it.

"But supposing he escape these accidents, which make repentance impossible, a dangerous sickness has other circumstances enough to make it very uneasy: for the organical faculties of the mind cannot but be dulled and prejudiced by the discomposure of the spirits, by which their functions are to be exercised; and the sense of pain, the troublesome prescriptions of physicians, the loathsome and bitter potions, the weakening operation of physic, the languishments produced by want of spirits, the restlessness proceeding from heat or want of sleep, the distracted importunities of those interested persons, especially if any of them be suspected to hover about the dying man's bed, as birds of prey that wait for a carcass, the sighs and tears of friends and relations that come to take their last farewell, and to embitter it the lawyer that must be directed to draw up the will, the divine that must be allowed to say something concerning the soul, and the affrighted conscience, that alone brings more disquiet than all the rest put together, do make a dying man's condition so amazing, so dismal, and so distracting, that to think this an opportune time to begin such a work (which may well enough employ the whole man in his calmest state of mind), is a madness as great as any, that even a death-bed can, by the translation of the humors into the brain, occasion; for my part, I think it so wild, and so unadvisable a thing to put off the beginning to provide all graces to a death-bed, that I think it uneasy enough so much as to exercise *then* those that were acquired *before;* men being in that state commonly unable so much as to reap the consolation they have been sowing all along a pious life."

(Our author then considers the condition—that though it be said, a true repentance cannot come too late, yet it is a hard thing to be certain, that so late a repentance is true. He then continues:)

"And as it is difficult, when a man already feels much punishment for sin, and sees himself in danger of more, to discern clearly upon what account it is, that he is sorry for what he has committed; so it must certainly be a state unspeakably anxious and uncomfortable to find one's self dragged to the grave, without knowing whether the last trumpet shall call him thence to heaven or to hell: and if he should be deceived in judging of the validity of his repentance, the fatal error would be remediless, and the mistake far sadder and more horrid than that of the Syrians, who, when they thought they were arrived victorious at Dothan, found themselves at the mercy of their enemies in Samaria, 2 Kings vi. 18. To conclude, he that resolves not to renounce his sins, till he thinks Christ ready to renounce him for them, may very probably lose his soul, and has most certainly lost his ingenuity; and that will appear a very sad loss for a man, that being by death denied the opportunities of actually leading a new and pious life, must derive his comfort from the assurance that he sincerely intends it."

"Still, a death-bed is a wonderful reasoner: many a proud infidel hath it humbled and refuted, without a word, who but a short time before would have defied all the ability of man to shake the foundation of his system. All is well, as long as the curtain is up, and the puppet-show of life goes on; but when the rapid representation draws to a close, and every hope of longer respite is precluded, things will appear in a very different light. Would to God I could say that that great and awful moment were as often distinguished by the dew of repentance as by the groan of despair."

Sir Humphrey Davy has well observed:

The laws of nature are all directed by Divine Wisdom, for the purpose of preserving life and increasing happiness. Pain seems in all cases to precede the mutilation or destruction of those organs which are essential to vitality, and for the end of preserving them; but the mere process of dying seems to be the falling into a deep slumber; and in animals, who have no fear of death dependent upon imagination, it can hardly be accompanied by very intense suffering. In the human being, moral and intellectual motives constantly operate in enhancing the fear of death, which, without these motives in a reasoning being, would probably become null, and the love of life be lost upon every slight occasion of pain or disgust: but imagination is creative with respect to both these passions, which, if they exist in animals, exist independent of reason, or as instincts. Pain seems intended by an all-wise Providence to prevent the dissolution of organs, and cannot follow their destruction. I know several instances in which the process of death has been observed, even to its termination, by good philosophers; the instances are worth repeating. Dr. Cullen, when dying, is said to have faintly articulated to one of his intimates: "I wish I had the power of writing or speaking, for then I would describe to you how pleasant a thing it is to die." Dr. Black, worn out by age, and a disposition to pulmonary hemorrhage, which obliged him to live very low, whilst eating his customary meal of bread and milk, fell asleep, and died in so tranquil a manner, that he had not even spilt the contents of the spoon which he held in his hand. And Sir Charles Blagden, whilst at a social meal with his friends, Monsieur and Madame Berthollet, and Gay Lussac, died in his chair so quietly, that not a drop of the coffee in the cup which he held in his hand was spilt.

THE LAST MOMENTS AND WORDS OF DISTINGUISHED PERSONS.

Some of the following brief accounts of the closing scenes in the lives of men of genius may tend to show how far a predominant passion or favorite pursuit may influence the mind, even in the latest hour of life. In the majority of instances, "the ruling passion strong in death" is found to be exemplified.

Rousseau, when dying, ordered his attendants to place him before the window, that he might once more behold his garden, and bid adieu to nature.

Addison's dying speech to his son-in-law was characteristic enough of the man, who was accustomed to inveigh against the follies of mankind, though not altogether free from some of the frailties he denounced. "Behold," said he to the dissolute young nobleman, "with what tranquillity a Christian can die."

Roscommon uttered, at the moment he expired, two lines of his own version of *Dies iræ*.

Haller died feeling his pulse, and when he found it almost gone, turning to his brother physician, he said, "My friend, the artery ceases to beat," and died.

Petrarch was found dead in his library, leaning on a book.

Bede died in the act of dictating.

Herder closed his career writing an ode to the Deity, his pen on the last line.

Waller died repeating some lines of Virgil.

Metastasio, who would never suffer the word "death" to be uttered in his presence, at last so far triumphed over his fears, that, after receiving the last rites of religion, in his enthusiasm he burst forth into a stanza of religious poetry.

Lucan died reciting some words of his own *Pharsalia*.

Alfieri, the day before he died, was persuaded to see a priest; and when he came, he said to him, with great affability, "Have the kindness to look in to-morrow. I trust death will wait four-and-twenty hours."

Napoleon, when dying, and in the act of speaking to his clergyman, reproved his sceptical physician for smiling, in these words—"You are above these weaknesses, but what can I do? I am neither a philosopher nor a physician; I believe in God, and am of the religion of my father. It is not every one who can be an atheist." The last words he uttered—Head—Army—evinced clearly enough what sort of visions were passing over his mind at the moment of dissolution.

Tasso's dying request to Cardinal Cynthia was indicative of the gloom which haunted him through life: he had but one favor, he said, to request of him, which was that he would collect his works, and commit them to the flames, especially his *Jerusalem Delivered*.

Leibnitz was found dead in his chamber, with a book in his hand.

Clarendon's pen dropped from his fingers when he was sick with the palsy, which terminated his life.

Chaucer died ballad-making. His last production he entitled, "A Ballad made by Geoffry Chaucer on his death-bed, lying in great anguish."

Barthélemy was seized with death while reading his favorite Horace.

Sir Godfrey Kneller's vanity was displayed in his last moments. Pope, who visited him ten days before he died, says, he never saw a scene of so much vanity in his life; he was sitting up in his bed, contemplating the design he was making for his own monument.

Wycherley, when dying, had his young wife brought to his bedside, and having taken her hand in a very solemn manner, said, he had but one request to make of her, and that was, that she would never marry an old man again. There is every reason to believe, though it is not stated in the account, that so reasonable a request could not be denied at such a moment.

"Bolingbroke," says Spence, "in his last illness, desired to be brought to the table where we were sitting at dinner: his appearance was such that we all thought him dying, and Mrs. Arbuthnot involuntarily exclaimed, 'This is quite an Egyptian feast!'" On another authority, he is represented as being overcome by terrors and excessive passion in his last moments; and, after one of his fits of choler, being overheard by Sir Harry Mildmay complaining to himself, and saying, "What will my poor soul undergo for all these things!"

Keats, a little before he died, when his friend asked him how he did, replied, in a low voice, "Better, my friend, I feel the daisies growing over me."

The pious Gerson, the chancellor of the church and university of Paris, had the terror of his last moments assuaged by the prayers of three hundred children supported and educated by his charity, and who were congregated in his house, from the threshold to his bedchamber. "Now, O God," he exclaimed, in a transport of holy joy, as he closed his eyes in death, "thou dost let thy servant depart in peace! The soul that is accompanied to eternity by the prayers of three hundred children, may advance with humble hope into the presence of their Father and their God."

Schiller, when dying, was asked how he felt. "Calmer and calmer," he replied. Perhaps, this serenity was mainly due to the state of his body; for that degree of physical weakness which no longer suffers the will to employ the muscles, but yet arrests not the internal action of the brain, is usually attended by an indescribable calm of mind. If, indeed, the conscience be reconciled to God, it is complete; for then the torment of conflicting affections is over, the soul sees only that it is heir to a rich and eternal inheritance. Thus, a tranquil ecstasy is often witnessed at the death-bed of the Christian:

> Is that a death-bed where the Christian lies?
> Yes, but not his; 'tis Death itself there lies.—*Coleridge.**

Sir James Mackintosh lived like a philosopher, and died like a Christian. Not long before he ceased to speak, his daughter said to him, "Jesus loves you." He answered slowly, pausing between each word, "Jesus Christ—love—the same thing!" After a long silence, he said, "I believe!" She asked, "In God?" He answered, "In Jesus." On her inquiring how he felt, his last word was, "Happy!"

Sir Walter Raleigh, according to the Bishop of Salisbury, who attended him on the scaffold, was "the most fearless of death that ever was known, the most resolute and confident, *yet with reverence and conscience.*"

---

* Dr. Moore states that when the vital flame was flickering, the heart was faltering with every pulse, and every breath was a convulsion, he has said to a dying believer, who had not long before been talking in broken words of undying love, "Are you in pain?" and the reply, with apparently the last breath, was, "It is delightful!" In another person, in whom a gradual disease had so nearly exhausted the physical powers that the darkness of death had already produced blindness, the sense of God's love was so overpowering, that every expression for many hours referred to it in rapturous words, such as, "This is life—this is heaven—God is love—I need not faith—I have the promise." It is easy to attribute such expressions to delirium; but this does not alter their character, nor the reality of the state of the soul which produces them. Whether a dying man can maintain any continued attention to things through his senses, we need not inquire. It is enough for him, if, in the spirit, he possess the peace and joy of believing.—*The Use of the Body in relation to the Mind*, pp. 427, 428.

Maccail, the expiring Scottish probationer, exclaimed, with foretaste of the bliss of Paradise, "Farewell, sun, moon, and stars; farewell, kindred and friends—farewell, world and time—farewell, weak and frail body:—welcome eternity—welcome angels and saints—welcome Saviour of the world, and welcome God, the Judge of all."

"I do not mean to be killed to-day," were the words of "the great" Turenne, a few minutes before he was struck down in battle by a cannon-ball. What short-sightedness!

Edward Moore, in his periodical paper, *The World*, took leave of his readers in a humorous account of his own death, which really took place two months afterward.

George, the first Lord Lyttelton, who, after being a sceptic, became a zealous believer, said to his son-in-law, Lord Valentia, on taking leave of him,—"Be good, be virtuous, my lord, *you must come to this.*"

Bishop Hough's dying words to some of his friends and neighbors who attended him in his last moments were, "We part to meet again, I hope, in endless joys."

A correspondent of *Notes and Queries* has been at the pains of collecting these memorable and note-worthy "last words" of great persons. To these a few additions have been made.

"Tête de l'armée." (Napoleon.)
"I have loved God, my father, liberty." (De Staël.)
"Let me die to the sound of delicious music." (Mirabeau.)
"Is this your fidelity?" (Nero.)
"A king should die standing." (Augustus.)
"I must sleep now." (Byron.)
"Kiss me, Hardy." (Nelson.)
"Don't give up the ship." (Laurence.)
"I'm shot if I don't believe I'm dying." (Thurlow.)
"Clasp my hand, my dear friend, I die." (Alfieri.)
"God preserve the Emperor." (Haydn.)
"Let the light enter." (Goethe.)
"All my possssions for a moment of time." (Elizabeth.)
"What, is there no bribing death?" (Beaufort.)
"Monks, monks, monks!" (Henry VIII.)
"Be serious." (Grotius.)

"In tuas manus, Domine." (Tasso.)

"It is small, very small" (clasping her neck). (Anna Boleyn.)

"I feel as if I were myself again." (Walter Scott.)

"It is well." (Washington.)

"Independence forever." (Adams.)

"A dying man can do nothing easy." (Franklin.)

"Don't let poor Nelly starve." (Charles II.)

"I have endeavored to do my duty." (Taylor.)

"There is not a drop of blood on my hands." (Frederick V.)

"I resign my soul to God, my daughter to my country." (Jefferson.)

"It is the last of earth." (J. Q. Adams.)

"Dont let that awkward squad fire over my grave." (Burns.)

"Lord, make haste." (H. Hammond.)

"Precious salvation." (Sir J. Stonehouse.)

"Remember" (the charge to Archbishop Juxon to bid Charles II. forgive his father's murderers). (Charles I.)

"I shall be happy." (Archbishop Sharp.)

"God's will be done." (Bishop Ken.)

"Amen." (Bishop Bull.)

"I have peace." (Parkhurst.)

"Come, Lord Jesus." (Burkitt.)

"Cease now" (Lady Masham was reading the Psalms). (Locke.)

"I thank God I was brought up in the Church of England." (Bishop Gunning.)

"O Lord, forgive me specially my sins of omission." (Ussher.)

"Lord, receive my spirit." (Ferrar, Cranmer, Hooper, G. Herbert.)

"Thy will be done." (Donne.)

"This day let me see the Lord Jesus." (Jewell.)

"In te speravi: ne confundar in eternum." (Bishop Abbot.)

"God will save my soul." (Burghley.)

"This is death." (George IV.)

"Lord, take my spirit." (Edward VI.)

"What? do they run already? Then I die happy." (Wolfe.)

"God bless you, my dear" (Miss Morris). (Dr. Johnson.)

"What I cannot utter with my mouth, accept, Lord, from my heart and soul." (F. Quarles.)

"Then I am safe." (Oliver Cromwell.)

"Let the earth be filled with His glory." (James, Earl of Derby; Bishop Broughton.)

"I go to my God and Saviour." (P. Heylyn.)

"My days are past as a shadow that returns not." (R. Hooker.)

"Let me hear once more those notes so long my solace and delight." (Mozart.)

"I wish the true principles of the government carried out. I ask no more." (Harrison, ninth President of the United States.)

"For my coming down, let me shift for myself" (on the scaffold). (Sir Thomas More.)

"In me behold the end of this world with all its vanities." (Sir P. Sidney.)

"I do not suffer, my friends; but I feel a certain difficulty in existence." (Fontenelle, in his 100th year.)

THE SOUL GOING FORTH FROM THE BODY.

Sir Thomas Browne refers to this phenomenon when, in his *Religio Medici*, he says: "It is observed, that men sometimes, upon the hour of their departure, do speak and reason above themselves. For then the soul begins to be freed from the ligaments of the body, begins to reason like herself, and to discourse in a strain above mortality."

Sir Kenelm Digby, in his Observations on Sir Thomas Browne's *Religio Medici*, quotes from Roger Bacon, "a separated and unbodied soul:" and Browne mentions a remarkable heresy of the Arabians—"that the souls of men perished with their bodies, but should be raised again at the last day: not that I did absolutely conceive a mortality of the soul, but, if that were (which faith, not philosophy, hath yet thoroughly disproved), and that both entered the grave together, yet I held the same conceit thereof, that we all do of the body, that it rise again. Surely, it is but the merits of our unworthy natures, if we sleep in darkness until the last alarm. A serious reflex upon my own unworthiness did make me backward from challenging this prerogative of my soul; so that I might enjoy my Saviour at the last, I could with patience be nothing almost unto eternity." Origen was called from Egypt to make head against this rising sect of minute philosophers, and so successfully disputed against them in full council, that they abandoned their errors, and returned to the received doctrine of the Church. Origen himself, however, fell into the error, that not only the souls of men, but the devils themselves, should be discharged from tortures after a certain time—" that God would not persist in his vengeance forever, but, after a definite time of his wrath, would release the damned souls from torture." (*Religio Medici.*) But Genebrard endeavors to clear Origen of this charge.

Webster, in his *Display of supposed Witchcraft*, writing of corpses bleeding in the presence of murderers, argues:—" If we physically consider the union of the soul with the body by the mediation of the spirit, then we cannot rationally conceive that the soul doth utterly forsake that union, until by putrefaction, tending to an absolute mutation, it is forced to bid farewell to its beloved tabernacle; for its not operating *ab extra* to our senses, doth not necessarily infer its total absence. And it may be, that there is more in that of *Abel's blood crying unto the Lord from the ground*, in a physical sense, than is commonly conceived, &c."

The appearance of the Departure of the Soul is thus mentioned as a known fact in one of the works of the celebrated mystic, Jacob Böhmen. In *The Three Principles*, chap. 19, "Of the going forth of the soul," he observes:

"Seeing that man is so very earthly, therefore he hath none but earthly knowledge; except he be regenerated in the gate of Deep. He always supposeth that the Soul (at the deceasing of the Body) goeth only out at the Mouth, and he understandeth nothing concerning its deep Essences above the Elements. *When he seeth a blue Vapor go forth out of the Mouth of a dying Man* (which maketh a strong smell all over the chamber), then he supposeth that is the Soul."

In the Folk-lore of *Notes and Queries*, No. 20, a curate of Exeter relates that on visiting a poor man, who was daily expecting his death from a very painful disease, his wife, one morning, informed the narrator that she thought he would have died during the night, and consequently she and her friend unfastened *every lock in the house.* The reason given was—that every bolt or lock fastened was supposed to cause uneasiness to the soul, and hinder its departure; consequently, upon the approach of death, all the boxes, doors, &c., in the house were unlocked.

Another correspondent relates that, according to popular belief, a considerable interval *invariably* elapses between the first semblance of death, and what is considered to be the departure of the soul. About five minutes after the time when death, to all outward appearances, has taken place, "the last breath" may be seen to issue with a vapor or "steam" out of the mouth of the departed. Hogarth, in his Tailpiece, has represented the figure of Time breathing forth his last—a puff of breath, with the word "Finis" proceeding from his mouth!

In some parts of Holland, when a child is dying, persons shade it by the hands from the parents' gaze; the soul being supposed to linger in the body as long as a compassionate eye is fixed upon it. Thus, in Germany, if he who sheds tears when leaning over an expiring friend, or bending over the patient's couch, does but wipe them off, he enhances, they say, the difficulty of death's last struggle. We find this poetical superstition recorded in *Mary Barton, a Tale of Manchester Life.*

In Bishop Hale's *Breathings of the Devout Soul*, we find:

In this life, in this death of the body, O Lord, I see there are no degrees, though differences of time. The man that died yesterday is as truly dead as Abel, the first man that died in the world: and Methuselah, that lived nine hundred and sixty-nine years, did not more truly live, than the child that did but salute, and leave the world. But in the life to come, and the second death, there are degrees: degrees of blessedness, to the glorified; degrees of torments, to the damned; the least whereof is unspeakable, unconceivable. O Thou, Thou art the Lord of Life and Death, keep my soul from those steps that go down to the chamber of death; and once set it, for higher I dare not sue to go, but over the threshold of glory and blessedness.

THE PASSING BELL.

We gather from the two following extracts the object of this bell, which was tolled when the soul was *passing* from this life, and has been described as "the melancholy warning of the death-crier."

In a statute passed towards the reign of Henry VIII., it is ordered "that clarks are to ring no more than the passing bell for poare people, nor less for an honest householder, and he be a citizen; nor for children, maydes, journeymen, apprentices, day-laborers, or any other poare person."

In 1662, the Bishop of Worcester asks in his visitation charge:— "Doth the parish clerk or sexton take care to admonish the living, by tolling of a passing bell, of any that are dying, thereby to meditate of their own deaths, and to commend the other's weak condition to the mercy of God?"—*Annals of Worcester*, 1849.

Sir Walter Scott asserts, in his *Border Minstrelsy*, that the custom was then (1803) still retained in many villages in Scotland.

We find frequent allusions to this practice. Sir Symonds D'Ewes* mentions, in 1624, the bell tolling for an individual whom he visited, and who lived some hours afterward. The canon, however, is express on the subject: "And when any person is passing out of this life, a bell shall be tolled, and the minister shall not then slack to do his last duty." At one period, the sound of the Passing Bell was heard in every parish, and in most of the Visitation Articles the custom was enjoined. Nor can any reasonable objection be raised against it, as it was allowed by the Church of England. The question in Visitation Articles usually appeared in this form: "And when any person is passing out of life, doth he, upon notice given thereof, toll a bell, as hath been accustomed, that the neighbors may thereby be warned to recommend the dying person to the grace and favor of God?" Probably, such a custom would now, by some persons, be called popish; yet few practices were more likely to advance the interests of true religion in a parish.

At Dewsbury, in Somerset, is a sort of Christmas Passing Bell; that is, a bell tolled on Christmas Eve, as at a funeral; and any one asking whose bell it was would be told it was the devil's knell. The moral of this is, that the devil died when Christ was born. The custom was discontinued for many years, but was revived by the vicar in 1828. Among the sweet bells of Dews-

---

* There are few of us who care to recollect our ancestors as *bell-ringers;* but Sir Symonds d'Ewes, who was lord of the manor of Lavenham, in Suffolk, was a learned antiquary, and greatly attached to bell-ringing. Sir Matthew Hale, Lord Chief Justice of the Common Pleas, and William Cecil, Lord High Treasurer of England— were also *bell-ringers.* Indeed, *Campanology*, or *Tintinnalogy*, or the Art of Ringing, was formerly a gentleman's recreation.

bury is the famous "Black Tom of Tothill," which is said to have been an expiatory gift for a murder.

Bishop Hall has this touching Meditation *On the Tolling of a Passing Bell:*

How doleful and heavy is this summons of death! This sound is not for our ears, but for our hearts: it calls us not only to our prayers, but to our preparation; to our prayers, for the departing soul; to our preparation, for our own departing. We have never so much need of prayers, as in our last combat: then is our great Adversary most eager: then are we the weakest: then nature is so over-labored, that it gives us not leisure to make the use of gracious motions. There is no preparation so necessary as for this conflict: all our life is little enough to make ready for our last hour. What am I better than my neighbors? How often hath this bell reported to me, the farewell of many more strong and vigorous bodies than my own; of many more cheerful and lively spirits! And now what doth it, but call me to the thought of my parting? Here is no abiding for me: I must away too.

O Thou, that art the God of Comfort, help thy poor servant that is now struggling with his last enemy. His sad friends stand gazing upon him, and weeping over him; but they cannot succor him: needs must they leave him, to do this great work alone: none, but Thou, *to whom belong the issues of death*, canst relieve his distressed and over-matched soul. And, for me, let no man die without me: as I die daily, so teach me to die once: acquaint me beforehand with that messenger, which I must trust to. *Oh, teach me so to number my days, that I may apply my heart to true wisdom.*

BEAUTY OF DEATH.

He that hath bent him o'er the dead,
Ere the first day of death is fled—
The first dark day of nothingness,
The last of danger and distress—
Before decay's effacing fingers
Have swept the lines where beauty lingers,
And marked the wild angelic air,
The rapture of repose that's there—
The fixed yet tender traits that streak
The languor of the placid cheek—
And but for that sad shrouded eye,
That fires not—wins not—weeps not—now—
And but for that chill, changeless brow,
Whose touch thrills with mortality,
And curdles to the gazer's heart,
As if to him it could impart
The doom he dreads, yet dwells upon—
Yes—but for these—and these alone—

> Some moments—ay—one treacherous hour,
> He still might doubt the tyrant's power,
> So fair—so calm—so softly sealed
> The first—last look—by death revealed.

To these exquisite lines in *the Giaour*, in the context of which the aspect of Greece is compared to a beautiful corpse, Lord Byron appends a note, in which he remarks that "this peculiar beauty remains but a few hours after death." "But (says Mr. Leslie) I have been told, by those in the habit of making casts, that on the second day the expression is generally improved, and even on the third day it is often still finer. I have in several instances been ordered to make drawings of the dead, and though in every case I have entered the room where the body lay somewhat reluctantly, yet I have invariably felt reluctant to quit it."

"At Kreutzberg, near Brunn, there is a church, under the pavement of which lie, in one vault, the bodies of twenty-five monks, in open coffins. The dryness of the air has preserved them from decay, though the last buried has lain there for more than a century. I visited the church with a party of ladies, who at first hesitated to descend into the abode of the dead. We all, however, went down, each carrying a lighted taper, and such was the fascination of this singular scene, that we lingered in it for some time. The air was perfectly pure, and we seemed to be in another world, with its own eternal interests effacing for the time all other interests. It seemed to us a mistake that death should be represented by poets or by painters as a hideous phantom. We could not contemplate those withered faces of old men, for they seemed all old, and think of death otherwise than as a gentle friend. Their attitudes were varied, and all had a kind of grace which, though we knew it to be arranged by their friends, seemed perfectly natural. One, the gardener, had a chaplet of withered leaves round his head. All were clothed in the dress of their order; and their clothes, as well as their bodies, though the last were dried to mummies, appeared to be little decayed."

"Lord Byron says, 'In death from a stab, the countenance preserves its traits of feeling or ferocity, and the mind its bias to the last.' I can only say, that in all the casts I have seen from those whose deaths have been violent or painful, I have noticed the same repose of the features, and the same faint indication of a smile, that assists in constituting the beauty of death in other cases. Causes wholly unconnected with the state of mind or feeling at the time of dissolution, contribute, in individual cases, to beautify the features. The cast taken, very imperfectly, by Dr. Antommarchi, from the face of Napoleon, is more handsome than any bust or portrait of him; and, indeed, has the look of a much younger man than he appears in the latest portraits. This is easily accounted for. Illness has reduced the superabundant fleshiness of the lower part of his face, and brought it back to the condition of an early period; and death, by leaving the mouth slightly open, had destroyed that expression of selfish determination which the thin compressed lips give to every portrait of Napoleon. The profile of the cast is the most perfectly beautiful profile of a man I ever saw; and it should here be noticed that, as in this instance, the beauty added by death to a face originally of very fine proportions, has nothing to do with metaphysical causes, so I believe it is the case in every instance; the faint smile being caused by the last slight convulsion after all consciousness has ceased.

"The *beauty of death* is not easily explicable. How far its strange fascination may arise from the idea suggested of a repose compared with which that of the most tranquil sleep is agitation (says Leslie), I will not pretend to determine. I knew a man of the highest order of mind, a man of fine feelings, but of great simplicity, and far above all affectation, who, standing by the corpse of his wife, said—'It gives me very pleasurable sensations.' And yet, he truly loved her."—*Leslie's Autobiography.*

GRIEF FOR THE DEAD.

Archbishop Whately has these admirable remarks: "As for the grief which a man may be supposed to feel for the loss—the total and final loss—of some who may have been dear to him on earth, I have only this to remark, that a wise and good man in this life, in cases where it is clear that no good can be done by him, strives, as far as possible, to *withdraw* his thoughts from evil which he cannot lessen, but which still, in spite of his efforts, will often cloud his mind. We *cannot*, at pleasure, draw off our thoughts entirely from painful subjects which it is in *vain* to think of. The power to do this completely, when we will, would be a great increase of happiness; and this power, therefore, it is reasonable to suppose, the blest will possess in the world to come, and will be able, *by an effort of the will*, completely to banish and exclude every idea that might alloy their happiness."—*Scripture Revelations.*

It is an exquisite and beautiful thing in our nature, that when the heart is touched and softened by some tranquil happiness or affectionate feeling, the memory of the dead comes over it most powerfully and irresistibly. It would almost seem as though our better thoughts and sympathies were charms, in virtue of which the soul is enabled to hold some vague and mysterious intercourse with the spirits of those whom we dearly loved in life. Alas! how often and how long may those patient angels hover above us, watching for the spell that is so seldom uttered, and so soon forgotten!

It has even been observed that immoderate grief, if it does not exhaust itself by indulgence, easily assumes the character of superstition or weakness, or takes a type of insanity.

There is, in many minds, a fearful presentiment that great happiness cannot be of long duration; but if the prosperous periods of life are those which seem to form the natural climax and terminating point of life, they are those in which we can least bear the loss of others. The sudden removal of one who is in the very midst of his usefulness, in whose success we had "garnered up our hearts," creates a revulsion of feeling which poor humanity can ill support. It is the anticipation of re-union hereafter which throws the only light that can penetrate the gloom of the mourner's mind. He is yet to have a meeting beyond the grave; and whilst this idea mitigates grief, it renders the prospect of death itself less terrible. It was in this way that Mrs. Garrick endeavored to remove the terrors of death, after her loss of the great actor. Boswell tells us that in 1781, when Mrs. Garrick received company for the first time since her husband's death, she talked of him with complacency; and while she cast her eyes on his portrait, which hung over the chimney-piece, said that "death was now the most agreeable object to her."

INTERFERENCES OF THE DEAD WITH THE LIVING.

Isaac Taylor has a remarkable passage on this question, which, he considers, "ought not to be summarily dismissed as a mere folly of the vulgar." He says:

> "In considering questions of this sort, we ought not to listen, for a moment, to those frequent but impertinent questions that are brought forward with the view of superseding the inquiry; such, for example, as these: 'What good is answered by the alleged extra-natural occurrences?'—or, 'Is it worthy of the Supreme Wisdom to permit them?' and so forth. The question is a question, first, of *testimony*, to be judged on the established principles of evidence, and then of *physiology;* but neither of theology nor of morals. Some few human beings are wont to walk in their sleep; and during the continuance of profound slumber, they perform, with precision and safety, the offices of common life, and return to their beds, and yet are totally unconscious, when they awake, of what they have done. Now, in considering this or any such extraordinary class of facts, our business is, in the first place, to obtain a number of instances, supported by the distinct and unimpeachable testimony of intelligent witnesses; and then, being thus in possession of the facts, to adjust them, as well as we can, to other parts of our philosophy of human nature. Shall we allow an objector to put a check to our scientific curiosity on the subject, for instance, of Somnambulism, by saying, 'Some of these accounts have turned out to be exaggerated or totally untrue!' or, 'This walking in the sleep ought not to be thought possible, or as likely to be permitted by the Benevolent Guardian of human welfare?'"—*Physical Theory of Another Life.*

DEATH CUSTOMS.

In many parts of Britain is prevalent a superstition, preserved to us in an aphoristic form in the following distich:

> Happy is the wedding that the sun shines on;
> Blessed is the corpse that the rain rains on.

Otherwise thus:

> Sad is the burying in the sunshine;
> But blessed is the corpse that goeth home in rain.

In Brittany it is commonly believed that if any one draws a likeness of another, and carries it away with him, he holds, at any distance of time or place, an unlimited power over the original, whose death he may cause, at any time, by the destruction of the portrait!

In the Diary of the Rev. John Ward, 1662–1681, we find this curious entry: "Dr. Conyers dissected a person not long ago, that died for love in London; and they found (at least, as they fancied) *the impression of a face upon his heart.*"

ANTIQUITY OF BURIAL CLUBS.

Mr. Kenrick, in his ingenious work on *Roman Sepulchral Inscriptions*, adduces the following evidence of the existence of burial clubs among the Romans from a monument found at Lanuvium, a town of ancient fame for the worship of Juno Sospita, about nineteen miles from Rome, on the Via Appia. The inhabitants of this town appear, out of flattery toward the Emperor Hadrian, in whose reign the marble was erected, to have formed themselves into a college for paying divine honors to Diana and Antinous, with which they strangely combined that of a burial club, not forgetting the festivities which formed so important a part of all acts of religion among the Romans. To prevent disputes, the laws of the association were inscribed on marble, and probably set up in the temple of the two deities. An *amphora* of good wine was to be presented to the club by a new-member, the sum of 100 sesterces (about 15s.) was to be paid as entry money, and five asses (little more than 2d.) per month as subscription. Their meetings were not to take place oftener than once a month. If any one omitted payment for (so many) months (the marble is here mutilated), no claim could be made, even though he had directed it by will. In case of the death of one who had paid his subscription regularly, 300 sesterces (2l. 5s.) were allotted for his funeral expenses, out of which, however, 50 were to be set apart for distribution at the cremation of the body. The funeral was to be a walking one. If any one died more than twenty miles from Lanuvium, and his death was announced, three delegates from the college were to repair to the place where he had died, to perform his funeral, and render an account of it to the people. Fraud was to be punished by a fourfold fine. Twenty sesterces each were to be allowed to the delegates for travelling expenses, going and returning. If the death had taken place more than twenty miles from Lanuvium, and no notice had been sent, the person who had performed the funeral rites was to send a sealed certificate attested by seven Roman citizens, on the production of which the usual sum for the expenses was to be granted. No funeral of a suicide was to take place. There are many other rules tending to preserve order and promote good fellowship, but these are all which relate to the burial club. This curious document is an additional proof how much ancient life resembled modern life, when we obtain a view of it, as it were, *intus domique*, through the medium of its monuments.

"GOD'S ACRE."*

This is a phrase applied to the churchyard, or burial-place, to denote its sanctity. It is, of course, well known that in the ancient days of the Church, these burial-places were formed round the resting-places of famous saints. The same feeling may be traced in later days. The burial-ground appertaining to St. George the Martyr, Queen-square, Bloomsbury, is a long and narrow slip of ground behind the Foundling Hospital. A strong prejudice appears to have existed against this burial-place, and no person was interred here till the ground was broken for the pious Robert Nelson, author of *Fasts and Festivals*, whose character for piety reconciled others to the place, and other interments followed quickly.

There is a similar instance of this veneration in the history of Bunhill Fields, where, in the vault of his friend, Mr. Stradwick, the grocer, on Snow-hill, in whose house he died, is buried John Bunyan, author of *The Pilgrim's Progress*. Modern curiosity has marked the place of his interment with a brief inscription, but his name is not recorded in the Register. So numerous have been, and still are, the dying requests of his admirers to be buried as near as possible to the place of his interment, that it is not possible to obtain a grave near him, the whole surrounding earth being occupied by dead bodies to a very considerable distance.

---

* See an interesting work with this title, by Mrs. Stone.

"People like to be buried in company, and in good company. The Dissenters regarded Bunhill Fields' burial-ground as their *Campo Santo*, and especially for Bunyan's sake. It is said that many have made it their desire to be interred as near as possible to the spot where his remains are deposited."—*Southey*.

EMBLEMS ON TOMBS.

The devices which we see on old tombs distinguish, by their emblematic differences, the dead which they enclose. The legs of crusaders were crossed; the right hand of prelates was raised, as if in benediction ; bishops bore the crozier in the left hand, abbots in their right; less dignified priests bore a chalice ; kings and bishops had gloves on both hands. Officers of State and other noblemen are represented with a glove on the right hand, for the purpose of supporting a hawk, while the other glove is off and is held in the left hand. Lions at the feet typify vigilance and courage; and human heads may be seen under the feet of one of the figures in the Temple Church, denoting infidels slain in the Crusades. Dragons under the feet pierced, as for example by the staves of the abbots of Peterborough, express triumph over the devil; and sometimes an escalop-shell would be engraven under the cross, to denote that the occupant of the tomb had in lifetime performed a pilgrimage to the tomb of St. James at Compostella. There are recorded many instances of bad taste in tombs. It was, for example, a fashion at one time to represent on them a body in a state of corruption. There is one of a Duc de Croye, in a church near Louvain, where a skeleton is represented with the worms preying on it.

ANTISEPTIC BURIAL SOILS.

In certain Burial-places, human bodies are preserved for a century and more, which is attributed to the antiseptic properties of the soil. St. Michan's Vaults, Church Street, Dublin, possess this property. The soil and walls of this crypt are a compound of argillaceous earth and carbonate of lime. This admixture exercises a chemically absorbent influence on all ordinary earthy and atmospheric moisture. Every one knows that moisture is, perhaps, the greatest aid to decomposition. Amid the rains of winter or the heats of summer, the vaults of St. Michan, with the exception of one small chamber, are uniformly free from damp; and the consequence is the phenomenon referred to. The portion which appears damp is destitute of any animal remains but bones. In some of the dry compartments which are rarely opened, the ornamental appendages of certain coffins shine as brilliantly as when originally deposited there—a circumstance which strikingly attests the uncommon aridity of the walls and soil. The floor is covered with dust as dry as that overlying a country road in summer. Beneath the foundation is a bed of silicious sand. A nun, fully robed, was for half a century shown here, in high preservation.

A vault possessing antiseptic properties is also shown beneath the monastic chapel of the Kreutzberg, about two miles from Bonn. Here are the corpses of several poor monks in open coffins, the bodies dressed in cowl and cassock, as on the day of their dissolution. Here they were deposited between the years 1400 and 1718, and the extraordinary state of preservation in which they have remained during that extensive lapse of time has been attributed mainly to the dryness of the sandy soil which surrounds them. The worsted stockings and gray leather shoes of some are undecayed; and the nails upon their bony fingers, and the gray hair on their craniums, are perfect. Notwithstanding the bodies seem to be the size and weight of ordinary thin men, they are so light, that one can be raised with a single finger.*

Sand is an agent for correcting putridity; hence, probably, the practice of strewing floors with sand.

A correspondent of *Notes and Queries* relates (2d S., vi. 156): "When I was a boy I was told, and I heard it with a strange sensation of dread, that if an individual took up a handful of dust thrown from a newly opened grave, he might know whether a good or wicked person had been formerly buried there: for, said the informant, if the dust *stirs* in your hand, you may be sure that it

---

* See the description, by Mr. Leslie, at page 218.

had once formed a portion of the body of a wicked man or woman; for 'the wicked cannot rest anywhere,' not even in the grave!"

DECAY OF THE HUMAN BODY.

When putrefaction commences, there can, of course, be no longer any doubt of the departure of life—premising that the putrefaction is general, and not of a local kind. There is nothing more appalling and humiliating than the decomposition of the dead. We may, indeed, persuade ourselves, that the dead are only silent and immovable; but when changes gradually manifest themselves, and we can no longer recognize the familiar features we have so often looked upon, we see the greatness of that alteration, and feel what it is to die.

The peculiar cadaverous odor of the body is well known to most persons, and the appearances of incipient putrefaction need no explanation. The finer changes are, perhaps, best indicated by the placidity of the cornea, and the loss of transparency in the eye. These can seldom be mistaken by medical men, though death may undoubtedly take place before they are strikingly apparent. Amongst other indications of decomposition, the gravitation and transudation of the blood to the surface on which the body lies are important subjects for consideration, because they have been mistaken by persons ignorant of such matters for indications of injuries and bruises; indeed, they often present lines and marks closely resembling the extravasations produced by blows; hence they are termed sugillations, from the Latin *sugillatio*, a black mark.

M. Bouchut has, in a memoir on apparent death, for which he received a prize of 1,500 francs, replied to these questions: "What are the distinctive characters of apparent death? 2. What are the means to prevent premature interment?"

M. Bouchut states that the *sounds* of the heart, as indicated by the stethoscope, are never entirely wanting, except in real death; and that the longest interval between the loud beats of the heart is about six or seven seconds. He further insists on the complete dilatation of the pupil of the eye as a corroborative sign of death, remarking that, though contracted in the death-struggle, it afterward and speedily becomes dilated; so truly may we say that "*la pupille est la fenêtre de l'âme.*"

Even the alterations which take place after the body is committed to the grave have engaged the attention of medical inquirers. It seems not very probable that the features of the dead can be recognized after fourteen or fifteen days' interment; and in three or four months all vestiges of the face are destroyed.—*Abridged from Harrison on the Medical Aspects of Death.*

EMBLEM OF THE RESURRECTION.

We see the Phœnix, with a glory of rays round its head, perched upon the palm-tree, the Tree of Life, as a symbol of the resuscitated and glorified body, in the mosaics of various Roman apsides, as in those of the churches of the Saints Cosma and Damiano. We also see a similar bird perched upon the Tree of Life in the Paradise represented in the apsis of S. Giovanni Laterano. St. Augustin, however, considered the Peacock to be a symbol of the resurrection of the body, because its flesh was believed to be incorruptible. But the peacock never takes the place of the phœnix in the apsidial mosaics; nor does the phœnix ever take the place of the peacock on Christian sepulchral urns and other monuments.

Dr. Barlow, from whose communication to the *Builder* these observations are quoted, states it to be alleged that when the palm-tree has decayed, the Arabs cut it down to the roots, and burn it on the spot; and the ashes being covered with a layer of earth, a new shoot springs up, which in the course of a few years becomes a strong tree. It would seem that we have here the origin of the fabled phœnix rising renewed from the flames that consumed it, as the bird and the tree bear the same name. This is probably the reason why, in Christian symbolism, the phœnix with a glory of rays was employed to signify the glorified body in the resurrection.

Sir Thomas Browne, among his erudite guesses, describes the

Phœnix as a bird of Paradise, "and alike the emblem of the Resurrection and the Sun:" again, "that it was a palm-tree, and that it was only a mistake upon the homonymy of the Greek word *phœnix*, which signifies a palm-tree."—See Timbs's *Popular Errors Explained*, pp. 117–8.

The Church of St. Giles' in the Fields, London; has a "Resurrection Gate," with an elaborate bas-relief of the Day of Judgment. This curious work of art is stated to have been taken from the lich-gate of the former church.

FLOWERS ON GRAVES.

This rite scarcely belongs to the "Mysteries" of Death; its simplicity being an instinct of every stage of man's life—the very child seeking to

> Pluck the frail flowers that gayly bloom,
> And cast as they fade away,
> In garlands on its mother's tomb.

Or in the more touching couplet describing some children at play among the tombs—

> Alas! unconscious of the kindred earth,
> That faintly echoed to the voice of mirth.

A drooping flower is an emblem of early death, a thought which we remember to have seen amplified in some lines upon two young children of the Rev. Joseph Hamilton, D. D., interred at Hemel Hempstead, in Hertfordshire:—

> As fades the flower in early spring,
>   When tempests sweep the land,
> So droops the tender infant's form
>   When seized by death's cold hand.
> Farewell, sweet babes, the loss is ours,
>   For you are gone to rest;
> The Shepherd has but call'd his lambs,
>   To fold them to his breast.

One who felt acutely the sorrows as well as enjoyed the ecstasies of life, has sung:

> Flowers are the bright remembrancers of youth:
> They waft back with their bland and odorous breath
> The joyous hours that only young life knows,
> Ere we have learn'd that this fair earth hides graves.
> They bring the cheek that's mouldering in the dust
> Again before us, ting'd with health's own rose;
> They bring the voices we shall hear no more,
> Whose tones were sweetest music to our ears;
> They bring the hopes that faded one by one,
> Till naught was left to light our path but faith,
> That we too, like the flowers, should spring to life,
> But not like them again e'er fade or die.—*Lady Blessington.*

Of the Pagan custom of strewing graves with flowers, we find this beautiful record in Virgil; where Anchises, grieving for Marcellus, makes him say:

> Full canisters of fragrant lilies bring,
> Mix'd with the purple roses of the spring;
> Let me with fun'ral flowers his body strew:
> This gift, which parents to their children owe,
> This unavailing gift, at least, I may bestow.

The rose has been for ages the favorite flower for funereal purposes. Among the Greeks, the relatives of the deceased wore garlands of roses during the days of mourning, as emblematical of the shortness of life, which passes as quickly away as would the beauty of those roses which form the mourner's crown. The tombs of the dead were decorated with roses, under the idea that they possessed the power of protecting the remains of the deceased, and were peculiarly acceptable as an offering to their manes. The Greeks also used the amaranthus, which is commonly regarded as the flower now known by the name of "everlasting." Parsley and myrtle were likewise funereal plants. The Romans were so fond of the rose, that we find inscriptions which refer to legacies left in their wills for the express purpose of providing roses, with which their tombs were annually to be decorated. This custom has descended to our times.

Lord Byron writes from Bologna, June 7, 1819: "Here, as in Greece, they strew flowers on the tombs: I saw a quantity of rose-leaves and entire roses scattered over the graves at Ferrara. It has the most pleasing effect you can imagine."

The Romans are considered to have brought this custom into

Flowers on Graves. 225

England: such is the opinion of the Rev. Owen Manning, the historian of Surrey, in which county, at Ockley, it has been, until lately, the custom, from time immemorial, for betrothed lovers to plant rose-trees at the head of the grave of a deceased lover, should either party die before the marriage. Camden describes the churchyard as thickly planted with rose-trees, in his time; Aubrey records the same custom; and John Evelyn, who lived at Wotton Place, near Ockley, thus testifies the observance there —of the maidens yearly planting and decking the graves of their defunct sweethearts with rose-bushes. Now, the Romans were much at Ockley; the Roman road (Stane-street) passes through the village to this day; so that we are inclined to agree with Mr. Manning that the rose-planting at Ockley is a relic of a Roman custom.

At Barnes, in Surrey, on the south bank of the Thames, is an interesting observance of this flower rite. On the south side of the church, between two buttresses, enclosed by wooden rails, a few rose-trees are cultivated, in pursuance of the will of Mr. Edward *Rose*, citizen of London, who, according to a tablet affixed to the church wall, died in 1653, having bequeathed to the parish of Barnes, the sum of 20*l.* for the purchase of an acre of land, from the rent of which the churchwardens were enjoined to keep in repair the paling of the enclosure, and maintain a succession of rose-trees; the surplus funds to be applied for the benefit of the poor.

We find in a poem of the Saxons:

"Mark my hillock with the simple flower."

Shakspeare's Arviragus, in *Cymbeline*, says:

> With fairest flowers,
> Whilst summer lasts, and I live here, Fidele,
> I'll sweeten thy sad grave: thou shalt not lack
> The flower that's like thy face, pale primrose; nor
> The azur'd hare-bell, like thy veins; no, nor
> The leaf of eglantine, whom not to slander,
> Outsweeten'd not thy breath.
> * * * * *
> Yea, and furr'd moss besides, when flowers are none,
> To winter-ground thy corse.

And in *Hamlet* ("that piece of Shakspeare's which appears to have most affected English hearts"), the bewildered Ophelia sings:

> Larded all with sweet flowers;
> Which bewept to the grave did go,
> With true-love showers;

besides which we have the affecting flower-strewing scene.

The appropriateness of spring-flowers is thus touched upon by Herrick:

> Virgins promis'd when I died,
> That they would each primrose-tide,
> Duly morn and evening come,
> And with flowers dress my tomb;
> Having promis'd, pay your debts,
> Maids—and here strew violets.

In Wales, where the custom is observed to this day, the white rose is always planted on the grave of an unmarried female; the red rose is appropriated to any one distinguished for benevolence of character. Here, too, the bed, the coffin, and the grave are also strewed with flowers. We remember the rite at Hemel Hempstead, in 1809, where a young boy dying at school, the corpse and the open coffin, as well as the room in which it was placed, were strewed with flowers; and the schoolfellows of the deceased, 100 in number, were admitted to view the mournful scene.

The decoration of the corpse is mentioned by many poets. Shakspeare, in *Romeo and Juliet*, makes Friar Lawrence say:

> Dry up your tears, and stick your rosemary
> On this fair corse.

Sir Thomas Overbury concludes his character of "the fair and the happy Milkmaid," with: "Thus lived she, and all her care is that she may die in the spring-time, to have store of flowers stuck upon her winding-sheet."

The Vicar of Stratford-upon-Avon, in his Diary (1648—1679), says: "Wee poor men steal into our graves with no greater noise than can bee made by a sprigg of rosemary, or a black ribband."

Gay, in his *Shepherd's Week*—the Dirge Pastoral, &c., has this picture of the funeral of a village maiden:

To show their love, the neighbors far and near,
Followed with wistful look the damsel's bier.
Sprigg'd rosemary the lads and lasses bore,
While dismally the Parson walked before.
Upon her grave the rosemary they threw,
The daisy, butter-flower, and endive blue.
After the good man warn'd us from his text,
That none could tell whose turn would be the next;
He said, that Heaven would take her soul, no doubt,
And spoke the hour-glass in her praise—quite out.
To her sweet memory flowery garlands strung,
O'er her now empty seat aloft were hung.
With wicker rods we fenc'd her tomb around,
To warn from man and beast the hallow'd ground;
Lest her new grave the Parson's cattle raze,
For both his horse and cow the churchyard graze.

In a previous passage from the same poem we find this account of the superstitions of the death-bed, about a century and a half since:

When Blouzelind expired, the wether's bell
Before the drooping flock toll'd forth her knell;
The solemn death-watch click'd the hour she dy'd,
And shrilling crickets in the chimney cry'd;
The boding raven on her cottage sate,
And with hoarse croakings warn'd her of her fate;
The lambkin, which her wonted tendance bred,
Dropped on the plains that fatal instant dead;
Swarm'd on a rotten stick the bees I spy'd,
Which erst I saw when goody Dobson dy'd.

Jeremy Taylor says: "Though I should like a dry death, yet I should not like a dry funeral. Some flowers strewed upon my grave would do well and comely; and a soft shower to turn these flowers into a springing memory, or a fair rehearsal." The pious John Evelyn also says: "We adorn their graves with flowers and redolent plants, just emblems of the life of man, which has been compared in Holy Scripture to those fading beauties, whose roots, being buried in dishonor, rise again in glory."

But the Garden, with its flowers and evergreens, is altogether hallowed ground. "It speaks of a Christian people employed in an occupation, which, above all others, is the parable that conveys the deepest truths to *them*—which daily reads them silent lessons, if their hearts would hear, of the vanity of earthly pomp, of the beauty of heavenly simplicity, and purity, and lowliness of mind, of contentment and unquestioning faith—which sets before them, in the thorns and thistles, a remembrance of their fallen state—in the cedar, and the olive, and the palm-tree, the promise of a better country—which hourly recalls to their mind the Agony and the Burial of Him who made a garden the scene of both, and who bade us mark and consider such things, how they bud, and 'how they grow,' giving us in the vine a type of His Church, and in the fig-tree of His Coming." (*Quarterly Review.*)

In Roman Catholic burial-grounds, the planting and decorating of graves has been a rite from time immemorial; and in the Protestant public cemeteries of England, the same observance is now general; although it was rarely seen in our churchyards.

The yew-tree is indigenous to England; and when its longevity, its durability, and the perpetual verdure it presents, are taken into consideration, it is not surprising that the yew should have been recognized as an emblem of the immortality of the soul, and employed about churchyards to deck the graves of the deceased.

Sin and Punishment.

THE EARLIEST SIN.

THE earliest wide-spread sin was violence. That wilfulness of temper—those germs of wanton cruelty, which the mother corrects so easily in her infant, were developed in the earliest form of human society into a prevailing plague of wickedness. The few notices which are given of that state of mankind do not present a picture of mere lawlessness, such as we find among the mediæval nations of Europe, but of blind, gross ignorance of themselves and all around them. Atheism is possible now, but Lamech's presumptuous comparison of himself with God is impossible, and the thought of building a tower high enough to escape God's wrath could enter no man's dreams. We sometimes see in very little children a violence of temper which seems hardly human; add to such a temper the strength of a full-grown man, and we shall perhaps understand what is meant by the expression that the earth was filled with violence.—*Dr. Temple, on the Education of the World.*

THE GREAT SIN.—DESTRUCTION OF THE OLD WORLD.

Through the transgression of the angels, who were tempted by the beauty of the daughters of Eve to unite themselves to a species only a little lower than their own, the corruption of the human race, and the *enormity* of their crimes before God, were fearfully augmented. A new sin contaminated mankind: a monstrous progeny had birth, powerful for evil beyond ordinary human beings, "mighty men which were of old," and a stain, not arising from Adam's transgression, infected the mixed offspring, each bearing about with him not only a polluted human nature, "naturally engendered," but an unclean spirit, supernaturally engendered.

It may be permitted for us to conjecture that it was *this* offence and stain, beyond all others, which provoked the Almighty to destroy the old world, in order that he might utterly exterminate those semi-angelic families, which else, by gradual intermixture, would have polluted the whole race of man.

The mythologists, many of whose fables were certainly based on authentic traditions, appear to have heard, through the descendants of Noah, of this forbidden intercourse—these "mighty men." They seem to allude to it in the story of the *giants* or *demigods*, the sons of Cœlus and Terra, of heaven and earth, who rebelled against the Ruler of heaven, sought to invade his realms, and were by him cast down and buried beneath the earth.—*Bishop Courtenay on the Future States: Appendix.*

SPECIAL PROVIDENCES.

The followers of Mahomet and the inhabitants of Eastern countries are said to believe in the special interference of Providence in each particular case: hence they value but little human life. If a man is in peril, they do not exert themselves to extricate him; but they argue that if God wishes it, the man will surely die. No reasonable man can doubt the truth of the proposition in this form, but in their neglect they assume the whole case; and the question we have to consider is, whether the Creator does, by a special act, will the death of a man, or any other event which takes place on the globe, or has the world been constructed in obedience to laws? Natural science, deduced from the observation of facts, appears to indicate that every thing in this great globe is governed by fixed and immutable laws, and that nothing happens either by chance, or by the special interposition of Providence, apart from these general views.

One of the three letters written by the Duke of Wellington *from the field of* Waterloo was a brief note, which, having enumerated some who had fallen, ended thus emphatically:—" I have escaped unhurt; the FINGER OF PROVIDENCE WAS ON ME." What the impulse was which dictated these extraordinary words, we leave to the opinion of those who read them. . . . When the dreadful fight was over, the Duke's feelings, kept so long at the highest tension, gave way; and as he moved among the groans of the wounded, and the reeking carnage, and heard the rout of the vanquished and the shouts of the victors, fainter and fainter through the gloom of night, he wept, and soon after wrote the words which we have quoted from his letter. It is in such trying hours that man feels his frail mortality, instinctively turns to God, and referring his actions to the will of Him who guides and governs all things, with reverence says: "The finger of Providence was on me."

It was on the eve of this bloody contest that the great commander uttered these memorable words: "Next to the calamity of losing a battle is that of gaining a victory."

NEMESIS OR RETRIBUTION.

Nemesis Sacra is the Scripture doctrine of Retribution on Earth, or the doctrine of punishment for sin even in this life. The subject has been elaborately investigated in "A Series of Inquiries, Philological and Critical," in which the general conclusions arrived at are thus expressed:

That the afflictions of this life, however they may be overruled in favor of the good, so as to become the instruments of eternal blessedness, are primarily chastisement for sin, agreeably to that famous maxim, "Nisi peccata non flagella."

That retribution is not less apparent in the New Testament than in the Old, among pagans than the believers in revelation.

That probably every transgression, whether committed by the righteous or the wicked, the penitent or impenitent, is punished in a greater or less degree in this life, whether by the positive infliction of evil, or the negation of good. At least, there is no record in Scripture of any grave offence against the law, moral or divine, without the record also of its chastisement. But if there were many, the mere omission would not impugn the truth of the doctrine; for as the holiness of God cannot change, his judicial administration must be in constant activity.

That according to the magnitude of the transgression, so varies the punishment, from the tremendous penalty of excision in the midst of sin to the mildest forms of visitation, but that since both generally fall within the ordinary course of human experience, they pass unobserved.

That in public visitations, while the impenitent are crushed, an opening is made for the escape of the righteous and those disposed to become righteous; or, at any rate, the evil is in some way overruled in their favor.

That when chastisement is not thus overruled, but is permitted to afflict the penitent, that permission is for a gracious purpose. Thus it led David to repentance, and perfected the holiness of Job; it became salvation to Manasseh, and equally so to Nebuchadnezzar; while to the impenitent it is not merely a judgment, but a curse, often involving utter destruction. Thus it proved to Pharaoh and to Ahab, to Ahaziah and Belshazzar. Afflictions, therefore, being to the former evidence of the Divine love—designed to purify from the remaining corruptions within, and to render meet for " the inheritance of the saints in light," —should be welcomed not only with gratitude but with joy. In many cases they are a privilege as well as a blessing: "For unto you it is given in behalf of Christ, not only to believe on Him, but also to suffer for His sake."

That there are afflictions which bring with them more joy than sorrow. What Christian deserving of the name has not felt the keen thorns of repentance? And who that has felt them, would exchange them for the most exquisite of worldly pleasures?

That though we read much in the New Testament of the sufferings of Christ's followers, as if they were inseparable from the profession of Christianity, by far the greater portion of them must be attributed to times of peculiar trial, when the Jews passed from country to country to move the Gentiles against the new converts, rather than to the inevitable lot of the Christian in every age and country. In ordinary times, he has all the advantages of the worldling, and many of which the worldling never dreamed. Eternal truth assures us that "godliness is profitable for all things, having the promise of the life that now is, as well as of that which is to come."

That unless we could read the heart, and comprehend in all its details the moral state of a man—whether affliction is likely to harden or improve him—we cannot tell whether any special manifestation of it be designed in judgment or in mercy. Owing, however, to the mixed character of every human being, we may safely assume that it generally partakes in a greater or less degree of both. We have sinned, and therefore we are punished: we often sigh after greater purity, and therefore the very chastisement is made instrumental to that effect.

It should, however, be added, that although the author of the above work has exhibited in it much learning and critical acumen, his reasoning is, in many cases, based upon bold alterations of the authorized version of the Scriptures which will be much questioned by scholars.

Nemesis, in the Greek mythology, is a female divinity, who appears to have been regarded as the personification of the righteous

Representations of the Devil. 233

anger of the gods. Herodotus was deeply impressed with an ever-present Nemesis, which allows no man to be very happy, or long happy with impunity. It has also been described as a degree of good fortune sure to draw down ultimately corresponding intensity of suffering from the hands of the envious gods. Or, in other words, it is that every-day presentiment which forebodes suffering or evil as sure to follow any piece of good fortune.

Mr. J. A. St. John, in his able work, *The Nemesis of Power*, interprets Nemesis as "the personification of Justice, and as, therefore, engaged equally in rewarding and in punishing. Her movements are slow, but irresistible; and she is ever at work in human society, insuring ultimate triumph to the Good, and perdition to the Wicked. She may be regarded, therefore, as the inseparable attendant on Power, to uphold and encourage it when exercised for the benefit of mankind, to repress and chastise it when perverted to their injury or destruction."

REPRESENTATIONS OF "THE DEVIL."

The devil, as he has been commonly *depicted*, is a form of a composite character, chiefly derived from the classical superstitions of Greece and Rome.

The devil, as usually described, and still in magic-lantern exhibitions portrayed, is cloven-footed and horned, tailed and black, and carries a pitchfork which corresponds with the two-pronged sceptre of Pluto, King of Hell. Mythologists make the important distinction, that the sceptre of Neptune, indeed, was a trident, or had three teeth; but the sceptre of Pluto had only *two*. Not only his pitchfork but his blackness, the devil owes to Pluto; who, from his disadvantageous position beneath the surface, is named Jupiter *niger*, the black Jupiter. (*Sen.*) Cf. "*atri* janua Ditis" (*Virg.*), "nigri regia cæca dei," (*Ov.*)

The tail, horns, and cloven feet of the evil one are due to the Greek satyri, and to their equivalents the Roman fauni. These, as we all know, had *horns*, and *tails*, and *cloven feet*. But be it borne in mind, as a connecting link, that the word rendered "satyrs" in the Old Testament, has by some been understood to signify demons or *devils*. (Is. xiii. 21; xxxiv. 13.) Hence the confusion of the attributes.

Considering the many fearful representations of Satanic power which we find in Scripture, does it not signally indicate the influence of folk-lore, and the abiding operation of popular tradition, when we thus find our worst enemy known vernacularly to this day rather as the embodiment of bygone superstitions, than as a spiritual adversary, not to be combated save by weapons drawn from the Christian armory?—*Notes and Queries*, 2d S., No. 201.

In the year 1789, there appeared in England a translation from the French of a Jesuit, Bougeant, entitled *A Philosophical Amusement upon the Language of Beasts*. Bougeant was sent to the prison of La Flèche for publishing this work, but was soon released. His theory is, that the soul of every living animal, man excepted, is *a devil:* every fly, every locust, every oyster, every infusorium, is animated by a devil. He admits transmigration, or the number of evil spirits in his system would be perfectly bewildering.

The personality and existing power of Satan seem to be very much lost sight of in the present day, though plainly declared in Scripture, which always represents him as being now at large, as "Prince of the power of the air,"—while the current tradition has him now bound in Hell, into which he is to be cast at a time yet future, according to the testimony of all Scripture. People are thus put off their guard against his wiles, and led captive by him at his will.—See, on this subject, generally, a very valuable lecture delivered to a Society in Cork, by the Rev. M. Chester, Vicar of Ballyclough, Mallow—and an essay by Mr. Maitland, of Gloucester, on the same subject.—Note to *Truths for the Times: On the Intermediate State.* By the Rector of Clonmore. 1860.

PICTURE OF HELL.—UTTER DARKNESS.

Cowley, in his *Davideis*, book i., sings:

> Beneath the silent chambers of the earth,
> Where the sun's fruitful beams give metals birth,
> Where he the growth of fatal gold does see,
> Gold which above more influence has than he;

Picture of Hell—Utter Darkness.

> Beneath the dens where unfletcht tempests lie,
> And infant winds their tender voices try,
> Beneath the mighty ocean's wealthy caves,
> Beneath the eternal fountain of all waves,
> Where their vast court the mother-waters keep,
> And undisturb'd by moons in silence sleep,*
> There is a place deep, wondrous deep, below,
> Which genuine night and horror does o'erflow;
> No bound controls th' unwearied space, but Hell,
> Endless as those dire pains that in it dwell.†
> Here no clear glimpse of the Sun's lovely face
> Strikes through the solid darkness of the place;
> No dawning morn does her kind reds display;
> One slight weak beam would here be thought the day.

In a previous Ode—*The Plagues of Egypt*—Cowley has this passage upon the fate of Pharaoh:

> What blindness or what darkness did there e'er
> Like this undocil King's appear?
> What e'er but that which now does represent,
> And paint the crime out in the punishment?
> From the deep baleful caves of hell below,‡
> Where the old mother Night does grow,

---

* To give a probable reason of the perpetual supply of waters to fountains, it is necessary to establish an abyss or deep gulf of waters, into which the sea discharges itself, as rivers do into the sea, all which maintain a perpetual circulation of water, like that of blood in a man's body; for to refer the originality of all fountains to condensation, and afterwards dissolution of vapors upon the earth, is one of the most unphilosophical opinions in all Aristotle. And this abyss of waters is very agreeable to the Scriptures. Jacob blesses Joseph with the blessings of the heavens above, and with the blessings of the deep beneath; that is, with the dew and rain of heaven, and with the fountains and rivers that arise from the deep; and Esdras, conformably to this, asks, what habitations are in the heart of the sea, and what veins in the root of the abyss? So, at the end of the Deluge, Moses says that God stopt the windows of heaven, and the fountains of the abyss.

And undisturb'd by moons in silence sleep. For I suppose the moon to be the principal if not the sole cause of the ebbing and flowing of the sea, but to have no effect upon the waters that are beneath the sea itself.

† This must be taken in a poetical sense; for else, making Hell to be in the centre of the earth, it is far from infinitely large or deep; yet, on my conscience, wherever it be, it is not so strait, as that crowding and sweating should be one of the torments of it, as is pleasantly fancied by Bellarmin. Lessius, in his book *De Morib. Divinis*, as if he had been there to survey it, determines the diameter to be just a Dutch mile. But Ribera (upon and out of the Apocalypse) allows Pluto a little more elbow-room, and extends it to 1,600 furlongs, that is, 200 Italian miles. Virgil (as good a divine for this matter as either of them) says, it is twice as deep as the distance betwixt heaven and earth. Hesiod is more moderate. Statius puts it very low, but he is not so punctual in the distance: he finds out a hell beneath the vulgar one, which Æschylus mentions also. The Scripture terms it *Utter Darkness*.

The room in St. James's Palace, formerly appropriated to the game of Hazard, was remarkably dark, and conventionally called, by the inmates of the palace, "Hell"; whence, and not, as generally supposed, from their own demerits, the term became applied to gaming-houses generally.

‡ Chap. v. 21. Even darkness that may be felt. The Vulgar, *Tum densa* (tens-

Substantial Night, that does declaim
    Privation's empty name,
Through secret conduits monstrous shapes arose,
Such as the Sun's whole force could not oppose,
    They with a solid cloud
    All heaven's eclipsed face did shroud.
Seem'd with large wings spread o'er the sea and earth,
To brood up a new chaos his deformed birth.
And every lamp and every fire,
Did at the dreadful sight wink and expire,
To the empyrean source all streams of light seem'd to retire,
The living men were in their standard houses buried;
    But the long night no slumber knows,
    But the short death finds no repose.
Ten thousand terrors through the darkness fled,
And ghosts complain'd, and spirits murmured;
And fancie's multiplying sight
Viewed all the scenes invisible of night.

THE WHEEL OF ETERNAL PUNISHMENT.

As the wicked (says Drexelius) delight to consume their days in a circle of pleasure, God will appoint them a circle, but it shall be a circle of torments, which will never have an end. This was foretold by holy David: "Thine arrows," says he, "went abroad; the voice of thunder was heard round about." (Ps. lxxvii. 17, 18.) Famine, war, pestilence, disease, calamities, death, and all other afflictions, under which we often languish in this life, are the arrows of the Lord; these, however, soon fly over us; they swiftly pass from one another; but the voice of His thunder, the voice of His anger and heavy displeasure, like a wheel that is always in motion, shall sound about the infernal regions from everlasting to everlasting.*

---

bræ) *ut palpari queant.* Whether this darkness was really in the air, or only in their eyes, which might be blinded for the time; or whether a suspension of light from the act of illumination in that country; or whether it were by some black, thick, and damp vapor which possessed the air; it is impossible to determine. I fancy that the darkness of hell below, which is called *Utter Darkness*, arose, and overshadowed the land; and I am authorized by the *Wisdom of Solomon*, chap. xvii. v. 14, where he calls it as Night that came upon them out of the bottom of inevitable hell; and therefore was the more proper to be (as he says after) as an image of that darkness which should afterwards receive them.

* Hence the mythological fable of the punishment of Ixion, the son of Phlegyas, King of Thessaly, who treacherously murdered his father-in-law. For this crime he was abhorred and shunned by the neighboring princes, when Jupiter, from pity, took him up to heaven. Provoked at his ingratitude and criminality, the sovereign of

The Wheel of Eternal Punishment.

This wheel, as if filled with gunpowder, when once it takes fire, shall burn to all eternity. "A fire is kindled in mine anger, and shall burn unto the lowest hell." (Deut. xxxii. 22.) There is another circle which is likewise eternal,—a continual changing from the extremes of heat and cold. "Drought and heat consume the snow-waters, and so does the grave those which have sinned." (Job xxiv. 19.) This is more expressly intimated to us by the "weeping and gnashing of teeth," which are mentioned by St. Matthew.

Upon the above passage the Rev. H. P. Dunster, the editor of D. Dunster's translation of the *Reflections on Eternity of Jeremiah Drexelius*, notes:

"That a continual changing from the extremes of heat and cold forms a portion of the punishment of the damned is a very common notion among the old writers, and is founded upon one or two passages in holy writ." The idea has been beautifully embodied by Milton, in *Paradise Lost*, b. ii.:

> Thither by harpy-footed fairies hal'd
> At certain revolutions, all the damn'd
> Are brought; and feel by turns the bitter change
> Of fierce extremes, extremes by change more fierce,
> From beds of raging fire to starve in ice
> Their soft ethereal warmth, and there to pine
> Immovable, in fix'd and frozen round,
> Periods of time, thence hurried back to fire.

Shakspeare also describes the same, in *Measure for Measure*, Act. iii.

> Ay, but to die, and go we know not where;
> To lie in cold obstruction, and to rot;
> This sensible warm motion to become
> A kneaded clod; and the delighted spirit
> To bathe in fiery floods, or to reside
> In thrilling regions of thick-ribbed ice.

Olympus struck him to Tartarus by lightning, and ordered Mercury to tie him with serpents to *a wheel, which, turning continually round*, rendered his punishment eternal;

> Ixion and Pirithous I could name,
> And more Thessalian chiefs of mighty fame.
> *Dryden's Virgil*

THE FALLEN ANGEL.

With admirable union of pathos and sublimity has Milton represented the fallen angel exclaiming,—

> Farewell, happy fields,
> Where joys forever dwell; Hail, horrors, hail
> Infernal world! and thou profoundest Hell,
> Receive thy new possessor; one who brings
> A mind not to be chang'd by place or time.

The Crucifixion of our Lord.

CRUCIFIXION was the common mode of punishment among the Persians, Carthaginians, and Romans; and the latter, at the urgent and tumultuous solicitations of the Jews, were the executioners in the Crucifixion of Jesus Christ.

The cross was the punishment inflicted by the Romans—on servants who had perpetrated crimes; on robbers; assassins; and rebels; among which last Jesus was reckoned, on the ground of his making himself *King* or Messiah (Luke xxiii. 1–5, 13–15).

The words in which the sentence was given, were as follows: "*Thou shalt go to the cross.*" The person to be punished was deprived of all his clothes, excepting something around the loins. In this state of nudity, he was beaten, sometimes with rods, but more generally with whips. Such was the severity of this flagellation that numbers died under it. Jesus was crowned with thorns, and made the subject of mockery; but nothing of this kind could be legally done, or, in other words, insults of this kind were not among the ordinary attendants of crucifixion. They were owing, in this case, solely to the petulant spirit of the Roman soldiers.

The criminal, having been beaten, was subjected to the further suffering of being obliged to carry the cross himself to the place of punishment, which was commonly a hill near the public way, and out of the city. The place of crucifixion at Jerusalem was a hill to the north-west of the city.

The cross, *a post*, otherwise called *the unpropitious or infamous tree*, consisted of a piece of wood erected perpendicularly, and intersected by another at right angles near the top, so as to resemble the letter T. The crime for which the person suffered, was inscribed on the transverse piece near the top of the perpendicular one.

There is no mention made in ancient writers of any thing on which *the feet* of the person crucified rested. Near the middle, however, of the perpendicular beam, there projected a piece of wood, on which he *sat*, and which served as a support to the body; the weight of which might otherwise have torn away the hands from the nails driven through them. Here we see the ground of certain phrases—as, " To ride upon the cross;" "to be borne upon the cross;" "to rest upon the sharp cross," &c.

The cross, which was erected at the place of punishment, and firmly fixed in the ground, rarely exceeded 10 feet in height. The nearly naked victim was elevated to the small projection in the middle; the hands were then bound by a rope round the transverse beam, and nailed through the palms. Hence the expressions: "to mount upon the cross;" "to leap upon the cross;" "to bring one upon the cross," &c.

The Jews, in the times of which we are speaking, viz., whilst they were under the jurisdiction of the Romans, were in the habit of giving the criminal, before the commencement of his sufferings, a medicated drink of wine and myrrh. (Prov. xxxi. 6.) The object of this was to produce intoxication, and thereby render the pains of crucifixion less sensible to the sufferer. This beverage was refused by the Saviour, for the obvious reason that he chose to die with the faculties of his mind undisturbed and unclouded. It should be remarked that this sort of drink, which was, probably, offered out of kindness, was different from the vinegar, which was subsequently offered to the Saviour by the Roman soldiers. The latter was a mixture of vinegar and water, denominated *posca*, and was a common drink for soldiers in the Roman army.

The degree of anguish was gradual in its increase, and the crucified person was able to live under it, commonly till the third, and sometimes till the seventh day. Pilate, therefore, being surprised at the speedy termination of the Saviour's life, inquired in respect to the truth of it of the centurion himself, who commanded the soldiers. In order to bring their life to a more speedy termination, so that they might be buried on the same day, the bones of the two thieves were broken with mallets; and in order to ascertain whether Jesus was really dead, or whether he had merely fallen

The Crucifixion of our Lord. 241

into a swoon, a soldier thrust his lance into his side (undoubtedly his *left* side), but no signs of life appeared. If he had not been previously dead, a wound of this kind in his side would have put a period to his life, as has been shown, both by the physician Eschenbach, and by Gruner. The part pierced was the *pericardium:* hence lymph and blood flowed out.

There is sufficient proof that the physical cause of the death of our blessed Saviour was the rupture of His sacred heart, caused by mental agony. Dr. Macbride, in his *Lectures on the Diatessaron*, quotes from the *Evangelical Register* of 1829 some observations of a physician, who considers the record concerning the blood and water as explaining (at least to a mere scientific age) that the real cause of the death of Jesus was *rupture of the heart, occasioned by mental agony*. Such rupture, it is stated, is usually attended by instant death, without previous exhaustion, and by the effusion into the pericardium of blood, which, in this particular case, though scarcely in any other, separates into its two constituent parts, so as to present the appearance commonly termed blood and water. Thus the prophecy, "Reproach hath broken my heart" (Psalm lxix. 20), was fulfilled, as were so many others, in the momentous circumstances of the Crucifixion, to the very letter.

Dr. Stroud, by the publication, in 1847, of his *Treatise on the Physical Cause of the Death of Christ*, is considered to have thrown a new light upon this solemn inquiry. In this work, the doctor's application of the science of physiology is brought into juxtaposition with the light of revelation; and the two establish the conclusion, that the bursting of the heart from mental agony was the physical cause of the death of Christ. (Selected and condensed from three communications to *Notes and Queries*, 2d Series, No. 25.)

The Head, the Hope, the Supporter of those who gave their bodies to be burnt drank Himself of a bitter cup. Of all the devices of cruel imaginations, Crucifixion is the master-piece. Other pains are sharper for a time, but none are at once so agonizing and so long. One aggravation, however, was wanting, which, owing to the want of knowledge in painters, is still, we believe, commonly supposed to have belonged to the punishment. The weight of the body was borne by a ledge which projected from the middle of the upright beam, and not by the hands and feet, which were probably found unequal to the strain. The frailty of man's frame comes at last to be its own defence; but enough remained to preserve the pre-eminence of torture to the cross. The process of nailing was exquisite torment, and yet worse in what ensued than in the actual infliction. The spikes rankled, the wounds inflamed, the local injury produced a general fever, the fever a most intolerable thirst; but the misery of miseries to the sufferer was, while racked with agony, to be fastened in a position which did not permit him even to writhe. Every attempt to relieve the muscles, every instinctive movement of anguish, only served to drag the lacerated flesh, and wake up new and acuter pangs; and this torture, which must have been continually aggravated until advancing death began to lay it to sleep, lasted on an average two or three days.—*Quarterly Review*.

With these harrowing details in the mind's eye, a painting of the Crucifixion is sometimes viewed by unthinking persons, who ill appreciate the painter's art, and least of all, Christian art,—such persons, we' say, look upon this sublime work merely as a representation of physical suffering. We have heard Albert Durer's grand picture of the Crucifixion, in one of the churches of Nurenberg, and made familiar to us by the finely executed German prints, objected to on the above account; but the mind of the devout Christian regards it not as a scene on earth, but "as the universal frame of Nature giving testimony to Christ's divinity." (See *Things not generally Known*, First Series, page 98.)

The Socrates of Plato blessing the executioner who in tears administered to him the cup of poison, is a noble conception: but how poor compared with Jesus, the Son of God, "in the midst of excruciating tortures praying for his merciless tormentors!" How touchingly are these sufferings described in the following stanzas from "Christ's Passion," by Cowley, "taken out of a Greek Ode, written by Mr. Masters, of New College, in Oxford:"

> Methinks I hear of murther'd men the voice,
> Mix'd with the murtherers' confused noise,
>   Sound from the top of Calvary;
> My greedy eyes fly up the hill, and see
> Who 'tis hangs there the midmost of the three:
>   Oh, how unlike the others He!
> Look how he bends his gentle head with blessings from the tree!
> His gracious hands ne'er stretch'd but to do good,
>   Are nail'd to the infamous wood;
>   And sinful man does fondly bind
> The arms, which he extends t' embrace all human kind.

Unhappy man, canst thou stand by, and see
  All this, as patient as he?
  Since he thy sins does bear,
  Make thou his sufferings thine own,
  And weep, and sigh, and groan,
  And beat thy breast, and tear
  Thy garments, and thy hair,
  And let thy grief, and let thy love
  Through all thy bleeding bowels move.

Dost thou not see thy Prince in purple clad all o'er,
  Not purple brought from the Sidonian shore
    But made at home with richer gore?
Dost thou not see the roses, which adorn
  The thorny garland by him worn?
  Dost thou not see the livid traces
  Of the sharp scourge's rude embraces?
  If thou feelest not the smart
  Of thorns and scourges in thy heart,
  If that be yet not crucify'd,
Look on his hands, look on his feet, look on his side.

Open, oh! open wide the fountains of thine eyes,
  And let 'em call
Their stock of moisture forth, where it lyes,
  For this will ask it all.
  'Twould all (alas!) too little be
  Though thy salt tears came from a sea:
  Canst thou deny Him this, when He
Has open'd all his vital springs for thee?
Take heed; for by his side's mysterious flood
  May well be understood
That He will still require some waters to his blood.

We add two commemorations in meditative verse:

LOQUITUR CRUCIFIXUS.

    O man, look what shame for thee
    Willingly I take on me:
    See my bodie scourged round,
    That it forms but all one wound,
    Hanging up 'twixt earth and sky,
    Mocked and scorned by all goes by.
    See my arms stretched wide and open,
    And my sinews torne and broken.
    See upon the cross I hang,
    View these nails with bitter pang,
    Which my own weight doth not tear,
    But thy weighty sins I bear.

The Crucifixion of our Lord.

See my head, O me, forlorne,
Pierced deepe with cruel thorne,
Which so long thereon hath stood
That the twig runs down with blood.
View my feet, and see my side,
Pierced and plowed with furrows wide.
See, all comfort from me taken,
Both of heaven and earth forsaken;
And not one, with word or deed,
Pities me while here I bleed.
Yea, they all that stand in hearing,
Mocke me for my patient bearing,
And with scoffs augment my sore,
When with bitter paine I roar.
Eli! Eli! I am dying!
Hark! they mocke me too for crying.
This I beare for thine amiss:
Was there ever paine like this?
Yea, and I do most fear that,
Lest thou, man, shouldst prove ingrat.
Now thou dost but make me smart;
But in that thou killst my heart.

From " Diuers Deuout and Zealous Meditations."—Harleian MSS.

THE CROSSE OF CHRIST.

Rise, O my soul, with thy desires to heaven,
  And with divinest contemplation use
Thy time, where time's eternity is given;
  And let vain thoughts no more my thoughts abuse,
But down in midnight darkness let them lie;
So live thy better, let thy worst thoughts die.

And thou, my soul, inspired with holy flame,
  View and review, with most regardful eie,
That holy crosse, whence thy salvation came,
  On which thy Saviour and thy sin did die;
For in that sacred object is much pleasure,
And in that Saviour is my life, my treasure.

To Thee, O Jesu! I direct mine eies,
  To thee my hands, to Thee my humble knees;
To thee my heart shall offer sacrifice,
  To thee my thoughts, who my thoughts only sees;
To thee myself—myself and all, I give;
To thee I die, to thee I only live.—*Sir Walter Raleigh.*

KNOWLEDGE OF GOD BEFORE THE TIME OF CHRIST.

Not a single philosopher had any idea of a God of such an exalted character, as to be the agent in the construction of the Universe, till Anaxagoras, the disciple of Hermotimus. This philosopher came to Athens in the year 456 before Christ, and first taught that the world was organized or constructed by some *mind*, or mental being, out of matter, which it was supposed had always existed. Socrates, Plato, and others, adopted, illustrated, and adorned this opinion.

Aristotle, on the contrary, supposed the world to have existed *in its organized form* eternally, and that the Supreme Being, who was co-existent, merely put it in motion.

The Epicureans believed that a fortuitous concurrence of atoms was the origin of all things. Many were *atheists;* many were *sceptics,* who doubted and assailed every system of opinions.

Those who maintained the existence of a framer or architect of the world (for no one believed in a *creator* of it), supported the opinion of the existence of *an animating principle in matter,* which originated from the supreme architect, and which regulated the material system.

Things of minor consequence, especially those which influenced the destiny of man, were referred by all classes to the government of the *gods,* who were accordingly the objects of worship, and not the Supreme Architect. Paul gives a sufficiently favorable representation of this defective knowledge of God. (Rom. i. 19-24.) After all, it may be the subject of an inquiry, whether Anaxagoras or Hermotimus had not learnt some things respecting the God of the Hebrews from those Jews, who were sold as slaves, by the Phœnicians, into Greece (Joel iii. 6); or from the Phœnicians themselves, who traded in Ionia and Greece; and whether these philosophers did not thus acquire that knowledge, which was thought to have originated with themselves. Perhaps they derived their notions of an Eternal Architect from the doctrine of the Persians respecting Hazaraum, or *the endless succession of time,* and Ormuz, who acted the part of the creator of the world. However this may be, we observe on this topic—

1. That the Hebrews remained firm to their religion, *before* their acquaintance with Grecian philosophy, although many receded from it after forming such an acquaintance.

2. The philosophic doctrine respecting the architect of the world rested on arguments of so subtle a kind, that they could not have been understood by the Jewish populace, and therefore could not have been applied by them, to confirm their minds in religious truth. According to Cicero, *De Natura Deorum*, lib. i. 6, such was the contention, even among the learned, with respect to the *doctrine of the gods*, that those who had the most strength and confidence on their side were compelled to *doubt.—Dr. Jahn's Manual of Biblical Antiquities*, pp. 862–3.

"CHRIST THE MORAL SAVIOUR."

Baron Bunsen, whose Biblical Researches occupy so large a share of the public mind, stands at the furthest pole from those who find no divine footsteps in the Gentile world. He believes in Christ, because he first believes in God and in mankind. In this he harmonizes with the Church Fathers before Augustin, and with all our deepest Evangelical schools. In handling the New Testament he remains faithful to his habit of exalting spiritual ideas, and the leading characters by whose personal impulse they have been stamped on the world. Other foundation for healthful mind or durable society he suffers no man to lay, save that of Jesus, the Christ of God. In Him he finds brought to perfection that religious idea which is the thought of the Eternal, without conformity to which our souls cannot be saved from evil. He selects for emphasis such sayings as, "*I came to cast fire upon the earth, and how I would it were already kindled! I have a baptism to be baptized with, and how am I straitened until it be accomplished!*" In these he finds the innermost mind of the Son of Man, undimmed by the haze of mingled imagination and remembrance, with which his awful figure could scarcely fail to be at length invested by affection. The glimpses thus afforded us into the depth of our Lord's purpose, and his law of giving rather than of receiving, explain the wonder-working power with which he wielded the truest hearts of his generation, and correspond to his life and death of self-sacrifice. This recognition of Christ as the moral Saviour of mankind may seem to some Baron Bunsen's most obvious claim to the name of Christian.—*Dr. Williams ; Essays and Reviews.*

[Christian Charles Bunsen, the profound scholar, passed from among us, at a patriarchal age, at Bonn, on Nov. 28, 1860, and was buried on Dec. 1. The coffin was wreathed with evergreens, intermingled with garlands of flowers, most of them presented by friends ; besides a bunch of flowers and a wreath which the Princess of Prussia had a few days previously sent to the Baron as a mark of sympathy and remembrance. The coffin being placed in the centre of the library, and the clergy and mourners having arrived, a favorite hymn of the Baron was played on the organ : the body was then borne by the handles by his sons, son-in-law, and secretaries, who were relieved by students of the University, and was thus carried to the grave, where the family and connections of the deceased sprinkled earth upon the coffin ; it was then left on the platform over the grave, covered with flowers, and not lowered to its last resting place till all the mourners had departed.

The End of the World Foretold.

An epidemic terror of the end of the world has several times spread over the nation. The most remarkable was that which seized Christendom about the beginning of the eleventh century, when in France, Germany, and Italy, fanatics preached that the thousand years prophesied in the Apocalpyse, as the term of the world's duration, were about to expire, and that the Day of Judgment was at hand. This delusion was discouraged by the Church, but it spread rapidly among the people. The scene of the Last Judgment was expected to be at Jerusalem, where, in the year 1000, a host of pilgrims, smitten with terror as with a plague, awaited the coming of the Lord.

"There may," says Dr. Williams, "be a long future during which the present course of the world shall last. Instead of its drawing near the close of its existence, as represented in Millenarian or Rabbinical fable, and with so many more souls, according to some interpretations of the Gospel of Salvation, lost to Satan in every age and in every nation, than have been won to Christ, that the victory would evidently be on the side of the Fiend, we may yet be only at the commencement of the career of the great Spiritual Conqueror even in this world. Nor have we any right to say that the effects of what He does upon earth shall not extend and propagate themselves in worlds to come. But under any expectation of the duration of the present secular constitution, it is of the deepest interest to us, both as observers and as agents, placed evidently at an epoch when humanity finds itself under new conditions, to form some definite conception to ourselves of the way in which Christianity is henceforward to act upon the world which is our own."—*Essays and Reviews.*

The Epistle of St. James, from his prophetical office, possesses a special interest from its conveying to us a picture of the end of the world. Dr. Wordsworth, in his Commentary upon this Epistle, says:

"The last days of Jerusalem are, as we know from Christ Himself, prophetical and typical of the last days of the world. The sins of the last days of Jerusalem will be the sins of the last days of the world. Hollow professions of religion, empty shows and shadows of faith, partiality and respect of persons, slavish idolatry of riches, observance of some of God's commandments, with open and impious defiance of others; arrogant assumption of the office of religious teaching, without due call and authority; encouragement and patronage of those who set themselves up to be spiritual guides; sins of the tongue, evil speaking against man and God; envying and strife, factious and party feuds, wars and fightings; adulteries, pride, and revelry; low worldliness, and presumptuous self-confidence; a Babel-like building up of secular plans and projects, independently of God's will, and against it; vain-glorious display of wealth; hardheartedness toward those by whose industry that wealth is acquired; self-indulgence and sensuality; an obstinate continuance in that evil temper of unbelief which rejected and crucified Christ:—these were the sins of the last days of Jerusalem as described by St. James; for these she was to be destroyed by God; for these she was destroyed; and her children were scattered abroad, and have now been outcasts for near two thousand years. Here is a prophetic warning to men and nations, especially to wealthy commercial nations in the last times."

The following eloquent exposition of this great question is abridged from the *Saturday Review*, April 14th, 1860:

The belief that all human affairs will at some time or other be terminated by one tremendous dramatic catastrophe—that the whole history of the human race leads up to that result, and that the epoch at which it will take place is capable of being foretold —commends itself so powerfully to the imagination of mankind, and is met with under so many different forms in various countries, and at various epochs of human history, that it is well worth while to consider what are the natural foundations on which it rests. It is most unquestionably true that, in times and countries where there has been any intellectual activity at all, men have shown a disposition to attribute to the history of the human race a sort of dramatic unity. Traces of this tendency are to be found in the classical visions of ages of gold, silver, brass, and iron—in the Hindoo cycles and avatars—in the ancient Rabbinical traditions, to which a certain number of idle pretenders to learning still profess to attach importance in our own days—and in the eagerness with which the Christian world has in all ages deduced from the Bible, not merely the general doctrine (which is not discussed here), that the present dispensation will conclude at a given time, and in a visible and, so to speak, dramatic manner, but the specific opinion that that final consummation was at hand on many different occasions. Every one knows that certain classes of society in the present day receive the expression of this opinion not only with favor, but with a sort of avidity; and most of us are probably aware that at particular periods—as, for example, at the beginning of the eleventh century—the conviction that the end of the world was actually approaching prevailed so universally as to produce very serious effects indeed upon the current business and proceedings of society. There are, indeed, some arguments produced in favor of specific predictions upon the subject which are so feeble that they can hardly weigh with any one qualified to appreciate the answers to them, though they are at times urged with a dishonesty which requires exposure; but the sentiment which gives these arguments their real weight is a very different and a far more important matter, and deserves closer and more sympathetic examination than it usually receives.

The tendency of men to believe that the world will come to an end, and to dally with, and in some degree to welcome the anticipation, is only one form of their impatience of the conditions under which they think and live, and the impatience is one which is neither ignoble nor altogether unreasonable. Rude ages and populations are, to an immense degree, opposed by the routine of daily life, and in more cultivated times a somewhat similar result is produced by the wide diffusion of scientific methods of thought and observation. The thought presses on the mind that the thing that hath been the same shall also be—that the world and all that is in it, and all other worlds by which it is surrounded, are a huge dead machine, grinding on eternally according to its own principles, and coming back perpetually at regular intervals to the same result.

The conception of the End of the World is a welcome one. It is a sort of opportunity for the spiritual nature of man to defy its

The End of the World Foretold. 251

material antagonist. It is a grand and an elevating thought that at some time, and under some circumstances, all that we see, and touch, and weigh, and measure, will cease to be; and that the spirits of men will be recognized, whether for good or for evil, as the real substances of which the heavens and the earth are the mere accidents. Every generation is guided, and to a great extent governed, by ideal conceptions; and the conceptions which influence any given age are indicated by the abstract words which find most favor with it. In our own times, phrases like "progress," and "civilization," point to a view of life which to many minds is utterly intolerable. They imply some such dream as this —The time will come, and is now coming, when war shall be unknown, when crime shall cease, when comfort shall be universal, and when life, almost freed from disease, shall be prolonged some years beyond its present limit. Every year will bring forth inventions which will economize labor, and diffuse the knowledge of principles that will give an ease, a gentleness, and a regularity to life which exists at present only amongst affluent and privileged classes. Such is the sort of ideal which in a thousand ways is hinted at.

The world in which we live is a moral problem already, and one which is at times distressing, but such a lubberland as that could only be made tolerable by the prospect of its speedy end. That men really passed through six thousand years of trial and suffering in order that there might be at last a perpetual succession of comfortable shopkeepers, is a supposition so revolting to the moral sense, that it would be difficult to reconcile it with any belief at all in a Divine Providence. The expectation that the world—that is, that human society—will some day come to an end, is based upon the belief that man is something more than the complement to brute matter, and that it is he who imparts dignity and interest to the planet in which he lives, and does not receive his importance from it. It follows from such a belief that the narrow and limited range of human faculties, the ceaseless strife and bottomless confusion of human passions, the struggle between moral good and evil—each of which, as far as the human eye can see, is not only antagonistic but necessary to the other—are not mere processes tending to work out their own solution here in some future generation, but tremendous and awful mysteries which can never be reconciled until some final decision and judgment is pronounced upon them.

GEOLOGICAL FUTURE OF THE UNIVERSE.

On the whole, the groups and systems of the geologist—imperfectly intrepreted as they yet undoubtedly are—present a long series of mineral mutations, and of vital gradation and progress. Not progress from imperfection to perfection, but from humbler to more highly organized orders, as if the great design of Nature had been to ascend from the simple conception of *materialism* to the higher aims of mechanical combination, from *mechanism* to the subtler elimination of mind, and from *mentalism* to the still nobler attribute of *moralism*, as developed alone in the intellect and soul of man. From the lowly sea-weeds of the silurian strata and marsh-plants of the old red sandstone, we rise (speaking in general terms) to the prolific clubmosses, reeds, ferns, and gigantic endogens of the coal measures; from these to the palms, cycads, and pines of the oolite; and from these again to the exogens or true timber-trees of the tertiary and current eras. So also in the animal kingdom: the graptolites and trilobites of the silurian seas are succeeded by the higher crustacea and bone-clad fishes of the old red sandstone; these by the sauroid fishes of the coal measures; the sauroid fishes by the gigantic saurians and reptiles of the oolite; the reptiles of the oolite by the huge mammalia of the tertiary epoch; and these in time give place to existing species, with man as the crowning form of created existence. This idea of graduation implies not only an onward change among the rock-materials of the earth, but also, as plants and animals are influenced in their forms and distributions by external causes, new phases and arrangements of vitality—the creation of new species, and the dropping out of others from the great scheme of animated nature. And such is the fact even with respect to the current era. The mastodon, mammoth, and other huge pachyderms that lived from the tertiary into the modern epoch, have long since become extinct, leaving their bones in the silts and sands of our valleys.

Geological Future of the Universe.   253

The elk, urus, bear, wild-boar, wolf, and beaver are now extinct in Britain; and what takes place in insular districts must also occur, though more slowly, in continental regions. The dodo of the Mauritius, and the dinornis of New Zealand, are now matters of history; and the same causes that led to the extinction of these, seem hurrying onward to the obliteration of the beaver, ostrich, elephant, kangaroo, and other animals whose circumscribed provinces are gradually being broken in upon, by new conditions.

Such facts as these, taken in connection with the physical changes that are occasionally taking place on the surface of the globe, necessarily lead to speculations as to the conditions and phases of the Future.* Respecting these, however, it were in vain to offer even the widest conjecture. Subjected as our planet is to the numerous modifying causes already described, we know that vast changes are now in progress, and that the present aspect of nature will not be the same as those she must assume in the eras that are to follow. But what may be the nature and amount of these changes, what the new conditions brought about by them, or what the races of plants and animals adapted by these conditions, science has yet no available means of determining. This only the philosophical mind rests assured of, that be the future vicissitudes of the globe what they may, they will continue to be the harmonious results of Law and Order; and that, as throughout the whole of the future, the great COSMICAL DESIGN which geology now labors to reveal, will be steadily upheld by the Omniscient omnipotence of Him " with whom is no variableness, neither shadow of turning."—*Advanced Text-Book of Geology*, by DAVID PAGE, F. G. S.

---

* In the widespread attention recently paid to the study of unfulfilled prophecy, certain writers have been ignorantly charged with prophesying the End of the World; whereas they foretell what is written rather than attempt to foretell what is about to come to pass. They pretend to no interior inspiration; but state their conclusions as inferences from the inspired record, accepting it alone as their only premises, and leaving to their readers to acquiesce or otherwise in their deductions. Thus, the Rev. Dr. Cumming shows, very forcibly, the year 1867 as the eve of the world's long predicted Millennial Rest; and he quotes an array of names who concur with him in looking to 1867 as a great crisis—a testing crisis—intersected by the various lines of prophetic dates.—See " The School of the Prophets," *Times*, Nov. 8, 1859, a comprehensive view of the subject admirably adapted for its place.

Man after Death.

THE DEAD KNOW NOT ANY THING.

ARISTOTLE thought that the Dead are affected in the other world, by the honor or reproach which is variously ascribed to their memory in this.

How forcibly is this strange belief of the Stagirite falsified in this Scriptural evidence "of Man's Ignorance of the Men and Things of this World after his departure hence:"

> Thou destroyest the hope of man: thou prevailest forever against him, and he passeth: thou changest his countenance, and sendest him away: his sons come to honor, and he knoweth it not; and they are brought low, but he perceiveth it not of them.—*Job* xiv. 19, 20, 21.
>
> But the dead know not any thing, neither have they any more a reward, for the memory of them is forgotten: Also their love and their hatred, and their envy is now perished; neither have they any more a portion forever in any thing that is done under the sun.—*Ecclesias.* ix. 5, 6.
>
> Doubtless, thou art our father; though Abraham be ignorant of us; and Israel acknowledge us not.—*Isa.* lxiii. 16.

PRAYERS FOR THE DEAD.

The vain custom of offering prayers to God on behalf of the Dead existed at a very early period after the death of the primitive teachers of Christianity. Tertullian (A. D. 200) says that the custom prevailed before his time. During the third and fourth centuries, prayers were offered for the Dead with the belief that they benefited the departed in many ways. Dr. Burton speaks apologetically of this practice: he says, in effect, that in the second and third centuries, Christians were agreed that the soul was, in its disembodied state, not insensible or asleep, but in a place apart, where it enjoyed a foretaste of the happiness which awaited it hereafter. It was also believed by a large portion of Christians that the resurrection of the righteous would take place before the final resurrection of all mankind at the day of judgment. When they spoke of the first resurrection, they meant that the righteous would rise and reign with Christ upon earth a thousand years, at the end of which period the general resurrection would take place. Burton assumes, that it was natural for them to add to this belief, that the souls of the righteous, while they were in their separate abode, were anxiously looking forward to the time of the first resurrection, when they would be released from their confinement; and their surviving friends did not think it improper to make it a subject of prayer to God, that He would be pleased to hasten the period when those who had departed in His faith and fear might enter into His heavenly kingdom. Dr. Burton assumes that this was the only sense in which prayers were offered for the dead; that the primitive Christians did not think their prayers could affect the present or future condition of those who were departed.

The testimonies, however, of the Christian fathers, prove that this is a very partial view of the practice. It is clear that the prayers were directed to the following particulars:—That God would receive such persons to Himself; that He would grant them forgiveness of all remains of sin and imperfection; that He would allow them an early share in the millennial reign of Christ on earth, and favor at the Day of Judgment (when they supposed that all men would pass through a fire of purgation), and an augmentation of their reward and glory in the state of final blessedness. It is certain also that prayers were offered for those who had died in sin, in hope of mitigating their sufferings, or rendering their condemnation more tolerable. The Church of England, at one time, encouraged this practice. In an ancient service-book, in the place of the present "Thanksgiving," there occurs the following: "We commend unto Thy mercy, O Lord, all other Thy servants, which are departed hence from us with the sign of faith, and now do rest in sleep of peace: Grant unto them, we beseech Thee, Thy mercy and everlasting peace," &c. The practice is, however, strongly condemned in the Homilies, and any passages in the Common Prayer which tended to encourage this erroneous and unscriptural usage, have been expunged.—*Ecclesiastical Dictionary*, by the Rev. JOHN FARRAR.

THE CONDITION OF MAN AFTER DEATH.

That the ancient Hebrews, that the Patriarchs themselves, had some idea of a future life, is evident; although we must acknowledge their information on the subject to have been limited and obscure.

1. From the distinction which is made between the subterranean residence denominated *Sheol*, and the *grave*, or place of interment for the body.*

2. That they believed in the existence of the spirit after the death of the body, is evident likewise from the credit which they were disposed to give to the art of necromancy, by means of which the Jews believed that the *spirits of the dead* were summoned back to the present scene of existence.†

The objection which is sometimes made, viz., that persons whose minds are under the influence of superstition are very inconsistent with themselves and in their opinions, does not avail any thing in the present case; for it would, in truth, be a miracle of inconsistency, if those persons who believed that departed spirits were no longer existing, should, nevertheless, give full credit to the ability of such non-existent spirits to reveal the mysteries of the future.

The belief of the ancient Hebrews, therefore, on this subject was, that the *spirits* of the dead were received into *Sheol*, which is represented as a large subterranean abode,‡ into which we are told that the wicked were driven suddenly, their days being cut short; but the good descended into it tranquilly, and in the fulness of their years.

---

* Gen. xxv. 8; xxvii. 35; xlix. 33; l. 2-10; Numb. xx. 24-26; Deut. xxxi. 16; xxxiv. 7; 1 Kings xi. 43.
† Lev. xix. 31; xx. 6, 7, 26, 27; Deut. xviii. 11; 1 Sam. xviii. 3, 10; 2 Kings xxiii. 24; 1 Chron. x. 13; Is. xix. 3; xxix. 4; lvii. 9; comp. Zech. xiii. 2-6.
‡ Gen. xxxvii. 35; comp. Numb. xvi. 30-33; Deut. xxxii. 22.

The Condition of Man after Death.

This very spacious dwelling-place for those who have gone hence, is often described as sorrowful, and as the land of darkness and the shadow of death, Job x. 21; Ps. vi. 5; lxxxviii. 11, 12; cxv. 17; Is. xxxviii. 18; but in Is. xiv. 9, *et seq.*, it is represented as full of activity; and in other places, as we may learn from Job xxvi. 5, 6, and 1 Samuel xxviii. 7, more than human knowledge is ascribed to its inhabitants, which is, indeed, implied in the trust which was reposed in necromancers. In this abode, moreover, the *Departed Spirits* rejoice in that rest so much desired by the Orientals (Job iii. 13); and there the living hope to see once more their beloved ancestors and children; and there also the servant is at length freed from his master, and enjoys a cessation from his labors: "There the wicked cease from troubling, there the weary be at rest."—Job iii. 13–19.

That the ancient Hebrews believed the good and the bad to be separated in Sheol, although it might be inferred from their ideas of the justice and benignity of God (Matt. xxii. 32), cannot be proved by any direct testimony. The probability, however, that this was the case, seems to be increased, when it is remembered that the author of the book of Ecclesiastes, who in chapter iii. 18, speaks somewhat hesitatingly of the immortality of the soul, says, in chapter xii. 7, that "*the spirit shall return to God who gave it;*" [and, although he nowhere in express terms holds up the doctrine of future rewards and punishments, yet he informs us in chap. xiii. 14, of something very similar to it, viz., "*That God shall bring every good work into judgment, with every secret thing, whether good or evil.*"]

We have not authority, therefore, to say positively that any other motives were held out to the ancient Hebrews to pursue the good and to avoid the evil, than those which were derived from the rewards and punishments of this life. That *these* were the motives which were presented to their minds in order to influence them to pursue a right course of conduct, is expressly asserted in Isaiah xxvi. 9, 10, and may be learnt also from the imprecations which are met with in many parts of the Old Testament.

The *Mehestani*, who were disciples of Zoroaster, believed in the immortality of the soul, in rewards and punishments after death, and in the resurrection of the body; at the time of which resurrection, all the bad would be purged by fire, and associated with the good. (See Zend-Avesta; comp. Ezek. xxxvii. 1–14.)

There is some uncertainty respecting the passages in Daniel, xi. 2, 3, 13; but it is possible that they may be a confirmation of the doctrine of the resurrection of the dead; and it is very clear that Haggai (ii. 23) speaks of some state of glory after the termination of the present life. (Compare Zech. iii. 7.) These sentiments of the later prophets, which are perfectly in unison with what is said of the justice and clemency of God in other parts of the Old Testament, were at length adopted by the Jews generally, with the exception of the Sadducees, against whom they are defended in the apocryphal books of Maccabees and Wisdom.

Thus the Jews were gradually prepared to receive that broader and fuller light which Jesus shed upon them: see 2 Tim. i. 10.— *Dr. Jahn's Manual of Biblical Antiquities*, pp. 363–5.

Bishop Hall (*Invisible World:—Of the Souls of Men*) says:

That the soul, after separation from the body, hath an independent life of its own, is so clear a truth, that the very heathen Philosophers, by the dim light of nature, have determined it for irrefragable : In so much as Aristotle himself (who is wont to bear ill for his opinion of the soul's mortality) is confidently reported to have written a book of the *Soul* separate, which Thomas Aquinas, in his (so late) age, professes to have seen; sure I am that his Master *Plato*, and that heathen Martyr, *Socrates* (related by him) are full of divine discourses of this kind. In so much as this latter, when *Crito* was asking him how he would be buried: I perceive (said he) I have lost much labor, for I have not yet persuaded my *Crito*, that I shall fly clear away, and leave nothing behind me; meaning that the soul is the man, and would be ever itself, when his body should have no being; And in *Xenophon* (so *Cicero* cites him), Cyrus is brought in saying *Nolite arbitrari*, &c. Think not, my dear sons, that when I shall depart from you, I shall then cease to have any being; for even while I was with you, ye saw not the soul which I had, but yet ye well saw, by those things which I did, that there was a soul within this body : Believe ye, therefore, that though ye shall see no soul of mine, yet it shall still have a being. Shortly, all but a hateful Epicurus have agreed to this truth : and if some have fancied a transmigration of souls into other bodies; others a passage to the stars which formerly governed them; others to I know not what Elysian fields; all have pitched upon a separate condition.

In the work entitled *Mortal Life, and the State of the Soul after Death*, we read: "If man, or rather the soul of man, did not live in a former state, then the Almighty *creates* a new soul for every person who is born. There is, in short, a constant creation of souls. Our material frames may continue their kind—similar bodies to themselves—by the delegated power of God; but they cannot be supposed to create souls. We commonly believe that God creates souls at the time these bodies are produced which they are to inform." Mr. Samuel Blair also records his opinion that " the soul is a real creation as well as the body, although a different substance ;"* and Lord Brougham remarks, that " while the material world affords no example of creation, of mind this cannot be said ; it is called into existence perpetually before our eyes."† Dr. Cromwell considers all these notions greatly below right, and even reverent, ideas of the operations of the Deity. Dr. Millingen, on the other hand, considers that "we are born with a soul ;" but then arises the question, at what period the immortal essence joins the embryonic existence. Another theory is, that "whenever a body is completely organized, there is a general law in nature, by which, without any particular interposition of the Deity, a soul immediately attaches itself to it ;" but this, Dr. Priestley adds, " supposes the pre-existence of all human souls ; which, indeed, was the original doctrine of the soul, and what he thinks to be necessary to make the system complete and consistent."‡

Dr. Cromwell then refers to the opinion of modern physiologists, that soul and body, unitedly, may, after all, be only a proper reproduction ; for that, allowing the soul to be essentially distinct from, it may be an essence comprehended by, one of those minute *cells*, in which every organized fabric, animal or vegetable, has been discovered to originate. (See Morell's *Elements of Psychology*, Part I.)

Examples are not less rife (says Dr. Cromwell), of the immaterialistic faith that the human soul comes immediately from God, and is of the very nature—indeed, so to speak, a very fraction— of God. It is beyond question that this doctrine prevailed with all such of the ancients as held that of the immateriality of the soul. The Indian or Egyptian philosopher never doubted it: it

* *Mind and Matter*, p. 188.
† *Disc. Nat. Theology*, p. 110.
‡ Priestley in Correspondence with Price, p. 872.

reigned from Plato, if not from Pythagoras, to Seneca and Epictetus among the Greeks and Romans; and it was a marked feature of the new Platonism of Alexandria. Plotinus, dying, exclaimed, "I am struggling to liberate the *divinity* within me." The pious James Montgomery sings:

> The sun is but a spark of fire,
> A transient meteor in the sky;
> The soul, immortal as its Sire,
> Shall never die.

"We are all emanations from the Infinite Essence," says Morell; and Mr. Blair states that he once heard an eloquent preacher say in the pulpit, "the soul is a part of God himself, and is deathless and indestructible;" thus nearly repeating Plutarch: "The soul is not God's mere work, but a part of himself: its creation was not by him, but from him, and out of him."

Dr. Cromwell urges that the progress of physiology indicates that psychology will hereafter not alone be based upon, but moulded by it; and foretells that in due time will follow the common admission that the capacities called those of the Mind, are, by a law of the human creature, "determined by the size, form, and constitution of the Brain, the form, size, and qualities of which are transmitted by hereditary descent."

"TO THE HOLY SPIRIT.

A remarkable instance of sacred poetry becoming the household words of the poor is presented in the following, from Herrick's "Noble Numbers," which, some fifty years since, was repeated by a poor woman in the ninety-ninth year of her age, named Dorothy King. This beautiful Litany and four others she had learned from her mother, who was apprenticed to Herrick's successor in the vicarage of Dean Prior, in Devonshire. She called them her prayers, which, she said, she was in the habit of putting up in bed, whenever she could not sleep. She had no idea that these poems had ever been printed, and could not have read them if she had seen them.

HIS LITANY,

To the Holy Spirit.

In the hour of my distress,
When temptations me oppress,
And when I my sins confess,
    Sweet Spirit, comfort me!

When I lie within my bed,
Sick in heart, and sick in head,
And with doubts discomforted,
    Sweet Spirit, comfort me!

When the home doth sigh and weep,
And the world is drown'd in sleep,
Yet mine eyes the watch do keep,
    Sweet Spirit, comfort me!

When the passing-bell doth toll,
And the furies in a shoal,
Come to fright a parting soul,
    Sweet Spirit, comfort me!

When the tapers now burn blue,
And the comforters are few,
And that number more than true,
    Sweet Spirit, comfort me!

When the priest his last hath pray'd,
And I nod to what is said,
'Cause my speech is now decay'd,
    Sweet Spirit, comfort me!

When (God knows) I'm toss'd about
Either with despair or doubt,
Yet before the glass be out,
    Sweet Spirit, comfort me!

When the tempter me pursu'th
With the sins of all my youth,
And half damns me with untruth,
    Sweet Spirit, comfort me!

When the flames and hellish cries,
Fright mine ears, and fright mine eyes,
And all terrors me surprise,
    Sweet Spirit, comfort me!

> When the judgment is reveal'd,
> And that open'd which was seal'd,
> When to thee I have appeal'd,
> Sweet Spirit, comfort me!

LIFE AFTER DEATH.—REUNION OF THE SOUL AND BODY.

The unequal distribution of good and evil in this world proves that there must be another state, where the good will be rewarded and the wicked punished: since, it is not possible that a Being of perfect justice and holiness, of infinite wisdom and power, should have so ordered things that obeying him and our own conscience should ever make us miserable, and disobeying them prove beneficial to us on the whole. Strongly as this argument proves the doctrine of a life after death, it is considerably strengthened by the universal agreement of mankind, with but few exceptions. Not only Jews, but all the nations of the world, learned or unlearned, ancient or modern, appear to have been persuaded that *the souls of men continue after death.*

The full reward of good persons deceased is not yet bestowed upon them, nor the full punishment of the wicked inflicted; since these things are to follow the General Resurrection. The state of those that die in the Lord is not a state of insensibility; since our Saviour describes the soul of Lazarus as "carried by angels into Abraham's bosom," and there "comforted;" and he promised the penitent robber upon the cross, that he should be "that day with him in paradise:" hence, this cannot be a state of insensibility, but of happiness.

That the bodies of all men shall be raised up again, and reunited to their souls, is reasonable: for God is infinite both in power and knowledge; and it is, unquestionably, as possible to bring together and enliven the scattered parts of our body again, as it was to make them out of nothing, and give them life at first. This doctrine is probably implied in that general promise made to our first parents, that "the seed of the woman should bruise the serpent's head," destroy his power, and consequently take away the curse under which he had brought mankind. For as part of the curse consists in the death of the body, it cannot be completely taken away but by the resurrection of the body. ("That which thou sowest is not quickened, except it die.")

Abraham had so strong a belief in this, that he was willing, on the Divine command, to sacrifice his son; reasoning, as the Epistle to the Hebrews teaches us, "that God was able to raise him up, even from the dead."

Job says: "I know that my Redeemer liveth, and that he shall stand at the latter day upon the earth. And though after my skin this body be destroyed, yet in my flesh shall I see God." Elijah being taken up alive into heaven, must also have given an expectation that the body, as well as the soul, was to partake of future happiness.

It is a question about which commentators are much divided, whether Job expresses in these words his firm belief of a resurrection in the body to happiness after death; or only of God's interposition in his favor before he died, to vindicate his character from the unjust imputations of his friends. The truth was not yet revealed.

Mind could not then grasp the doctrine of the Resurrection of the flesh, still less (of course) could language consciously express it; and yet it may have been a thing spiritually discovered by the faithful, from the first hour that the promise of a Redeemer was given. Dim, indistinct, impalpable, in short, a mystery, so far as intellectual apprehension was concerned, it may nevertheless have wrought upon the spirit with an influence scarcely less mighty than it does now, when it is read in the full light of the risen Jesus.

That which, in fact, "was from the beginning of the Word of Life," we upon whom the ends of the world are come have heard, yea, have, in a manner, "seen with our eyes, and have looked upon, and our hands have handled." For the life which Job discerned, if at all, so dimly, distantly, and indistinctly—the life of the body after the soul has fled from it, and it has mingled with the dust—that life has been manifested to us in Christ, who is the life; and we have seen it, though not with our own eyes, with the eyes of Christian forefathers, with whom, through the Spirit, we are one in the Communion of Saints.—*Job, a Course of Lectures, by J. E. Kempe, Rector of St. James's.*

The Intermediate State.

The Intermediate State is the condition of the righteous immediately after their departure from this life, and *between* that event and the General Resurrection. That this will be a state of repose from the sufferings that mortality is heir to, may be thought sufficiently plain from the declaration of St. John in the Revelation, that to those who "die in the Lord," their death will be the introduction to a state of undisturbed tranquillity: they will "rest from their labors." That it will be their immediate introduction to a state of *enjoyment* also, may, perhaps, be inferred from the clause, "and their works do follow them;" that is, the rewards consequent on their former works.

But there is stronger foundation for the opinion that the righteous will enter upon a state of enjoyment immediately after their dissolution. From the parable of the rich man and Lazarus —the former in torments, and the latter in Abraham's bosom,—it is inferred that death is at once followed by a condition of conscious comfort or torment; for the parable supposes the continuance upon earth of the "five brethren" of the rich man, in a state of prolonged trial and responsibility, at the same time that it represents Lazarus as "comforted," and the rich man as "tormented." It is, therefore, argues Bishop Mant, to be understood as describing, on the part of those who were dead, the condition which they were allotted before the Day of Judgment.

The Bishop maintains, also, that the language of our blessed Redeemer to the dying malefactor on the cross, recognizes the same notion. But the completest exposition of the doctrine of Holy Writ on this subject is considered by Dr. Mant to be found in the following collect in the "Order for the Burial of the Dead" —one of the most impressive portions of that admirable service of our scriptural Church:

The Intermediate State. 265

Almighty God, with whom do live the spirits of them that depart hence in the Lord, and with whom the souls of the faithful, after they are delivered from the burden of the flesh, *are in joy and felicity;* we give Thee hearty thanks, for that it hath pleased Thee to deliver this our brother out of the miseries of this sinful world; beseeching Thee that it may please Thee of thy gracious goodness, shortly to accomplish the number of thine elect, and to hasten thy kingdom; that we, with all those that are departed in the true faith of thy holy name, may have *our perfect consummation and bliss,* both in body and soul, in thy eternal and everlasting glory; through Jesus Christ, our Lord. Amen.

Still, this is but an instalment of enjoyment, and will be succeeded by another state of yet superior happiness, "when the trumpet shall sound, and the dead shall be raised incorruptible, and we shall be changed;" and when the crown of righteousness shall be given to "all those who love the Lord's appearing"— "by the Lord, the righteous Judge," in the presence of assembled men and angels, "on that day." (2 Tim. iv. 8.) Such is the argument of Bishop Mant, which must carry conviction by its clearness and simplicity.

Archbishop Whately, in his *Scriptural Revelations*, having considered the prevailing view of the subject, goes on to say:

"The only alternative—the only other possible supposition—is, that the soul remains in a state of profound sleep—of utter unconsciousness—during the whole interval between the separation from the body by death, and its reunion at the Resurrection. One objection to the reception of this supposition in the minds, I apprehend, of many persons—an objection which affects the imagination, though not the understanding—is, that it seems as if there were a tedious and dreary interval or non-existence to be passed, by such as should be supposed to sleep, perhaps for some thousands of years, which might elapse between their death and the end of the world. The imagination represents a wearisome length of time during which (on this supposition) those that sleep in Christ would have to wait for His final coming to reward them. We fancy it hard that they should be lost both to the world and to themselves—destitute of the enjoyments both of this life and of the next, and continuing for so many ages as if they had never been born.

"Such, I say, are the pictures which the *imagination* draws; but when we view things by the light of the *understanding*, they present a very different aspect. Reason tells us (the moment we consider the subject), that a long and a short space of time are exactly the same to a person who is insensible. All our notion of time is drawn from the different impressions on our minds succeeding one another: so that when any one loses his consciousness (as in the case of a fainting fit, or of those recovered from drowning, suffocation, or the like) he not only does not perceive the length of the interval between the loss of his consciousness and the return of it, but *there is* (*to him*) *no such interval;* the moment at which he totally lost his sensibility seems (and is, to him) immediately succeeded by the moment in which he regains it. . . . It will often happen, when any one sleeps very soundly, that the moment of his waking shall appear to him immediately to succeed that of his falling asleep; although the interval may have been many hours. Something of the same kind has been observed in a few instances of madness, and of apoplexy; in which all the ordinary operations of the mind having been completely suspended for several years, the patients, on the recovery of their senses, have been found totally unconscious of the whole interval, and distinctly remembering and speaking of, as having happened on the day before, events which occurred before the seizure; so that they could hardly be brought to believe that whole years had since elapsed." (The author of the work here adds in a note—"a case occurred within my own knowledge, not long ago, of a sick person who fell into a kind of trance which lasted several weeks; and immediately on her revival she asked for some grapes, which had been brought into her room just before she became insensible.")

"From considering such instances as these," he goes on to say, "as well as from the very nature of the case, any one may easily convince himself, that if ever a total insensibility takes place, so that all action of the mind is completely suspended, the time during which this continues, whether a single minute, or a thousand years, is, to the person himself, *no time at all.* In either case, the moment of his reviving must appear to him immediately to succeed that of his sinking into unconsciousness; nor could he possibly be able to tell afterwards, from his own sensations and recollections, whether his state of suspended animation had lasted an hour, a day, or a century.

"To all practical purposes, that is, to each, a long or a short time, which is such to his perceptions. Some of you may probably have known what it is to pass a night of that excessive restlessness, which accompanies some particular kinds of illness. Such persons will easily remember (what no one else can fully conceive) how insufferably tedious a single night will in such a case appear;—how enormously long the interval seemed to be between the times of the clock's striking;—how they seemed to feel as if morning would never arrive. And if it has happened that the next night the patient was completely relieved, and slept quite soundly, the very same number of hours, which the night before had seemed to him an age, would appear but a moment. The clock, indeed, he is well aware, has made the same movements in the one case as in the other; but relatively to the sick man himself, and as far as his feelings are concerned, the one night will have been immensely shorter than the other.

"The long and dreary interval, then, between death and the Day of Judgment (supposing the intermediate state to be a profound sleep), *does not exist at all, except in the imagination.* To the party concerned there is *no interval whatever;* but to such person (according to this supposition) the moment of his closing his eyes in death, will be *instantly* succeeded by the sound of the last trumpet, which shall summon the dead; even though ages shall have intervened. And in this sense the faithful Christian may be, practically, in paradise the day he dies. The promise made to the penitent thief, and the Apostle Paul's wish 'to depart, and to be with Christ,' which, he said, was 'far better' than to remain any longer in this troublesome world, would each be fulfilled to all practical purposes, provided each shall have found himself in a state of happiness in the presence of his Lord, the very instant (according to his own perception) after having breathed his last in this world."

OPINIONS CONCERNING THE STATE OF THE DEAD.

It may next be important as well as interesting to examine a few of the ancient notions upon this great question.

Origen taught, that "Such as depart out of this life after the common course of death, are disposed of according to their deeds and merits, as they shall be judged to be worthy; some into the place which is called hell, others into Abraham's bosom, and through *divers other* places and mansions." St. Hilary taught otherwise. *All the faithful*, according to him, were to be in Abraham's bosom, while the wicked are "hindered from coming by the gulf interposed between them." Lactantius taught, that *all the souls, both of the righteous and the wicked*, should be "detained in one common custody, until the time come when the great Judge doth make trial of their doings;" *i. e.* by exposing them to a mysterious flame which shall burn the wicked, and do service to the righteous, who have "something in them that will repel or put back the force of the flame!" And the Greek Church, differing from the rest in this, taught that (according to Luke xiii. 28, 29, 30) men entered Abraham's bosom at the resurrection. "The body is buried in the earth, but the soul goeth in unknown places, waiting for the future resurrection of the dead: in which, O gracious Saviour, make bright thy servant, place him together with the saints, and refresh him in the bosom of Abraham." We need not mention the opinion of St. Ambrose, who was not taught by the *Apostles* to say that "they that come not unto the first resurrection, but are removed out of the second, shall be burned (in purgatorial fire) until they fulfil the times between the first and the second resurrection; or if they have not fulfilled them, they shall remain longer in punishment." Nor need we attach much weight to that of Augustin, who taught that souls went into certain "hidden receptacles," into which the souls of God's children might carry some of their lighter faults, which would *hinder them from attaining heaven;* but from which they might be *released* by the *prayers and almsdeeds of the living.*—(Authorities from *Tracts for the Times*, No. 72.)

Let any one (says Bishop Courtenay), who maintains that these individual writers, or churches, were in possession of an oral apostolic tradition concerning the dead, state what that tradition contained, and what it did not; and inform the world how he, by the light of reason, can distinguish the truth of God, as contained in uninspired writings, from the errors of man.

Bishop Courtenay's able work, *the Future States*, was originally published in 1833, and reprinted in 1857. In the latter edition the author explains: "Time has not changed the writer's belief, that the soul of man is naturally mortal—being, when separate from the body, naturally incapable of independent consciousness; that without the Redeemer it can have no life, and that, even through the Redeemer, it has none until the Day of Redemption. He cannot accept the popular notion, that 'the saints which sleep' are all awake, and that 'the dead' are now alive."

The Bishop then proceeds, on a question of the interpretation of certain unfulfilled prophecies, to modify and retract an opinion formerly maintained. There are not a few persons who suppose, that the soul of a believer, upon its separation from the body, is immediately in a heavenly state, with Christ and the holy angels, and the saints of all former generations; and that, secondly, at the commencement of the Millennium, the body being restored to the soul, it lives and reigns with Christ, on the present earth, with greater glory still; and that, in the third place, having, at the expiration of the thousand years of triumph, been put upon its trial, and solemnly "judged out of the things written in the books," and ascertained to be "found written in the Book of Life," it enters upon its final and eternal condition.

Thus are *two intermediate states*, possibly of many thousand years' duration, interposed between the present world, and that promised in the closing pages of the Divine revelation.

The second of these supposed intermediate states, it is thought, will be preceded by a general conversion of the Jews, and the resurrection of Abraham, Isaac, and Jacob, and all the prophets, and all the saints without exception,—of whom those who are the seed of Abraham shall occupy the land of Israel, enjoying the visible presence and personal government of the Lord Jesus Christ.

Persuaded that these anticipations will not be realized, the Bishop has endeavored to show that all the Divine promises to Abraham and his seed shall be fulfilled in a heavenly Canaan, after the present heaven and earth have passed away. This interpretation of the prophecy he would now so far retract, as to admit that a conversion of the Jewish people to the Christian faith, and their consequent restoration to the land whence they have been banished, will precede the Millennium: a retraction, however, in no wise affecting the main positions, that "it is appointed unto men once to die; and after that—the judgment," and that not until the judgment can they, unless in rare and exceptional cases, "enter into the Life Eternal."

PARADISE AND HEAVEN.

"Paradise," writes Dr. Hales, "is the region appropriated to good souls." The learned Parkhurst observes, that "Paradise is the blessed state of faithful souls between death and the resurrection. Such is the sense of Paradise in the New Testament." Dr. Whitby remarks—"Our Saviour must have used the word Paradise in the same sense in which the Jews understood it, the place of happiness into which pious souls, when separated from the body, are immediately received." And Bishop Horsley says: "Of this place (Paradise) we know little, except that to those who die in the Lord it is a place of comfort and rest; not a Paradise of eternal sleep and senselessness, but a place of happy rest and tranquil hope."

"To him that overcometh," our Lord declareth by St. John, "I will give to eat of the tree of life that groweth in the midst of the Paradise of God." This (says Bishop Courtenay) is evidently a promise of a reward after the General Resurrection,* when the redeemed shall be permitted to eat of the precious fruit mentioned in the last chapter of the Apocalypse. The same place of bliss was beheld in vision by St. Paul, who was "caught up into Paradise," and there heard unutterable words. Into the same place, the believing robber† was probably admitted as soon as Jesus himself entered it. But notwithstanding the weight due to the expression, "*To-day*, thou shalt be with me in Paradise," it may be questioned whether our Lord entered into Paradise before his ascension, or at the earliest before his resurrection. For was He in the place to which St. Paul was "caught up," in a region belonging to those new heavens which are eventually to "come down from God,"—at the very time of his descent into Hades? Was he,—was his human soul,—at once above earth and below it, of whom St. Paul says that "he who ascended *first* descended into the lower parts of the earth?" This seems improbable; and Bishop Courtenay considers, that if a strict interpretation of the expression "to-day" be contended for, there is no alternative but to place Paradise below, in *Hades*, into which our Lord's human soul most certainly descended. The Bishop admits the inconvenience of the alternative; and adds, "Paradise is *probably above*, and was entered by our Lord in his ascension. The question is certainly obscure; but whatever may be understood by Paradise, it can never be shown that Christians in general have a better claim to be admitted to the privilege of the robber,† than they have to be translated or transfigured with Enoch, Elijah, and Moses."

That Paradise is not Heaven appears from this fact—that throughout the Scriptures, from the beautiful Prayer of Solomon, at the consecration of the Temple, "Hear Thou *in Heaven, Thy dwelling-place*:" to the prayer of our Saviour Himself, "Our Father, which art *in Heaven*:" heaven is pointed out as peculiarly God's throne. Further, we are informed that "No man hath ascended up to heaven, but He that came down from heaven, even the Son

---

* For the other rewards for those who overcome, are not immediately consequent on death. The departed saints have not yet received "power over the nations,"—to break them in pieces at "the end"—nor attained that consummate glory of "sitting with Christ on his throne."

† Not thief, but robber, or bandit, such as carry on their wicked trade in Italy and Spain at the present day.

of man which is now in heaven." (John iii. 13.) "David is not ascended into heaven." (Acts ii. 34.) Again, after our Saviour's resurrection, when He appeared unto Mary, His words were, "Touch me not, *for I am not yet ascended to my Father.*" He had been in Paradise, but had not yet ascended to God.

HEATHEN PHILOSOPHY OF THE IMMORTALITY OF THE SOUL.

In an able tract on *Futurity*, written by Mr. W. Merry, of Berkshire (and which, fortunately for the spiritual interests of its readers, has had an extensive circulation), the writer takes a view of the State of the Soul after Death, differing from that of Bishop Courtenay. To the inquiry of unspeakable interest—What becomes of man's spirit when no longer animating his mortal frame, the writer of the above tract replies: "The Spirit lives! Abraham and his descendants, who had died and were buried, *still lived;* God was still their God, and so declared to be *because* He is not the God of the dead, but of the *living.*" Mr. Merry's view of Job's declaration altogether differs from that of Dr. Courtenay. "How emphatically" (says the former) "does Job, 1,500 years before our Saviour appeared on earth, express his faith not only in the immortality of his spirit, but in the resurrection of his body." The value of the words, "I know that my Redeemer liveth," *et seq.*, is weighty indeed, when we read in an earlier chapter (Job i. 8) the character of Job in God's sight. "And the Lord said, Hast thou considered my servant Job, that there is none like him in the earth, a perfect and an upright man, one that feareth God and escheweth evil?"

Dr. Hammond has thus briefly expressed the sum of human knowledge upon this vital question: "The souls of the just are already in the hands of God, and it is certain that their bodies will be raised and again united to them by his Almighty power."

Although we owe to Revelation the reality of this solemn fact, it was believed in heathen philosophy before our Saviour's appearance on earth. Notwithstanding there exist no ancient writings approaching, even by many hundred years, the antiquity of the Bible, we know that 500 years previously, down almost to the commencement of the Christian era, that is, from the age of

Socrates to that of Cicero (omitting all uncertain mention of Pythagoras, a century earlier), the immortality of the soul, and its happiness or misery after death, were reasoned upon and maintained. Socrates, when condemned to death by the thirty tyrants of Athens, for " not acknowledging the gods which the state acknowledged," and for " introducing new divinities," passed his last moments in calm and confident argument with his friends, respecting the nature of the new and immortal existence about to open to him. " I should be inexcusable," he observed, " in despising death, if I were not persuaded that it will conduct me into the society of great and good men;" and, in reply to the question of his friend Crito, as to his burial, he says, " Is it not strange, that after all that I have said to convince you that I am going to the society of the happy, that Crito still thinks that this body, which will soon be a lifeless corpse, is Socrates? Let him dispose of my body as he pleases, but let him not mourn over it as if it were Socrates." So likewise, and in the same strain, does Cicero speak of death, as the *glorious day* when he shall go into the great assembly of spirits, and shall be gathered to the best and bravest of mankind who have gone before him.

Mr. Merry adds:

That the human mind should thus have arrived by philosophical deduction, assisted probably by tradition, however faint and remote, gathered from the Egyptians, and running back to Patriarchal origin, is not here brought forward as an evidence of truth; but as showing how gratefully sensible we should be, of the inestimable advantage enjoyed by the Christian over the Heathen world. That prospect of futurity, which was dimly perceived, and by the most learned only, the masterminds of the Grecian and Roman empires, is in our own day brought home with joyful certainty to the cottage-door of the humblest and the poorest.

The philosophy which Plato, and, after him, Cicero, define to be "Scientia rerum Divinarum et humanarum cum causis," was a well-conceived and pleasing hypothesis; but vouchsafes to *us* immutable truths, established on the sure evidence of the Bible, and which are open to all who have ears to hear, the unlearned and the learned.

If we do not recognize this Platonic doctrine, what becomes of the dictum which our polished Essayist has put into the mouth of the noble Roman, in the classic play of *Cato:*

> It must be so—Plato, thou reason'st well—
> Else whence this pleasing hope, this fond desire,
> This longing after immortality ?
> Or whence this secret dread, and inward horror
> Of falling into naught ? Why shrinks the soul
> Back on itself, and startles at destruction ?
> 'Tis the divinity that stirs within us;
> 'Tis heaven itself that points out an hereafter,
> And intimates eternity to man ;
> Eternity ! thou pleasing, dreadful thought !
> Through what variety of untried being,
> Through what uew scenes and changes must we pass ?
> The wide, th' unbounded prospect lies before me.
> . . . . If there's a Power above
> (And that there is all nature cries aloud
> Through all her works),
> He must delight in virtue;
> And that which he delights in must be happy.—*Addison.*

THAT MAN MUST BE IMMORTAL.

Bishop Courtenay, in his able work on *The Future States*, considers, at some length, the opinion that Man must be immortal, drawn from the wonderful skill and care shown in his structure. He argues, that for all we know, these contrivances may be, in themselves, as important as the end—human existence and welfare ; and that the importance of the end may depend on its being effected by means of such contrivances. Next, that if human existence were itself, and without reference to the means, the highest of all ends, the analogy of inferior nature shows that even the greatest things are perishable : and further, that if man be destined, through the excellence of his nature, for perpetuity, the *species*, not all the individuals of the species, will continue : and while there are, moreover, considerable difficulties in the way of the supposition, that the species would attain a higher degree of perfection in a disembodied state than in the present world. And, finally, that nearly equal solicitude has been manifested by the Creator in providing for the welfare of the inferior creation; and this, notwithstanding that man is at the head of that creation, and is the sole creature capable of comprehending and admiring the works of God, and of recognizing the Maker with gratitude and veneration,—not with a view, solely or chiefly, to the gratification of the human race. The beautiful diversity of structures, and of other contrivances, which we find actually to prevail in the animal and vegetable kingdoms, is indeed calculated to excite pleasure and wonder in the minds of all, gratitude and veneration in those whose thoughts ascend to the First Cause; but it would be inconsistent with those very feelings so to limit the Creator's bounty and contract the dimensions of the scheme of nature;—as unreasonable as to suppose that the stars were set in heaven only to give light to our globe, or display to us the extent of creative power.

If all, or the greater part of the arguments (continues the Bishop), which have been here employed, in proof of the dependence and connection of mind on organized matter, and on animal life, be correct, there arises, in the opinion of the writer, a very strong presumption that the death of the body will cause a cessation of all the activity of the mind, by way of natural consequence; to continue forever, *unless* the Creator should interfere; and restore, by a fresh exertion of His power, either the soul alone, or the soul and body together.

In the next Book—"Moral Evidence of a Future Life"—Dr. Courtenay argues that the light of the *moral* faculties of man, appearing to be more immediately derived from a celestial source than any other which the Father of Lights has conferred on us, seems peculiarly calculated to assist in the investigation of the more abstruse and mysterious parts of His designs; and may reveal to our hopes, though dimly and doubtfully at best, things beyond the reach of mere intellect; but which Revelation alone can fully disclose. When, by the aid of these faculties, we come to understand, in some degree, the true moral condition of man; and his relations to God, not as a Maker only, but as a moral Governor, who interferes with all events, in the history both of nations and individuals; and, notwithstanding the apparent abandonment of all the *details* of that history to the operation of blind natural causes, brings about in the end, through their instrumentality, great moral purposes of his own; and when, rendered more confident by this addition to our knowledge, we attempt to decide *for wha ends* this human race, seemingly so perishable, was

That Man must be Immortal.

called into existence, we are led to extend our views beyond this world, the hope of immortality becomes no longer a baseless vision.*

"Man we believe to be immortal," says the eloquent author of *The Physical Theory of Another Life*, "Man we believe to be immortal (revelation apart), not because his mind is separable from animal organization; but because his intellectual and moral constitution is such as to demand a future development of his nature. Why should that which is immaterial be indestructible? None can tell us; and on the contrary we are free to suppose that there may be immaterial orders, enjoying their hour of existence, and then returning to nihility."

In contemplating man as a moral being, we ultimately obtain, though not without many occasions of misgiving, more ample and encouraging views of the Divine economy, and see reason to think that man was created for purposes which cannot all meet their accomplishment in this world, and will find it in another; and to conjecture that after death the Creator may again put forth His power, in order to restore the spirit that had returned to him,† and rebuild the structure that could not preserve itself from decay.

---

* The line of argument here alluded to is followed out by Dr. Chalmers, in his *Bridgewater Treatise*, in the chapter—On the Capacities of the World for making a Virtuous Species Happy.

† It is strange that any one should consider the predicted "return of the spirit (or life) to God who gave it," as an assurance and promise of immortality. As long as the *breath of life* remains in them (for "the spirit" means no more), His creatures live; when the Giver resumes it, they die. So in Job, chap. iii. v. 34: "The Spirit of God hath made me, and the breath of the Almighty hath given me life." And (chap. xxxv. v. 14), "If God gather unto Himself his spirit and his breath, all flesh shall perish together, and man shall turn again unto 'dust." The breath of life breathed into the nostrils of Adam was *animal* merely. For compare Genesis, chap. vii. v. 18: "All (animals) in whose nostrils was the breath of life, of all that was in the dry land, died."

The Christian Resurrection.

"THE Christian's hope," says Archbishop Whately, " as founded on the promises contained in the Gospel, is the *Resurrection of the Body*."* Again, Isaac Taylor assures us that " what the Christian Scriptures specifically affirm, is the simple physiological fact of *two species of corporeity* destined for (assigned to) Man: the first, that of our present animal and dissoluble organization; the second, a future spiritual structure, imperishable, and endowed with higher powers and many desirable prerogatives."†

The assertions of Scripture, plainly interpreted, show that Holy Writ instructs man to expect no future life that shall be unconnected with and independent of *physical* restoration. Death, for the period of his cold reign, is the cessation of *all* vitality, and, consequently, the actual though not final extinction, along with every corporeal power, of the soul. Scripture and philosophy, however, unite in the non-encouragement of certain notions associated with the decease of relatives and friends, to not a few of whom consolation comes with the thought that the soul of him or her departed *is* in Heaven—not waiting for the Judgment that should decide its fate. To not a few, moreover,

> It is a beautiful belief,
> That ever round our head
> Are hovering, on angel wings,
> The spirits of the dead.

The beauty is, however, but poetical; and a firm faith in the Christian Resurrection should not be the less sustaining; for, agreeably to Christianity, the period of the separation of the beloved one taken and the sorrowing one left, is computable alone

---

* *Scripture Revelations of a Future Life.*
† *Physical Theory of Another Life.*

by the further length of the sorrower's stay in this world; the moment of death being to both the virtual moment of re-union. Whenever " *total insensibility* takes place, the time during which this continues, whether a single minute or a thousand years, is to the person himself no time at all: in either case, the moment of his reviving must appear to him immediately to succeed that of his sinking into unconsciousness; nor could he possibly be able to tell afterward whether this state had lasted an hour, a day, or a century."*

What eloquence and pathos are blended in the following passage from the *Breathings of the Devout Soul*, by Bishop Hall:

What a comfort it is, O Saviour, that thou art *the first fruits of them that sleep !* Those that die in thee, do but sleep. Thou saidst so once of thy Lazarus, and sayest so still of him again: he doth but sleep still. His first sleep was but short; this latter, though longer, is no less true : out of which he shall no less surely awaken at thy second call, than he did before, at thy first. His first sleep and waking was singular; this latter is the same with ours: we all lie down in our bed of earth, as sure to wake as ever we can be to shut our eyes. In and from thee, O blessed Saviour, is this our assurance, who art *the first fruits of them that sleep*. The first handful of the first-fruits was not presented for itself, but for the whole field wherein it grew: the virtue of that oblation extended itself to the whole crop. Neither didst thou, O blessed Jesu, rise again for thyself only; but the power and virtue of thy resurrection reaches to all thine: so thy chosen vessel tells us, *Christ, the first fruits, and afterward, they that are Christ's at his coming;* 1 Cor. xv. 23. So as, though the *resurrection be of all the dead, just and unjust,* Acts xxiv. 15; yet, to rise by the power of thy resurrection is so proper to thine own, as that thou, O Saviour, hast styled it the *resurrection of the just;* Luke xix. 14; while the rest shall be dragged out of their graves, by the power of thy godhead, to their dreadful judgment. Already, therefore, O Jesu, are we risen in thee; and as sure, shall rise in our own persons. The locomotive faculty is in

---

* *Scripture Revelations.*

the head: thou, who art our Head, art risen; we, who are thy members, must and shall follow. Say, then, O my dying body, say boldly unto death, *Rejoice not over me, O mine enemy, for though I fall, yet I shall rise again:* Micah vii. 8. Yes, Lord, the virtue of thy first-fruits diffuseth itself, not to our rising only, but to a blessed immortality of these bodies of ours: for as thou didst rise immortal and glorious, so shall we by and with thee; *Who shall change these vile bodies, and make them like to thy glorious body:* Phil. iii. 21. The same power that could shake off death, can put on glory and majesty. Lay them down, therefore, O my body, quietly and cheerfully; and look to rise in another hue: thou art *born in corruption,* thou shalt be *raised in incorruption;* thou art *sown in dishonor, thou shalt be raised in glory;* thou art *sown in weakness, but shalt be raised in power;* 1 Cor. xv. 42, 43.

Baron Bunsen, in the second volume of *the Divine Government in History,* seems to imply that if he recoils from the fleshly resurrection and Judaic millennium of Justin Martyr, he still shares the aspirations of the noblest philosophers elsewhere, and of the firmer believers among ourselves, to a revival of conscious and individual life, in such a form of immortality as may consist with union with the Spirit of our Eternal lifegiver.—(*Dr. R. Williams; Essays and Reviews.*) In the same able work, Dr. Temple, in his eloquent essay on the *Education of the World,* says:

"The spirituality of God involves in it the supremacy of conscience, the immortality of the soul, the final judgment of the human race. For we know the other world, and can only know it, by analogy, drawn from our own experience. With what, then, shall we compare God? With the spiritual or the fleshly part of our nature? On the answer depends the whole bent of our religion and of our morality. For that in ourselves which we choose as the nearest analogy of God, will, of course, be looked on as the ruling and lasting part of our being. If He be one and spiritual, then the spiritual power within us, which proclaims its own unity and independence of matter by the universality of its decrees, must be the rightful monarch of our lives; but if there be Gods many and Lords many, with bodily appetites and animal passions, then the voice of conscience is but one of those widespread delusions, which, some for a longer, some for a shorter period, have, before now, misled our race."

RESURRECTION OF THE SAME BODY.

This expression is used to denote the revivification of the human body after it has been forsaken by the soul, or the reunion of the soul hereafter to the body which it had occupied in the present world. It is admitted that there are no traces of such a doctrine in the earlier Hebrew Scripture. It is not to be found in the Pentateuch, in the historical books, or in the Psalms; for Ps. xlix. 15 does not relate to this subject; neither does Ps. civ. 29, 30, although so cited by Theodoret and others. The celebrated passage of Job xix. 25, *et seq.*, is quoted:

> For I know that my Redeemer liveth, and that he shall stand at the latter day upon the earth:
> And though after my skin, worms destroy this body, yet in my flesh shall I see God;
> Whom I shall see for myself, and mine eyes shall behold, and not another; though my reins be consumed within me.

This passage has been strongly insisted upon in proof of the early belief of this doctrine; but the most learned commentators are agreed, and scarcely any one at the present day disputes, that such a view of the text arises either from mistranslation or misapprehension, and that Job means no more than to express a confident conviction that his then diseased and dreadfully corrupted body should be restored to its former soundness; that he should rise from the depressed state in which he lay to his former prosperity; and that God would manifestly appear (as was the case) to vindicate his uprightness. That no meaning more recondite is to be found in the text, is agreed by Calvin, Mercier, Grotius, Leclerc, Patrick, Warburton, Durell, Heath, Kennicott, Döderlein, Dathe, Eichhorn, Jahn, De Wette, and a host of others. That it alludes to a resurrection is disproved thus:

1. The supposition is inconsistent with the design of the poem and the course of the argument, since the belief which it has been supposed to express, as connected with a future state of retribution, would in a

great degree have solved the difficulty on which the whole dispute turns, and could not but have been alluded to by the speakers.

2. It is inconsistent with the connection of the discourse; the reply of Zophar agreeing not with the popular interpretation, but with the other.

3. It is inconsistent with many passages in which the same person (Job) longs for death as the end of his miseries, and not as an introduction to a better life. (iii.; vii. 7, 8; x. 20, 22; xiv.; xvii. 11, 16.)

4. It is not proposed as a topic of consolation by any of the friends of Job; nor by Elihu, who acts as a sort of umpire; nor by the Almighty Himself in the decision of the controversy.

5. The later Jews, who eagerly sought for every intimation bearing on a future life which their Scriptures might contain, never regarded this as such; nor is it once referred to by Christ or his apostles.—*From Dr. Kitto's Encyclopædia of Biblical Literature.*

In 1856 there appeared a tract entitled, "The Resurrection of the same Body not an article of the Christian Faith;" containing the remarks of John Locke upon this subject, extracted from his *Reply to the Bishop of Worcester's Answer to his Second Letter.* The same tract contains the opinions of Bishop Newton; Archbishop Whately; Bishop Watson; Dr. Burton;—and Dr. Burnet, Master of the Charter-House. The opinion of the latter is very concise:

"*Whether we are to rise with the same bodies we lie down with in the grave.* Thereby we mean the numerical body, with the same matter and the same particles. This is a most celebrated question, though, in my opinion, more curious than necessary: it is not of any great consequence to us whether we shall have the same particles, or others of equal dignity and value, or what shall become of our *cast-off** carcasses when we shall live in light with angels."

---

* But as we neglect the hairs cut off from our beards, so, when the Divine Spirit goes out from a man, what will become of the receptacle? Whether fire shall burn it, or beasts tear it in pieces, or the earth cover it, no more belongs to him than what happens to a new-born child.—*Sen. Epist.*

The Future States.

THE DAY OF JUDGMENT.

HUMAN philosophy (says Bishop Courtenay), both natural and moral, has been proved by experience as unable to approach the truths revealed in Scripture concerning the Day of Judgment, as to decide the fate of a disembodied soul. It can, indeed, furnish some reasons for conjecturing that our present earth shall finally be broken up and ruined, if not actually annihilated. (See pages 248-252.) But that all shall be *together* abolished, that one period shall be the fulness of time for all, is contrary to every anticipation. "The day of the Lord," nevertheless, shall come as a thief in the night, suddenly as the deluge; and the *heavens* shall be rolled together as a scroll, the *elements* shall melt with fervent heat, and *all things*, being on fire, shall be dissolved; the *earth and heavens* shall flee away before the face of God, and no place be found for them. So it is written, so it is decreed.

* * * * *

The principles upon which judgment shall be executed on the "Dreadful Day," are yet more remote from human conjectures than is the universality of the judgment. That our earth and all visible worlds shall on one and the same day be abolished utterly; that nevertheless the human race, even all in whose nostrils has ever been the breath of life, shall in bodily form survive that awful period; that new heavens and a new earth shall be created, not to be destroyed, but to endure for all eternity; these are truths which, one and all, baffle the researches and should humiliate the pride of human philosophy. But it is a still greater wonder (an apparent *evil*, too, more extensive and more desperate than any which philosophy can detect; and which in all our inquiries concerning the origin of evil should be carefully kept in sight), that *a few only* of mankind shall rejoice in the restitution of all things; *a few only* shall receive the gift of eternal life; while the many, not being rescued by the Redeemer from their natural fate, shall go away into *eternal punishment*, and suffer *a second death.*

On this subject of future punishment, both as regards its duration, and the number of those to whom it will be awarded, God's Revelation far surpasses our conjectures. For His dealings with man partake of His own infinity. No moral reasonings, no alarm of a guilty conscience, could enable a heart unvisited by the grace of God to draw so broad a line of distinction, to divide the human race into classes so unequal in amount, and whose destinies should differ infinitely. The actual extent of human depravity and guilt, and, consequently, the severity of punishment, would not have been known, but for Revelation. That all had so far erred, and altogether become abominable, that a superhuman sacrifice was necessary to atone for their guilt, and a supernatural impulse upon their hearts to enable them to please God, are truths beyond reason, yet on which turns the whole history of man, present and future; and by which alone can be explained the wide distinction which shall be made hereafter. With God there shall be no neutrality, for man no middle state, less blissful than heaven, more tolerable than hell; for none shall be accepted but through the Redeemer: for the rest remains only " a fearful looking for of judgment and fiery indignation."

Cowley, in his Pindaric Ode—*The Resurrection*—draws this fearful picture of the Last Great Day. After telling us that Virgil shall see the whole World burnt to ashes like Troy, he proceeds:—

> Whom Thunder's dismal noise[*]
> And all that Prophets and Apostles louder spake,

[*] The Poet notes: "No natural effect gives such impressions of Divine fear as Thunder; as we may see by the examples of some wicked Emperors, who, though they were atheists, and made themselves gods, yet confessed a greater Divine power when they heard it, by trembling and hiding themselves. And Lucretius speaks it of Epicurus, as a thing extraordinary and peculiar of him, that the very sound of Thunder did not make him superstitious. Yet the Prophets and Apostles' voice is truly termed louder; for, as St. Paul says, the Voice of the Gospel was heard over all the habitable world."

And all the creatures' plain conspiring voice
Could not, whilst they liv'd, awake,
This mightier sound shall make
When dead t' arise
And open tombs, and open eyes,
To the long sluggards of five thousand years,*
This mightier sound shall wake its hearers' ears.
Then shall the scattered atoms crowded come
Back to their ancient home,
Some from Birds, from Fishes some,
Some from Earth, and some from Seas,
Some from Beasts, and some from Trees.
Some descend from Clouds on high,
Some from Metals upward fly,
And where th' attending soul naked and shivering stands,
Meet, salute, and join their hands.
As dispers'd soldiers at the trumpet's call
Haste to their colors all.
Unhappy most, like tortur'd men,
Their joints new set, to be new rack't again.
To mountains they for shelter pray,
The mountains shake, and run about no less confus'd than they.

THE HAPPINESS OF HEAVEN.

The Happiness of Heaven will be a happiness of vision and of knowledge; and we shall there pass from the weakness of our native ignorance, from the dark and twilight of our former notions, into the broad light of an everlasting day—a day which shall leave nothing undiscovered to us, which can be fit for us to know. Reason, being then unclogged from the body, shall have its full flight, and a free, uncontrolled passage into all things intelligible. We shall then surmount those beggarly rudiments and mean helps of knowledge, which now by many little steps gradually raise us to some short speculation of the nature of things; our knowledge shall be then intuitive and above discourse, not proceeding by a long circuit of antecedents and consequents, as now, in the vale of imperfection, it is forced to do; but it shall then fully inform the

---

* The ordinary traditional opinion is, that the World is to last six thousand years, and that the seventh thousand is to be the Rest or Sabbath of thousands: but I could not say sluggards of six thousand years, "because some of them would be found alive who had not so much as slept at all. The next perfect number (and verse will admit of no broken ones) was five thousand." By this license, however, the World loses one thousand years!

whole mind, and take in the whole object, by one single and substantial act.

Again, we are told, that in a future and a higher state of existence, the chief occupation of the blessed is that of praising and worshipping the Almighty. But is not the contemplation of the great works of the Creator, and the study of the ordinances of the great Lawgiver of the universe, in itself an act of praise and adoration? and if so, may not one at least of the sources of happiness which we are promised in a future state of existence—one of the rewards for a single and reverential pursuit after truth in our present state of trial,—consist in a development of our faculties, and in the power of comprehending those laws and provisions of Nature with which our finite reason does not enable us at present to become cognizant?

The Recognition of each other by the Blessed.

EVIDENCES OF THE RECOGNITION.

Bishop King, in a poem entitled the *Exequy* (17th century), thus apostrophizes the person whose departure from this life was the occasion of the composition:

> Never shall I
> Be so much blessed as to descry
> A glimpse of thee, till that day come
> Which shall the earth to cinders doom,
> And a fierce fever must calcine
> The body of this world like thine,
> (My little world!) that fit of fire
> Once off, our bodies shall aspire
> To our souls' bliss: then we shall rise
> And view ourselves with clearer eyes
> In that calm region, where no night
> Can hide us from each other's sight.

After some intervening passages, the poem concludes thus:

> The thought of this bids me go on,
> And wait my dissolution
> With hope and comfort. Dear (forgive
> The crime!) I am content to live
> Divided with but half a heart
> Till we shall meet and never part.

These quaint lines exemplify an opinion which prevails very generally among Christians: namely, that in the future state of happiness of the blessed, they who have known and loved each other in this world will be the subjects of *mutual recognition*, and will be *reunited* and *associated* with each other, and contribute to *each other's delight* in that condition of perpetual blessedness.

Bishop Mant observes that very little is said in Holy Writ,

which can be judged to bear directly upon this subject; but, in the absence of this specific testimony, he does not desire to discredit the opinion, since it is calculated to enhance the innocent delights, and to alleviate the unavoidable sufferings of this present life; and to improve us in virtue, as well as to further our consolation and enjoyment. Scripture does not contain any thing that militates against the opinion; but, on the contrary, makes it highly probable.

Under the Old Testament, comfort was derived from the persuasion, that in a future life a *reunion* would be effected of those ties of affection which had been severed in this life. In what affecting language David explains the motives of his conduct, first during the illness, and then after the death, of his child: "While the child was yet alive, I fasted and wept: for I said, Who can tell whether God will be gracious to me that the child may live? But now he is dead, wherefore should I fast? Can I bring him back again? I shall go to him, but he shall not return to me." (2 Sam. xii. 23.) From his own explicit avowals, David comforted himself with the assurance, that the child whom God had taken from him in this life, he would restore to him in the life to come.

From several passages in the *Epistles*, Dr. Mant derives a very considerable probability that St. Paul anticipated on the last day a personal knowledge of those on his part, and a personal reunion with them, with whom he had been connected in this life by the ties of personal offices and kind affection. That the recognition would be mutual, seems to be a matter of course. And it may, Dr. Mant apprehends, be further assumed, that the same faculty of recognition which would exist at the "day of Christ," and the commencement of the future state of existence, would be perpetuated during its continuance; and that a faculty which should be allowed to St. Paul, and to those with whom he was thus connected, would not be withholden from others, who had stood in relations of mutual attachment and endearment whilst on earth.

The language of our Lord with reference to the Day of Judgment also renders this recognition of each other extremely probable.

The Transfiguration of our Saviour, as recorded by St. Matthew xvii. and St. Mark ix., is not the only proof of this recognition.

Recognition by the Blessed.

Moses and Elias were talking with Jesus. Moses and Elias must then have been alive: not two unknown but two *specific* persons. It cannot properly be said that "Peter and James, and John his brother,". the disciples present, *recognized* those whom they had never known in life; but the *identity* of Moses and Elias is declared, and that of course involves the question of recognition. Again, in the parable of Lazarus in Abraham's bosom,* and the rich man in torment, identity of persons, and recognition after death, are presented to us as facts in the understood order of Providence.

That these are indeed the facts, may be clearly comprehended also from the *definite* and *distinctive* position of man in the sight of God. "Fear not, I have redeemed thee, I have called thee by *thy name*." (Is. xliii. 1.) "I will not blot out his *name* out of the book of life, but I will confess his name before my Father and before His angels." (Rev. iii. 5.) St. Paul speaks of those whose names are in the book of life; and St. James of those whose names are *not* in the book of life. And numerous other passages might be quoted to show that the Christian especially will stand before God in heaven as personally and as individually known and distinguishable from his fellow-beings as he now stands before God and man on earth. The deduction is obvious: where individuality exists, recognition is a necessary consequence. If, with our present limited faculties, men know each other after long absence, and change from youth to age, is it possible that redeemed men, with the enlarged perceptions of a higher existence, can fail to recognize the earthly friends who were the faithful solace of their life's pilgrimage?—*On Futurity, by W. Merry.*

The mutual recognition of the redeemed in glory is demonstrated in a calm and convincing spirit by the Rev. J. A. Killeen, in his popular work entitled *Our Friends in Heaven*. The Scriptural argument is ably conducted throughout; and in the Appendix to the work, the doctrine of mutual recognition after death is shown to be a truth acknowledged by the heathen Homer (always understood to express the views and feelings of his age and country) : he uniformly describes the departed as recognizing each other, and conversing together in their disembodied condition. Thus, when Ulysses is permitted to visit the world of spirits, his mother recognizes him; so also, the soul of Achilles

---

* Alluding to the custom of those days, when men reclined at length side by side, at their feasts, instead of sitting. Thus, also, St. John is described as "leaning on Jesus's bosom," at the last supper.

recognizes Ulysses; and the prophet Tiresias not only recognizes him, but predicts his coming fortunes. In Hades, Achilles recognizes Agamemnon, from whom he receives an account of what had occurred on earth since his decease. Here, too, Ulysses sees the souls of the suitors he had slain. Achilles, too, talks with Ulysses, comparing his former with his present state, and wishes to know from his earthly visitant whether his son strove to "rival his father's godlike deeds."

So also we find Sophocles make *Antigone*, when about to endure a cruel death, exclaim,

> Oh! my deep dungeon! my eternal home!
> Whither I go to join my kindred dead;
> But still I have great hopes I shall not go
> Unwelcomed, to my father, nor to thee,
> My mother!—Dear to thee, Eteocles,
> Still shall I ever be.

Æschylus, in his *Persæ*, represents the soul of Darius as still possessing the thoughts and feelings of his former life; and in the address which he delivers, this departed spirit is exhibited as retaining a perfect recollection of his former history.

Socrates, in his apology before his judges, thus bears testimony to the doctrine of mutual recognition and companionship in the life to come: "Will it not be unspeakably blessed, when escaped from those who call themselves judges, to appear before those who truly deserve the name, such as Minos, Rhadamanthus, Æacus, and Triptolemus, and to associate with all who have maintained the cause of truth and righteousness; or again to converse with Orpheus and Musæus, and Hesiod and Homer; at how much would any of you purchase this? Be assured I would choose to die often, if these things be true; for to me delightful would be the communion with Palamedes, Ajax the son of Telamon, and others of the ancients who died in consequence of an unjust sentence pronounced upon them!"

Virgil describes Æneas as visiting the realms of the departed, and there recognizing, and being recognized by, the spirits he met:

> The gladsome ghosts in circling troops attend,
> And with unwearied eyes behold their friend,

> Delight to hover near, and long to know
> What business brought him to the realms below.—*Æneid.* vi.

His father Anchises

> Meets him with open arms and falling tears.
> "Welcome," he said, "the gods' undoubted race,
> O long expected, to my dear embrace.
> 'Tis true, computing time, I now believed
> The happy day approached—nor are my hopes deceived."
> *Æneid,* vi.

Cicero (*de Senectute*) declares his belief in the doctrine of recognition thus emphatically:

"I feel impelled by the desire of joining the society of my two departed friends, your illustrious fathers, whom I reverenced and loved. I desire not only to meet those whom I myself knew, but those of whom I have heard or read, or regarding whom I myself have written. Oh, illustrious day, when I shall go hence to that divine council and assembly of souls, when I shall escape from this crowd and rabble; for I shall go not only to those illustrious men of whom I have before spoken, but also to my Cato, than whom one more excellent or illustrious in goodness was never born. He himself consoled me, judging that our distance and parting would not long continue."

"Thus," says Mr. Killeen, "we find that the poets and philosophers of both Greece and Rome comforted themselves with the hope of recognition and reunion after death. They did not consider that death destroyed either friends or friendship; and they looked forward to spending an eternity of love with them in the Elysian plains, the Hesperian gardens, or the far-off Islands of the Blest."

The reverend author then shows that this belief in a future recognition has not been confined to the *ancient* Pagans. The Heathen of modern times have adopted the same doctrine. Dr. Robertson records that upon the death of a Cazique, or American chief, certain of his wives, favorites, and slaves, were put to death and interred with him, that he might appear with the same dignity in his future station. The burning of Hindoo widows was founded on a similar belief: they prayed to abide in heaven with their husbands as many years as there were hairs on their heads. 'Porphyry tells us that the Hindoo Gymnosophists, or barefooted philosophers, were wont to *send messages to their departed friends* by those who were about to commit suicide. The natives of Dahomey entertain the same belief: when the King is anxious to send to his forefathers an account of any remarkable event, he delivers the message to the person who happens to be nearest to him, and then orders his head to be chopped off immediately, so that as a courier he may convey the intelligence to the King's friends in the land of spirits. In Guinea, when a King dies, many persons are slain, that they may live again with him in another world.

"Similar customs and ideas have been found existing among the Danes, the Chinese, the Brazilians, the people of Macassar and Japan, all which, though often defiled by superstitious and cruel rites, betoken the aspirations of the human spirit, and prove that humanity, even in its most degraded phases, still retains the purest of its social affections, and longs for everlasting friendship with those it loves."*

The Members of the Primitive Church were remarkable for their *love of their dead*, which they strongly showed by sacrifices, by honorable burial, and by visiting their tombs—thus aiming to realize a secret and invisible communion with their deceased friends, and to come, as it were, into a sort of spiritual contact with their dead. Hence they loved to have their burial-places around their churches. Neander says that the anniversary of the decease of their friends was observed as *a birthday to a nobler existence.* That on this day "it was usual to partake of the Supper of the Lord, in the consciousness of an inseparable communion with those who had died in Christ;" and he adds, "a gift was laid on the altar in their names, as if they were still living members of the Church." Cyprian consoled his church at Carthage, when multitudes had been swept away by pestilence—with this healing:

"We ought not to mourn for those who, by the summons of the Lord, are delivered from the world, since *we know they are not lost, but sent before us*—that they have only taken their leave

---

* *Our Friends in Heaven.* Appendix, 8th Edit.

of us, in order to *precede us*. We may long for them as we do for those who are on a distant voyage, but not lament them. Why do we not ourselves wish to depart out of this world, or why do we mourn our departed ones as lost? Why do we not hasten to see our country, to greet our parents? There await us a vast multitude of dear ones—fathers, mothers, and children—who are already secure of their own salvation, and anxious only for ours. What a mutual joy to them and us, when we shall come into their presence and embrace!"—*Church History*, vol. i.

THE TRANSLATION OF ENOCH.

The history of the prophet to whom the book of Enoch is attributed, or rather whose visions it relates, is recounted as follows in Gen. v. 18-24: "Jared, at the age of 162, begat Enoch; who, at the age of 65, begat Methuselah, and afterwards walked with God 300 years, and begat sons and daughters. All the days of Enoch were 365 years. He walked with God, and was not, for God took him." (Compare Ecclesiasticus xliv. 16; Heb. xii. 5.) The translation of Enoch has been compared with the ancient mysterious burial at sunrise of noble and comely youths who prematurely died. They are said to have been not really dead, but carried up alive to the region of light, in consequence of their being loved by the Supreme Being. The story of Ganymede is an instance. (See the learned disquisition on the subject in Montfaucon's *Religion des Gaulois*, tom. ii. p. 305, &c.; and in his *Explication des Textes difficiles*, tom. i. p. 132.) Hence the well-known axiom, "He whom the gods love dies young." Plutarch, *De Consolatione Philosoph.*

The *Translation of Enoch* has been commemorated by Thomas Peyton, a learned and pious poet, in his *Glasse of Time*; published in 1620:

> God re-ascends, and lets the world alone,
> Takes Enoch vp, that liu'd therein to mone,
> Waile, grieve, lament, the abuses which he saw
> Committed were against the conscience, law
> Of noble stature, in that sinful age;
> Small hope to mend, when hope could not assuage

> The furious current of this streamé and tide
> To good (sweete saint) with these foule men to bide.
> The angels bright, and all the powers diuine,
> Before thy face in glittering robes do shine,
> Their number more than are the stars and sands,
> With golden censers in their pure white hands,
> Winged with fame to mount the highest heauens,
> Ranck't all in order, must'ring iust by seauens,
> Descending sweetely on thy louely brest,
> To bring both soule and body to their rest.
> By safe conueyance, in a chariot fram'd
> Of burnisht gold, the horse with loue inflam'd
> Mount vp the aire with stately stomach fierce,
> And at the last the brazen wall doth pierce;
> Where like a Prince that Paradise had gain'd
> Of Eue and Adam thou art entertain'd,
> With farre more love within so braue a field,
> Then all the world and all therein can yeeld;
> There thou dost liue when they are wrapt in dust.
> The seuenth from them, tipe of our Sabaoth iust.

"MARRIAGES ARE MADE IN HEAVEN."

The origin of this beautiful proverb is thus explained:

Normal marriages being so innocent of all premeditation by *man*, can only be ascribed to the will of "the angel" espoused, or to fate, in either case (for ce qui femme veut, Dieu le veut) to the will of Heaven. After marriage, another sense may appear in the saying, viz.: that expressed in the words of St. Francis de Salis: "Marriage is a state of continual mortification;" and hence a sacrament for human salvation. Again, in suggesting the meaning of this phrase, we are led to the well-known beautiful myth of Plato, according to which, in a true marriage, the two counterparts have met by destiny, and form a perfect *homo*. The account in Genesis (chap. ii.) is not to a dissimilar effect. In this view, marriages are those whom God has joined only. (Mark x. 9.) In a literal sense, the phrase in question clearly expresses an impossibility; since in heaven are no marriages (Mat. xxii. 30), according to the usual interpretation; though some may take refuge in the beautiful evasion of Swedenborg—who says that in the next world the married couple will become one angel.

Had not this saying an *astrological* foundation? Sir Kenelm Digby says of his own marriage:

> In the first place, it giveth me occasion to acknowledge and admire the high and transcendent operations of the celestial bodies, which, containing and moving about the universe, send their influence every way and to all things; and who, although they take not away the liberty of free agents, yet do so strongly, though at the first secretly and insensibly, work upon their spiritual part by means of the corporeal, that they get the mastery before they be perceived; and then it is too late to make any resistance. For from what other cause could proceed this strong knot of affection, which, being tied in tender years, before any mutual obligations could help to confirm it, could not then be torn asunder by long absence, the austerity of parents, other pretenders, false rumors, and other the greatest difficulties and oppositions that could come to blast the budding blossoms of an infant love, that hath since brought forth so fair flowers and so mature fruit? Certainly, the stars were at the least the first movers, &c.—*Private Memoirs of Sir K. Digby*, 1811, pp. 10, 11.

"THE BUSINESS OF THE SAINTS IN HEAVEN."

What a singular book is this, by father Lewis Henriquez: printed at Salamanca in 1631. He attempts to prove, in the twenty-second chapter, "That every saint shall have his particular place in heaven; and Christ a most magnificent palace! That there shall be large streets, great piazzas, &c."—He says in the twenty-fourth chapter, "That there shall be a sovereign pleasure in kissing and embracing the bodies of the blest; that there shall be pleasant baths, and that they shall bathe in each other's sight. That they shall swim like fishes; and sing as melodiously as nightingales, &c."—He affirms, in the forty-seventh chapter, "That the men and women shall delight themselves in masquerades, feasts, and ballads;"—and in the fifty-eighth, "That the angels shall put on women's habits, and appear to be saints in the dress of ladies, with curls and locks, waistcoats and fardingales, &c." See the "*Moral practice of the Jesuits*," by the doctors of Sorbonne; it has been translated into English, and published in 1671.—*Spence's Anecdotes. Supplement*, 1757.

THE NEW HEAVENS AND EARTH.

Bishop Mant, in his volume on the *Happiness of the Blessed*, refers to several passages in St. Paul's Epistle to the Hebrews, indicating the *excellence* of the future residence of the blessed. Thus, he figuratively speaks of it as "Mount Sion," "the joy of the whole earth" (Ps. xlviii. 2); and he further mentions it, by a different modification of the same figure, as "the city of the living God, the heavenly Jerusalem." He elsewhere refers to the same celestial abode, in speaking of Abraham sojourning "in the land of promise, as in a strange country, dwelling in tabernacles with Isaac and Jacob, the heirs with him of the same promise; for he looked for a city which hath foundations, whose builder and maker is God." (Heb. xi. 10.) He then speaks of God having prepared a city for the descendants of Abraham who died in the faith; and of the descendants of Abraham after the Spirit, or the members of the Christian Church, the same Apostle says: "Here we have no continuing city, but we seek one to come." (Heb. xiii. 14.)

All these passages point to the superior excellence and value of that celestial abode which is prepared for God's faithful servants in the world to come. But the book of Revelation of St. John supplies *individual features* of the magnificence, beauty, and enjoyment of "the holy city, prepared as a bride adorned for her husband," "having the glory of God."

"And the foundations of the wall of the city were garnished with all manner of precious stones. . . . And the twelve gates were twelve pearls; every gate was of one pearl; and the street of the city was pure gold, as it were transparent glass." "And the city had no need of the sun, neither of the moon, to shine in it; for the glory of God did lighten it, and the Lamb is the light thereof. And the nations of them which are saved shall walk in the light of it; and the kings of the earth do bring into it their glory and honor." And it had "a pure river of water of life, clear as crystal, proceeding out of the throne of God and of the Lamb. And in the midst of the street of it, and on either side of the river, was the tree of life, which bare twelve manner of fruits, and yielded her fruit every month; and the leaves of the tree were for the healing of the nations."

In whatever manner such portraits as these are to be understood; whether it be that the most beautiful and splendid productions of the earth will be enjoyed in full perfection by the inhabitants of the heavenly state; agreeably to the idea ascribed to Raphael by our great poet,

> What if earth
> Be but the shadow of heaven, and things therein
> Each to other like, more than on earth is thought;
>
> *Paradise Lost.*

or that the representations of heavenly things are set before us in a figurative manner, as calculated to impress us with a more lively sense of their value and delightfulness, when shadowed forth under the images of those things which are esteemed on earth most precious and delightful; in either case they seem intended to place most expressively before our thoughts the *beauty* and *magnificence* of the future abode of the blessed,

> —The pleasant garden, and the crystal stream,
> The tree of life, which bears on every bough
> Fruits fit for joy or healing; on the brow,
> Of glorious gold a living diadem;
> On thrones which blaze with many a radiant gem;
> The branching palms; the raiment white as snow;
> Are these the joys that heaven's abodes bestow?
> Or may they rather earth-formed figures seem
> Of heavenly bliss? To me it matters not,
> If I but reach the mark, whate'er the prize
> Of God's high calling. Be content that what
> Is told, is told us by the only Wise:
> And blest, supremely blest, must be the lot
> Which Christ hath purchased, and which God supplies.
>
> *Bishop Mant.*

"We look (says St. Peter) for new heavens and a *new earth*, wherein dwelleth righteousness." And it seems evident that the proper abode of man will be *not in the new heavens, but on the new earth*. For St. John writes, "And I saw a new heaven and a new earth, for the first heaven and the first earth were passed away; and there was no more sea."

By the new earth, and the holy city, the new Jerusalem, which St. John saw coming down *from* God, *out* of heaven, the future place of abode of the followers of Christ, of all who shall have attained unto immortality, we must not understand a merely spiritual world, or state, but literally a *place* of happiness, and (perhaps it may not be incorrect to say) a *substantial* seat of bliss.

May we not (asks Bishop Courtenay) be permitted to conjecture that this great city shall become THE ABODE OF ALL LIVING

BEINGS: not only of angelic creatures and of the redeemed from the present earth, but of all *the rational and beatified inhabitants of all now existing worlds;* and that its foundations shall extend beyond the "flaming walls of the world" that now is, through spaces immeasurable by mortal man? For the New Jerusalem shall not, like the old, occupy a small part of the earth, but rather, like the Christian church, as foreseen by Isaiah, when "the earth shall be filled with the knowledge of the Lord, as the waters that cover the depths of the sea,"* it shall be co-extensive with the plain on which it stands. All abominable and condemned things shall be not *without* Jerusalem, yet *upon* the earth, like the gehenna of the Jews, where the dead and the filth of the city were consumed with fire; but beyond both, far from the Divine presence. Yet shall the immense tracts of the new earth be traversed with ease by the gloriously embodied spirits that inhabit them, for "there shall be no more sea,"—nothing, it may be, to impede the interchange of happiness and intimate communion of saints; and they, wandering where they will, even to the uttermost parts, shall still be led by the hand of God, still bask in the full splendor of "uncreated rays," still be sitting with Christ in his throne, even as he also is set down with the Father in his throne.

The philosopher may argue, upon principles merely physical, upon the blending of mind and matter, and the modifications of matter, which shall enter into the constitution of the glorified bodies, or of the earth which they shall inhabit. To such arguments Bishop Courtenay thus forcibly replies:

Yet, when we learn from Revelation that a change shall be effected in the bodies of the saints at the last day, in which every thing that is of the earth and earthy,—the whole nature, as it would seem, of the first man, a creature of the dust—shall be rejected; and that on the same Great Day the elements shall be dissolved, the earth burned up, and the whole material heavens, including even light, apparently the purest and most imperishable of material things, shall be utterly abolished, there is much ground for doubt whether any thing partaking of the nature of matter will be suffered to remain: if, indeed, we may not hold the abolition of *all* matter for certain, since "all things that are made," and "which can be shaken," will be removed at the Great Day. And perhaps nothing has been revealed concerning the

* So in Lowth's translation.

future state of the blessed, which more strongly shows the spirituality of their condition, than this abolition of material light. The city shall inhabit, shall enjoy, without the aid of the solar heavens, a perpetual day:

> Nor sun nor moon they need, nor day nor night,
> God is their temple, and the Lamb their light.

It is difficult to suppose that any thing resembling the emanation of material rays is intended, though such a notion is encouraged by the appearance of Christ at his transfiguration, when "his face did shine as the Sun, and his raiment was white as the light" (Matt. c. xviii.); and without some supposition of the kind, the vision of the heavenly Jerusalem fades completely from before the eye of the imagination.

* * * * * *

The future existence of the blessed then will be, not in the present visible heavens;—for these, though they constitute the material throne of God, and are the stage and proper sphere of the agency of many angelic beings, are but symbols and figures of the true, and will at a destined period pass away, and give place to *new* heavens; nor will it consist simply in a spiritual communion with the Father of Spirits, without any certain locality;—for men will still be embodied, and enjoying a certain corporeal proximity to Christ, after the likeness of whose glorious body they will be fashioned, having "spiritual bodies," and whether with any remnant of materiality we know not—but their future life will be ON THE NEW EARTH AND IN THE HOLY CITY.

One of the latest flights of scientific conjecture is the following, by Sir David Brewster, in his eloquent advocacy of the doctrine of "More Worlds than One," arguing for their peopling, as "the Abodes of the Blest:"

Man, in his future state of existence, is to consist, as at present, of a spiritual nature residing in a corporeal frame. He must live, therefore, upon a material planet, subject to all the laws of matter, and performing functions for which a material body is indispensable. We must consequently find for the race of Adam, if not for races that may have preceded him, a material home upon which they may reside, or by which they may travel, by means unknown to us, to other localities in the universe. At the present hour, the inhabitants of the earth are nearly *a thousand millions;* and by whatever process we may compute the numbers that have existed before the present generation, and estimate those that are yet to inherit the earth, we shall obtain a population which the habitable parts of our globe could not possibly accommodate. If there is not room, then, on our earth for the millions of millions of beings who have lived and died upon its surface, and who may yet live and die during the period fixed for its occupation by man, we can scarcely doubt that their future abode must be on some of the primary or secondary planets of the solar system, whose inhabitants have ceased to exist like those on the earth, or upon planets in our own or in other systems which have been in a state of preparation, as our earth was, for the advent of intellectual life.

Adversaria.

STUDY OF THE BIBLE.*

How utterly impossible it would be in the manhood of the world, to imagine any other instructor of mankind than—the Bible. And for that reason, every day makes it more and more evident that the thorough study of the Bible, the investigation of what it teaches and what it does not teach, the determination of the limits of what we mean by its inspiration, the determination of the degree of authority to be ascribed to the different books, if any degrees are to be admitted, must take the lead of all other studies. He is guilty of high-treason against the faith who fears the result of any investigation, whether philosophical or scientific or historical. And therefore nothing should be more welcome than the extension of knowledge of any and of every kind—for every increase in our accumulations of knowledge throws fresh light upon the real problems of the day. If geology proves to us that we must not interpret the first chapters of Genesis literally; if historical investigation shall show us that inspiration, however it may protect the doctrine, yet was not empowered to protect the narrative of the inspired writers from occasional inaccuracy; if careful criticism shall prove that there have been occasionally interpolations and forgeries in that Book, as in many others; the results should still be welcome. Even the mistakes of careful and reverend students are more valuable now than truth held in unthinking acquiescence. The substance of the teaching which we derive from the Bible will not really be affected by any thing of this sort; while its hold upon the minds of believers, and its power to stir the depths of the spirit of man, however much

* For these two extracts the editor is indebted to *Essays and Reviews*.

weakened at first, must be immeasurably strengthened in the end, by clearing away blunders which may have been fastened on it by human interpretation.

* * * * * * *

Though the study of the Bible must be for the present and for some time the centre of all studies, there is, meanwhile, no study of whatever kind, which will not have its share in the general effect. At this time, in the maturity of mankind, as with man in the maturity of his powers, the great lever which moves the world is knowledge, the great force is the intellect. St. Paul has told us "that though in malice we must be children, in understanding we ought to be men." And this saying of his has the widest range. Not only in the understanding of religious truth, but in all the exercise of the intellectual powers, we have no right to stop short of any limit but that which nature, that is, the decree of the Creator, has imposed on us. In fact, no knowledge can be without its effect on religious convictions; for if not capable of throwing direct light on some spiritual questions, yet in its acquisition knowledge invariably throws light on the process by which it is to be, or has been, acquired, and thus affects all other knowledge of every kind.

If we have made mistakes, careful study may teach us better. If we have quarrelled about words, the enlightenment of the understanding is the best means to show us our folly. If we have vainly puzzled our intellects with subjects beyond human cognizance, better knowledge of ourselves will help us to be humbler. Life, indeed, is higher than all else; and no service that man can render to his fellows, is to be compared with the heavenly power of a life of holiness. But next to that must be ranked whatever tends to make men think clearly and judge correctly. So valuable, even above all things (excepting only godliness), is clear thought, that the labors of the statesman are far below those of the philosopher, in duration, in power, and in beneficial results. Thought is now higher than action, unless action be inspired with the very breath of heaven. For we are now men, governed by principles, if governed at all, and cannot rely any longer on the impulses of youth or the discipline of childhood. We quote these able remarks from Dr. Temple's *Education*.

Professor Jowett, in a paper on the *Religious Tendencies of the Age*, observes:

There is a wide distinction between the interpretation and the application of Scripture. The latter is of much wider extent than the former. "Interpretation is the province of few; it requires a finer perception of language, and a higher degree of cultivation, than is attained by the majority of mankind. But applications are made by all, from the philosopher reading *God in History*, to the poor woman who finds in them a response to her prayers, and the solace of her daily life. In the hour of death we do not want critical explanations; in most cases, those to whom they would be offered are incapable of understanding them. A few words, breathing the whole sense of the Christian world, such as, 'I know that my Redeemer liveth' (though the exact meaning of them may be doubtful to the Hebrew scholar); 'I shall go to him, but he shall not return to me;' touch a chord which would never be reached by the most skilful exposition of the argument of one of St. Paul's Epistles."

SERPENT WORSHIP.

There is scarcely a heathen nation that has not adopted some deity in the form of a serpent. Among those who were foremost in this form of idolatry were the Egyptians, who built chapels underground, where they carefully fed and worshipped them. In the time of Herodotus, serpents were kept tame at Thebes, adorned with jewels, and consecrated to Jupiter. When they died they were buried with divine honors, and placed in urns in the temple of Jupiter.* And, according to Ælian, they were admitted into the houses of the Egyptians, and there treated as household gods. It is said that Jotham, king of Israel, built much on the wall of Ophel, that is, the serpent God; and this animal was the form under which the Cnaphis or Agathodæmon of the Egyptian pantheon was worshipped by the inhabitants of the Thebaid.

But, although this creature was worshipped by many nations

---

* Eutropius, lib. ii. He states also that another serpent was worshipped in a tower at Miletus, in Egypt, where there was a priest and other officers attending it. It was fed daily with meal and honey.

in the east, the Babylonians, Arabians, Scythians, Phœnicians, Macedonians, and many others; yet in India, and more particularly on the coast of Malabar, this form of worship attained its greatest height of absurdity. The king of Calicut, who was formerly the most powerful of all the Malabar princes, and whose title was no less than " God upon earth," was so much enslaved by the worship of this creature as to have temples built purposely for them, where they were held sacred and made the guardians of all their houses, persons, and property. So highly was the serpent considered in the east, that wherever it was figured or painted, the place was held sacred, and the ground consecrated; and the most exalted honor that could be conferred upon a hero was to style him "born of a serpent." Thus, Alexander the Great, who suffered himself to be called God, and Scipio Africanus, were both said to be born of serpents. So likewise was the companion of Cadmus, the giant in Homer, and a certain prophet in Pausanias; nay, whole tribes went by the name of serpent. This was the case with some people inhabiting Cyprus and around the Hellespont. Even in the primitive church there was a sect called Ophites, because they worshipped the serpent that betrayed Eve, and therefore ascribed supernatural knowledge to that animal.

But the most probable origin of Serpent worship would seem to take its rise in the corrupt and perverted constructions which were put upon the history of Adam and Eve by heathen nations, many of which seem to have received sufficient intimation of this event. and of the record made by Moses, to account for many strange perversions which we read of in mythology. Indeed, in the Phœnician theology the creation is described almost in the same manner as that of the Pentateuch.

SYMBOLICAL FIGURES FROM NINEVEH.

The visitor to the British Museum who curiously examines the winged bulls, lions, and other mysterious figures from Nineveh, can scarcely fail to be convinced that they are not mere sculptural ornaments, but symbols of certain mysteries and ceremonies of the primeval religion of Assyria. The era of these sculptures is so remote, and the traditions respecting them so obscure, that the inquiry into their signification is difficult, and the conclusions arrived at unsatisfactory; still, some attempt has been made to penetrate the mystery which surrounds them. The chief mythological figures are the winged bull with a man's face; the winged lion with a man's face; the winged man with a fir-cone in one hand and a square basket or vessel in the other; and a man with the head and wings of an eagle or hawk. The hypothesis which Mr. Ravenshaw, in a paper read to the Asiatic Society, maintains with respect to them is, that they are, as already surmised by Mr. Layard, the originals of the cherubim of Ezekiel; that they were likewise the originals of the apocalyptic beasts of St. John; and that, slightly modified, they were afterward adopted, and are now used, as the symbols of the four Evangelists. Further, that they were originally invented by the Magi and Chaldeans as astronomical symbols of the equinoctial and solstitial points; that they represent in fact the four seasons—spring, summer, autumn, and winter; and perhaps also the four winds and the four elements.

In support and illustration of these views, the writer enters into an examination of the passages in the Old Testament and in other writings, regarding the cherubim, showing that there is no authority in Scripture for supposing them to be bodiless infants, and comes to the conclusion that the face of a cherub was in reality the face of a bull. At an early period of the Christian Church these winged animals were adopted as the symbols of the Four Evangelists. The winged lion was assigned to St. Mark, as the symbol of strength; the winged ox to St. Luke, as the symbol of sacrifice; the eagle and chalice to St. John, as the symbol of contemplation; and the winged man with a cup and hatchet to St. Matthew, as the symbol of power. The employment of these figures as astronomical symbols formed the next branch of inquiry, and the conclusions were, that the colossal bulls are symbols of the sun in Taurus, or the vernal equinox; that the winged man is Mitra or Serosh, the guardian of the autumnal equinox; and the winged man-lion and eagle-headed man the symbols of the solstices, being the four cherubim who watched the gates of Heaven, and upheld the Zodiac.

As regards the other mythological figures, it is probable that the man with a goat in his arms represents the constellation Capricorn, and the fish-god, that of Pisces. All the names of the gods found in the Nineveh inscriptions will probably, on further inquiry, prove to be the names of constellations, stars, or planets, chosen as the guardian angels of nations, kings, or individuals. The mystic tree, which forms so conspicuous an object in the sculptures, has evidently some astronomical signification. The number of its rosettes or leaves vary considerably, but never exceed thirty; and the winged circle, or the new moon and some stars, are generally seen above it. Hence it seems probable that these trees were orreries showing the month, day, or season which is being celebrated by the winged figures or priests who are represented in connection with them. The winged circles or eyes, which are frequently placed above the sacred tree, and seem to form the principal object of adoration, so closely resemble the winged globes on the portals of the Egyptian temples, that it is difficult to disbelieve the identity of their origin. At first they were probably typical of time, but came afterwards to be looked upon as the symbols of Ormuzd, the active creator and source of all good. These speculations may appear more curious than profitable; still it cannot be uninteresting to inquire what were the ideas of men 3,000 years ago, when the earth was comparatively young; to learn what were the traditions of Asia as to the origin and destiny of the human race, and what notions were then entertained as to the Creator and Governor of the universe.

EVIDENCES OF CHRISTIANITY—CHANGES IN OPINION.

If we compare the general tone, character, and pretensions of those works which, in our schools and colleges, have been regarded as the standard authorities on the subject of "the Evidences," we must acknowledge a great change in the taste or opinions of the times from the commencement of the last century to the present day; which has led the student to turn from the erudite folios of Jackson and Stillingfleet, or the more condensed arguments of Clarke *On the Attributes*, Grotius *de Veritate*, and Leslie's *Method with the Deists*, the universal text books of a past generation—to the writings of Lardner and Paley; the latter of whom, in the beginning of the present century, reigned supreme, the acknowledged champion of revelation, and the head of a school, to which numerous others, as Campbell, Watson and Douglas, contributed their labors. But more recently, these authors have been in a degree superseded, by a recurrence to the once comparatively neglected resources furnished by Bishop Butler; of so much less formal, technical, and positive a kind, yet offering wider and more philosophical views of the subject; still, however, not supplying altogether that comprehensive discussion which is adapted to the peculiar tone and character of thought and existing state of knowledge in our own times.

* * * * * *

At the present day, the "evidential" view of miracles, as the sole or even the principal external attestation to the claims of a Divine revelation, is a species of reasoning which appears to have lost ground even among the most earnest advocates of Christianity. It is now generally admitted that Paley took too conclusive a view in asserting that we cannot conceive a revelation substantiated in any other way. And it has been even more directly asserted by some zealous supporters of Christian doctrine that the external evidences are altogether inappropriate and worthless.

CHRISTIAN REVELATION—WHY FIRST GIVEN TO THE WEST.

It has been customary to argue that, *à priori*, a supernatural revelation was to be expected at the time when Jesus Christ was manifested upon the earth, by reason of the exhaustion of all natural or unassisted efforts for the amelioration of mankind. The state of the world, it has been customary to say, had become so utterly corrupt and hopeless under the Roman sway, that a necessity and special occasion was presented for an express divine intervention. Our recently enlarged ethnographical information shows such an argument to be altogether inapplicable to the case. If we could be judges of the necessity for a special divine intervention, the stronger necessity existed in the East. There immense populations, like the Chinese, had never developed the idea of a personal God, or had degenerated from a once pure theological creed, as in India, from the religion of the Vedas. Oppressions and tyrannies, caste-distinctions, common and enormous vices, a polluted idolatrous worship, as bad as the worst which disgraced Rome, Greece, or Syria, had prevailed for ages.

It would not be very tasteful, as an exception to this description, to call Buddhism the gospel of India, preached to it five or six centuries before the Gospel of Jesus was proclaimed in the nearer East. But on the whole it would be more like the realities of things, as we can now behold them, to say that the Christian revelation was given to the western world, because it deserved better and was more prepared for it than the East. Philosophers, at least, had anticipated in speculation some of its dearest hopes, and had prepared the way for its self-denying ethics.—*Dr. Williams: Essays and Reviews.*

THE HOLY THORN AT GLASTONBURY.

This miraculous tree grew in the grounds of the famous abbey of Glastonbury, in Somerset. The tradition is briefly, that when Joseph of Arimathea came to Britain, to preach Christianity, A. D. 63, Arviragus, then king, gave them the isle of Avalon, in Somerset, afterwards called by the Saxons Glastonbury. On Joseph's arrival, having a hawthorn-stick in his hand, he stuck it in the ground, when it grew and blossomed on Christmas-day, to the great amazement of the people. Several thorns of this kind were in after ages planted in the neighborhood, which budded and blossomed in the depth of winter; and some ten years since, a thorn of this kind, which was observed not to have a single blossom on it on Christmas-eve, was seen in blossom next day.

Warner, in his *History* of the Abbey, states that the Thorn had two trunks, or bodies, till the reign of Queen Elizabeth, in whose days a saint-like Puritan taking offence at it hewed down the biggest of the two trunks, and had cut down the other body in all likelihood, had he not been miraculously punished by cutting his leg, and one of the chips flying up to his head, which put out one of his eyes. . . . The remaining trunk is described to have

The Holy Thorn at Glastonbury. 307

been as great as the ordinary body of a man, that it was a *white thorn*, but was so cut and mangled in the bark, by people cutting their names on it, that it was a wonder how the sap and nutriment were conveyed to the root and branches, which were also maimed and broken by comers. Yet the arms and boughs were widely spread, and bore haws as plentifully as others do.

In a word, the blossoms of this tree were such *curiosities* beyond seas, that the Bristol merchants carried them into foreign parts: it grew upon (or rather near) the top of a hill in a pasture bare and naked of other trees, and was a shelter for cattle feeding there, by reason whereof, the pasture being great, and the cattle many, round about the tree the ground was bare and beaten as any trodden place. Yet this trunk was likewise cut down by a "military saint" in the time of Charles I. In 1826, however, when Warner wrote, there were divers trees from it by grafting and inoculation, preserved in the town and country adjacent: amongst other places, there was one in the garden of a currier in the principal street of Glastonbury; a second at the White Hart inn; and a third in the garden of William Strode, Esq. "There is (adds Warner) a person about Glastonbury, who has a nursery of them, who, Mr. Paschal tells us he is informed, sells them for a crown apiece, or as much as he can get."

Collinson, in his *History of Somersetshire*, states that besides the Holy Thorn, there grew in the Abbey churchyard, on the north side of St. Joseph's chapel, a walnut-tree which never budded forth before the feast of St. Barnabas (June 11); but on that very day shot forth leaves and flourished. This tree disappeared, and in its place grew a very fine walnut-tree of the common sort. It is strange to say how much this tree was sought after by the credulous; and though not an uncommon walnut, King James, Queen Anne, and many of the nobility of the realm, even when the times of monkish superstition had ceased, gave large sums of money for cuttings of the original tree.

Glastonbury too was famous for its Mineral Waters, which, according to Holinshead, cured King Arthur of his wounds. Their fame slept for ages; but in 1751, at Glastonbury, a man who had been thirty years afflicted with asthma, dreamed that he was told if he drank of certain waters near the Chain Gate, seven Sunday mornings, he should be cured; which he accordingly did, became well, and attested the cure upon oath. This was rumored abroad, and it was computed that 10,000 persons shortly afterwards visited Glastonbury to drink the waters there, for "various distempers."

THE CHRISTIAN MISSION.

In this beneficent work, we see the necessity of grasping the marvels of God's love and comprehending somewhat of the mysteries of the everlasting counsels of our redemption, of the love of Christ, and the sympathy of the Cross, which penetrates each individual soul. The eye of God is over every one, under the greatest tumult and confusion of worldly trouble; and His tender compassion is as full to each one of the innumerable souls of men as if that single soul was alone on a desert island. When this great truth of the tender care of God for each soul is realized, this further idea must be grasped—viz.: that the Church of Christ, His witness on earth, if she is faithful to her mission, must reproduce among men this tender loving care of her Lord. Compassion for the weak, the tempted, and the fallen, must be her special care. The world passes these by with scorn; but in all ages the Church has strewed Christendom with hospitals, penitentaries, lazar-houses, and infirmaries, while her children have ministered —aye, the noblest born—in prison and by the sick-bed, and even the purple pride of kings bent to wash the feet of outcasts. Where such things die out, all true service dies also; and then a cold unsympathizing world reasserts its accursed supremacy. When a great religious enterprise is proposed, the world always suggests difficulties, calls it ill-timed, disturbing to family arrangements and comforts; and as rubbing so unceremoniously the brightness of a tinselled decency it calls it unpractical, fanciful, exaggerated, romantic. Yes, it must be so; for to such a temper what an exaggeration is the Cross! what a mystery that the Eternal Son should hang on it! how incomprehensible that unchanging love can, in the hour of its agony, remember the dying malefactor! The Church is ever contending against this spirit; and blessed is that branch of the Church stirred up to any special protest which, stretching beyond that of a martyred band, should revive the dying embers of a nation's love. To a certain extent such is the nature of all Missionary zeal. However accidentally fashionable, all such fashions are esteemed by the world a waste, an extravagance, an absurdity. Such acts in reality give us clearer visions of the Cross, closer access to it, more of its saving power. This good work tends to break up the dead level of respectability, and the yet deeper lethargy of questioning unbelief, healing intestine divisions, abating party spirit, and fanning to a flame the flickering emblems of our love to God and man. Note its special characteristics. First, it is the highest intellect of our Universities going forth, for the love of Christ, to bless the most ignorant and the most barbarous. Secondly, it is the Church going forth in the completeness of her Apostolic organization to spread the Gospel among the outcasts of her people. These are the ventures of faith which win an Apostle's crown, not only for their leader but for all whence they spring. This movement is, first a sign of good amidst our suspicions, divisions, hard language about one another, strong scepticism as to the truth of God, showing the energy yet inherent in our branch of the Church. Secondly, it strengthens and revives our home-life, it being true now, as in all ages of the Church, that "There is that scattereth and yet increaseth," and that "The soul of the bountiful shall be made fat." We have kept the good deposit at once in doctrine, in discipline, and in succession : we may say our English prayers and read our English Bibles in peace; we consecrate an unmutilated Eucharist, maintain an unmutilated creed, set forth the Cross of Christ simply, yet cling dutifully to His Body, the Church ; cherish the glorious memory of His departed saints, inherit the transmitted authority of His undying Apostleship. Oh! in this coming Communion wrestle with God, dear brethren, in prayer for yourselves, for those going out,[*] and resolve not to let Him go unless He bless us. Think of the greatness of this enterprise, of the dangers to be encountered, the blessings to be conveyed, and the souls to be saved! Think of your own need,

[*] From a Sermon preached in Canterbury Cathedral, October, 1860, by Samuel, Lord Bishop of Oxford, upon the departure of the Oxford and Cambridge Mission for Southern Africa.

your coldness, your lukewarm service, your lack of love, restrained prayers and chilled thanksgivings, and, thinking thus, pray mightily; for intercession opens many a heart. To the assurance of God's abiding presence, what shall we add that shall not weaken these words? Oh! thou shalt know in that desert land the secret of His presence; thou shalt see, as men see not in their peaceful homes, the nail-pierced hand, and the crowned brow; and thou shalt find, as all great saints have found, that He is better than all else; when all leave thee He shall be closest to thee, shall change labor to rest, suffering into ease, anguish into glory, and, if need be, the martyr's suffering to a martyr's victory.

THE TRUE COURSE OF CHRISTIAN LIFE.

There is a kind of religious teaching which is very apt to betray souls. The first direction given to men of all characters is to set out with a firm persuasion of their reconciliation with God, and the enjoyment of everlasting happiness. This is surely an inverted order of things. For our right to the comfort of the promise made to believing Christians, can only be ascertained by the agreement of the temper of our minds and the course of our lives, with the Scripture characters of those privileged persons, to whom those promises are appropriated; and to expect men to arrogate that comfort to themselves, previously to any degree of holy conformity in disposition and conduct to those descriptive characters, is to take the children's bread, and give it unto dogs; is to act without gospel, warrant or authority, to prescribe rashly, and fatally to mislead the souls of men. This kind of teaching too often leads to nothing better than a bold, presumptuous confidence. Whereas, even with evidence of the best sort attending this course, the true Christian will always proceed on his course trembling with rejoicing. Dr. Arnold draws the picture: "To-day, penitent, justified, and full of assurance—to-morrow, it may be, cast down, and full of humiliation, and godly fear. So it will be, and so it must be; till *having finished our course*, and the work of the tempter being ended, and his power stopped for ever, we may find there is a peace to be no more disturbed, a rest to be no more broken, an assurance to be no more troubled with fear."

TRUE AND FALSE BUDDHISM.

In Germany, England, and elsewhere, it has lately been the fashion to nickname a certain class of freethinkers, *Buddhists ;* but this term is altogether inapplicable in the present case, and is founded upon a general misapprehension, which has been thus ably exposed in a letter addressed to *The Times* journal, by Colonel Sykes, F. R. S., the celebrated Hindostanee scholar :

They who adopt this erroneous view, instead of going to primitive Buddhism, accept as its genuine religious tenets those embodied in works which were written in a language foreign to Buddhist literature ; whether sacred or profane, promulgated in a foreign country, and of a date from 1,100 to 1,200 years after Buddha's first preaching. They adopt Burnouf's exposition of Buddhism, as derived from books met with in Nepaul, and written in Sanscrit. Equally they trust to Hinang Tsang's fables of the seventh century, and to the practices and beliefs at present existing in China and other Buddhist countries. As well might they pronounce primitive Christianity from the lives of the Roman Catholic Saints of the Middle Ages; from the opinions of the Anabaptists of the sixteenth century ; or those of the Mormons of the present time. One thousand years after Buddha's advent, Fa Hian travelled in India for the purpose of collecting Buddhist books, and observing the state of Buddhism. He found the religion declining and corrupted ; but in the seventh century, when Hinang Tsang travelled in India, Buddhism was fast declining into childish legends and superstitions, and modern Brahminism was rising in its place.

It was in this corrupt state that Buddhism found its way to Nepaul about the eighth century ; and its dogmas were for the first time recorded in Sanscrit, as the multitudinous impressions upon rocks, pillars, and copper-plates, in Pali, attest ; and the books taken from India to China by the Chinese travellers, between the fourth and seventh centuries, were equally in Pali, as they exist to this day in Pali, although written in the Chinese character. This fact is attested by Dr. Gutzlaff, in the catalogue of the Chinese books published in the Journal of the Royal Asiatic Society. With these proofs that the use of Sanscrit for Buddhist works was a comparatively modern innovation, Burnouf and others are content to receive their impressions of Buddhist doctrines, instead of going to the sermons preached* or the discourses delivered by Buddha himself, to the proceedings of the three councils held after his death, and to the Dipawanse and Mahawanse.

To the profound scholar who printed the text of the two first "Ushtakas" of the *Rig Veds*, the world is indebted for the proofs that Brahminism, in its modern acceptation, had no existence before Buddhism. That scholar has shown us that there were no images, no proofs of caste in its modern exclusiveness; that the elements were personified and invoked, and offerings made, at first of a simple character, but afterwards animals were offered in sacrifice in the manner of the Jews; and at last in such profusion, in hecatombs even, that the rivers of blood which flowed appear to have shocked Buddha; and his chief object seems to have been to put a stop to these sacrifices, and to spare animal life, and in consequence the Buddhists repudiated all sacrifices. Gentleness, kindness, peace, harmony, philanthropy, love of virtue, and abhorence of vice, are the characteristics of Buddhism, and its code of ethics equals that of any other religion. But it has been sought to throw upon Buddhists the stigma of Atheism, Materialism, and a belief in the annihilation of the Soul. These accusations have their origin in the mystical transcendentalisms of a comparatively modern and corrupted state of Buddhism, and which have not any authority from the preachings or discourses of Buddha himself. Buddha constantly refers to a First Cause, another world, and a state of rewards and punishments after death. Buddha's own hymn on his becoming Buddha, testifies to his belief in God. He speaks of the Builder and Architect who made him and controlled his transmigrations; and the Rev. Mr. Gogerly, in his translation of the *Damina Parida*, written in Pali,

---

* *Turnour's Translations, Journal of the Asiatic Society of Bengal,* vol. vii. page 693.

makes Buddha repeatedly speak of the present and future world
—viz., "The sinner suffers in this world, and he will suffer in the
next world: in both worlds he suffers," &c. Again, "The virtuous man rejoices in this world, and he will rejoice in the next
world. In both worlds he has joy," &c. Here is the founder of
the religion talking of the present and a future world, expressing
his belief in a state of rewards and punishments, &c.—" greatly
will he (the sinner) suffer in the regions of torments, and greatly
will he (the virtuous man) rejoice in Heaven,"—necessarily,
therefore, expressing his belief in a power or being to dispense
rewards and punishments. Surely there must be some distortion
in reasoning to pronounce such a believer an Atheist! Supposing
that the Buddhist may believe in God, it has been maintained that
he disbelieves the immortality of the soul. The Rev. W. Hardy,
however, says,* "Materialism, Atheism, and the entire cessation of
exietence stand or fall together: if the two former could be proved,
the third would follow as a matter of course,"—that is to say, to
believe in annihilation is to believe in Materialism and Atheism.
The charge of "annihilation" is founded upon a comparatively
modern interpretation of the Buddhist doctrine of Nibutti ("Nirvana" in Sancrit), or absorption into the First Cause. And what
is this Nibutti, but that the soul, having quitted its human tenement, and passed through its multiplied transmigrations, all of
which are probationary processes, in case it attains to absolute
perfection it is again received into that Being from whom it originally emanated; but short of that perfection, the soul remains
separate and apart, wandering through its prescribed habitations,
until it does attain to perfection. Now, though this doctrine may
shock the Christian's idea of the immaterial condition of man in
another world, it is certainly neither Atheism, Materialism, nor
Annihilation.†

---

* *Eastern Monachism*, p. 308.
† Remarkable is Baron Bunsen's generous vindication of the first Buddhist Sakya against the misunderstandings which fastened on him a doctrine of atheism and annihilation. The penetrating prescience of Neander seems borne out on this point by genuine texts, against the harsher judgment of recent Sarscrit scholars. He judged as a philosopher, they as grammarians.—*Dr. R. Williams; Essays and Reviews*, p. 90.

PLATONIC LOVE.

It is to be regretted that all young men are not more familiarly acquainted with the teaching of the first man who asserted the Immortality of the Soul on solid arguments, resting on truth and experience. Plato taught that all human felicity would find abundant increase, if men cultivated the godlike intellectual faculties, rather than pursued material and sensual pleasures. He held that there was a divine spark in every man, which was always cherished by the divine power, and which would not be extinguished in the soul, if man himself would but protect it from the blasts of a sensual and passion-driven world. The subjection of the irascible and concupiscible passions, and the cultivation of the rational and moral powers, were the two supports of a system which is more fully developed in the *Republic* of Plato. When Byron rhymed about the "confounded fantasies" of Plato, the poet knew nothing of the great son of Ariston, nor of his system. It is these "confounded fantasies" that Cowper has woven into a briefer, but not a better, system than that of Plato. Indeed, it is Plato's system condensed:

> Pleasure, admitted in undue degree,
> Enslaves the will, nor leaves the judgment free;
> 'Tis not alone the grape's enticing juice
> Unnerves the moral powers, and mars their use:
> Ambition, avarice, and lust of fame,
> And woman, lovely woman, does the same.
> The heart surrendered to the ruling power
> Of some ungoverned passion, every hour,
> Finds by degrees the truths that once bore sway,
> And all their deep impressions wear away;
> So coin grows smooth, in traffic current passed,
> 'Till Cæsar's image is effaced at last.

Cowper knew, as we all know, that there came a Teacher with whom the ablest in the schools may not be compared; but the English poet had better appreciation of Greek and Roman philosophers than Byron ever had. Cowper did not accuse any of them of "confounded fantasies," when he said:

> How oft, when Paul has served us with a text,
> Has Epictetus, Plato, Tully, preached!

> Men that, if now alive, would sit content
> And humble learners of a Saviour's worth,
> Preach it who might. Such was their love of truth,
> Their thirst of knowledge, and their candor too.
>
> Dr. Doran; *Notes and Queries*, 2d S. No. 115.

"Love," we are told, "is of God," (1 John iv. 7,) and is at once characteristic of the Christian and of Heaven. Christ says, "By this shall all men know that ye are my disciples, if ye love one another." So far from being a merely animal emotion, which is to be destroyed by death, it is the bond that binds each to the other, and all to Jehovah, and can only find its free exercise in Heaven:

> They sin who tell us Love can die;
> With life all other passions fly—
> All others are but vanity.
> In Heaven ambition cannot dwell,
> Nor avarice in the vaults of hell;
> Earthly, those passions of the earth,
> They perish where they have their birth.
>   But Love is indestructible.
> Its holy flame forever burneth,
> From Heaven it came, to Heaven returneth;
> Too oft on earth a troubled guest,
> At times deceived, at times oppress'd,
>   It here is tried and purified,
> Then hath in heaven its perfect rest.
> It soweth here in toil and care,
> But the harvest time of love is there.—*Southey*.

PLATONISM AND CHRISTIANITY.

Professor Blackie, in his erudite paper on Plato, (*Edinburgh Essays*, 1856,) after showing that both the English and the Scottish mind labor under a special incapacity of comprehending the work of the great apostle of idealism, continues:

"Nevertheless there is one door through which the English mind has a more free and open access to Platonic philosophy, viz., Religion; and it is really astonishing, when we reflect seriously, how little this avenue has been made use of. Learned Germans have written valuable books on 'the Christian element in Plato;'[*]

---

[*] The Christian Element in Plato, and the Platonic Philosophy Unfolded and Set Forth. By Dr. C. Ackermau, Archdeacon at Jena. Translated by S. B. Asbury, B. A. Edinburgh, T. and S. Clark.

and it is a well-known fact that many of the most authoritative of the Greek fathers spoke of the philosophy of the Academy, in the very same language that St. Paul used in reference to Judaism, as being a schoolmaster to bring the Greek world to Christ. Nor does it require a very profound glance to see how Platonic philosophy and Christian faith, in their grand outlines, characteristic tendencies, and indwelling spirit, are identical; identical, at least, in so far as a thing of Hebrew, and any thing of Hellenic origin, can be considered as presenting varieties of a common type. The prominence given to the doctrine of the immortality of the soul, in all Plato's works, as contrasted with the position of the same doctrine in the system of Aristotle and other Greek philosophers —the atmosphere of a pure and unworldly emotion, that, like airs from Paradise, floats through the blooming bowers of the Academy; the single-hearted dedication of the soul to truth, beauty, and holiness, as things essentially divine, for their own sake, to the utter contempt of all the inferior springs of action that lie in the words expediency, policy, utility, and worldly wisdom: these, with other characteristics that lie on the very surface of the Platonic books, are things essentially Christian, and are felt, by every person of well-cultivated moral sensibility, to be much more closely allied to the Gospel of John than they are to Aristotle, John Locke, or Doctor Paley."

Professor Blackie accounts for so little advantage having been taken of Platonic meditation by reason of the strange peculiarities of the English mind, which has robbed our scholarship of all capacity to develop its best elements, and our theology of all desire to form any alliance with the highest forms of scholarship. Notwithstanding the close connection of our churches with our universities, Plato, the element in purely academical learning most essentially Christian, is neglected, owing to "the tyrannical force of the English character," and the narrow pedantic routine of our universities. "Our scholarship and our theology were alike deficient in the philosophical element; and without this neither Greek nor theology could lead the normal English academical or ecclesiastical man into the essentially speculative domain of Plato. Hence in the most Christian and the most classical country of Europe, the works of the man who wrote the noblest Greek, and taught the most Christianizing of doctrines, were practically ignored. * * * * * *

"Some of the persons who opposed its introduction, 'had they known anything about him,' would have eschewed Plato with more jealousy, even as Cardinal Bellarmin is reported to have done, '*just because he was so very closely allied to Christ.*' Such likeness (it was feared by timid souls) might have given rise to a dangerous mistake."

RELIGION HAPPILY ADAPTED TO THE MIND OF MAN.

We find this cheerful picture of practical Christianity in one of the nervous sermons of Dr. South:

"If religion were to bear only upon the unmistakable bottom of divine authority, we might propose to ourselves an idea, what could be fittest to answer and employ those faculties of man's mind that are capable of religious obligation. Reason would continue such a religion as should afford both sad and solemn objects to amuse and affect the pensive part of the soul; and also such glorious matter of bright representations as might feed its admiration and entertain its more sprightly apprehensions; for the temper of all men in the world is either sad or composed, joyful or serene: and even the same man will find that he is wholly acted upon in the general tenor of his life by the vicissitudes and interchanges of these dispositions. Accordingly Christianity, in those great matters of fact upon which it is founded, happily complies with man's mind by this variety of its subject. For we have both the sorrows and glories of Christianity, the depressions and the triumphs, the mourning and the hosannas; we have the affecting sadness of Christ's fasting, his bloody agony, his crucifixion, and the bitter scene of his whole passion in its several parts and appendages. On the other side: we gaze at his miracles, admire his transfiguration, joy at his supernatural resurrection, and that which is the greatest complement and consummation of all—his glorious ascension. The first sort of them naturally suit with the composed, fixed, and monastic disposition of some minds, averse from all complacency and freedom; the second invite the joys of serener minds, happier constitutions, and brisker meditations. Nay, such a divine checkerwork shall we find in the whole contexture of the story of our religion, that we have the light still with the advantage of the shades, and things exhibited with the recommending vicinity of their contraries: so that it is observed, that in the whole narrative of our Saviour's life, no passage is related of him, low or weak, but it is immediately seconded and, as it were, corrected by another high and marvellous. No sooner was Christ humbled to a manger, but the contempt of the place was taken off by the glory of the attendance and ministration of angels: his submission to that mean and coarse ceremony of circumcision was ennobled with the public attestation of Simeon concerning him: his fasting and temptation attended with another service of angels: his baptism, with a glorious recognition, by a voice from heaven. When he seemed to show weakness in seeking fruit upon that tree which had none, he manifested his power by cursing it with deadness by a word. When he seemed to be overpowered at his attachments, he then exerted his mightiness in causing his armed adversaries to fall backwards, and he healed Malchus with a touch. When he underwent the last and violent infamy of crucifixion and death, then did the universal frame of nature give testimony to his divinity, and the temple rending, the sun darkening, and the earth quaking; the whole creation seemed to sympathize with his passion. And when afterwards he seemed to be in the very kingdom and dominion of death, by descending into the grave, he quickly confuted the dishonor of that by an astonishing resurrection, and by an argument *ex abundantiá* proved the divinity of his person, over and over, in a miraculous ascension."

Religion, whether natural or revealed, has always the same beneficial influence on the mind. In youth, in health, and prosperity, it awakens feelings of gratitude and sublime love, and purifies at the same time that it exalts; but it is in misfortune, in sickness, in age, that its effects are most truly and beneficially felt: when submission in faith and humble trust in the divine will, from duties become pleasures, undecaying sources of consolation; then it creates powers which were believed to be extinct, and gives a freshness to the mind, which was supposed to have passed away forever, but which is now renovated as an immortal hope: then it is the pharos, guiding the wave-tost mariner to his home, as the calm and beautiful still basins or fiords, surrounded by tranquil groves and pastoral meadows, to the Norwegian pilot escaping from a heavy storm in the North Sea, or as the green and dewy spot, gushing with fountains, to the exhausted and thirsty traveller in the midst of the desert. Its influence outlives all earthly enjoyments, and becomes stronger as the organs decay and the frame dissolves; it appears as that evening star of light in the horizon of life, which, we are sure, is to become in another season a morning star; and it throws its radiance through the gloom and shadow of death.

POWER OF RELIGION OVER DIFFICULTIES.

There can scarcely be a more direct instance of the practical value of the Bible to man, in his secular as well as his sacred concerns.

When Sir George Grey, some twenty years ago, was on his expedition through the unexplored country of Southern Australia, his position and prospects, upon one occasion, had become alarming, and he was undecided as to which of three plans he should adopt. But he determined not to decide hastily, and in order more fully to compose his mind, *he sat down and read a few chapters in the Bible.* "By the influence thus imparted," observes he, "I became perfectly contented, and again rising up, pursued my way along the beach to the party. It may be here remarked by some, that these statements of my attending to religious duties are irrelevant to the subject, but in such an opinion I cannot at all coincide. In detailing the sufferings we underwent, it is unnecessary to relate the means by which those sufferings were alleviated; and after having, in the midst of perils and misfortunes, received the greatest *consolation from religion,* I should be ungrateful to my Maker not to acknowledge this, and should ill perform my duty to my fellow-men, did I not bear testimony to the fact, that under all the weightier sorrows and sufferings that our frail nature is liable to, perfect reliance upon the goodness of God, and the merits of our Redeemer, will be a sure refuge and a certain source of consolation."

ATTRIBUTES OF THE DEITY.

Mr. Bowdler, in his posthumous work, *The Religion of the Heart*, says:—

"I have often been struck with our presumption in defining the Attributes of the Deity—a subject with which, like most of which we are ignorant, we make rather too free. The usual ideas entertained of our Maker amount to little more than this: we take all those qualities contributing, as we think, to our perfection, and adding infinity to them, fancy we have an adequate idea of the 'Ens Entium.' Whereas it is not clear that there is the least similitude between the nature of the creature and his Creator; and it is morally certain that an infinite variety of perfections must dwell in Him, of which no seeds are yet sown in us. The more direct path appears to be the same which we adopt in common life; to draw our inferences concerning His nature and character, from the manifestations of it in the affairs of this world, and in express revelation, remembering only the humility with which we should enter on a subject so awful and incomprehensible. Were the mysteries of the Eleusinian Ceres enveloped in darkness, and shall JEHOVAH be the subject of our petulant speculations ?*

"Methinks the contradictions into which we so often fall, might teach us more humility: we can only consider the attributes of our Maker singly, and in exalting one, we perpetually degrade another: yet it is curious, that the attribute which we most frequently disallow, is that which is most fully evidenced—his omnipotence. Pope says:

> Of systems possible, if 'tis confest,
> That Wisdom infinite *must* form the best—

laying down this truth as the foundation of his system. Cannot God then be at once All-wise and Almighty? Yet if this postulate be granted, his powers are limited indeed; for then it is im-

---

* It seems scarcely reconcilable with our notion of the fitness of things—that the created should by the Creator be endowed with power to call into question His attributes.

possible for him to create above one system, supreme excellence being one. Even Lord Bacon, in his celebrated confession of faith, supposes it to have been impossible for God to have created any thing which would have seemed good in his eyes, unless washed by the blood of the Lamb slain before the foundation of the world. Cannot God be at once, then, All-pure and Almighty? Like flatterers, ignorant of their trade, we debase where we mean to exalt."

ON ATHEISM—BY SOUTH.

The true cause of that Atheism (says South), that scepticism, and cavilling at religion, which we see, and have cause to lament in too many in these days, proceeds not from any thing that is weak or wanting in our religion to support it, and enable it to look the strongest arguments, and the severest and the most controlling reason, in the face; but men are atheistical because they are first vicious; and question the truth of Christianity, because they hate the practice; and therefore, that they may seem to have some pretence and color to sin freely, and to surrender up themselves wholly to their sensuality, without any imputation on their judgment, and to quit their *morals* without any discredit to their *intellectuals*, they fly to several stale, trite, pitiful objections and cavils, some against religion in general, and some against Christianity in particular; and some against the very first principles of morality, to give them some poor credit and circumstance in the pursuit of their brutish courses.

PREPARING FOR ANOTHER WORLD.

Who is there that hath not heard some honest, painstaking man say, when old age is coming on, "I will retire from business, and prepare for another world,"—or some such words? Yet, well meant as this may be, it is a great error to suppose that the common engagements of this world are a hindrance to our preparation for the next; for Scripture and reason show that we were sent into this probationary state to the end that our souls might learn experience among the diverse circumstances of active life, so as to know good from evil, and never to hazard the falling from glory, when once attained, by any such mistake as was committed by those spirits who kept not their first estate.

*　　*　　*　　*　　*　　*

When we entertain any doubt as to the soundness of our opinions, there is nothing which doth so strengthen and clear our apprehension, as the recurring to what Lord Bacon doth well term the great book of God's works. Now we all know that when Adam fell from his first estate, God imposed on him a law, which experience showeth to be still the law of human nature, that "in the sweat of his brow he should eat bread." No man can propound to himself that the loving Father of all his works would either inflict a punishment for vengeance rather than for amendment on the first offender, or replenish the surface of this globe with beings disqualified, by the very law of their existence, from the pursuit and attainment of their ultimate good: we may, therefore, reasonably conclude that the toil imposed on man was intended to be the strengthener and safeguard of his virtue, and to guide his frailty in the true path to life eternal. We see it to be the appointment of God,—for what he suffereth is so far his appointment, that he might prevent it, and doth not;—I say we see it to be the appointment of God that millions must go forth to their daily toil, if they mean to eat their daily food; nay, the very necessity for food, which is the cause of this labor, is especially created by God. Then, if such be the order written in the book of His works, we must, unless we are determined to shut our eyes, and not read therein, conclude that retirement and inaction are not the circumstances best fitted for the development of the spiritual life within; which doth rather thrive and flourish upon the fulfilled duty of each day; even if it were no more than the conscientiously doing an honest day's work for the allotted day's pay, whether seen or not: and in like manner, vice pineth and dieth in the mind, when quiet sleep, the result of labor, filleth the hours which are not given either to active employ, or to the exercise of those kindly social affections which so readily twine about the heart, when the space for their enjoyment is short, and the zest of their enjoyment is not dulled by satiety.

Instead, therefore, of seeking a discharge from all duty, as well as the means of improving the soul, whose true life is the fulfilment of duty, we should endeavor rather, as age approaches, to cut out for ourselves occupation sufficient for the diminished powers of the body, such as shall give room for the exercise of that concern for others, and carelessness of self, which form the best grace of youth, and which may still hover, like a bright halo, round the head of age, making gray hairs lovely, and giving earnest, even in this life, of what will be the society of "just men made perfect" in the next.*

Bishop Hall tells us that Edward, Earl of Norwich, had wont to animate himself against the encounter with our last enemy, Death, by the heavenly thought, that in the very instant of his soul's departing out of his body, it should immediately enjoy the vision of God. And certainly so it is. The spirits of just men need not stand upon distances of place, or space of time, for this beatifical sight; but so soon as ever they are out of their clay lodging, they are in their spiritual heaven, even while they are happily conveying to the local: for since nothing hindered them from that happy sight, but the interposition of this earth, which we carry about us, the spirit being once set free from that impediment, sees as it is seen, being instantly passed into a condition like unto the Angels; well, therefore, are these coupled together by the blessed Apostle, who, in his divine rapture, hath seen them both: Ye are come (saith he) unto Mount Sion, and unto the City of the living God, the heavenly Jerusalem; and to an innumerable company of Angels, and to the spirits of just men made perfect.

* * * * *

How full and comfortable is that profession of the great Apostle, who, when he had sweetly diverted the thoughts of himself and his Corinthians from their light afflictions to an eternal weight of exceeding glory, from things temporal, which are seen, to those everlasting, which are not seen, adds: "For we know that if

* *Abridged from An Exposition of Vulgar and Common Errors, by Thomas Brown Redivivus.* 1854.

our earthly house of this Tabernacle be dissolved, we have a building not made with hands, eternal in the heavens;" more than implying, that ours is no sooner off from the temporal things, than it is taken up with eternal objects; and that the instant of the dissolution of these clay cottages is the livery and seizin of a glorious and everlasting mansion in heaven.— *The Invisible World : Of the Souls of Men.*

REMOTENESS OF UNIVERSAL CHRISTIANITY.

The present tendencies of the world are not (says Bishop Courtenay) towards a universal reign of Christianity. A variety of Scriptural proofs might be adduced in proof of this point; but one will be fully sufficient. The book of Revelation informs us that in fact we are not to expect a universal reign of Christianity, as the result of causes now in operation. It contains an account of the chief events in the spiritual history of the world, commencing with the infancy of Christianity, or at some period yet future, and carried up to the general Judgment and the dissolution of the earth by fire. And it presents a succession of awful pictures of human wickedness and Divine wrath. The seals, the trumpets, the vials, are all charged with the righteous judgments of God, inflicted in punishment of the rebellions then existing. Nowhere can we discover a season wherein the wicked shall cease from troubling, and receiving a meet recompense of trouble, until the "thousand years" commence, during which Satan shall be bound, and the souls of martyrs shall live, and reign with Christ over the emancipated Kingdoms. It would seem, then, that, notwithstanding the influence of Christianity, the knowledge of the Lord shall *not* " cover the earth, as the waters that cover the depths of the sea," before the close of this dispensation ; but that the general tendencies of the world are towards greater and greater sinfulness, until the conquests of the prince of darkness are terminated by a special interposition of the Almighty, and the usurper is cast down from his throne.

And we know not that sin will wholly cease, even during the

millennium; while we are expressly told (a fact which is often most wonderfully disregarded by expositors of prophecy), that multitudes, "the number of whom is as the sand of the sea," shall enlist themselves in the service of the Devil during the short post-millennial season of liberty which shall precede his everlasting condemnation.—*Bishop Courtenay on the Future States: Appendix.*

ETERNAL PUNISHMENTS.

The doctrines respecting future punishments have been much controverted in all ages of the Church; and even those who acknowledge "everlasting punishment" maintain that *everlasting* signifies only to the end of its proper period. (See *The word Eternal*, and *The Punishment of the Wicked*, by the Rev. F. D. Maurice.) Jeremy Taylor has this emphatic passage upon the unsatisfactoriness of the primitive doctors upon this head:

"Concerning this doctrine of theirs, so severe and yet so moderated, there is less to be objected to than against the supposed fancy of Origen (who was charged with saying, the pains of the damned should cease, and that they shall return into joys, and back again to hell, by an eternal revolution); for it is a strange consideration to suppose an eternal torment to those to whom it was never threatened, to those who never heard of Christ, to those that lived probably well, to heathens of good lives, to ignorant and untaught people, to people surprised in a single crime, to men that die young in their natural follies and foolish lusts, to them that fall in a sudden gaiety and excessive joy, to all alike; to all infinite and eternal, even to unwarned people; and that this should be inflicted by God, who infinitely loves his creatures, who died for them, who pardons easily, and pities readily, and excuses much, and delights in our being saved, and would not have us to die, and takes little things in exchange for great: it is certain that God's mercies are infinite, and it is also certain that the matter of eternal torments cannot truly be understood; and when the schoolmen go about to reconcile the Divine justice to that severity, and consider why God punishes eternally a temporal sin, or a state of evil, they speak variously, and uncertainly, and unsatisfyingly."—*Christ's Advent to Judgment, Sermon* 3.

Taylor had previously stated that Origen was not the first that said the pain of the damned should cease; for Justin Martyr maintained that so far from the soul's dying, "the souls of the godly in a better place, of the wicked in a worse, do tarry the time of judgment; then they that are worthy shall never die again, but those that are designed to punishment, shall abide so long as God please to have them to live and to be punished."

Mr. Maurice argues that these doctrines could not be unknown to the translators of our Bible, or the framers of our Articles.

BOYISH OR MANLY HAPPINESS—WHICH PREFERABLE?

A distinguished clergyman writes: "I have no recollection in my boyish days of quiet happiness, but of many fears, perturbations, &c., and a continual longing for the dignity and the independence of the manly state. Now that I am a man, and verging towards an old one, I find my vessel suffers but little from the short gusts and ripplings of the passions; but is borne along under a tattered sail by the steady trade-wind of solicitude. When I was a boy, my pleasures and cares were selfish; now I care and think more for others than myself. Here I exult in some little advantage from the comparison; and yet, after all, the *prospect* is the chief subject of comparison. That of a boy is full of change and novelty. That of an elderly man admits of little variety and no novelty, but the great one of all—a new existence! The conclusion of this long sermon is, that a thoughtful boy may be happy without religion, but a thoughtful man cannot."

GOD'S ANCIENT PEOPLE.

Eighteen hundred years have passed since two Hebrew disciples, journeying by the way, heard themselves addressed with that awakening rebuke, "O fools, and slow of heart to believe all that the prophets have spoken" (Luke xxiv. 25). May we not hear, as it were, the same heavenly voice speaking alike to Jew and Gentile, and reproving our dulness of understanding and our blindness of heart? What if these things are marvels; what if we cannot discern with certainty the mode and time for the accomplishment of the divine purposes affecting the ancient people; what is the whole of their history, from Egypt to the dispersion, but a series of perpetual wonders? Take but the smallest fraction of their personal records, analyze the successive events, and they resolve themselves into as many miracles. Witness the division of the sea; the angels' food; the rock that followed them; the garments which waxed not old, and the feet that swelled not; the opening of the earth, the fire from heaven; the parting of the waters of Jordan; the walls of Jericho; the sun standing still in the valley of Ajalon. All the events connected with them—the earliest and the latest—while they show remarkably God's power, are nevertheless full of mystery. What more mysterious than that there should spring from one "as good as dead, as many as the stars of the sky in multitude, and as the sand which is by the sea-shore innumerable?" (Heb. xi. 12.) What more mysterious than the way by which they were led out of Egypt on the exact day foretold four hundred and thirty years before? (Exod. xii. 40, 41.) What more mysterious than the providential ordering by which they were brought back from the captivity of Babylon at the precise termination of the predicted seventy years? (Jer. xxv. 11, 12; xxix. 10; compared with Ezra i. ii.) What more marvellous than the downfall of their temple, the aptest type of their national history, within forty years of our Lord's prophecy? once the wonder of the world, now not one stone left upon another; once the glory of all lands, now without a mark or token to tell the traveller of its site. Or what more marvellous than their own career as a people? once the sole depositaries of God's truth, the subjects of a direct theocracy, the witnesses of a perpetual miracle, now "an astonishment, a proverb, and a byword among all nations" (Deut. xxvii. 37), whither the Lord has led them; once the freest of all nations, so that their boast was, that they were never in bondage to any man (John viii. 33), yet brought successively under the yoke of Chaldeans, Medes, Greeks, and

Romans. Nay, in its present crisis of penal degradation and dispersion, how mysterious is this people! There is a dignity in their very disgrace and infamy. Though cast down, yet not dejected utterly; though stricken sorely, yet not annihilated; aliens and vagabonds, but not swept away from the face of the earth. Christian men can never look at them without associations of solemn interest and awe. They cannot but remember, that of them, as concerning the flesh, Christ came; that of them was the goodly fellowship of the prophets; that of them was the glorious company of the apostles. Would we could add that of them, too, was the noble army of martyrs! And, though subjected to whip and scourge, and scorn and contumely, their enemies and they who have been the instruments of their punishment have been themselves abased; Egyptians, Assyrians, Babylonians, Syro-Macedonians, and Romans, have all in their turn been razed from the list of principalities and powers. Yet they, the hated ones, they yet survive.

* * * * *

"Though God has made a full end of all the nations whither he has driven them, he has not made a full end of them." (Jer. xiv. 28.) Hath he smitten him, as he smote those who smote him? or is he slain according to the slaughter of them that are slain by him? (Is. xxvii. 7.) Truly, we may say, all these things are wonderful, too wonderful for us to know: they are mavellous in our eyes; but we must add, nevertheless, with all the certainty and assured belief of men who have seen with their eyes, and heard with their ears, and to whom their fathers have told it, "this hath God wrought."—*Bishop (Sumner) of Winchester.*

LATIN OR MEDIÆVAL CHRISTIANITY.[*]

The Pontificate of Gregory the Great (590–604) marks the final Christianization of the world. Heathenism was utterly extinct. The Christian hierarchy has full possession of the minds of men. Ecclesiastical Latin is the only language of letters; art,

[*] From a review of D . Milman's *Latin Christianity*: *Times*, 1859.

so far as it exists at all, is exclusively Christian. But the transition from the primitive Gospel has become no less striking than the triumph over Paganism. The creeds of the church now form but a very small portion of Christian belief. The Almighty Father has receded, as it were, from human vision into a vague sanctity; the divine Saviour himself occupies but a comparatively small portion of the heart of the worshipper, absorbed with other objects of reverence, more open (as it seemed) to human sympathies. The shrines and the relics of martyrs are now the favorite resort of the great multitude of the believers. Hero worship—the heroism being of the monastic type—is in the ascendant. Legends of saints rival, if they do not supplant, the narratives of Scripture in the possession of the popular mind. The ordinary providence of God gives place to a perpetual strife between evil spirits and good angels about the person of every individual believer. No protection against the former is so effective as the presence of the departed saints, especially if in the vicinity of their own places of sepulture. Happy the churches which possessed the inestimable treasure of the body, or even a portion of the body, of an early confessor. The sacred talisman was an effectual security against calamity; nay, its virtue extended even to the absolving from sin. Relics have attained a self-defensive power; profane hands which endeavored to remove them withered; the chains of St. Paul sometimes refused to yield filings—an inestimable gift, when they could be procured, for a barbaric king. The taunt which the Christian writers of earlier times threw out against their Pagan adversaries, that their temples were most of them tombs of dead men, could now be retorted with interest. The possession of the bones of Orestes was not more ardently coveted by the Lacedæmonians than the remains of departed worthies by Gregory himself, intellectually as well as spiritually, by the confession of all, the model of his age. He himself obtained an arm of St. Andrew and the head of St. Luke from Constantinople, although to the petition of the Empress Constantia he refused any thing beyond a cloth which had touched the sacred body of St. Paul at Rome. Thus, moulding together elements derived from all sources—Jewish, Pagan, and Christian—arose the vast and complicated system of mediæval Christianity, a system as little to be despised as the offspring of fraud as to be justified as a genuine development of the primitive Gospel.

ORIGIN OF THE LITANY.

The proceedings of Gregory in the early part of his pontificate, to avert from his people the miseries of pestilence and famine, are highly characteristic of the zealous Christian pastor and the paternal ruler. His estates in Sicily supplied the corn which kept the poor population of Rome from perishing. In the mean time he constantly addressed them from the pulpit, and encouraged them by his presence. The origin of that kind of service which goes by the name of Litany, or Processional, dates from this time. The whole population of Rome was marshalled in seven bodies, and traversed the streets with prayers and penitential hymns. The clergy and the sacred virgins, the widows and the children, the laity, rich and poor, all had their assigned share in this solemnity. The cry of the whole city literally ascended to the throne of the Almighty. The pestilence was not stayed; no less than 80 victims fell dead during the procession; but neither the faith of the people nor of their bishop failed, and after ages moulded this fact into a picturesque tradition, which contemporary accounts do not justify, that as the last troop of suppliants reached the monument of Hadrian, the Destroying Angel was seen to sheathe his sword. The statue which crowns the castle of St. Angelo, as it is now called, commemorates the miracle.

VITAL FORCE—WHAT IS MATERIALISM?

Dr. W. Brinton, in a lecture on physiology, delivered by him at St. Thomas's Hospital, London, observes:

The charge of Materialism is difficult to deal with, mainly because of the sophistical sense in which the word has been used, and the odium it has therefore come to convey. The only decently scientific hypotheses which represent the material and its antagonist theory, are both of them, so far as I dare venture to judge, as perfectly compatible with religion as are the Books of Euclid. Indeed, I question whether they are not quite compatible with each other—whether the difference be not in great degree one of terms or words, rather than of ideas. One side, for example—well represented by one of the most able physiologists of the day, Dr. Carpenter,—is inclined to assume the existence of a force or forces, so unlike any thing we meet with in the inorganic creation—that is, so characteristic of Life—as to be fitly named *vital*. These forces ceasing at death, allow the substances they previously tenanted and governed to fall back, as it were, into the domain of the ordinary laws of matter, in obedience to which they now decay and disperse into the world around them. The other side, which I will instance by the illustrious Valentin, regard Life and Organization as sustained in great measure by the same laws as those which, in different degrees and modes of working, operate in the inorganic world. Declining to separate the physical and chemical phenomena of dead and living nature by a line of demarcation hitherto not definitely proved to exist, and confidently resting on the innumerable and undoubted facts which prove that such forces as heat, light, magnetism, chemical affinity, are every moment operating in the living body, it supposes that even the most peculiar and fleeting of these operations which we sum up as Life, are effected, in obedience to natural laws, by the use of forces everywhere present.

Of the theologian who should call this "Materialism," I would ask, "How does it affect revealed religion, or infringe our common creed?" Its supporters, in assuming that "the vital functions are the result of an infinitely wise plan of organization," do but modify, and indeed modify by exalting, our notions of the infinite wisdom they explicitly acknowledge. The materials, so to speak, they regard as fewer, simpler, more general, less heterogeneous, than had hitherto been imagined. Scientifically, they must only gain their position more fully by proving it more fully than they have yet done. But, theologically, if there be any difference, surely it is that the simpler the materials, the more unimaginable must be the skill and wisdom of the workmanship.—*Lancet*, Nov. 10, 1850.

MYSTERIES AND MIRACLES.

Mysteries are those great and hidden things of our religion, whose truth we are assured of by divine authority; but the manner of their being surpasses our understanding: such as the Plurality of Persons in the Divine Unity; God manifest in the Flesh; the operation of the Holy Spirit in the hearts of believers; the Spiritual Presence of Christ in the Eucharist; and the uniting our scattered parts from the dust of death.—*The Centaur not Fabulous*, by Dr. Young.

Ignorant sceptics are accustomed to attempt to justify their doubt of Miracles by their non-occurrence in the present times. Such persons overlook, in reading the Scriptures, the striking difference between the dispensations of God in the time of our Saviour and his apostles, and in our own. Then miracles were wrought on the bodies and minds of Christians, in order to establish the truth of the Gospel. That object being effected, miracles became rare, or ceased altogether.

The Pilgrim's Progress.

In 1858 there was published *The Ancient Poem of Guillaume de Guileville, entitled " Le Pelerinage de l'Homme," compared with the " Pilgrim's Progress" of John Bunyan :* edited from Notes collected by the late Mr. Nathaniel Hill. De Guileville was a French monk, who was born in 1295, and died about 1360. His writings were popular in England, portions of them having been translated by Chaucer and Lydgate. That Bunyan knew directly any thing of De Guileville does not appear, but it is clear that he was acquainted with those fragments of the old chivalrous literature which were still handed about in the form of cheap books. Whether any portions of De Guileville himself survived in this shape may well be doubted; but as De Guileville himself confessedly borrowed from the *Romance of the Rose*, nothing is more likely than that a common element may be found in De Guileville and in Bunyan.

It is, however, absurd to say this resemblance supports a charge of plagiarism between the *Pelerinage* and the *Pilgrim's Progress*. The general idea of representing the Christian's course under the figure of a pilgrimage is so obvious that it could hardly fail to occur to many minds independently, especially in days when pilgrimages were things of daily occurrence. De Guileville and Bunyan are by no means the only authors who have worked out the idea. And, besides the general similarity of idea, a certain resemblance could hardly fail to occur in the details of the story. Of any Pilgrim's Progress the groundwork must be found in certain Scriptural phrases and descriptions. The Celestial City in the Apocalypse must of necessity be the pilgrim's goal. Then much of the detail must be drawn from mediæval history or romance. The fiends and personified vices against which the Christian has to contend, naturally assume the form of the giants and ogres of mediæval romance—of the Turks and Saracens of mediæval reality. The pilgrim fought his way to Jerusalem—so the Christian fights his way to Heaven. St. Paul's parable of the Christian armor, St. John's picture of the combat between Michael and the Dragon, stood ready to be pressed into the service. There was thus a vast mass of floating material ready to the hands of all writers of pilgrimages, and of which all writers of pilgrimages availed themselves. But we see no ground for supposing that Bunyan borrowed from De Guileville, or did more than draw upon a common stock of ideas and images, which, even in De Guileville's time, were not absolutely new.

But there is nothing in all this which at all derogates from originality. Granting that Bunyan borrowed his idea from De Guileville, there is nothing which lays him open to the charge of "plagiarism." Whatever Shakspeare, Æschylus, Homer, or Bunyan borrowed from anybody else, they fairly made their own. De Guileville's allegory is dead—Bunyan's is alive. De Guileville may have dug up some dry bones and arranged them in the form of a skeleton—Bunyan is the real enchanter who gave them flesh and blood, and the breath of life. And this is even more remarkable when we consider that what was natural in the days of De Guileville had become somewhat unreal in the days of Bunyan. In Bunyan's time people no longer went on pilgrimages, least of all people of Bunyan's own way of thinking. De Guileville may well have sent more than one pilgrim on an actual journey to Jerusalem —Bunyan would doubtless have dissuaded any Bedford burgess from such an undertaking, as being little better than one of the works of the flesh. Bunyan's theology is of course Calvinistic; and one cannot but see, with Lord Macaulay, that the real battles and the real persecutions of his own time have helped to give much of their life to his descriptions of imaginary battles and persecutions. But, nevertheless, the costume of Bunyan's book is essentially Crusading and not Covenanting. This may well arise from the fact of Bunyan's drawing from the common stock of all pilgrim-mongers. But it may also have something to do with that great characteristic difference between an early and a late literature. In Palestine, in early Greece, in mediæval Europe, poetry consisted very much in describing to people what they themselves said and did every day. We, for the most part, in any thing professing to be poetical or romantic, sometimes of set purpose, sometimes because we cannot help it, get as far as possible from the realities of our own life.*

The *Pilgrim's Progress*, in its invention and plan, is generally supposed to have been the child of John Bunyan's own fancy; and he has, in his advertisement, strongly vindicated his claim to it. The necessity of this vindication, at least, proves that the matter was called in question in his own time; and the following extract contains at once his defence, and his own account of the origin and execution of the work:

> Some say the Pilgrim's Progress is not mine,
> Insinuating as if I would shine,
> In name and fame by the book of another;
> Like some made rich by robbing of his brother;
> Or that so fond I am of being sire,
> I'll father bastards, or if need require,
> I'll tell a lie in print to get applause;
> I scorn it, John such dirt-heap never was,
> Since God converted him. Let this suffice
> To show why I my pilgrim patronise.
> It came from mine own heart; so to my head
> And then into my fingers trickled;
> Then to my pen, from whence immediately
> On paper I did dribble it daintily.
> Manner and matter too were all my own;
> Nor was it unto any mortal known,
> Till I had done it—nor did any then
> By books, by wits, by tongues, or hands, or pen,
> Add five words to it, or write half a line:
> Therefore, the whole, and every whit is mine,
> And for this, thine eye is now upon,
> The matter in this manner came from none
> But the same heart and head, fingers, and pen,
> As did the others. Witness all good men;
> For none in all the world without a lie,
> Can say that this is mine, excepting I.

Notwithstanding these declarations, concerning the general truth of which I feel no doubt (says Dr. Adam Clarke), his whole plan, both in this work and his *Holy War*, the latter especially,

* Abridged from the Saturday Review, Dec. 4, 1858.

being so very similar to Barnard's religious allegory, called the *Isle of Man, or Proceedings in Manshire*, first published in 1627; and also to that most beautiful allegorical poem, by Mr. Edmund Spenser, oddly called *The Faëry Queen;* there is much reason to believe that one or other, if not both, gave birth to the book in question. This must be granted, unless it could be rationally supposed, which is not likely, that Mr. Bunyan never saw the book of Spenser, or that of Barnard. But, although the general idea should be allowed, to be suggested by the authors already mentioned, yet the imagery, the coloring, the language, and the true evangelical direction of the whole, are Bunyan's, and Bunyan's only. It would not be difficult, however, to draw a parallel between those works and those of our author, and show many corresponding personages throughout, especially in Mr. Barnard's *Isle of Man*.—We quote the above from a memoir of Bunyan, by Dr. Adam Clarke, who concludes by subscribing to the opinion of Mr. Addison, that had John Bunyan lived in the time of the Primitive Fathers, he would have been as great a Father as any of them.

The translation of *The Voyage of the Wandering Knight* (originally written in French by John Cartheny), n. d., but dedicated to Sir Francis Drake, would appear most likely to have given Bunyan the idea of composing, if not the ground-work of, the *Pilgrim's Progress*. Mr. Offor, the editor of Bunyan's work, however, states there to be no ground for supposing that Bunyan ever saw this *chevalier errant*. Still there are many apparent similarities; and a manuscript note in the edition of the *Wandering Knight* preserved in the Grenville Library of the British Museum, bears the following note upon the inside of the cover: "There can be no doubt that this is the original of Bunyan's *Pilgrim's Progress*."

Mr. Offor says: "The foulest and most unfounded slander upon the fair fame of Bunyan has appeared in *Freeman's Journal*, in which it is asserted that Bunyan copied his *Pilgrim's Progress* nearly verbatim from an old Popish work on purgatory, called *The Pilgrimage of the Soul*, which commences after the body is dead, and goes through all the imaginary pains of that fraudulent invention, so profitable to the priests, called purgatory, scarcely one sentence of which has the slightest similarity to Bunyan'. *Pilgrim's Progress*, excepting that it is a dream."—*Notes and Queries*, Second Series, No. 199.

It is a curious fact, and not very generally known, that a complete design of a *Pilgrim's Progress* is to be found in Lucian's *Hermotimus:* it is not to be imagined that Bunyan could have seen it there, from the limited educational advantages he possessed; yet the obvious allegory occurred to his mind, unschooled as it was, in a similar arrangement with that suggested by Lucian.—*Notes to the Pilgrim's Progress converted into an Epic Poem*, Parsonstown, 1844.

Bunyan had some providential escapes during his early life. Once he fell into a creek of the sea, once out of a boat into the river Ouse, near Bedford, and each time he was narrowly saved from drowning. One day, an adder crossed his path. He stunned it with a stick, then forced open its mouth with a stick and plucked out the tongue, which he supposed to be the sting, with his fingers; "by which act," he says, "had not God been merciful unto me, I might, by my desperateness, have brought myself to an end." If this, indeed, were an adder, and not a harmless snake, his escape from the fangs was more remarkable than he himself was aware of. A circumstance, which was likely to impress him more deeply, occurred in the eighteenth year of his age, when, being a soldier in the Parliament's army, he was drawn out to go to the siege of Leicester, in 1645. One of the same company wished to go in his stead; Bunyan consented to exchange with him, and this volunteer substitute, standing sentinel one day at the siege, was shot through the head with a musket-ball. "This risk," Sir Walter Scott observes, "was one somewhat resembling the escape of Sir Roger de Coverley, in an action at Worcester, who was saved from the slaughter of that action by having been absent from the field."—*Southey*.

Bunyan's Allegory has been translated into Chinese, each page being engraved on wooden blocks.

Appendix.

TRADITIONAL ANECDOTES, CURIOUS CUSTOMS, ETC.

THERE is a very strange legend connected with the Lambton family: one of the ancestors, a Crusader, to rid the neighborhood of a monster serpent, consulted a witch, who counselled him how to slay the creature, upon his vowing to kill, if successful, the first living thing he met. "Should you fail to keep this oath," said the witch, "the Lords of Lambton, for nine generations, shall never die in their beds." The Knight then arranged with his father, that upon the sound of his bugle, a favorite greyhound should be set loose, who would fly to him, and thus become the sacrifice. The Knight, after a desperate contest, slew the monster, and sounded the bugle; when the old Lord, overjoyed at this victory, instead of releasing the greyhound, rushed forward to embrace his son, who would not shed the blood of his father. He again blew the bugle, and the greyhound, now released, came bounding forward, and the Knight plunged his sword into its heart. But the vow was broken, and destiny was not to be eluded; and strange to say, how much so ever of the story may be true, *for nine generations, no Lord of Lambton died quietly in his bed.* There are two stone figures in the garden-house at Lambton Castle, illustrative of this legend.—See the narrative in Sir Bernard Burke's *Family Romance*, vol. ii.

When Lord Bacon, as he himself records, dreamt in Paris, that he saw "his father's house in the country plastered all over with black mortar," his feelings were highly wrought upon, and he made no doubt that the next intelligence from England would apprise him of the death of his father. His apprehensions the

Appendix. 339

sequel proved to be well grounded; for his father actually died the same night in which he had this remarkable dream.

The royalist Sir Richard Fanshawe and his Lady chanced, during their abode in Ireland, to visit a friend, the head of a sept, who resided in his baronial castle, surrounded with a moat. One midnight, Lady Fanshawe was awakened by a supernatural scream, and beheld by moonlight a female face, and part of her form, hovering about the window of the bedchamber, at a considerable height from the moat. The face was young and handsome, but pale; the hair loose and dishevelled, and the costume that of the ancient Irish. The figure disappeared with two shrieks. In the morning, Lady Fanshawe told her host what she had witnessed, when he thus accounted for the apparition. "A near relative of my family (said he) expired last night in the castle. We concealed our certain expectation of the event from you, lest it should throw a cloud over the cheerful reception which was your due. Now, before such an event happens in this family and castle, the female spectre whom you have seen is always visible. She is believed to be the spirit of a woman of inferior rank, by marrying whom, one of my ancestors degraded himself; and whom afterward, to expiate the dishonor done to his family, he caused to be drowned in the castle moat."

In the park of Chartley, near Lichfield, is preserved the breed of the indigenous Staffordshire cow, of sand-white color, with black ears, muzzle, and tips at the hoofs. In the year of the battle of Burton-bridge, a *black calf* was born; and the downfall of the house of Ferrers happening about this period, gave rise to the tradition, which to this day is current—that the birth of a particolored calf, from the wild breed in Chartley Park, is a sure *omen of death* within the same year to a member of the lord's family; and by a noticeable coincidence (says the *Staffordshire Chronicle*, July, 1835), a calf of this description has been born whenever a death has happened in the family of late years. The decease of the seventh Earl Ferrers and his Countess, of his son, Viscount Tamworth, and of his daughter, Mrs. W. Joliffe, as well as the deaths of the son and heir of the eighth Earl, and his daughter Lady Frances Shirley, were each preceded by the ominous birth of a calf. In the spring of 1835, an animal perfectly black was calved by one of the weird tribe, in the park of Chartley, and was shortly followed by the death of the Countess, the second wife of the eighth Earl Ferrers. This family tradition has been effectively wrought into a romantic story, entitled *Chartley ; or the Fatalist.*

In a letter of Philip, the second Earl of Chesterfield, it is related, that on a morning in 1652, the Earl saw an object in white, like a standing sheet, within a yard of his bedside. He attempted to catch it, but it disappeared. His thoughts turned to his Lady, who was then at Networth, with her father, the Earl of Northumberland. On his arrival at Networth, a footman met him on the stairs, with a packet directed to him from his wife, whom he found with Lady Essex, her sister, and Mr. Ramsey. He was asked why he had returned so suddenly. He told his motive; and on opening the letter in the packet, he found that his lady had written to him requesting his return, for she had seen an object in white, with a black face, by her bedside. These apparitions are stated to have been seen by the Earl and Countess *at the same moment*, when they were forty miles asunder!

Dr. Johnson, when sailing in the Hebrides, between Rasay and Sky, in a large boat, with Boswell and other friends, fell into this conversation on Death. Johnson observed that the boastings of some men as to dying easily were idle talk, proceeding from partial views. Boswell mentioned Hawthornden's "Cypress Grave," where it is said that the world is a mere show, and that it is unreasonable for a man to wish to continue in the show-room after he has seen it. Let him go cheerfully out, and give place to other spectators.—*Johnson.* "Yes, sir, if he is sure he is to be well after he goes out of it. But if he is to grow blind after he goes out of the show-room, and never to see any thing again, or if he does not know whither he is to go next, a man will not go cheerfully out of a show-room. No wise man will be contented to die, if he thinks he is to go into a state of punishment. Nay, no wise man will be contented to die, if he thinks he is to fall into annihilation; for, however unhappy any man's existence may be, he would yet rather have it than not exist at all. No, there is no rational principle by which a man can die contented, but a trust in the mercy of God, through the merits of Jesus Christ."

Appendix. 341

When Dr. Johnson was struck with palsy, in June, 1783, after the first shock was over, and he had time to recollect himself, he attempted to speak in English. Unable as he found himself to pronounce the words, he tried what he could do with Latin, but here he found equal difficulty. He then attempted Greek, and could utter a few words, but slowly and with pain. In the evening he called for paper, and wrote a *Latin Hymn*, addressed to the Creator, the prayer of which was, that so long as the Almighty should suffer him to live, he should be pleased to allow him the enjoyment of his understanding; that his intellectual powers and his body should expire together—a striking instance of fortitude, piety, and resignation!—*Sir James Prior's Life of E. Malone.*

How satisfactory it is to know that the last sonnet which the pious Mrs. Hemans composed—and that on her last bed of suffering—was the Sabbath Sonnet:

> How many blessed groups this hour are bending,
>   Thro' England's primrose meadow paths, their way
> Towards spire and tower midst shadowy elms ascending,
>   Whence the sweet chimes proclaim the hallowed day.
> The halls, from old heroic ages gray,
>   Pour their fair children forth; and hamlets low,
> With whose thick orchard blossoms the soft winds play,
>   Send out their inmates in a happy flow,
> Like a free vernal stream. I may not tread,
> With them, those pathways—to the feverish bed
>   Of sickness bound: yet, oh! my God! I bless
> Thy mercy that with Sabbath peace hath filled
> My chastened heart, and all its throbbings stilled
>   To one deep calm of lowliest thankfulness.

Lord Byron was told by the commander of a packet, that being asleep one night in his berth, he was awakened by the pressure of something heavy on his limbs; and there being a faint light, he could see, as he thought distinctly, the figure of his brother, who was at that time in the same service in the East Indies, dressed in his uniform, and stretched across the bed. Supposing it to be an illusion of the senses, he shut his eyes, and made an effort to sleep. Still the pressure continued; and still, as often as he ventured to take another look, he saw the figure lying crosswise, in the same position. To add to the wonder, on putting his hand forth to touch the figure, he found the uniform in which it appeared to be dressed, *dripping wet*. On the entrance of one of his brother officers, to whom he called out in alarm, the apparition vanished; but in a few months after, Captain Kidd received the startling intelligence, that *on the above night*, his brother had been drowned in the Indian seas. Of the supernatural character of this appearance, Captain Kidd himself did not appear to have the slightest doubt.—*Moore's Life of Byron.*

Grimaldi, the father of the celebrated "Joe," the clown, had a vague and profound dread of the 14th day of the month. At its approach he was always nervous, disquieted, and anxious: directly it had passed, he was another man again, and invariably exclaimed, in his broken English, "Ah! now I am safe for another month." But it is remarkable that Grimaldi actually died on the 14th day of March, and that he was born, christened, and married on the 14th of the month.

Mrs. Crowe relates that on board one of Her Majesty's ships lying off Portsmouth, the officers being one day at the mess-table, a young Lieutenant R. suddenly laid down his knife and fork, pushed away his plate, and turned extremely pale. He then rose from the table, covered his face with his hands, and retired. The president of the mess, supposing him to be ill, sent to inquire after him. At first, Mr. R. was unwilling to reply: but on being pressed, he confessed that he had been seized by a sudden and irresistible impression, that a brother he had in India was dead. "He died," said he, "on the 12th of August, at six o'clock; I am perfectly certain of it." No argument could overthrow this conviction, which, in due course of post, was verified to the letter. The young man had died at Cawnpore, on the day above named.

Watching for the Dead on St. Mark's and Midsummer Eve was formerly customary in Yorkshire. On St. Mark's Eve (April 24), persons would sit and watch in the church porch, from 11 o'clock at night till one in the morning. In the third year (for it must be done thrice), the watchers were said to see the spectres of all those who were to die the next year pass by into the church.

The same custom on Midsummer Eve is thus noticed in the *Connoisseur*, No. 56: "I am sure my own sister Hetty, who died just before Christmas, stood in the church porch last Midsummer

Appendix.

Eve, to see all that were to die in that year in our parish: and she saw her own apparition." In the *Athenian Oracle*, vol. ii., p. 515, we find: "On last —— Eve, nine others, besides myself, went into a church porch with an expectation of seeing those who should die that year; but about eleven o'clock, I was so afraid that I left them; and all the nine did positively affirm to me, that about an hour after, the church-doors flying open, the minister (who, it seems, was much troubled that night in his sleep), with such as should die that year, did appear in order, which persons they named to me; and they appeared all then very healthful, but six of them died in six weeks after, in the very same order that they appeared." Mrs. Bray relates that at Tavistock, Devon, two brothers sat up one Midsummer Eve, in the church porch, from an idea that if, at twelve o'clock at night, they looked through the keyhole of the door, they would see all those who were to die that year walk into the church from the opposite doorway. They fancied they saw themselves in the funeral procession! Certain it is that they both died within a very short time from this watching.

What a dream of beauty and tenderness has Dr. Faber, with true poetic soul, figured in his wild dirge upon the barks of the Charwell, over his "blighted love, and his chosen's bier."

>
> The dew falls fast, and the night is dark;
> The trees stand silent in the park.
> The fatal lights have all died out,
> And naught is heard but a lone owl's shout;
> The mists keep gathering more and more,
> But the stream is silent as before.
> > From bridge to bridge with tremulous fall
> > .The river droppeth down,
> > And it washeth the base of a pleasant hall
> > On the skirts of Cambridge Town.
>
> Why should I think of my boyhood's bride,
> As I walked by this low-voiced river side?
> And why should its heartless waters seem,
> Like a horrid thought in a feverish dream?
> But it will not speak, and it keeps its bed
> The words that are sent us from the dead.
> > The river is green, and runneth slow,
> > We cannot tell what it saith;
> > It keepeth its secrets down below—
> > And so doth death.

LITERARY HISTORY OF MADMEN.

In the year 1860, M. Octave Delepierre published an ingenious and interesting work, the object of which is to prove that "madness enters in some measure into most of the great minds with which history makes us acquainted; and that it often becomes very difficult to establish the difference which predispositions to madness present, from certain conditions known as those of reason." The authority of M. Lélut is invoked to prove that Pythagoras, Numa, Mahomet, and others, whose influence has been of such vast amount in the world, were all in some measure affected in mind: "they were simply men of genius and enthusiasm, with partial hallucinations." The good dæmon which so often whispered counsel in the ears of Socrates, and the amulet discovered after death in Pascal's pocket, have convinced M. Lélut, who has ingeniously attempted to convince others, of the insanity of these great philosophers.

Strange is the supposition which regards as madmen so many of the great men who have left their stamp upon the history of the world. Numa was mad, inasmuch as he professed that a certain nymph appeared to him in a cavern, which he called Egeria.* Notwithstanding which, however, some may be of opinion that of the two hypotheses—the first, that Numa was mad, and yet capable in his madness of thinking out much legislative wisdom, and of establishing many prudent institutions; the other, that Numa, being of sound mind, was politician enough to perceive that superstition was the most powerful instrument by which to impress new doctrines upon a primitive people—the latter has about it a far greater appearance of probability. Even if Numa were mad, was not the nymph still a lie? And the wisdom which he somehow acquired not a lie? A madman's delusion, though it be true for him, is not true for the universe, and cannot therefore but die with its author. So Numa's wise laws have had their influence and are still working in the world, while the temporary accessories

* See *Egeria*, a poem of graceful thought and nervous fancy, by Charles Mackay, LL. D.

Appendix. 345

by which they were rendered acceptable to the barbarian mind have long since vanished.

Mahomet mad too! because, amongst other things, the angel Gabriel was said to have paid visits to him. When Pococke inquired of Grotius where the proof was of that story of the pigeon trained to pick peas from Mahomet's ear, and to pass for an angel dictating to him? Grotius answered that there was no proof! Now, the word this man spoke has been the life guidance of one hundred and eighty millions of men these twelve hundred years. These hundred and eighty millions were made by God as well as we. "A greater number of God's creatures believe in Mahomet's word at this hour than in any other word whatever."* And we are asked to believe that it was the wisdom of madness!

Of Cromwell's grievous madness there will be little doubt in certain minds. Did not a spectre appear to him in the open day, or some strange woman open the curtains of his bed at night, and predict to him that he should be king of England? And a Huntingdon physician told Sir Philip Warwick that he had often been sent for at midnight; Mr. Cromwell was full of hypochondria, thought himself near dying, and had "fancies about the town cross." Moreover, he was subject to uncontrollable fits of laughter on serious occasions. "One that was at the battle of Dunbar told me that Oliver was carried on by a Divine impulse. He did laugh so excessively as if he had been drunk. The same fit of laughter seized him just before the battle of Naseby."†

Again, there was once a "report raised by the devil, that Mr. Whitefield was mad," and he himself says, "he might very well be taken to be really mad, and that his relations counted his life madness." Here is an account from his journal, of what seems to have been a compound of indigestion and nightmare, wherein may be discernible by certain mortals something of a mad ring: "One morning rising from my bed, I felt an unusual impression and weight upon my chest. In a short time the load gradually increased, and almost weighed me down, and fully convinced me that Satan had as real possession of my body as once of Job's. . . . I fancied myself like a man locked up in iron armor; I felt great heavings in my body, prayed under the weight till the sweat

* Carlyle. † Aubrey's *Miscellanies*.

came. How many nights did I lie groaning under the weight, bidding Satan depart from me in the name of Jesus."

But why continue a list, which by a "specialty" criticism might be made to include almost every great actor in this mad world—George Fox stitching for himself a leathern suit; Ignatius Loyola, "that errant, shatter-brained visionary fanatic," as Bishop Lavington calls him; St. Francis, founder of the Franciscans, who was wont to strip himself naked in proof of his innocence, and to appear in fantastical dresses; and many others in whom appears a mixture more or less of fanaticism and imposture.

Perhaps if there is one man to whom a reader of English history would point, as having entertained wide and philosophical views instead of having faith in the expediency-doctrine of the moment —that man is Edmund Burke. "He possessed (says Coleridge) and had sedulously sharpened that eye which sees all things, actions, and events in relation to the laws which determine their existence, and circumscribe their possibility. He referred habitually to principles; he was a scientific statesman."

When the far-seeing sagacity of Burke, in foretelling the unhappy results of the French Revolution, first struck into the minds of his party, from which he had been separated, it was reported that he was in a state of mind bordering on insanity, especially after he had in the House of Commons addressed to the chair, with much vehemence of manner, the words of St. Paul: "I am not mad, most noble Festus; but speak the words of truth and soberness." Burke's niece ventured to name to him the above absurd rumor, when he very sensibly replied: "Some part of the world, my dear—I mean the Jacobins, or unwise part of it—think, or affect to think, that I am mad; but believe me, the world twenty years hence will, and with reason too, think from their conduct that they must have been mad."

These rumors, however, gained strength, particularly after the death of Burke's son: he was said to wander about his grounds kissing his cows and horses; but his affection for domestic animals had been remarkable from his early manhood, and Reinagle painted him patting a favorite cow. This picture brought from London to Beaconsfield an old friend, to ascertain the truth or falsehood of the story—when Burke, without knowing the object of his

Appendix.

visit, unsuspiciously showed him portions of the *Letters on a Regicide Peace*, which he was then writing. The circumstance of his being seen to throw his arms round the neck of his son's favorite horse, to weep and sob convulsively as he kissed the animal, had, however, a greater share in substantiating the rumor than had Reinagle's picture.

Lord Chatham, contemporary with Burke, was also alleged to have been insane. Horace Walpole fosters this scandal, and the fact of the Earl placing himself under Dr. Addington, originally a "mad doctor," strengthened the rumor; but Addington had been the village doctor at Hayes, where Lord Chatham resided. His ill-managed expenditure and his freaks of extravagance backed the report, which, after all, was little better than an invention of Chatham's political enemies.

The hallucinations and madness of Tasso, of Benvenuto Cellini, of the painter Fuseli, of Cowper, of Swift, and of many others whose names press under the pen, exhibit a picture of the human mind which would almost make us agree with Aristotle, that it is the fame of a good poet to be mad.

That Swift not only expired "a driv'ler and a show," but lived a madman, is what the world generally believes; but Mr. W. R. Wilde, F. R. C. S.,* having stated all that is really known of Swift's sufferings and disease, asserts that up to the year 1742, Swift showed no symptom whatever of mental disease, beyond the ordinary decay of nature. Towards the end of that year the cerebral disease under which he had long labored, by producing effusion, &c., destroyed his memory, rendered him at times ungovernable in his anger, and produced paralysis; but all this was the result of physical disease. It cannot be doubted that his not speaking was not the result of either insanity or imbecility, but arose either from the paralysis of the muscles by which the mechanism of speech is produced, or from loss of memory, such as frequently appears in cerebral disease; for he would often attempt to speak, but could not recollect words to express his meaning, when he would shrug up his shoulders, and sigh heavily. We have also the evidence of one of the few eye-witnesses of the Dean's con-

* The closing years of Dean Swift's Life. By W. R. Wilde, F. R. C. S. Second Edition, 1849.

dition at this period—that he never yet talked nonsense, or said a foolish thing. The disease under which he labored so long might be termed "epileptic vertigo," such as that described by Esquirol, an affection to which it is well known many men of strong intellect have been subject. For the last few years of his embittered existence—from his 75th to his 78th year—his disease partook so much of the nature of senile decay, or the dementia of old age, that it is difficult to define by any precise medical term his actual state. Mr. Wilde has very carefully examined the question; and although, to this day, it is difficult to persuade the great mass of the people in Dublin that the Dean was not one of the first inmates of his own madhouse (although the building was not erected till many years after his death)—yet there is nothing to confirm the assertion, promulgated by Johnson, that Swift's "madness was compounded of rage and fatuity;" or that Swift expired "a driv'ler and a show."*

To return to M. Delepierre's work. *Religious Madmen* differ in many essential points from others in their aberrations: their objects are the emotions, the passions, and the instinctive impulses of the soul. A Jesuit named Paoletti, who, in the middle ages, wrote against Thomas Aquinas' doctrine concerning Predestination and Freewill, and who had been in confinement five years when he wrote, composed a treatise in which he "demonstrated that the aborigines of America were the direct descendants of the devil and one of the daughters of Noah; consequently it was absolutely impossible that they should ever obtain salvation or grace."

Simon Morin, who had published an absurd book, was arrested by order of the French Parliament, and was ordered to be sent to a madhouse for the rest of his days. But having abjured his follies he was released, and soon after published another book, in which he maintained that he was no other than the Son of Man. He was condemned, in 1662, to be burnt alive with his books, and his ashes to be cast to the wind. So Simon Morin and his hetero-

---

* It is remarkable that the last sufferings of Sir Walter Scott—one of Swift's biographers, and certainly not the most lenient one—present a striking parallel to the case of Swift in nearly every particular except in point of duration. When Scott was in his 58th year, he first began to feel those premonitory symptoms of incipient disease of the brain under which Swift labored from the time he was 28. Many of Sir Walter's symptoms, in the two closing years of his life, resemble those of Swift; and the post mortem symptoms are very much alike.— *Wilde.*

doxy were extinguished. On the other hand, St. Francis, the founder of the Franciscans, who saw visions "as of an angel with six burning wings, bearing a figure nailed upon the cross," and who, at any rate, was at one time chained down in a dark room by his parents, and was "deemed to be mad both by the learned and vulgar,"—he was canonized.

Proceeding to the second division—*Literary Madmen*, we find that they do not occupy themselves with deep speculations on abstruse subjects: they rarely go below the surface of things, and are concerned rather with the mode of expression of common ideas than with the nature of the ideas themselves. Their intellectual powers being less concentrated than in those who are occupied with philosophy or theology, the exhaustion is much less. Many belonging to this class are persons who, in madness, are still afflicted with the itching humor of writing. Yet some there are who, out of decay, emit bright phosphorescence of genius, and compose in good style what a professed philosopher may read with advantage: the writings of Nathaniel Lee, born about the end of the seventeenth century, have been praised by Addison One night, when Lee was composing one of his dreams in his cell in Bedlam, a cloud passed before the moon, by the light of which he was writing, when he suddenly cried out: *Jove, snuff the moon.* Dryden relates how this same Lee once replied to a bad poet who had made the foolish remark, that it was very easy to write like a madman: "It is very difficult to write like a madman, but it is very easy to write like a fool."

Alexander Cruden became insane while at college, through his love being rejected by a young lady: he was sent to an asylum, but shortly after recovered; and after he was set at liberty, he wrote his *Concordance*, a work of surprising research. He was three times placed in confinement; and after his release on the last occasion, despairing of obtaining what he deemed justice for his wrongs, he wrote to his sister, and several of his friends, proposing, with the utmost simplicity, that they should in an easy way afford him a slight compensation—by subjecting themselves to imprisonment for a time in Newgate. Heavenly voices, towards the end of his life, informed him that he had a divine mission; and he demanded that he should be recognized of the King in Council, and that he should be created by Act of Parliament, "Corrector of the People."

Living at the same time as Cruden, was a certain Christopher Smart, who, after a brilliant career at Cambridge, unhappily became insane. During his confinement he wrote, by means of a key, on the panels of his chamber, a poem of nearly a hundred stanzas to the "Glory of David, King and Prophet."

Philosophical Madmen are in a somewhat similar position to that of theological madmen: they are mostly vain persons who have lost their way in matters too deep for them; and by reason of their vanity, and of the nature of the subject of their pursuits, are as difficult to deal with as those who speculate on religious mysteries. A deplorable instance of this class is afforded by Thomas Wirgman, who, after making a large fortune as a goldsmith and silversmith, in St. James's-street, London, squandered it all as a regenerating philosopher. He had paper made specially for his books, the same sheet consisting of several different colors; and as he changed the work many times while it was printing, the cost was enormous; one book of 400 pages cost 2,276*l*. He published a grammar of the five senses, which was a sort of system of metaphysics for the use of children, and maintained that when it was universally adopted in schools, peace and harmony would be restored to the earth, and virtue would everywhere replace crime. He complained much that people would not listen to him' and that, although he had devoted nearly half a century to the propagation of his ideas, he had asked in vain to be appointed Professor in some University or College—so little does the world appreciate those who labor unto death in its service. Nevertheless, exclaimed Wirgman, after another useless application, "while life remains I will not cease to communicate this blessing to the rising world."

Political Madmen.—Davesney or Davenne, *temp.* Louis XIV., was of opinion that of right he ought to supplant that monarch, and mount the throne: and he proposed two plans of deciding the question. "Call the Cardinal, the Regent, the Duke of Orleans, the Princes Beaufort, and those who are deemed most holy in the world; have a furnace kindled; let us all be thrown into it, and he who comes out uninjured, like a renovated phœnix from the flames, let him be regarded as the protégé of God, and be ordained prince of the people." Fearing however, naturally enough, that so severe a test might not be acceptable, he proposes another. "Let the Parliament sentence me to death for having dared to speak the truth to princes. Let them execute me, and if God does not protect me from their hands in a supernatural way, let the memory of me be extinct. If God preserves me not from the hands of the executioners, nothing shall be done to them; but if a supernatural arm tears me from their clutches, let them be sacrificed in my place."*

* Selected and Abridged from an able Paper, by Henry Maudsley, on Delepierre's *Histoire Littéraire des Fous*, in the *Journal of Mental Science*, No. 84. With several interpolations.

GENERAL INDEX.

ABERNETHY on Life, 61.
Abodes of the Blest, 297.
Abstraction, Mental, 109.
Adaptation of Color to the Wants of Animals, 48.
Addison's Cato quoted, 278.
ADVERSARIA, 299-332.
Age, Old, and Death, 178.
Angels, Notions of, 77.
Angels, popular ideas of, 82.
Apple-tree, Eve's, 46.
Aristotle on the Soul, 59.
Arnold, Dr., his death, 196.
Arundel, Philip, Earl of, his death, 164.
Atheism, Dr. South on, 321.
Attributes of the Deity, 320.
Author of our Being, the, 16.
Average of Human Life, 49.

Bacon, Lord, dream of, 388.
Baillie and Brodie on Death, 192.
Beauty of Death, 212.
"Beginning," the, of Creation, 24.
Being, Chain of, 89.
BELIEF AND SCEPTICISM, 130-145.
Belief, Weak, 138.
Bell, the Passing, 210.
Bible, Study and Interpretation of the, 299.
Bichat, M., his definition of Life, 16.
Blumenbach on Ethnology, 80.
Bolingbroke, Lord, his Infidelity, 141.
Bowdler, Mr., on the Attributes of the Deity, 320.
Brain in Childhood, 118.
Brain, Working of the, 98.
Brewster, Sir David, "Worlds to come," 297.
Brodie, Sir B., on Duality of Mind, 73; Memory, 99; Mental Processes, 94; Mind preceding Death, 186; Nervous System, 96.
Brougham, Lord, on Mind, 98.
Buddhism, True and False, 311.
Bulwer Lytton on the Pre-existence of Souls, 70.
Bunsen, Baron, his Biblical Researches, 246; Creation, 26.
Bunson, Baron, death and funeral of, 247.
Burial Clubs, Antiquity of, 217.
Burial Soils, Antiseptic, 219.
Burns and Byron, melancholy, 112.

"Business of the Saints in Heaven," 298.
Byron, his superstition, 171.

Cain, how he killed Abel, 47.
Cawnpore, death at, 342.
Ceylon, Paradise in, 47.
Chain of Being, the, 89.
Chance, What is it? 158.
Change-bearing Laws of Nature, 20.
Change in Opinion, 304.
Chartley Tradition, 339.
Chemistry cannot create an Organic germ, 38.
Chesterfield, Lord, appearance to, 340.
Child father to the Man, 127.
Childish Desires, 132.
Childless, to die, 146.
Chrisom Child and Cloth, 183.
Christ, Death of, 241.
"Christ's Passion," by Cowley, 242.
Christian Life, true course of, 310.
Christian Mission, the, 308.
CHRISTIAN RESURRECTION, THE, 276-280.
Christian Revelation, 305.
Christianity, Evidences of, 308.
Christianity, Mediæval, 328.
Christianity, Universal, Remoteness of, 324.
Clairvoyance, on, 92.
Climacterics, on, 51.
Coleridge, his definition of Life, 16.
Coleridge, his unbelief, 139.
Color and Wants of Animals, 48.
Consumption and Longevity, 57.
Contrition of the Ancients at Death, 181.
Courtenay, Bishop, on the Intermediate State, 268.
Courtenay, Bishop, on Man's Immortality, 274.
Creation of Matter, 21.
Creation, the Mosaic and Geologic, 22.
Creation, views of the, 26.
Cromwell *on the Soul and the Future Life,* 59.
Cross, the, 289.
"Crosse of Christ," 244.
CRUCIFIXION OF OUR LORD, 239-247.
Crucifixion, punishment of, 239.

Darkness, Utter, 234.
Darwin's Theory of Species, 27.

General Index.

Daubeny, Prof., on Man, 57.
Davy, Sir Humphrey, on Spiritual Natures, 83.
Day of Judgment, the, 281.
Dead, Prayers for the, 254.
Dead, State of the, 267.
Dead, Know not any thing, 254.
Death, Beauty of, 212.
Death Customs, 217.
Death, Premonitions of, 168.
Death and Sleep, 179.
Death, state of Mind preceding, 186.
Death at Will, 179.
Death-bed, the, by Feltham, 198.
Death-bed Repentance, 199.
Decay of the Human Body, 221.
Decay of Memory, 105.
Deity, Existence of the, 18.
Destruction of the World, 229.
Development Theory, the, 33.
"Devil," representations, 233.
Dickens, Charles, on Pre-existence of Souls, 71.
Discipline of the Intellect, 126.
Divine Eternity, the, 18.
Divine Perfections, the, 19.
Domesticity of Character, 15.
D'Orbigny on the Creation, 27.
Drowning, sensations in, 125.
Duality of Mind, 71.
Dying Christian to his Soul, 195.

Emblems on Tombs, 219.
Embryo under the Microscope, 32.
Emerson on the Soul, 158.
Emotion and the Intellect, 110.
END OF THE WORLD FORETOLD, 248–258.
Enoch, Translation of, 291.
Eve's Apple-tree, 46.
"Excelsior," 77.
Experience, Fallible, 136.

Faber, Dr., dirge by, 343.
Falstaff, Sir John, his death described, 183.
Family Likenesses, 48.
Fanshawe, Lady, and Spectre, 339.
Flowers in Coffins, 296.
Flowers on Graves, 228.
Foote, Samuel, death of, 166.
Fragments of Time, 58.
Funeral, Village Maiden's, 227.
FUTURE STATES, THE, 281–284.
Futurity, Mr. Merry on, 271, 272, 287.

Galvanized Human Body, 96.
Garden, hallowed ground, 227.
Gay Melancholy, on, 118.
Genesis of the Earth and Man, 25.
Genius, What is it? 108.
Glastonbury, Holy Thorn at, 306.
"God's Acre," 218.
God's Ancient People, 326.
"Great Book," the, 125.
Grey, Sir George, on the Consolation of Religion, 319.
Grief for the Dead, 212.

Grimaldi, his dread of Friday, 342.
Growth, Real, 185.

Hamilton, on Faith, 130.
Hamilton, on Phrenology, 55.
Happiness of the Blessed, by Bishop Mant, 285.
Happiness—Boyish or Manly, 326.
Happiness of Heaven, 288.
Harrison, Mr. Bower, on the Phenomena of Death, 187.
Haydon, the painter, presentiment of, 173.
Hearts, Broken, 197.
Heart Disease, Death from, 196.
Heavens and Earth, New, 294.
Hell, Picture of, 234.
Hemans, Mrs., her last Sonnet, 341.
Herschel, Sir John, on Species, 20.
High Spirits, a presage of Evil, 150.
Hogarth, his "Tail-piece," 166.
Holy Spirit, to the, 260.
Hours fatal to Life, 162.
How Man dies, 187.
Hunter, John, death of, 167.
Hypochondriac authors, 121.

Identity, Personal, 87.
Immortality of the Soul, see Soul.
Impressions, Permanent, by Spiritual Powers, 85.
Impressions, Persistence of, 102.
Impulses, Insane, 116.
Infidelity, Renunciation of, 142.
Insane, how treated by the Egyptians, 124.
Insane Impulses, 116.
Intellect, Discipline of the, 126.
Intellectuality and Insanity, 120.
Interferences of the Dead with the Living, 215.
INTERMEDIATE STATES, 264–275.
Intolerance and Unbelief, 137.
Intuitions, what are they? 107.
Ixion and his Wheel, 286.

Jehovah and the Eternal, 18.
Jerusalem, the New, 296.
Jews, history of the, 326.
Job, and the Resurrection, 263.
Johnson, Dr., on Death, 240.
Johnson, Dr., Latin Hymn by, 341.
Judgment Day, the, 281.

Kidd, Capt., and supernatural appearance, 341.
Kingdoms of Nature, the, 41.
Knowledge of God before the time of Christ, 244.

Lambton Family Tradition, 338.
Lardner, Dr., on Personal Identity, 87.
Last Moments and Words of distinguished Persons, 202.
Latin Christianity, 328.
Leighton, Archbishop, Death of, 177.
Leslie, the painter, on the Beauty of Death, 213.
Liebig on the Development Theory, 33.
Life after Death, 262.

General Index. 355

Life Assurance, on, 55.
Life not greater than its Reflex, 128.
Life, Origin of, 27.
LIFE AND TIME, 15–58.
Life, the Tree of, 44.
Life, What is it? 15.
Likenesses, Family, 48.
Litany, Origin of the, 330.
Litany to the Holy Spirit, by Herrick, 261.
Loquitur Crucifixus, 248.
Lyttelton, Lord, Death of, 174.

Madge Wildfire, Gay Melancholy of, 118.
Madmen, Literary History of, 344.
Madness, What is it? 119.
MAN AFTER DEATH, 254–268.
Man after Death, Condition of, 256.
Man and his Dwelling-Place, 85.
Man, his Future Existence, 297.
Man, that he must be immortal, 278.
Man's proper place in Creation, 57.
Man's Reluctance to think of God, 183.
Marriages made in Heaven, 292.
Materialism of the Development Theory, 143.
Materialism and Spiritualism, 87.
Materialism, What is it? 330.
Matter, Creation of, 21.
Melancholy, or Poetic Feeling, 111.
Memory, Decay of, 105.
Memory, how it takes place, 101.
Memory, Value of, 104.
Memory, What is it, 99.
Mental Abstraction, 109.
Mental Processes of which we are unconscious, 94.
Mesmerism and Somnambulism, 90.
Metempsychosis, the, 144.
Microscope, revelations of, 82.
Miller, Hugh, on the Creation, 28.
Milton, on the Pre-existence of Souls, 69.
Mind and Body, 93.
Moments, Last, of distinguished Persons, 202.
Mortality, Gompertz's Law of. 49.
Mosaic and Geologic Creation, 22.
Mysteries and Miracles, 332.

Nature, the Kingdoms of, 41.
Nature, Numbers in, 42.
NATURE OF THE SOUL, 59–75.
Nemesis of Power, 233.
Nemesis, or Retribution, 231.
Nervous System, Changes in, 96.
New Heaven and Earth, 294.
Nineveh, Symbolical Figures from, 302.
Norwich, Earl of, and Death, 323.
Numbers in Nature, 42.

Operation of Mind, 125.
Our Friends in Heaven, by the Rev. J. Killeen, 289.
Oxford, Bishop of, Anecdote by, 126.
Oxford, Bishop of, on the Christian Mission, 309.

Paradise and Heaven, 269.
Parents of the Human Race, 32.
Passing Bell, the, 210.
Personality of God, 67.
Petty, Mr., premonition of his death, 168.
PHENOMENA OF DEATH, 162–228.
Phœnix, the Emblem, 222.
Phrenology, Hamilton on, 55.
PILGRIM'S PROGRESS, 333–337.
Plato, the Christian Element of, 315.
Plato on the Soul, 60.
Platonic Love, on, 314.
Platonism and Christianity, 315.
Plurality of Worlds, 37.
Power of Religion over Difficulties, 319.
Pre-existence of Souls, 68.
PREMATURE INTERMENT, 155–161.
Premonitions of Death, 168.
Preparing for another World, 321.
Prophecies of World's End, 258.
Punishments, Eternal, 325.

Reason, Perverted, 119.
RECOGNITION OF EACH OTHER BY THE BLESSED, 285–298.
Registration and Memory, 104.
Religion happily adapted to the Mind of Man, 317.
Religion, Power of, over Difficulties, 319.
Remoteness of Universal Christianity, 324.
RESURRECTION, THE CHRISTIAN, 276–280.
Resurrection, Emblem of the, 222.
Resurrection of same Body, 279.
Revelation, What is it? 131.
Rogers, S., and Clairvoyance, 92.
Roses on Graves, 224.
Rowe, Elizabeth, Hymn by, 74.

St. Hilaire, his definition of Life, 15.
Sceptics, Confessions of, 138.
Sceptics, how men become, 187.
Scott, Sir Walter, on the Pre-existence of Souls, 70.
Serpent Worship, on, 301.
Sin, the Earliest, 229.
Sin, the Great, 229.
SIN AND PUNISHMENT, 229–238.
Sleep and Death, 179.
Smith, Sir J. E., on the Vital principle, 38.
Soldiers and Sailors, superstitions of, 169.
Somnambulism, on, 90.
Soul after death, 256.
Soul and Body, Re-union of, 262.
Soul, does it sleep, 181.
Soul going forth from Body, 208.
Soul, Immortality of, 271.
Soul, the Imprisoned, 62.
Soul and the Magnetic Needle, 62.
SOUL, NATURE OF THE, 59–75.
Soul, Symbols of the, 65.
Souls, Portage of, 82.
Souls, Pre-existence of, 68.
Souls, Transmigration of, 75.
Southey on the Pre-existence of Souls, 68.
Space and Time, 50.
Special Providences, 230.

General Index.

Spiritual Life, 76–92.
Spiritual Natures, 88.
Spiritual Reclamation, McCormack on, 76.
Statistical Results, curious, 54.
Stiffness of Death, 193.
Study of the Bible, 299.
Superstition, What is it? 146–154.
Swift, Dean, mental infirmity of, 122, 347.
Sykes, Colonel, on Buddhism, 311.
Symbols of the Soul, 65.

"Thirteen to Dinner," 152.
Time, Fragments of, 53.
Trance, Legends and Anecdotes of, 155.
Transfiguration proof of Recognition, 286.
Translation of Enoch, 291.
Tree of Life, the, 44.

Unity of the Human Race, 80.
Universe, Geological Future of, 252.
Utter Darkness, 234.

Vital Force, on, 330.
Vital Principle, Animal and Vegetable, 33.

Voltaic Battery, Electric Eel, and Brain of Man, 95.

Wandering Jew, the, 160.
Watching for the Dead, 342.
Weak Belief, 133.
Wellington, Death of, 89.
Wellington at Waterloo, 230.
West, Christian Revelation, why first given to the, 305.
What is Superstition? 146–154.
Whately, Archbishop, on Darwin's Theory of Species, 29.
Whately, Archbishop, on the Intermediate State, 265.
Wheel of Eternal Punishment, 236.
Wigan, Dr., on Duality of Mind, 71.
Winchester, Bishop of, on the Jews, 326.
Wolsey, Cardinal, Death of, 168.
Wordsworth on the Pre-existence of Souls, 69.
World, another, preparing for, 321.
World, Destruction of the, 229.
World, the End of, Foretold, 243–253.
Worlds, Plurality of, 87.

Youth Melancholy, 113.

ABOUT THE AUTHOR

John Timbs (17 August 1801 – 6 March 1875), English antiquary, was born in Clerkenwell, London. He was educated at a private school at Hemel Hempstead, and in his sixteenth year apprenticed to a druggist and printer at Dorking. He had early shown literary capacity, and when nineteen began to write for the Monthly Magazine. A year later he became secretary to Sir Richard Phillips, its proprietor, and permanently adopted literature as a profession. He was successively editor of the *Mirror of Literature*, the *Harlequin*, the *Literary World*, and sub-editor of the *Illustrated London News*. He was also founder and first editor of *Year-Book of Science and Art*. His published works amounted to more than one hundred and fifty volumes. In 1834 he was elected a fellow of the Society of Antiquaries of London.

Some of his work was published under the pseudonym, **Horace Welby**, and was continued to be re-edited and republished well after his death.

- *Signs before death, and authenticated apparitions: in one hundred narratives, collected by Horace Welby (1825)*
- *Arcana of science and art: or, An annual register of useful inventions and improvements, discoveries and new facts, in mechanics, chemistry, natural history, and social economy (1828)*
- *Harlequin. A journal of the drama (1829)*
- *Laconics (1829)*
- *Literary world: a journal of popular information and entertainment (1839)*
- *Table-wit, and after-dinner anecdote (1840)*
- *Things not generally known, familiarly explained. A book for old and young (1856)*
- *Curiosities of history (1857)*
- *School-days of eminent men. I. Sketches of the progress of education in England, from the reign of King Alfred to that of Queen Victoria. II. Early lives of celebrated British authors, philosophers and poets, inventors and discoverers, divines, heroes, statesmen &c \ (1858)*
- *Curiosities of science (1859)*
- *Stories of inventors and discoverers in science and the useful arts. 1860*
- *Popular errors explained and illustrated (1862)*

- *Century of anecdote from 1760 to 1860 (1864)*
- *Romance of London. Supernatural stories, sights and shows, strange adventures, and remarkable persons (1865)*
- *Something for everybody; and a garland for the year 1866*
- *Club life of London 1866*
- *English Eccentrics and Eccentricities (1866, in two volumes)*
- *Mysteries of life, death, and futurity (1868)*
- *Mountain adventures in the various countries of the world 91869)*
- *Wonderful inventions: from the mariner's compass to the electric telegraph cable (1870)*
- *Abbeys, castles, and ancient halls of England and Wales (1872)*
- *Thoughts for times and seasons (1872)*
- *Doctors and patients (1873)*

www.ingramcontent.com/pod-product-compliance
Lightning Source LLC
Chambersburg PA
CBHW020730160426
43192CB00006B/180